A Desert Becomes A Garden

A DESERT BECOMES A GARDEN
The Autobiography of Kim Jin-hong

Published by YBM/Sisa
55-1 Jongno 2-ga, Jongno-gu
Seoul 110-122, Korea

Kim Jin-hong: durekim@chollian.net
Doorae Office USA: (323) 730-0333 (phone)

YBM/Si-sa website: www.ybmsisa.co.kr
YBM/Si-sa Internet bookstore: www.book.ybmsisa.com
(82+2) 2000-0515 (phone)

First English Edition Published in 2002
Printed in the Republic of Korea

ISBN 89-17-15778-5 (hardbound)
ISBN 89-17-15777-7 (paperback)

*This book
is dedicated to
people everywhere
who have vision and hope
for
the betterment of mankind
and
who work to achieve it.*

A DESERT BECOMES A GARDEN

THE AUTOBIOGRAPHY OF KIM JIN-HONG

KIM JIN-HONG

YBM Si-sa

Contents

PART THREE DARKNESS UNTO LIGHT

Preface to the English Edition

In Korean there is a saying: The passage of time is like an arrow in flight. Thirty years have passed since I, as a young urban missionary, moved to the Cheonggye-cheon slum of Seoul. Paul the Apostle said, "By the grace of God, I am what I am...." The years have passed quickly. I feel that I, too, am what I am, by the grace of God. I know that I have been blessed, as I look back on those three decades and see the result.

Hwalbin Church, the church I founded in Cheonggye-cheon, opened its doors on October 3, 1971, a day that coincided with Korea's National Foundation Day, which in Korea is referred to as the day the heavens opened and Hwan-ung, the mythical founder of Korea, descended to earth. I chose that day for the foundation of the church because I wanted my work to affect the hopeless of the slum as if the doors of heaven had been thrown open, showing them the way.

In Mark 1:11 it is written that before Jesus Christ undertook his mission on earth, "...he saw heaven being torn open..." and he heard a voice. People in the slum lead wretched lives, with no hope for a better future. Through my mission, I wanted them to witness the kingdom of God and to feel his presence, as I did, myself, when I was in prison in 1974-1975. In a cold cell that measured a mere 25 square feet, I experienced the kingdom of God and felt him reach out to me. My prayer for my readers is that regardless of where you are or what your circumstances, in your lifetime you have a spiritual encounter with God.

Today's world is obsessed with materialism, physical pleasure, and indolence. Although they are widespread, these obsessions contradict the nature of mankind. God created man to experience joy only if he places greater value on spirituality than on worldly goods and pleasures. People who fail to learn this lesson will never escape misfortune, discord, alienation, anger, and pain. The only way to overcome the misery of the worldly life is through God and Jesus Christ.

My ministry has always centered on the community—the urban poor in the 1970s, farmers in the 1980s, and the Doorae Community Movement (DCM) in the 1990s. Now, over the threshold of the new millennium, I am concentrating my missionary activity, through the Doorae Church, in China and in North Korea. The DCM has grown, developed, and flourished, much like a child coming of age. As I write this, the movement continues to grow and mature. This growth surely has a purpose, which I believe derives from the same principles as those laid out in Ephesians 4:12-13:

> ...to prepare God's people for works of service, so that the body of Christ may be built up until we all reach unity in the faith and in the knowledge of the Son of God and become mature, attaining to the whole measure of the fullness of Christ.

Despite its shortcomings, I hope that this book contributes to "building up the body of Christ" and that it helps the reader attain "the whole measure of the fullness of Christ."

KIM JIN-HONG
SEOUL, KOREA
AUGUST 2002

Acknowlegments

It is a pleasure for me to write this page, acknowledging the contribution of the people responsible for producing this translation of my autobiography. Theirs was not an easy task, for a variety of reasons, not least of which was adapting a book that is quintessentially local in focus, that is, directed at the Korean community in Korea and abroad, making it understandable and interesting for a wider non-Korean audience.

The person whose idea it was to prepare this translation, who has supported it from the beginning, and without whom it would never have been completed, is Y.B. Min, the founder and chairman of YBM/Si-sa, the largest English language publisher in Korea. Thank you is not adequate to express my appreciation for his generous support for this work and for a range of Doorae Community activities.

Special thanks also go to So-young Lee, who directed the translation effort from concept to final product, organized the translation, participated in the editing and refinement of the text, and oversaw the production. Ms. Lee's editorial skills are matched by her skills in working with people, where she gained consensus to resolve issues that involved differences of opinion among people who held strongly to their views.

I extend my gratitude, also, to others who worked on the project, whether as translators or editors, and who approached the task with energy and dedication. Steve Stupak worked hard to ensure that the language of the text was both accurate and appropriate, and that non-Koreans could understand the environment and conditions in which the work developed.

Sue Chang, as copy editor, did a wonderful job of cleaning up a lot of loose ends, working out inconsistencies, and introducing clarifications.

Among translators, Soo-mi Kim, Kyung-hee Chang, and Sang-yoon Kang worked hard to generate a product that others then massaged and molded to produce a final text. Pastor Hae-kwon Kim, a Doorae scholarship recipient, read and amended important details in the manuscript.

Ms. Lee's production team, consisting of Hee-jung Han, Jung-ae Choi, Hyun-sook Lee, and Hee-kyung On, worked from raw text files to produce a book that is attractive and inviting to the reader, a quality that every author can recognize and every reader can appreciate.

Translators' Note

This work was originally published in serialized form in a Korean monthly magazine. Its popularity as a serial prompted the author to have it published in book form, with only minimal editing. Translating a serial is very different from translating a work that begins as an intact whole.

Each chapter of a serial has to be able to stand alone. The reader does not have the benefit of being able to go back twenty pages to refresh his or her recollection of something that was explained earlier. To have removed this quality of serialization from the work entirely would have destroyed much of its immediacy and vitality. In preparing this translation, in this regard we purposely followed the original. We believe that what it may detract from the continuity of the narrative, it more than makes up for in drawing the reader into the story. We hope you agree.

Life in Korea over the years of Pastor Kim's lifetime has not been easy. The people with whom Pastor Kim has always worked are on the lowest rung of society's ladder. These are not the refined of Korea's Christian flock. They are people for whom the line between life and death is often very thinly drawn. Their actions, their language, and their values reflect the tenuous grip many of them have on survival. Readers may sometimes be shocked by the words and the deeds of the personalities in this book. Although we have removed certain of the more offensive language, we have not removed it all. In leaving it in, we wanted the reader to understand the environment in which Pastor Kim operated, and to have a feeling for the selfishness, the vulgarity, and the wickedness that pervades the life of many of the people with whom Pastor Kim came into contact.

With regard to Korean language, we retained some of the artifacts of Korean culture, such as *soju*, a popular grain drink, *hyeongnim*, the title for an older brother, and *won*, the unit of currency, and others because they are clear reflections of the environment. We hope they add to the reader's sense of involvement in the story. To the degree possible, we kept to the original text, deleting only some of the passages that were repetitious as the result of serialization.

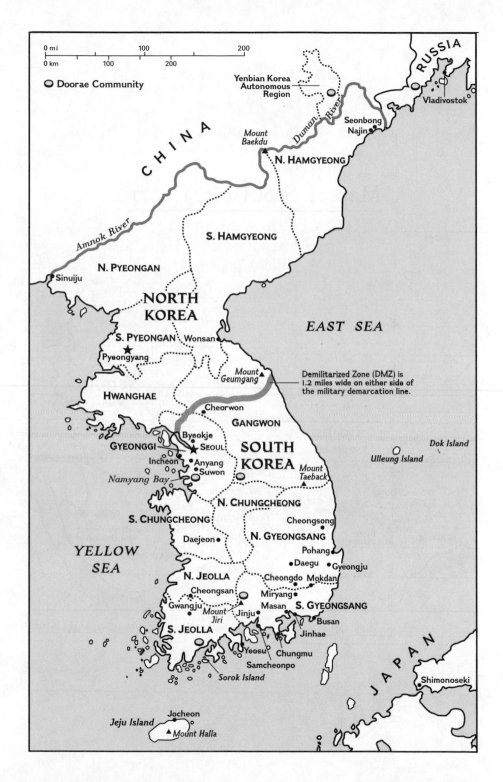

Map of Seoul circa 1971

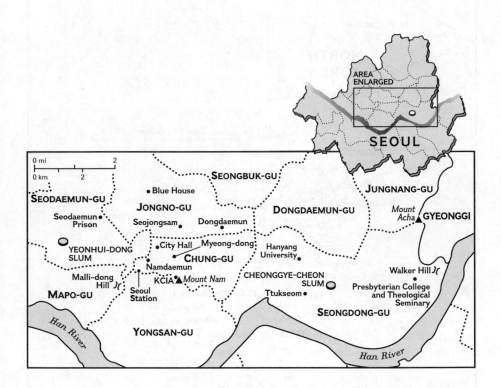

AREA ENLARGED

SEOUL

0 mi 2
0 km 2

SEONGBUK-GU

• Blue House

SEODAEMUN-GU

JONGNO-GU

JUNGNANG-GU

Seodaemun
Prison •

Seojongsam •

DONGDAEMUN-GU

• Dongdaemun

Mount
Acha ▲ GYEONGGI

YEONHUI-DONG
SLUM

• City Hall

Myeong-dong •

Hanyang
University •

CHUNG-GU

• Namdaemun

Malli-dong
Hill)(

KCIA ▲ Mount Nam

CHEONGGYE-CHEON
SLUM

Walker Hill)(

Presbyterian College
and Theological
Seminary

MAPO-GU

Seoul
Station

• Ttukseom

SEONGDONG-GU

YONGSAN-GU

Han River

Han River

PART ONE

Searching

1

My Spirit's Roots

I WAS BORN IN CHEONGSONG, North Gyeongsang province, in the south of Korea. My birthplace, Sabusil, lies in the most secluded of the valleys of Andeok-myeon.* I first saw the light of day in the early summer of 1941, a time when people were busy harvesting barley and planting rice. I was the third child in our family, a sister having preceded me by two years and a brother by four.

At the time, we were living in Japan. My father was working as a taxi driver in Tokyo, a job he took seriously and at which he worked hard.

My mother returned to Korea for my birth, but, with me in arms, went back to Tokyo shortly afterward. Our home was in Shinjuku. Although I lived there for five years, I do not remember it, except for a vague recollection of a knoll that was in front of our house and the surrounding landscape.

In the fall of 1945, after the Japanese colonial rule in Korea ended as a result of Japan having lost the war, we joined hundreds of other families on a repatriation voyage to our native land. By "we," I mean my mother, my by-then three siblings, including a younger brother, and me.

My father stayed behind. That was the last I saw of him. A few years later he died of an illness. His ashes were returned to Korea and, on a rainy day, we buried him on a mountainside. After the burial, a rainbow appeared in the sky. My mother broke into tears and said, "That rainbow carried your father off to heaven."

---

*A *myeon* is a rural administrative district.

3

My family—Mother, younger brother, older brother, me, and sister—after our return to Korea.

Oddly, I remember nothing of my father. I was five when we parted. You might think that there would be some faint memory I could attach to him, but there is not. My mother always told us that despite my father's lack of formal education, he was well read and had great insight. When we were small, my mother would often tell us stories of great men—Yi Sun-sin, Tolstoi, Toyohiko Kakawa, and Kancho Uchimura. I wondered where she had learned all those stories and one day I asked her.

"Your father taught them to me," she said. "He used to buy me books and always encouraged me to read. We'd write down our impressions of what we'd read and would share them with each other."

Because of my father's influence, my mother made sure all of her children got into the habit of reading. If ever she caught us sitting about idly or just chatting, she would reprimand us. "There is no future for anyone who wastes time. That's why Korea lags behind Japan. Our people don't read enough," she would say.

Thanks to my mother, I acquired the habit of reading and to this day I feel uneasy if I don't have a book in my hand.

WHILE I AM ON THE SUBJECT OF MY FAMILY, perhaps I should say something about our background. My paternal grandfather had two brothers. They lived in the city of Gyeongju, but when their parents died, they could no longer stay in their house. They moved to a make-shift shack on the bank of a creek.

One day, in a heavy rain, high water swept their house away. The three brothers, now both orphaned and homeless, walked until they reached the remote village of Cheongsong, where they were taken in as servants by a farmer. There they grew up, but as adults, they could not find anyone willing to marry them. No parents in their right mind would allow their daughters to marry such unpromising men. Desperate men, however, take desperate measures, and my forebears were no exception.

One night the oldest brother took it upon himself to sneak into a widow's home. He wrapped her in the blanket she was sleeping with, put her in a big sack, and took her back to his place. This form of kid-napping was an old Korean custom, whenever a man wanted to marry a widow. That night he forced her to sleep with him, but at the crack of dawn got on his knees, apologized and begged forgiveness.

"I have committed a grave sin. My way was wrong, but I meant well. I leave it to you to decide. You can either leave and act as if nothing has happened or you can stay and become my wife. Although I have little to offer in the way of material things, you can be sure I have a good heart." Then he asked, "Could you agree to spend the rest of your life with me?"

Considering that the man had lived all his life as a servant, the intellectual level of his argument could not have been high, but despite his stammering and weak logic, the widow accepted his offer.

"The way things are," she said, "I might as well marry you. I have nothing. My only hope is that you'll be kind." She became the wife of my grandfather's oldest brother. As unpropitious as the "courtship" had been, the two nevertheless enjoyed a long and good marriage.

My grandfather's second brother resorted to an even more extreme measure in his pursuit of a bride. An elderly couple lived in the town with their only daughter. My great uncle would go to their house every day and threaten them, saying, "If you give me your daughter's hand in marriage, I will take good care of both of you for the rest of your lives.

But if you refuse, I will set your house on fire, throw myself into the flames, and we will all die." Of course, the elderly couple protested. "You worthless thief! How could we ever let our darling daughter marry the likes of you? Never set foot on our threshold again," they would tell him.

This did not dissuade him, however. Day in and day out, every morning he would show up at their door with the same words and every morning would meet with the same response. This went on for six months. At long last, the man's unabated threats caused the couple such concern that the daughter relented, saying, "Father, Mother, I'm willing to marry this fellow. This way I can be sure to provide a comfortable life for you both." Although at first the couple vehemently opposed the union, they finally came around. Amazingly, after such a rocky start, that marriage, too, was a great success.

Finally, it was my grandfather's turn to marry. His story, however, was different, although not as you might expect. While working in his masters' rice paddies one day, he was approached by an American missionary. Speaking Korean, the missionary said, "Hello, young man! Why don't you take a break and come sit down. I'd like to talk to you." My grandfather walked over to the blue-eyed stranger and sat next to him on the bank of the rice paddy. Thus it was, at this chance meeting, that he was introduced to the Gospel. Then and there, he accepted Christ as his savior.

The life of a servant was not compatible with that of a practicing Christian. Bound to his duties on the farm, it was difficult to observe the Sabbath as a day of rest. To be able to attend church on Sunday, he would stay up all night the night before, chopping wood. In the rice-planting season, he planted by moonlight. Seeing this, as the seasons passed, his masters were so impressed with his unwavering dedication to both his work and his faith that they decided to have their daughter marry him. It was a union of the comfort of the middle class and the poverty of a servant.

MY PATERNAL GRANDPARENTS HAD THREE SONS, of whom my father was the youngest. I have often thought that my family's class mixture perhaps explains a dichotomy in my character—the refined and the vulgar coexisting—taking me from one extreme to the other.

My father, I would say, inherited only the good qualities of his parents. Growing up, I was always told that he had never been anything but a model child, even when he was young. Whenever she reprimanded us for misbehaving, my mother would always remind us of our father's example and urge us to follow it.

"Your father was such a good boy when he was your age. Why don't you take after him?" she would say.

At that I would retort, "What good was all that good behavior to him, if he died so young? We'll be a little naughty and maybe we'll live longer."

While his sincerity and kind heart may not have ensured him a long life, these qualities surely paid off when he was about to get married. It was against all odds for a poor man to marry a person such as my mother, who was from a well-to-do household. When the two families discussed the possibility of the young couple marrying, my maternal grandmother objected strongly because of my father's background. My mother, however, was not to be put off. "What difference does it make which family he comes from? What counts is who he is and how good he is. I want to marry him," she boldly asserted.

It was not common in those days for a young woman to stand up for herself and speak her mind. My mother had good reason to speak out, however, because she had known my father since elementary school and had always been fond of him. When they were in school together, she found him to be honest, sincere, and thoughtful. She was delighted when the parents of the two families began discussing the possibility of their marrying. She felt compelled to talk her parents into consenting. In the end, my mother's marriage into the Kim family proved to be a blessing for us.

My father was a good man, but his early death left the four of us fatherless for most of our childhood. My mother earned a living from sewing, which barely provided enough money to send her children through school and to college. We became who we are as adults thanks to my mother's determination to educate her children. On his deathbed in Japan, my father was reported to have said, "Tell my wife that it is my wish that she educate our children well, but if she cannot educate them all, at least Jin-hong should get a good education."

My mother's only possession was a sewing machine, which was

our sole source of income. She worked at her sewing day and night. We would go to sleep at night listening to the tick-tick-tick of the sewing machine and in our slumber would hear it throughout the night. Whenever important holidays drew near, her workload grew even heavier.

My mother had plans for her children. She had always wanted to make a pastor out of me. A day would not pass without her praying for the future of her children. We would sometimes awake to the sound of my mother at her dawn prayers, when she would pray for each of us, one after the other. When it came my turn, she would always say, "And the third, Jin-hong, may he become your servant, Lord."

I was not pleased with her prayer. Having seen the hardship of a pastor serving in a rural town, I would think to myself, "If I were a pastor, I could only eke out a meager existence."

Once, when on an errand I visited our pastor's house, I saw his wife alone, crying in the kitchen. I thought to myself then that the life of a pastor brings only tears to his wife. I raised my objection to my mother. "Mother, why do you always pray that I become a pastor?"

"My dear boy, do you know what a glorious thing the vocation of a pastor is?"

"No, I don't, but if it's so glorious and wonderful, have your other children take it up. I'd much rather become a general or a lawyer."

"No, I want you to become a pastor because you have a pastor's disposition. You may not know it now, but I know it's your calling. Your mother's prayers will be answered."

FOR A TIME WHEN I WAS IN COLLEGE I led what I can only call an intemperate life. One night, I had been out drinking with friends and came home very late and very drunk. I was in the bathroom and had begun to vomit when my mother came in and tapped me on the back.

"Come to your senses, little pastor," she said.

"Please, Mother! Don't 'little pastor' me. How can you talk about me being a pastor when you see the shape I'm in?"

"No. No matter what mess you make of your life now, one day you will become a pastor."

My drinking and my senseless ways went on for a couple of years after graduation. Finally, however, I resolved to enroll in a seminary and indeed did become a pastor. When I told my mother of my decision, she was overjoyed.

During my sophomore year at the seminary, I decided to move to a destitute neighborhood to serve the poor and the needy. Everyone else tried to discourage me, but she alone stood by me and gave me her unqualified support.

"If you are going to become a pastor, you have to be ready to serve and not expect to be waited on. Jesus taught us to help the needy and that's exactly what you should do. Your father would have done the same. You are so much like him," she told me.

DURING MY CHILDHOOD, when my mother would be up all night working at her sewing machine, she would often wake me sometime during the night and ask me to sing her a hymn. "Jin-hong, please sing me a hymn."

I would protest, "Why do you always get me up? Why don't you wake up the others?"

"It's because when you sing, you sing with so much feeling. Besides, as a pastor-to-be, you ought to be singing hymns."

"Which hymn would you like to hear, Mother?" I would ask.

"You know, the same as always, 'Nearer, My God to Thee,'" would be her reply.

In my half-asleep state, I would clear my throat and begin to sing Hymn 364, whereupon my mother would gently close her eyes and listen. At the end of the hymn, she would say, "How wonderful it is! You have a way with singing; you make it inspiring, my boy."

The day came when I had sung Hymn 364 so many times that I knew it by heart. Of course, back then I had no way of knowing that that hymn would become a great asset to me later in life and would sustain me in difficult times.

Growing older, I often had to struggle through hardship. Whenever I felt frustrated and overwhelmed, I would sing Hymn 364 to myself. By the time I would get to the fourth verse, the hymn would relieve my stress, and I would have regained my composure.

In 1974 I was in prison for having violated emergency measures that had been issued under the dictatorial rule of President Park Jeong-hui. One day, in the bitter winter cold, I was pacing back and forth in my cell, singing my mother's favorite hymn:

> Nearer, my God, to Thee, Nearer to Thee!
> E'en though it be a cross That raiseth me;

As I was singing, I heard someone banging on the wall in the cell next to mine.

"Sir? Whoever is singing. Sir?" a voice called.

I wasn't sure at first whether it was I who was being addressed, but as the banging continued, I hazarded a reply.

"Yes? Are you talking to me?" I asked.

"Yes, sir," came the reply.

"Who are you?" I asked.

"I'm in for assault and I'm waiting for my trial," the voice said.

"I see," I said. "Why are you calling me?"

"I'm sorry, sir, but could you please sing a little louder so I can write down the words? I can't make them out because you are singing too softly."

The voice was that of a young man.

"Singing louder is no problem," I said, "but why do you want to write it down?"

He then told me his story. He was the son of a pastor from a rural town. He told me how he had always resented his father for putting the family through poverty and hardship. His father refused to pursue his ministry in a city. Instead, they moved from one village to another, where he would always set up a church. Every time the church became established, his father would hand it over to a successor, and they would move on to another village where there was no church. Although he was sure his father was acting on conviction, it took a toll on the family. What was worse, the congregation often did not appreciate their pastor.

The young man told me how on several occasions he had witnessed the church elders and members of the congregation mistreating his father. There were times when he had felt like he was losing his mind and could not contain his anger. To get even with his father, he later became a hoodlum, fighting with anyone he could.

His tearful mother tried to talk him out of his destructive behavior. She would hold onto him and pray, taking his hands into her own, singing a hymn. The hymn that his mother would sing was the very hymn that I had been singing, Hymn 364.

Locked in a cell, awaiting the uncertain outcome of his trial, he could not hold back his tears when he heard me singing. Out of guilt, his heart ached for his mother, and after so many years of pent-up hatred for his father, he suddenly missed him, too. That was why he wanted to sing with me when I sang that particular hymn and why he wanted to write down the lyrics.

I was greatly moved by his story and started to sing the hymn more slowly, verse by verse, as he sang with me. Even with a stone wall between us, and never having met or seen him, I felt strong compassion for the young man. My heart poured out to him and we both wept while we sang:

> Nearer, my God, to Thee, Nearer to Thee!
> E'en though it be a cross That raiseth me;
> Still all my song shall be, Nearer, my God, to Thee,
> Nearer, my God, to Thee, Nearer to Thee.
>
> Though like the wanderer, The sun gone down,
> Darkness be over me, My rest a stone;
> Yet in my dreams I'd be, Nearer, my God, to Thee,
> Nearer, my God, to Thee, Nearer to Thee.

He continued to weep and our conversation ended. Two months passed and one day a woman in her fifties came to visit me. I did not recognize her.

I asked, "Have we met before? Are you sure I'm the one you're looking for?"

"Yes, indeed, sir. You don't know me, but do you recall singing a hymn to a young man in the cell next to yours?"

"I do," I replied. "You mean the pastor's son."

"Yes, that's right. I'm his mother," she said.

"Ah, then you'd be the pastor's wife."

"Exactly. The young man you taught the hymn to is our oldest son."

"It's a pleasure to meet you, ma'am, but what brings you here?" I asked.

"My son has just been released on probation. He came home a totally changed person. We don't detect in him the slightest shadow of his old destructive self. He has become a good man. I told him that he should go to prison more often. When I asked him what happened that had made such a difference in him, he told me about you, how you taught him the hymn, and how he wept when he sang it.

"At that very moment, he swore to himself that he would change and become a new person. When my husband learned how you helped turn our son's life around, he insisted that I come see you and express our gratitude. We can't thank you enough for what you did for our son and for our family. Thank you so much, sir." Tears rolled down the woman's face as she spoke. She wiped her eyes with her handkerchief. As I listened to her, I was touched and told her my mother's story.

"I, myself, think of my mother when I sing that hymn," I said. "Remembering my mother, who always asked me to sing it when I was growing up, helps me endure prison life."

Later I learned that the woman had left some spending money on deposit for me at the prison. They, themselves, had so little to live on, but it was their way of showing appreciation.

GETTING BACK TO MY MOTHER'S STORY, my father's last words had a strong influence on how she raised us. To comply with his wishes, she was uncompromising in her pursuit of the best education she could provide us. Not only did she encourage us to read around the house, she would scour the village for books and reading material for us. Considering that books were not easily come by, given her straitened situation, the task was doubly difficult. Tracking down anything she could find from the homes of friends and relatives, she would bring home every sort of book, from university textbooks, such as *Introduction to Law* and *Introduction to Psychology*, to novels and essays.

One genre that stands out in my mind was comic books. In those days, comic books were a rarity. I have no idea how my mother got hold of them, but she brought home a number of them for us to read. There was one in particular that left a strong impression on me. It was called *Prince of the Jungle*. The print and the drawings were far from polished and the story was poorly developed, but it had immense appeal for me as a boy. I read it over and over until I finally knew the story by heart and could recall all of the pictures, frame by frame.

This was the story. A boy by the name of Cheol-min and his family were aboard an airplane flying across Africa. The plane developed engine trouble and crashed in the jungle, killing everyone aboard except Cheol-min. As the orphaned child wandered helplessly about the jungle, he was befriended by the wild animals and nurtured by them until he grew up to become a mighty prince of the jungle. Cheol-min fostered justice in his jungle kingdom, protecting human and beast alike against attacks from outside, whether from man or beast. He was a true leader of the jungle kingdom.

As I read the story, I imagined that I was Cheol-min. Like him, I would wend my way through the jungle, amidst the roar of beasts, the drum beat of the natives, and the ground-trembling rumble of elephant footfalls. All this, of course, I did with the unrivaled gallantry of Cheol-min.

Daydreaming of my life as Cheol-min, my imagination grew day by day. The world of the jungle was everywhere—in my sleep, I dreamt of the jungle and of myself as a valiant Cheol-min, setting things right and ruling my jungle kingdom.

In farm villages in those days it was the children's job to take the cattle to graze. I was no exception. Every household in our neighborhood kept a cow, and when I arrived home from school, I would gulp down a bowl of cold cooked barley and head for a nearby mountain with our cow. Other children would tag along, bringing their cows.

Once we got there, we would let the cows graze in the meadow while we played. Sometimes we would jump into a stream and bathe in the cool water and other times we would play tag or hide-and-seek. When we became bored with our games, we would sit in a circle and tell stories. Whoever had the greatest repertoire of stories would rise as the star of the group. Armed with the story of the prince of the jungle, I knew I could not fail.

In the process of telling the story, I would embellish the original, adding flourishes and recounting Cheol-min's adventures with a loud voice and great gestures. My stage, the wide expanse of green meadow, gave the story an additional air of excitement. As the plot unfolded, I would produce the sounds and motions of the wild animals. Before I knew it, I would be sputtering saliva, making the drumming sounds of the natives. My mouth would froth as I shouted commands, leading my charges against savage invaders. Entranced by the story, the children would become one, groaning and lamenting in chorus as they sat witness to the twists and turns of Cheol-min's adventures.

An unexpected problem developed, however, since day in and day out I had to take our cow to graze, but my supply of stories was limited. A day did not pass without children nagging me to tell them another story. I had no choice but to invent new stories, ever taxing my imagination. My intent was to keep my friends entertained by coming up with new and exciting episodes.

Thanks to this cattle-grazing and storytelling, my imagination grew tremendously. Captivated by my stories, the children practically became addicted to them. After taking their cows home, they would come to my house in the evening and, once again, nag me to tell them stories. It didn't take long for me to realize that I was doing them a great favor and getting nothing in return. I thought to myself, there must be something in this for me. I came up with the idea charging admission to my storytelling sessions. The price would be one potato. No one would be admitted unless they brought a potato. That was it, one potato, one story.

My family was as poor as ever. We did not own any land and our sole income, then as before, was from my mother's sewing. Even as a child, I knew we were always in need of staples and vegetables, which I explained to my friends. No one objected and from that day on, potatoes flowed into our home, every night filling a basket. Thanks to my active imagination, potatoes became a regular feature on our dinner table.

My mother was very impressed with all this. "You're one of a kind! How do you manage to reap such a harvest without owning even one square foot of land? How you do it is beyond me!" she exclaimed one day.

2

Children Play War

I EXPERIENCED MY FIRST LOVE during elementary school. Although while it was happening, I thought it was an important milestone in my life, my experience was far from romantic or exciting. It was entirely one-sided, so I suppose the term "crush" would be more appropriate than "love."

There was a girl by the name of Ok-su who lived in our neighborhood. She and her family had returned to Korea from Japan in 1945 at about the same time my family did. She was pretty and smart. My mother and her parents were close friends and attended the same church. It was no wonder, then, that we got to know each other well. Whenever Ok-su and I would walk together, boys in the neighborhood would tease me about walking with a girl.

"Jin-hong-has-a-girl-friend, Jin-hong-has-a-girl-friend!" they would chant.

"Jin-hong and Ok-su are stuck on each other!"

Ok-su would blush whenever other children chattered at us, but, for my part, I did not mind.

One time we were cast in the lead roles in a school play. Ok-su was Princess Nak-rang and I Prince Ho-dong. At the end of the play the audience gave us a thunderous applause. Standing next to Ok-su, I could smell her sweet scent and felt like a million dollars.

Then, one day, I received heartbreaking news. Ok-su's father was taking the family back to Japan. Ok-su would be leaving. The minute I heard the news, I felt as if the whole world was collapsing around me.

I was devastated and lost all desire to go to school, or even to go on with life. I spent my days in an utterly depressed state.

Then, the dreaded day came for Ok-su to leave. She said her good-byes to everyone in class and walked out of school. I couldn't let her go like that so I rushed out and raced to meet her on the way home. I took a shortcut, hoping to catch her. I hid behind a tree along the way and waited for her. When she appeared, I approached her.

"Ok-su, are you really leaving?" I asked anxiously.

"Of course I am," she replied, too matter-of-factly.

Her answer was aloof and detached. The look on her face and the nonchalant way in which she passed by me hurt even more than the thought of her leaving. My anguish was greater than ever. If losing Ok-su were not enough, her insensitivity toward my feelings was unbearable. I felt like the most wretched person on earth. I walked into a barley field, lay down and cried my eyes out.

It was then that I made myself a promise. I would grow up to be a great success. Then I would go to her and ask her to marry me. That's right! I thought. If I'm going to have Ok-su as my bride, I must succeed in life. I shall succeed!

IN THE SUMMER OF 1950, when I was in the third grade, tragedy struck our country—the Korean War broke out. The war began with a flurry of police activity. At first they hurtled about in every which direction. Then, in panic, they dashed off toward the south, not to be seen again. Our town fell silent. Shortly thereafter North Korean troops moved in, singing martial songs. When that happened, even the stray dogs in our neighborhood curled their tails in fear. With their arrival, major tragedies unfolded daily, one after the other, in what otherwise was a small peaceful village. There were endless cries for help, gunfire and bombing, and the death of both people and animals.

One day my grandfather called to us, "Hey, everyone, come over here. Look, up in the sky!" We rushed to see what he was pointing at. High in the sky, we could make out what seemed to be United Nations aircraft, flying in formation. Heading north, the planes left white billowy vapor trails across the sky.

Grandfather's face lit up. He assured us that the war was coming to an end, now that the United Nations had joined the war.

"It will be only a matter of time before the North Koreans retreat. In the meantime, we need only be patient," he would say. A faithful Christian, my grandfather abhorred the communists. He waited earnestly, in silence, for the enemy to flee, even though many impoverished farmers and serfs were collaborating with the North Koreans and had been bossing other villagers around.

Shortly afterward, an airplane flew over, dropping leaflets. They said that UN forces had landed at Incheon and encouraged the people to muster strength and patience until the South prevailed.

In those days, Korea still had a form of serfdom. With the first wave of invasion from the North, the serfs in the farming community began to act strangely. The look on their faces seemed to suggest hope of liberation.

One day I overheard my mother and one of her parents' serfs talking. "A world where everyone is equal," I heard. "A new world," "A world without masters or serfs." These phrases cropped up in their conversation. My mother would respond in a composed manner, "Christianity is not compatible with Communism. When we all go up to heaven, there will be no masters or serfs. Here on earth, however, there are still masters and there are still serfs."

Without any knowledge of what Communism meant, I clasped my hands in prayer. "Dear God, I pray that you will keep my mother from falling into the hands of the communists."

UN bombers dropped their loads incessantly on our village during the entire time that the North Koreans occupied it. The villagers would take refuge in the valley to escape the bombing. There we would hide in caves and among the rocks.

During the attacks, great fireballs would volley from the sky and earth-splitting thunder would rumble through the valley. People would lie flat on the ground, holding their breath and trembling with fright. I would be squeezed in tightly among them, subjected to the same agony as everyone else. Annoyed at the sound, however, once I raised my head toward the sky. In fear and frustration, I blurted out, "Damn it! This booming will kill us long before any of the bombs do."

Everyone burst out laughing. After a good laugh, people chimed in, "You're right, Jin-hong! The bombs won't strike us dead, but the booming will!" My comic remark that day somehow pierced the tension, and put people at ease. Surprisingly, they relaxed and began to chat and talk with one another. It was from this incident that I first understood the power of humor.

The war continued and more and more young men were drafted into the army. Upon receiving a draft notification, a family would immediately start a flood of tears, with people wailing over the thought of losing their sons and husbands. Everyone believed that enlisting in the armed forces in wartime meant certain death.

As the war dragged on, bags of ashes found their way back the homes of war casualties. Each delivery of ashes would generate another bout of lamentation for the entire town. Fresh graves would be added to the village cemetery.

WARTIME DID NOT STOP CHILDREN FROM PLAYING, but it did change the way we played. We began to imitate the mayhem and destruction that we saw around us.

Violent language and behavior became increasingly evident in our interactions. Whereas earlier we might have said, "Would you stop that?" now we would say, "I'll kill you, if you don't knock it off!" Our language grew coarser each day, as we were exposed to the horrifying sight of corpses exposed to the elements.

Initially, we tied a rope to a cornstalk, making a sling, and carried it on our shoulder, pretending it was a rifle. We chose sides and fought battles. Soon the cornstalk was replaced by a gun, carved out of wood. The toy gun was in turn replaced by a real rifle, and we armed ourselves with an entire array of ordnance salvaged from battlefields.

What started out as child's play turned into a war between children of different villages. We sorted ourselves into units: an artillery unit, a commando unit, and an attack unit. We held training exercises and planned our strategy before going into battle.

The artillery unit's major weapon was a trench mortar, armed with a cartridge filled with gunpowder and pieces of red-hot charcoal. For good measure, we rammed spent .30 caliber shells down on top of the coals. The gunpowder would soon explode, and the charcoal and machine gun shells would catapult out the end. Needless to say, this was a major piece of hardware for the artillery unit.

During these battles, the artillery unit would be at the front, hurling projectiles at the enemy. Next, the commando unit would march forward and launch their assault. Finally, the attack unit would charge, amid shouts and clamor. The team that lost the battle would flee and any of the enemy who lagged behind would be captured as prisoners of war. When they were our prisoners, we would lock them up in a storage shed, burnt out from the war. Sometimes, we would let them go after a while. Other times they would stay in the shed until their parents came looking for them and let them out.

One day the older kids talked me into becoming the commander. They picked me because I was considered the bravest and the smartest of the children my age. Flattered by the attention, I accepted, not knowing what I was getting into. To this day, it embarrasses me to think about it.

One autumn afternoon, on the offensive, our troop marched arrogantly into the enemy's territory, a neighboring village. The commando unit went in first, with me, as troop commander, in the lead.

The entrance to the village was on a downhill slope. Going down the hill, I looked right and left as I marched forward, leading the unit. I shuddered in fear and my heart raced, but there was no turning back. I hid my fear with loud shouting and continued on.

Suddenly, out of the blue, we were ambushed. Rocks were being hurled at us from behind a persimmon tree. In an unguarded moment, my comrade, standing next to me, fell down with a cry, covering his forehead with his hands, blood gushing out from between his fingers.

Overwhelmed with fear, we retreated, as rocks now showered down on us from all directions. Going uphill to escape the village was no laughing matter. It was the longest climb I had ever experienced.

Running for my life, I arrived home, frantic. My mother, who had been sewing, looked at me puzzled. I can imagine what I must have looked like, my clothes dirty and smeared, as if I had been wallowing in the mud.

"What have you been up to? And why are you so out of breath?"

"Oh, nothing much. I was playing."

"Why the fuss, then?"

"It's nothing, Mother."

I went in my room, as if nothing had happened. I didn't set foot outside our house for two days. I finally mustered the courage to go out. When I did, a different world was awaiting me. Kids in the neighborhood began to call me names and make fun of me.

"Commander-of-the-Commando-Unit-is-Commander-of-the Chicken-Unit, Commander-of-the-Commando-Unit-is-Commander of-the-Chicken-Unit."

Faced with unbearable shame and embarrassment, I went straight home and buried my head in my blanket.

The kid who had had his forehead bloodied had bean paste rubbed on the wound as a disinfectant and wrapped a bandage around his head. From then on, I would hide whenever I saw him. He must be in his fifties by now. I wonder about him from time to time, and whether he carries a scar on his forehead from that long-ago skirmish.

One night, my mother woke us all from our sleep. "Shhhhh!" she whispered, pointing out into our yard. In the serene moonlit brightness, we could see nothing, but my mother was staring at something. We held our breath and tried to see what she was pointing at.

There it was, in the middle of the yard. Shrubs were moving slowly. One, two, three . . . more than ten shrubs were slowly crossing our yard, one step at a time, as if they were alive. They were inching closer and closer to the command forces of the North Korean Army.

My mother whispered, "Children, they're our soldiers. The South Korean soldiers are coming in. We have to keep quiet or the North Koreans will find out." The shrubs were South Korean soldiers camouflaged with twigs and grass. Their advance forces were infiltrating the village.

Shortly afterward, loud shouting, followed by a thunderous barrage of weapons fire, broke the night silence. The sound was so intense that I thought my eardrums would break. When the gunfire ceased, I heard the moaning and groaning of injured soldiers. Among the North Korean soldiers were boys in their teens, with their bowels spilling out onto the ground, crying "Mother, Mother."

Our world changed as of the next day. The South Korean soldiers set up their headquarters in my grandfather's house, which bustled with activity, and villagers who had fled the war returned home, one by one. The corpses of the North Korean soldiers were buried under the persimmon tree in the village, and farmers went back to tilling the fields. The town returned to its pre-occupation routine.

MY MOTHER, IN THE MEANTIME, CONTINUED with her sewing. My brothers had gone to live at my uncle's house, so I was responsible for finding firewood for the family, while my sister did the cooking. Finding wood was my responsibility during my elementary-school days. Lugging a huge wooden frame on my back, one that towered above me, I would roam the mountains in search of firewood.

Because we were living in a single room off the servants' quarters in my grandparents' home, we borrowed a great many things from them. Every time I set out to find wood, I would borrow a hatchet and a saw. I did not always return the tools in one piece, however. Sometimes, they would be lost and other times broken. My grandmother often scolded me for my carelessness, which I always resented.

One afternoon, with the frame on my back, I was getting ready to go out when I was startled by my grandmother's yelling. "Jin-hong, you've taken every tool we own. Are you now taking more? I want you to bring back all the tools you've ever taken."

In a fit of anger, I turned toward my grandmother and dropped my pants. I pulled out my tiny member and, holding it in my hand, shouted, "Grandma, here's my tool. Is this enough to replace all your lost tools?"

Grandmother, who had been sitting barefoot in the living room, rushed out toward me, shouting, "Yes, you little twit. Give me that tool of yours!"

Frightened out of my wits, I quickly pulled up my pants, ran out and down the alley. That was the day my grandmother decided I was destined for greatness and stopped reproaching me for using her tools. She told my mother, "Raise Jin-hong well. He has immense potential. When I demanded that he return all my tools, he pulled down his pants and exposed himself. No one else would have done that! He has a future ahead of him, that boy of yours."

There was a time during my elementary-school years when rumor had it that I was a child prodigy. In Korean class one day, my teacher called on me and asked me to read aloud from our textbook. I did not have my book with me that day and, instead of borrowing one from a classmate, I recited the passage verbatim from having memorized it when I read it the night before. The teacher stared at me and asked, "Jin-hong, are you reading with no book in front of you?"

"Yes. I left my book at home today, but I read it last night, so I know what it says."

"My goodness! A child prodigy! We have a child prodigy in our school!" exclaimed the teacher. That day I became a child prodigy. So many people referred to me as a prodigy that even I came to believe it.

Only later, in middle school, after we had moved to Daegu, which was a much bigger city, did I realize that I was nothing special. In Daegu there were "child prodigies" on every street corner. After I graduated from college and moved to Seoul, an even bigger city, I discovered that not only was I not a prodigy, I was rather dull and even lazy. It dawned on me then that if I let myself dawdle the hours away, I would never amount to anything. The only way out of it would be to push and develop myself continually.

THERE IS ONE ASPECT OF MY CHILDHOOD that cannot be left unmentioned, and that has to do with my church. My family attended Bokdong Church. It was located in a deep valley and although remote, it nevertheless had a long history and had produced a number of future leaders. Next to the church building, which had a traditional Korean tile roof, stood a huge elm.

To this day, I think of that church as my home and I miss it more every year. As I grew older, whenever I felt the need to escape from the harshness of reality, I would daydream about my childhood church. It was a crutch that helped me get through lonely months in prison, painful times of illness, and the frustrations of carrying on with life.

The church would hold children's recitals on important holidays, such as Christmas, Thanksgiving, and Easter. At every event, I took the stage as a presenter, giving the opening comment and either singing a solo or taking part in a play. We also annually held outdoor Sunday services to celebrate Children's Day, the first week of May, when the congregation would assemble outdoors, with tables laden with sumptuous food. In the shade of chestnut and apple trees, it was wonderful to be out and alive. On those occasions, too, I would always be called upon to sing:

> A lark singing in the barley field.
> A maiden picking herbs gazes at the sky.

There is no way of spotting where it's coming from.
And only a swallow tail flies by.

People would applaud and praise my performance whenever I sang in public. Later, having strayed, these memories were instrumental in turning me back to the church. Such fond and enduring thoughts accumulated in my heart, sustained me during my years of despair.

Once, for our Thanksgiving service, I brought three of my friends to church. We always had a special snack after the service, where each family brought persimmons, apples, or rice cakes. Considering that in those days food was not plentiful, the Thanksgiving snack was a treat that children looked forward to, which explained the overflowing attendance of children at every Thanksgiving service.

On that particular day, however, food was short. One of the church members announced, "Those children whose parents are not regular members of the congregation may not have any rice cakes. They came today only for the food, not the service."

She then started checking all the children who had been lining up to get rice cakes. I felt so bad for my friends that my face turned crimson with embarrassment. I knew that what she was saying was wrong. If anybody was going to be left out of the eating, it should be the children of parents who are regular members of the church. We should yield our food to our guests, the newcomers, I thought. At that I decided to get out of line and not eat anything. My mother somehow learned about it and that night asked me.

"Jin-hong, my child, I hear you didn't eat anything at church today."

"No. I didn't."

"Why? Were you sick?"

"No, I was fine."

"Why, then? What was the matter?"

"Today I took Chun, Yeong-il, and Tae-sik to church."

"Good for you! Then what happened?"

"When it was time to line up for food after the service, they said that children who were not regular members of the church were not allowed to eat. None of my friends could have anything, so I didn't feel like eating either."

"You went all day without eating! Why didn't you go ahead and eat, Jin-hong?"

"I couldn't do that, Mother. How could I eat, all by myself, while my friends, who I had invited, could not? People shouldn't act like that in church. Jesus said to give, and if you give only to churchgoers and leave out the others, I think that goes against what Jesus is all about."

"You're right, my son. You're absolutely right. The church people were wrong to do that. I'll bring it up at the next board meeting. You must be starving. I'll boil you some potatoes."

My mother did raise the issue at the church meeting the following month. After much discussion, the board members concluded that it was a mistake to have deprived the visiting children of the Thanksgiving snack and that it should not happen again. I was pleased that my missing one meal in protest had had such an impact on our congregation.

3

Every Cloud Has a Silver Lining

WHEN I GRADUATED FROM elementary school, my mother had to decide whether I would continue my schooling. We had been living from hand to mouth and in our circumstances, it seemed out of the question for my mother to afford middle-school tuition.

My grandfather knew about our situation and took it upon himself to find me a job as an apprentice to a blacksmith. Then he tried to convince my mother that it was the right thing for me to do.

"Don't overwork yourself trying to send your children to school," he told my mother. "Send Jin-hong to the blacksmith's. It's all arranged, and he'll be able to fend for himself for life with the skills he'll learn there."

My mother would not hear of it. "I don't think so, Father. He's too smart to be satisfied with such a job, and besides, that's not what his father wanted for him. On his deathbed, he said that at the least he wanted Jin-hong to get an education. Even if it means that I starve, Jin-hong will continue his schooling."

"Why bring up someone who's no longer living? If your husband was so dedicated to his children's education, he should have stayed around to see to it himself. People can't be bound by the wishes of the dead."

At that, Grandfather stalked off in a huff. Having overheard their conversation, I would be forever grateful to my mother for her perseverance. I promised myself that I would study hard and be good to her and grow up to be a great man to repay her.

I began to go to church every morning, praying that the Lord would find a way for me to go to school. I was convinced that if I failed to go on with my education, I would never accomplish a thing. I was desperate.

"Dear Jesus, please allow me to get into a middle school so I can become a great man and work for my country, build up my family's reputation, and serve my mother. I will never accomplish anything if I become a blacksmith's errand boy. Jesus, I must go on with my education."

I FINALLY MANAGED TO ENTER MIDDLE SCHOOL. My mother had stuck by me against all the criticism from her relatives. School for me, however, was not an easy ride. For starters, I began without having paid my tuition. A month into the term, my teacher took me aside and told me to go home, get my tuition money, and pay at the business office before returning to class. I gathered my things and left the classroom.

I had nowhere to go, but I wasn't alone. Three of my classmates were dismissed in the same fashion. We went to a nearby stream and spent the rest of the day in the shade of an acacia tree. We went home when school let out later in the day, saying nothing to our parents.

Day after day, I would carry my satchel to school and go to class, just like the other kids and, day after day, my teacher would call me up to the front of the class and demand that I go home and get my tuition money. Then, I would walk out of the classroom with my three classmates and together we would head for the stream, where we would pass the time before returning to our homes at the end of the day. It was during this first year of middle school when, in the midst of this routine, I was asked to sing at the school's Foundation Day.

I was called in to the principal's office the day before the celebration. Without telling me why I had been called in, the principal asked me to sing a song. I sang an old popular song, "The Palace in Ruin." Although it was an adult song and not appropriate for a child to sing, he must have liked it because, to my surprise, he told me that he wanted me to sing that very song at the Foundation Day ceremony.

The celebration came off successfully and afterward I was allowed to stay in class, with the understanding that eventually the school would get its money.

My mother, meanwhile, had become frustrated because she could not afford our tuition. One day she packed up and, with my sister in tow, headed for Daegu to find work. After she left, I did not hear from her. Thus I spent my first semester at Andeok Middle School.

When summer vacation came around, I wrote to my mother. Starting off with "Dear Mother, please read what I have to say about my situation," I poured my heart out to her, going into great detail about the pathetic condition in which I found myself. I even drew pictures of my shoes with holes in them, my toes sticking out the front, my pants torn at the knees, and my shirt with tattered sleeves. I pleaded with her to allow me to go live with her and promised that I would earn my keep by doing any work I could, even selling newspapers and cigarettes on the street.

My mother must have been moved by my letter because in September she came to get me. She settled the account with the school's business office, paying all the overdue tuition and fees, requested transfer documents, and took me off to Daegu.

My mother and my older sister had been living in a slum. While my mother had gotten herself a job at a textile plant, my older brother worked at a printing office and my sister as a housemaid. I was happy that our family was together again.

I sold newspapers on the street during the day and attended Yeong-sin Middle School in the evening. I soon quit selling newspapers, however, and got myself a proper job delivering a newspaper, the *Hanguk Ilbo*, to subscribers. I would get up at four in the morning, take a stack of some one hundred newspapers, and set out on my route. Covering a long distance from Sinam-dong* to Sincheon-dong, then all the way to the rear gate of Gyeongbuk National University in Sangyeok-dong, my route was spread out over a wide area. By the time I finished, I was dizzy from hunger and exhaustion. Whenever I passed a restaurant, I would stand immobile, savoring the sweet smell of soup before going on my way.

One day, a passerby stopped me in the middle of my route. "Do you have an extra you can sell me?" he asked. While I should have said no, I couldn't bring myself to refuse him and hesitated. As I stood

---

* A *dong* is equivalent to a ward.

there, the man handed me twenty *won** and pulled a newspaper out from the bundle under my arm. I took the twenty *won* to a nearby store and bought myself a steaming hot bun stuffed with bean paste. It tasted heavenly and was a great treat for my stomach.

Following a fleeting moment of pleasure, I was quickly consumed with worry about how to make up for the missing paper because I had only enough papers for my route. After considering which house to skip, I decided on the one that seemed least likely to cause me trouble, but I was wrong because whoever didn't get a newspaper called the office to complain.

On a river bank in Daegu during middle-school years.

My supervisor reproached me for my failure and warned me that if anything like that happened again, I would be fired. I assured him, as well as myself, that it would never happen again. Nevertheless, in the days following, when I was once again tempted by a stranger with another twenty *won*. I would waver, listening to my conscience shout that what I was doing was not right. That voice was drowned out by my stomach calling for another bun with bean paste filling and before I knew it, my fingers had grabbed his twenty *won* and had handed over the newspaper. The next minute found me running again to a store to

---

* The *won* is the Korean unit of currency. See Appendix for a won: dollar conversion table for the years 1955-2000.

buy another bun. After repeated occurrences of this sort, an angry manager called me into his office.

Glaring down at me, he said, "I tried to be patient with you and look the other way while you kept pulling this stunt on me. I warned you that you would be fired if you didn't live up to your responsibilities. Now I've had enough of you. I feel like thrashing you, but I'll restrain myself."

He didn't restrain himself from firing me, however. Giving in to the temptation of the bean-paste-filled buns had cost me my job.

One day, my mother called us all to a family meeting. "Children, I have something to discuss with you. Our family has so many mouths to feed, yet so little to eat, we must come up with a solution. I know someone who works at an orphanage who tells me that they can take Jin-hong and Cheol-ung. There they will be fed and educated. I think they will be much better off than struggling at home with so little to eat. What do you think?"

My older brother and I acquiesced to her suggestion, but my sister and my younger brother, Cheol-ung, reacted strongly against it. My younger brother pleaded to stay with our mother, even if it meant being hungry. My sister argued that a family should stay together. She pointed out that so far her two little brothers had been growing up with kind hearts, despite the difficult circumstances. If they were exposed to harsh and cruel kids in the orphanage, they would be badly influenced. Once they turned bad, there would be no way of turning them around, regardless of how much money or food they got.

She convinced my mother. "You're absolutely right," Mother said. "We can't let poverty separate us. The saying goes that there's a way out, even when the sky falls. I'm sure none of us will starve." That ended the family meeting.

FEELING COMPELLED TO CONTRIBUTE to my family's livelihood, I next took a job at a glass factory. The job that was assigned to me, however, required more of me than I could give. Part of the manufacturing process required water, which I had to supply, in a bucket, from a stream below a dam. I was slow and people yelled at me for the slightest delay.

I did the best I could, but I simply was not strong enough for the job. Heat from the furnaces affected my voice and, by the end of the day, I could barely speak. My legs trembled from exhaustion. It was no wonder that when I went to school at night, after work, I would fall asleep in class.

My teacher, unaware of my daytime job, would hit me on the head and complain, "Do you come to school to sleep?" By then, however, nothing could have kept my eyes open. I have to do something about this situation, I told myself. I need to survive! If I fail, I might end up in the orphanage.

Despite my determination, something happened in my third month at the glass factory that forced me to quit. A line manager who was angry with me for causing a delay in the manufacturing process, knocked me down and beat and kicked me. I was totally defenseless and didn't dare let out a yelp. The beating ended only when other workers intervened to stop the raging man.

When I came home with my nose and mouth bleeding, my sister rushed toward me and asked what had happened. Wiping the blood off my face with a wet towel, tears rolled down her face as she listened to my account of the beating.

"Jin-hong," my sister said, "your job at the factory causes you too much pain. You have to quit. You're the kind of person who will succeed by studying, not by hard labor. Let's look for a job that'll let you work and study at the same time."

"Where could I find a job like that? Sure, my job at the factory is horrible, and I'd love to quit, but I have to work or Mother'll have to support us all by herself."

With tears in our eyes, my sister and I mumbled a few words to each other and then began to blubber and cry.

When I went to the factory to tell them I was quitting, they refused to pay me the two months wages they owed me. When I insisted upon being paid and explained that I was quitting because the work was too hard for me, they sneered at me for daring to demand pay when I hadn't even completed their probation period. I did not back down, but confronted them on several occasions afterward to demand my wages. My persistence paid off, and eventually they did pay me, however insubstantial the amount. After that experience, I was no longer able to sing. My voice was ruined.

I STAYED HOME UNTIL ONE DAY I DECIDED to visit a friend of my older brother's who worked at a bookstore. I proposed that if he would allow me to pick a book from the shelves each day, I would return it the next day in exactly the same condition as when I took it. I explained to him that I had been craving reading material, but had no way to pay for it. I begged him to help me. I finally prevailed upon him, but while he agreed to do as I asked, he warned me against returning the books stained or with dog-eared pages.

From that day on, I devoured books like a starving man at a banquet. That was the beginning of my reading period. Feeding my voracious appetite for books, I read and read, sometimes two books and sometimes three a day. My readings encompassed a wide range of topics, from *Les Misérables, Crime and Punishment,* and *Sanguo yanyi (The History of the Three Kingdoms)* to *Woman's Life* and *A Collection of Korean Literature.*

My relatives did not appreciate seeing me curled up in my room, buried in books.

"What a senseless boy! Leaving his poor mother to slave to support the family, while he spends his time reading scraps of paper."

Mother would respond, "Whatever he reads will be of use. You know how in the old days people said that a well-read son can never go wrong. Considering there are so many kids who get into trouble, I'm thankful that he reads."

Despite the sneering and taunting from relatives, those were truly happy days for me. Whenever I picked up a book, I became so engrossed in it that I felt as though I was the hero of the story. When I read *Sanguo yanyi*, I became Zhuge Liang, and when I read Lee Gwang-su's *Heuk (The Soil)*, I became Dong-hyeok. If I fell asleep while reading, in my dreams I would become the main character of the story.

Some of my favorite books were works by Dostoyevsky, and Hermann Hesse's *Demian*. To this day, I can return to the real world only after I have finished the last page of a book.

Instead of sleeping in class, to my teachers' continued disappointment, I now read in class. Although they reproached me for not paying attention, I could not let go of my book. I was considered strange and word got out to the other teachers. At one point, I had my book taken away for reading in class. I followed the teacher to his office and, in desperation, I begged him to return it. He finally did, but only after I gave my word that I would no longer read in class.

My reading period ended abruptly when my source was cut off. My brother's friend moved away, leaving me without a benefactor.

In the meantime, my sister, who had continued to study while working as a housemaid, had been admitted to a teacher's college in Daegu. My mother was elated with the news. Seeing how excited she was made me wonder what I could ever do that would please her as much.

My younger brother, who was three years my junior, was in elementary school at the time. One day, he came home from school looking dejected. I asked, "Did something happen at school? Why are you so down?"

He explained that he was unable to do his homework the night before because he did not have any textbooks and had been punished by the teacher. My heart went out to him and I began to think of how to get him the textbooks he needed.

After several days of pondering, I decided to shoplift them from a bookstore. I figured I could filch them from the shelves, when the owner was not looking.

There were a lot of bookstores lining the streets near Daegu City Hall. I walked along the street, searching for the store that seemed the busiest. I picked one that was bustling with customers, went in, and found the three books my brother needed.

As soon as I thought the storekeeper was distracted, I slid the books under my shirt and walked out quietly, trying to be inconspicuous. My heart beat wildly and my body was tense, as if someone was grabbing me from behind.

Looking straight ahead, I walked until I was some distance from the bookstore. Then, just when I thought I was safe, a rough hand grabbed me by the neck. "You little thief! Who do you think you are?" With that, the shop owner smacked me across the cheek. Sparks flashed in front of my eyes.

I handed him the three books and desperately begged him, rubbing my two hands together, "I'm sorry, sir. I'm truly sorry. Please, forgive me."

I will never forget how utterly wretched and defenseless I felt. He took pity on me and let me go. I walked away, defeated. That was my first and only experience at shoplifting.

Incidents in my life such as this one, may have contributed to my outlook that life is, in many ways, very sad. I think the only way for a person to overcome this inherent sadness is to lead a meaningful life.

When I arrived home, I was greeted by my brother, who rushed to meet me.

"What happened to your face? Did you get in a fight? It's all swollen, as if you've been stung by a bee!"

"No, I just bumped into something."

"What did you bump into that could have made it swell up like that? Are you sure you bumped into something?"

Unable to hide my tears, I ran to my room.

After my patron at the bookstore moved away, I borrowed books from the City Library, where I spent my days reading, until in the evening my empty stomach would tell me that it was time to go home.

4

Itinerant Wanderings

AFTER GRADUATING FROM MIDDLE SCHOOL, I attended evening class at Yeongsin High School. By then, my enthusiasm for reading had waned and I had discovered the excitement of the silver screen. Housed in the Town Hall and facing the Daegu Railway Station was the decrepit Daegu Army Theater.

It specialized in cowboy movies, which I found fascinating. It was not long before my fascination became an addiction, and I found myself skipping both classes and meals to go to the movies. To pay for my new-found vice, I sometimes even sold my school books.

While it called itself a theater, the facilities and equipment hardly qualified it as such. The foul stench of urine that hung in the air stung the nostrils. The film quality was so bad that vertical lines on the screen made every scene look as if it was taking place in the rain and the movies suffered from chronic interruptions, with films always getting cut off, disrupting their continuity.

I, however, did not mind the poor condition of the theater. Before voices on foreign films were dubbed, a narrator would explain to the audience what was happening on the screen.

I always enjoyed the narration more than the movie itself. "The villains are chasing John Wayne. A few steps ahead of him lies a cliff and certain death. What should Wayne do?" the voice intoned rhetorically. "Unwilling to accept defeat, he swiftly turns around, points his gun at the…"

At the height of the excitement, the power would go off with a loud "thunk!" The enraged audience would waste no time in hooting demanding catcalls.

"We want our money back! We're getting outa here!"

This great chorus of raucous disapproval that filled the theater would end only after power had been restored. Anticipating the resumption of the last scene, as the film started to roll again, we would be disappointed to find that John Wayne's gun was no longer in his hand and he was out of danger. The film would have jumped forward to a wholly unrelated segment.

For me, it was all the same. The narrator's deep voice would get me excited and seeing the heroes gun down the villains only increased the thrill.

After leaving my job at the glass factory, I turned to peddling. It was easier work and gave me more freedom. In the beginning, I peddled a Chinese medicinal mint called *eundan*.

Later, I took up ballpoint pens. In those days, ballpoints were a rarity because they had only recently been invented. I bought the pens from wholesalers and would go around to coffee shops and offices on weekends and sell them.

During my first year in high school, I started a cosmetics business. I carried my product, a low-quality homemade cosmetic cream, around in a pack on my back and sold it in residential areas. People called the cream by the generic name "tom-tom cream," because people who sold it often beat on a tom-tom to get the attention of customers.

I bought the materials to prepare the cream and mixed it at home. At the same time, I bought some secondhand cosmetics jars. I placed them in a big pot, filled the pot with water, added some caustic soda to clean them, and turned on the heat. After the jars had boiled a while, I cooled them one by one, scrubbed them as clean as I could with a toothbrush, and let them dry. Finally, I filled the jars with my tom-tom cream.

I, too, had a drum. To a rub-a-dub-dub, rub-a-dub-dub, I would deliver my spiel. "Cosmetics for sale! Top cosmetics that work wonders for a chapped face and hands. Don't miss this once-in-a-lifetime opportunity to buy high-quality cosmetics. Cosmetics here!"

I hawked my goods, walking through Daegu's narrow alleys. Sometimes I would spread them out on a mat along a busy street, conducting my business there.

"Ladies and gentlemen, I have the best-quality cosmetics," I would shout, to no one in particular. "Don't miss this. Get the best cosmetics available at half their original price. Only 100 *won* per jar."

Sales went well. On some days I would set up shop in the Yeongcheon Market and on others I would take trips to nearby towns. The market in Yeongcheon was open only one day a week. I would display the cosmetic creams on the ground. Although the jars all contained the same cream, I would set the best-looking jars aside, as if they were in some way special.

Occasionally, women who appeared to be well-off would come up to me, asking for a good-quality cream. Taking my cue, I would reach for the best-looking jar I had and state my claim, "This is the top of the line, ma'am." Unscrewing the lid, I would dip my finger in it and dab a dot of cream on her palm.

"This is not the same as the others. Different people have different needs," I would go on, "and a lady like you, ma'am, deserves the finest— this one."

Flattering her, I would quote a price three times that of the original. Taken in by my remarks, the woman would happily agree that the cream was of exceptional quality and would walk away with a purchase.

This sort of thing happened several times, and my younger brother, who one day happened to see me pulling this trick, asked in amazement, "Can you get away with that?"

"Don't worry, I know what I'm doing. This is what business is all about," I replied confidently, as if I were an expert on the subject.

DURING MY SECOND YEAR OF HIGH SCHOOL, I became a devotee of Schopenhauer's philosophy of pessimism and read his book *On Suicide*. Still selling cosmetics in the market, I would read whenever I found time. I relished every line:

> Whoever you are, you are sure to die, even though your life has been full of abomination and crime. Life is not so desirable a thing as to be protracted at any cost. The chief of all remedies for a troubled mind is the feeling that among the blessings which Nature gives to man there is none greater than an opportune death; and the best of it is

that every one of us can avail himself of it…. Not even to God are all things possible; for he could not compass his own death, if he willed to die, and yet in all the miseries of our earthly life this is the best of his gifts to man.

Life is better unborn or, if ever born, to be lived quickly.

In my gloomy world, reading Schopenhauer was like pouring oil onto a flame. Eventually his pessimism mastered my soul to such a degree that I felt forced to either make a brave choice and surrender my life or live on like a coward. I decided to commit suicide. To fulfill my mission I began to buy sleeping pills from drugstores around town. Once I had gathered enough pills to put myself into an eternal sleep, I would summon my courage and take my life. Or so I thought.

One day, my mother found the pills in one of my pockets and confronted me with them.

"Jin-hong, what're all these pills in your pocket? They look like sleeping pills. I hope you're not planning anything stupid," she said. "No, Mother, and why do you have to go through my pockets, anyway? There's nothing to worry about."

"Jin-hong, tell me the truth. You've been acting very strangely lately. It's your life, I know, but you also need to think about your mother who for years has deprived herself of food and sleep to feed and raise the four of you."

With that she unceremoniously tossed the pills into the rubbish. Of everything she said, it was the part about depriving herself of food and sleep that weighed on me most heavily. I could not deny it. I had no choice but to abandon my plan to put an end to my painful existence and continue my weary way through life.

Although I had given up the thought of committing suicide, my life became no less a burden, as I continued with my schooling. I would daydream during class and was consumed with boredom as the teacher went on about calculus, or whatever.

ONE DAY, I DECIDED TO TRAVEL. PENNILESS, I TOOK OFF, with only a toothbrush in my shirt pocket and a book of poetry by Hermann Hesse. I considered myself a modern-day Kim Sat-gat, a well-known early 19th-century satirist who roamed the countryside, reciting poetry. My wandering would last two years. During that time I was in and out of school. Lengthy absences caused me to be expelled four times, until finally Yeongsin High School refused to reinstate me. I transferred to Seonggwang High School, from which I finally managed to graduate.

As I set out on my journey, I generated income by peddling my cream. With a cosmetic box on my back and a small drum strapped on my chest, I would beat the drum while walking through rural villages. Local women would stop me from time to time. When they did, the conversation would go something like this:

"Young man, is your cream any good?"

"Yes, of course. It's excellent."

"Let me have one."

"Ma'am, you need to bring an empty cosmetic container, so I can fill it."

I would scoop the cream out from my box, as if I were scooping ice cream, and fill the empty containers. In exchange, I would be given a meal and, on some occasions, even be allowed to stay overnight in one of the small rooms that traditional Korean houses have off the vestibule. Whenever I was tired from walking all day, I would find a hill overlooking a village, sit down, and read Hesse:

ACROSS THE FIELDS

> Across the sky, the clouds move,
> Across the fields, the wind,
> Across the fields, the lost child
> Of my mother wanders.
> Across the street, leaves blow,
> Across the trees, birds cry.
> Across the mountains, far away,
> My home must be.

Cosmetic cream was a good winter business, but in summer the seasonal increase in the farm workload gave women little time to care for their skin. Then I would switch to needles and thread. Needles were the perfect product for an itinerant peddler. They were small and easy to carry, and were something that no one could do without for long. Everyone needed them. I would barter a pouch of needles for a meal and a spool of thread for overnight accommodation.

There were times when I stayed on at a farmer's house for days or weeks, helping out with farm chores. After spending a while with a family, I found that I would become attached to them. Keeping to the spirit of Kim Sat-gat, however, I would always tear myself away and move on, going from town to town and city to city.

ONE TIME DURING MY WANDERING I found myself near Miryang, in South Gyeongsang province, on my way to Masan. I was following the Nakdong River. It was during the summer rainy season and it had been raining on and off for several days. It was afternoon and rain was pouring down. To escape it, I retreated to a shed on the muddy riverside. It was adequate enough as a shelter because it had a door that closed and it held fresh straw from the summer harvest.

I took off my wet clothes, set them out on the straw to dry, and waited for the rain to let up. It didn't. Instead, it poured down in ever-greater volume, its monotonous cacophony punctuated at intervals by lightning and thunder. The sun went down and darkness stretched over the landscape, but the rain did not abate. Abandoning the idea of leaving the shed any time soon, I decided to stay the night. I fashioned myself a bed out of straw and went to sleep.

I don't know how long I had been asleep, but sometime during the night I awoke with a strange feeling. It was pitch black and water was flowing into the shed. Disoriented and afraid, I listened to the rainfall as the water violated the tenuous security of my makeshift quarters. I walked back and forth until finally the water was knee deep.

It was so dark, I had no idea what was around me, but I could feel the water rising. It occurred to me that my life could end in this shed, and I shuddered at the thought. I crawled as high up the pile of straw as I could and knelt to pray.

"Lord, please save me. Would it be right for me to drown here? If you save me from this water, I will become your faithful servant. Please, please save me." I begged and I pleaded, but by now the water surging in was becoming louder. I let my legs hang down from my perch atop the straw, thinking that when my feet touched the water, the end would not be far off. If that happens, should I try to swim? Should I go up onto the roof? I considered every alternative as I continued to pray.

"Oh, Lord, am I going to die here? Please reach out and deliver me. As you delivered Moses from the Nile, and the Israelites from the Red Sea, deliver me from the Nakdong."

As I prayed, I could hear the far-off thunder. At one point, with the lightning brightening the shed for a brief moment, I sensed that the water level was going down. I quickly dangled my feet over the edge of the straw. To my amazement, I felt no water. The water was receding. I could still hear the rain outside, coming down as hard as ever, but where I was, the situation was improving. I didn't know what was happening, but I was relieved. Through the night, I sat awake, listening to the rain.

When daylight came, I opened the door and stepped outside. "This is my Father's world, and to my list'ning ears, All nature sings, and round me rings the music of the spheres...." I poured out the hymn spontaneously.

I set out along the bank of the upper reaches of the river. A couple of miles downriver from the shed, I came upon a dam that had burst the night before. Seeing that, it all made sense—the miraculous lowering of the water level inside the shed, despite the continuing rain. The reservoir had emptied through the broken dam.

Although all the nearby fields were flooded, I could not help feeling great joy at being alive. As I continued along the riverbank, I came upon distressed farmers, despairing over their ruined fields. I tried my best to keep a serious demeanor before their tragedy, but inside I felt differently. The more I thought about it, the more amazing my experience had been. I knelt on the bank of Nakdong and gave thanks to the Lord. It didn't matter how the dam had burst, I was convinced that it was the Lord's response to my prayers.

Finishing my prayer of thanks, I decided that I should return home and study. I felt that Jesus had saved me because He wanted me to serve Him. Without studying, I would be of no use to Him. I couldn't continue to wander about with no purpose. I would go home and prepare myself to become Jesus' servant.

I got on a bus to return to Daegu. Greeting the bus driver in my most polite voice, I explained that I had no money because I had run away from home and had been penniless for a long time. I went on to say that I had decided to return home and that I would be grateful if he would give me a free ride. Those were the days when adults were generous to young people traveling without money and he let me board.

As the driver motioned his permission, I was elated and walked to the rear of the bus and sat down. I started singing, first "The Silla Moonlight," then "How Bright is the Fall Moon," and then I went on to sing "The Hill of Bau." In fact, for more than an hour I sang a collection of songs, ranging from pop to hymns. Finally, an elderly man sitting next to me admonished me, "Young man, if you want to sing, do it in your own home. Be considerate of others around you." I blushed with embarrassment and turned my head away.

Upon returning home, I told my mother my intention to get an education. She responded solemnly. "Raising four kids hasn't been easy. If you are to study, it would add to my burden, but if you're convinced that it's important for your future, then I will support you, whatever it takes."

When I returned to my old school, Yeongsin High, I was told that I had been officially dropped from the roll. I pleaded with my teacher that I would study hard, if only given the chance. The school relented and let me in. My commitment, however, was short-lived. Barely a month after I was reinstated, I found myself once again daydreaming in class.

This time I talked my friend, Yoon Hyeong-su, into going off with me. I took a job as a salesman for The Kim Cheol Advertising Research Center. Names can be deceptive. Despite the prestigious ring to the name, The Kim Cheol Advertising Research Center was nothing more than an over-the-counter drug direct-sales company that sent salespeople into the countryside to sell their products, which included rat poison and worm medicine.

Paired up with Hyeong-su, I made the rounds of open markets in rural towns, peddling the chemicals. The rat poison was supposedly harmless to people, yet fatal to mice. We settled in a high-traffic area, bustling with people, and hawked the poison the best we could.

While I harangued passersby with a sales pitch, Hyeong-su stood alongside me, demonstrating the safety of the poison by putting it in and out of his mouth. This was to show that it was harmless to humans and fatal only to small animals. Many farmers bought it, but to this day, I have no idea whether it actually worked.

Having cut my teeth as a pitchman with my cosmetics business, I spoke confidently and enthusiastically.

"Ladies and gentlemen, the eye is the jewel of your life. You need to go to the mountain to catch snakes, you need to go to the brook to catch crawfish, and you need to come to the market to buy medicine. Rid yourself of all the intestinal parasites that have set up house in your intestines and endanger your health. With just one of these tiny pills, unwelcome roundworms in your system will be sentenced to oblivion. Buy this and you will be healthy and will thank me. If you don't, it's your loss!

"Consider yourself lucky to have discovered this product right here in the market today. You probably owe this luck to your ancestors, for you have respected them well. How much do we, The Kim Cheol Advertising Research Center, ask for this great medicinal breakthrough? Just one thousand *won*! But are we actually going to charge you that much for it? No, we are not! We're slashing the price in half! You pay only five hundred *won*!

"Yes, you heard me right! We have a special promotion going on right now. For a time, just through the end of the year, we're offering our product at a special price, to promote it and to serve the health of the public."

As I spoke, Hyeong-su passed out the medicine and collected the money. Raising money in this way, however, was not easy. Not only was it difficult to find a place in the market, rainy days meant no business and, come farming season, farmers would be too busy to come to the market.

By the time we arrived at the Namji Market in South Gyeongsang province, we were completely exhausted. We did not have a dime between us. We squatted in front of a short-order cafe and rubbed our empty stomachs.

Hyeong-su said, "Jin-hong, we need to come up with something. We can't go on like this."

"I know, but it doesn't seem like there's anything we can do."

"No, I'm sure if we look, we'll find a way. I have an idea, but I don't know if you'll go for it."

"What is it? If it sounds good to you, why would I object? It's not as if I have any brilliant ideas of my own."

"No, but you're different from me."

"What are you talking about? How are we different?"

"You know, you believe in Jesus, and I don't."

"What does it matter what I believe in? The fact that we're hungry is the same for both of us."

"That's not what I'm talking about. It's just that people who believe in Jesus aren't supposed to do what I'm thinking of."

"What is it that you're making such a big deal out of?"

"I was thinking that we could pickpocket."

"What? Are you out of your mind? You mean steal someone's money? Don't even mention such nonsense."

"See. I knew you'd say that. It's because you believe in Jesus."

"No, it's not. It's not right to steal, whether you're a believer or not."

We held out for a few more hours, but there was nothing we could do to allay our hunger. I went along with Hyeong-su's idea after all.

"OK, let's try it. There's a saying that a man should try everything once."

We decided to do it just one time. We planned it so that I would distract our victim and Hyeong-su would take the money. Finally, a vulnerable-looking old lady appeared with money sticking out of her pocket. Hyeong-su winked at me and whispered, "Bump into her and distract her. I'll take the money."

My heart throbbed. I took a deep breath to gain composure and caught up with the old lady. Pretending to be gazing at the mountains off in the distance, I bumped into her. To stall her, I wrapped my arms around her shoulders and stammered, "Oh, I'm so sorry. You should be more careful, when you're in the market."

Hyeong-su quickly came onto the scene. He approached the old lady, extended his hand, but walked away abruptly. We met at a pottery house on the edge of the market.

"Did you pull it off?"

"I couldn't. Right when I was about to reach out, I felt someone pulling me by my collar from behind."

We decided to give it a second go. This time we would switch roles, and I would do the snatching. When a middle-aged woman appeared with her purse in her shopping basket in plain view, we knew right off that she was a perfect mark. Fixing his eyes on the purse, Hyeong-su glanced at me as if to say "go for it." I nodded back to show him that I understood and I tailed the woman.

Hyeong-su quickly passed ahead of her and went to the end of the alley. He turned around and came back toward her, bumping into her head on. I immediately rushed toward them, but as I reached out my hand to grab the purse, I felt as if everyone was looking at me. I just walked away. Again I met Hyeong-su in front of the pottery, as we had planned.

"Did you get it?"

"No, I couldn't possibly do it. I was too nervous."

"Yeah, me too. Let's give it up. We're not cut out for this."

"But we need to eat something. What can we do?"

"I have an idea, Jin-hong. Follow me!"

With Hyeong-su leading the way, we walked along a back alley of Namji Market. I wondered what scheme he was cooking up this time. He sauntered into an inn, with an aura of commanding presence.

When the caretaker showed up, Hyeong-su haughtily said, "*Ajumma*,* give us a clean room and send in a meal for two."

"Sure. Go into that room over there and I'll serve you supper in a little while."

"Could you keep these bags for us? They contain everything we own, so please be careful with them."

"Don't worry. They're safe with me."

I went along, without uttering a word, while Hyeong-su carried on with his scheme. When we were left alone at supper, I said to him. "You're making me nervous. What are you up to?"

"Don't worry. Everything is under control. All you have to do is eat well, sleep well, and do as I tell you."

After the meal, Hyeong-su fell fast asleep. I lay restless, listening to him snore through the night. After filling our stomachs with a good breakfast the next morning, Hyeong-su said, "Jin-hong, go and wait for me at the gazebo under that big tree on the other side of the hill."

"What about you? What are you going to do?"

Ajumma refers to a middle-aged woman.

44

"Don't worry. I can take care of myself. Just go and wait for me," he insisted. I did as I was told and walked up the hill and waited.

Hyeong-su arrived a while later, empty-handed. "Those bags may be pretty worn-out, but they should be worth our accommodation."

We resumed our journey, traveling from town to town along the south coast of South Gyeongsang province. One day, as we were walking along the road between Pohang to Gyeongju, Hyeong-su spoke to me in a serious voice.

"Jin-hong, I think it's time you went home."

"What are you talking about?"

"You and I are buddies, but I have a feeling that our lives are going in different directions. It's OK for me to live on as an itinerant peddler, but this life isn't for you. You belong in school."

"No, you're wrong. The last time I went home, I was determined to study, but after a month, I couldn't take it any longer and hit the road again. Don't you remember? I couldn't bring myself to concentrate. I'm no longer any good for studying. I'm too used to being footloose, just like Kim Sat-gat," I protested.

"I still think it'd be better for you to go back to school. Look at you. You still carry books around and read whenever you have a chance. That's proof that you should be home studying. We've had our share of good times in the real world. Now let's go home. You can go back to your studies and I'll come up with something to do."

Before going to sleep that night, I gave serious thought to what Hyeong-su had said and came to the conclusion that I should go home and return to my studies. The next morning, we caught a free ride on a train bound for Daegu.

WHEN I GOT HOME, I TOLD MY MOTHER that I once again wanted to go back to school. With much difficulty, she came up with the money to pay the tuition. At first the school denied my readmission, but after I promised to buckle down and put my life in order, they once more relented and admitted me.

Within a week, however, I was finding it extremely hard to remain in class. Nothing the teacher said registered in my head and a thousand distractions haunted me. My experiences on the road, all the places I had been, the towns, the marketplaces, the harbors, all danced before my eyes.

A mere month after I resumed my education, I dropped out and left for another journey.

This time I hopped a Seoul-bound train. Peddlers on the train were passing along the aisles. Talking to them, it occurred to me that peddling on a train would be a perfect job for me, since it would allow me to travel everywhere. I saw myself squeezing my way among crowds of passengers on the train, selling an array of snacks and beverages, ranging from dried squid, to caramel, sweet jelly, and *soju*.*

At the station in Seoul, I inquired about the job and went through the steps to become a train peddler. I started by selling the same items as everyone else. Passing along the narrow aisles, I shouted out, "Dried squid, caramel, *soju*, and soft drinks," but after a few days the boredom drove me to become more inventive. I decided to liven up my job and make it fun, and do something the customers could enjoy, as well.

I spiced up my sales pitch, mimicking the narrator's voice of the films I had watched at Daegu Army Theater. Sales tactics that I had picked up from selling medicine also came in handy.

"Greetings to all of you aboard the train. This is the railroad snack bar run by the Transportation Ministry. Are you weary from your long trip? Then I have good news for you. Not long ago this squid was frolicking in the Pacific Ocean. It traveled to Ulleung Island, where a local fisherman caught it, dried it, and sold it to me. Now you can eat it and take the skin home to patch your *janggu* (traditional Korean drum). It's tougher than what you're using now and will give a good solid sound.

"We have roasted chestnuts that are a specialty of Yeongcheon. You can eat the chestnuts and take the shells home to start your fire. It'll keep you warm and put you right to sleep on cold nights.

"We have Jinro *soju*. Share a glass or two with the people around you, and this dismal coach will become a virtual paradise."

I went from car to car, pitching my snacks. Customers appreciated my wit and began to buy more. Calling out what they wanted, they would comment, "You have a way with words, young man." My sales took off from the very beginning and consequently improved the treatment I received from my employer.

Soju is an inexpensive, popular grain drink, containing 25 percent alcohol.

Although things were going well for me, I had no intention of staying long on the job. I moved on, taking a train bound for the south-west corner of the Korean Peninsula, where I got off in the city of Yeosu, on the south coast. I strolled through the countryside, taking in the breathtaking view of the villages on the islands off the coast. This time I was carrying an anthology of Park Mok-wol's poetry:

THE WAYFARER

Crossing water on a ferry
onto the path through wheatfields.

The wayfarer goes like the moon
in the clouds.

A single road threads to the south
three hundred *li* * long.

The evening glow tints
each village where rice wine matures.

The wayfarer goes like the moon
in the clouds.

I felt the overwhelming emotion that the poet had described. I thought of myself as the wayfarer who walked the 300 *li* along the south coast, moving, as the moon moves through the clouds.

My travel took me to Sorok Island, a remote island for lepers. As I walked among them, I became exposed to their deformed bodies and to the wounds they carried within. They all had different personal histories, yet they shared a commitment to life. My experience with them caused me to reflect on my own life, which threw me into deep mental turmoil.

Are these lepers, plagued with distorted physiques, not struggling to live? And me with a healthy body, what am I doing with my life? I thought to myself.

All my talk about Kim Sat-gat suddenly seemed futile and I realized

---

* A *li* is a measure of distance equivalent to one-third of a mile.

how I had been frittering my life away. Contemplation led me to the conclusion that I needed to lead a more productive life. What, for me, could be a productive life?

Then I hit on it. I could become a doctor and return to help the lepers! It was time to put an end to my aimless life on the road, I thought. I would go home, study hard, and become a doctor. I would devote my life to serving the needy.

It had been several months since I had left home. When I informed my mother of my new determination to become a doctor, she said, "Whether you become a doctor or a pastor, it's all the same to me, as long as you stop wandering around and concentrate on your studies. A person has only a certain period in life that he can devote to studying. After that, you have to earn a living. If you waste your youth, you will regret it later."

I went back to Yeongsin High and once again asked to be readmitted. This time, however, my teacher adamantly rejected me.

"School is a place of instruction for healthy people. It's not a mental institution that can admit deranged people like you. If I accept you now, you'll only leave again, so just forget it."

I wouldn't take no for an answer. I followed him around and begged.

"Please give me another chance. It's all right, don't even put my name on the roll. Just let me sit in class. You'll see that this time I've really changed. After I prove myself, you can decide whether to formalize my attendance."

After my persistent entreaties, I was allowed into the classroom. I found that I had missed so much school that it was difficult to follow along in classes such as English and math. I became anxious and frustrated at what appeared to be an extremely remote possibility of my ever becoming a doctor.

Thinking about it a lot, I came to a conclusion. I went to a barber shop and had my head shaved. Then, I stopped by a secondhand bookstore and bought more than thirty books. Going home, I went to my room and pulled a blanket over the sliding door, completely blocking out the sunlight. To brighten the dimness, I lit a candle. I meditated in front of the candle for a short time and then I began to read. I had decided to stop my wandering once and for all and instead cultivate perseverance. Without resorting to a radical measure, I was sure I could not become a doctor.

With the candle burning in front of me, I sat erect in a posture that resembled that of a monk concentrating on moral teaching. A month went by, and I had successfully achieved what I yearned for—I could sit still and abstain from distracting thoughts.

On my second trip to the bookstore, I bought an English grammar book entitled *On Sentence Structure* by a Professor Yoo Jin. Beginning that day, I pored over the grammar book. I concentrated hard and read it seven times over. I even knew which pages explained a variety of selected headings, such as gerunds and prepositions.

UPON MY RETURN TO SCHOOL AFTER THIS HIATUS, my teacher was so angry that he told me never to set foot in his school again. As an alternative, I knocked on the door of Seonggwang High School. To my delight, I was admitted. From that day on, I studied day and night.

Having acquired confidence in English from my encounter with *On Sentence Structure,* I decided to attack math in the same way. I looked for a math book that suited my level and, after finding it, went to my mother to ask for the money.

She sat quietly before replying, "You really need this book, do you?"

"Yes, Mother. I've been away from school so long, I have only a poor understanding of the basics. I need to catch up and, as I see it, this is the only way."

"OK, then. Be patient. I'll try to get the money tomorrow."

My mother, who had left home at daybreak, did not return home until sundown. Pangs of hunger led me to the kitchen in the evening. I opened the earthenware jar where we stored rice. To my astonishment, there was only a handful of rice in a thin layer at the bottom. It once again reminded me of how utterly meager our existence was, just like in the old days. I told myself that I would study hard and grow up to make Mother happy. I then sat at my desk and resumed my study. Mother came back late that night and handed me the money, without saying a word. She then went to sleep.

Without commotion, I took the money and thanked her. I was soon back concentrating on my studies. Deep into the night, I happened to lay my eyes on Mother and noticed that she had a scarf over her hair.

I figured that she must have forgotten to take it off before going to sleep and approached her to remove it for her. As my hand reached to remove the scarf, I was numbed to see that her hair was not what it had been. She had but a few strands in front and on the sides.

Only then did it occur to me that Mother had sold her hair to provide me with the money.

I was crushed. Now, everything made sense. Mother went all over town the whole day to come up with the money, but was unsuccessful. She must have decided to cut her hair as the last resort. She had left her bangs intact and covered the rest of her head with a scarf to conceal it. Somberly, I returned to my desk, took a few deep breaths, and held my hands in prayer.

"Jesus, I want to study hard to become successful. I want to provide well for my mother after I grow up. Please keep her healthy until then."

That incident drove me to study even harder. Every time I grew tired of studying, I thought of my mother's hair. It was a constant reminder that I could not spare one moment in idleness. For several weeks, I did not have the heart to set my eyes on my mother's face. Pretending to be unaware of her hairlessness, I focused on my study.

I soon started going to church. Dongsin Church, which my sister and brother attended, was led by Pastor Park Yong-muk, a fine, spiritual pastor. I became involved in the high-school Sunday school and served as the student president twice. To this day, I beam at the pleasant memory of the church, which became a significant part of my youth.

After transferring to Seonggwang High School, my student life became more stable. I attended classes relatively conscientiously, compared to the old days, but I found it difficult to change my disposition to go against traditions and rules. I was often tardy and was bound to be absent whenever it rained. One day, my homeroom teacher called upon me and inquired, "Jin-hong, stand up. Why were you absent yesterday?"

"It rained yesterday."

"What? Are you saying that you don't come to class when it rains?"

"Yes. I don't come to school when it rains."

"Are you joking with me? Come to the front this minute!"

I dragged my feet along and stood in front of the podium, when the teacher smacked me on my face with his roster. I returned to my desk, rubbing my burning cheek and grumbled, "Damn him. What a loser this guy is. He can't see my greatness."

I inadvertently made my classmates burst out in laughter. Our teacher flew into a rage and yelled at me to return to the front of the class.

"What did you say? What did you say that made everyone laugh? You cursed me, didn't you?"

I remained seated at my desk and answered calmly.

"That's enough, teacher. Let's leave it at that."

My classmates burst out in laughter a second time. Now I was headed for real trouble. The teacher's outrage had hit the climax as he threw a fit in front of the class. Walking out of the classroom, he ordered me to come down to his office. Instead of following him, however, I went home.

During my high-school days, I once visited the Gyeongbuk University Hospital to motivate myself to persevere in my studies and to reaffirm my determination to pursue the medical profession. As I walked from place to place around the complex, looking into wards and examining rooms, I discovered what appeared to an insurmountable problem with my plan. The pungent odor of hospital disinfectants was so great that it made me nauseous to the point of developing a headache.

I thought to myself, "This is awful! I'll have to smell this, not for just one or two years, but for my entire life! Perhaps being a doctor isn't for me after all." However lofty my intentions were in serving the people on Sorok Island, I realized that my constitution was not compatible with the workplace.

I left the hospital with this thought and returned for a second visit, a few days later. Walking through the halls, I became convinced that I could never become accustomed to the odor of the disinfectants. At that, I gave up my dream of becoming a doctor and decided instead to go into law. Passing the bar exam, I thought, would be the quickest path to making my mother's life easier.

Beginning that day, I studied with renewed determination. I wrote on a piece of paper, "Kim Jin-hong, admitted to Seoul National University School of Law." I pasted the paper above my desk.

One day, on her way out, my mother said, "Jin-hong, I changed the briquette and left the vent open. Would you please close the vent after a while? I left your rice on the burner. Help yourself to it at dinner time."

I casually said OK, but soon forgot all about it because I was so engrossed in my studies. After a while, I was startled at the sound of my mother's cry from the kitchen.

"My goodness! What on earth has happened?"

I rushed to the kitchen, only to find it filled with thick smoke and the sharp smell of burnt food stinging my nose. The water in the rice had boiled away and caused the bottom of the pot to melt onto the briquette. My mother clicked her tongue and spoke to me harshly, "Why do you make such a big deal about studying? How could you be so blind and insensitive as to what's happening around you? Didn't you smell anything?"

"I'm sorry, Mother. I had no idea."

Having no recourse, I went back to my room. When I concentrate, I have a habit of becoming oblivious to everything else. When there's a book I want to read, I will read while I'm walking and sometimes fall into a pit or run into a post.

I fly often. I will be waiting for my flight, reading a book, and sometimes I become so absorbed that I lose track of time. I look up because around me everything becomes suddenly quiet, only to find that my plane has taken off.

Still, this is not a habit I want to break, because it is good to be able to concentrate. If I concentrate while reading, many years later I still remember what I read and can recall it for use in my presentations. Whatever I read and remember becomes a part of me.

Having decided against medicine and, later, against law, I decided to become a writer. Upon entering college, I declared myself a philosophy major because I thought that studying philosophy would best prepare me for my career. Not only because there were many writers in both East and West who had studied philosophy, but also because I believed that anyone who wants to reach people through literature requires a clear ideology.

In 1962 the college entrance exam was a national exam where students applied according to their major. Whether it was law or philosophy, an applicant would take a test in his major and would then apply to schools, depending upon the results.

The day I took the test, I had eaten a bowl of noodles and, as I was leaving the house, I said to my mother, "Mother, I'm about to go take the entrance exam."

"All right," was her reply.

"Uh, you should give me my lunch."

"There's no lunch. Just go."

"No, Mother. It's not like it's just any day. It's the day I take my college entrance exam. How can I go without lunch?"

"What do you expect me to do? And how are you going to get along in life, when you can't even get your own lunch? Eat or go hungry, you work it out."

I was at a loss for words, but I knew that although she sounded uncaring, her heart was probably breaking. I left without saying anything more. When lunchtime came, there was no problem not having packed a lunch. My friends' mothers had packed them more than they could eat and I was able to eat enough by going first to one, then to another, asking them to share. As it turned out, I ate too much and became drowsy during the afternoon math test.

I did well enough on the exam to be accepted by Seoul National University's Department of Philosophy, with ten points to spare. When the time came for me to travel to Seoul, however, I could not afford so much as train fare. Dejected, I stayed in my room. My mother came to me and suggested, "Jin-hong, why not think about going to Keimyung College?"

"Keimyung College? Why there?"

"The dean of Keimyung was your father's friend. I talked to him about your situation and he said you should consider it. He said that since you have a good entrance exam score, if you work hard, you're bound to do well anywhere you go. I agree with him. Don't you think it'd be better if you were to distinguish yourself in a school like Keimyung, rather than to go to Seoul and put up with all the problems you'd have there? I know you'd like to go to Seoul, but there's no way I can send you."

"Mother, I've studied hard to reach a goal and I can't rot away in a little school in the countryside."

"Why would you rot away? It's all up to you. There's a saying, 'Better to be the head of a chicken than the tail of an ox.' Rather than be last in Seoul, why don't you try to be first in the country?"

"Why do you think I'd be last in Seoul?"

"It's common sense that if you go to Seoul, you're going to be at a

53

disadvantage. It'd be difficult for you to concentrate on your studies and you couldn't excel."

"I still have a few days left until applications are due, so I'll think about it." After speaking with my mother, I gave it a lot of thought. Should I go to Seoul, even though it would be tough? Would I be able to achieve my potential in the country? After thinking about it for a few days, I remembered the proverb my mother had quoted, "Better to be the head of a chicken than the tail of an ox." I decided, OK, let's be the head in Daegu rather than the tail in Seoul!

On the day I went for my interview at Keimyung College, the dean asked me, "Jin-hong, with your exam score you could go to a good school in Seoul. Why do you want to come to our school?"

"I came here because I want to become the dean of this school!"

"Ah, then I guess I should step down," he chuckled.

"You can take your time," I said. "It'll take me a while."

Because of my test score, Keimyung College awarded me a four-year scholarship. With the scholarship, I was able to attend college without having to worry about how to pay tuition. Thus began my university career.

5

A Seeker's Journey

MY CHRISTIAN FAITH, WHICH I HAD inherited from my parents, began to waver when I entered college. I faced an identity crisis. According to psychologist Eric Erickson, children born into Christian families adopt the faith of their parents and follow it faithfully while they are young. As they grow older, however, and become aware of their own individuality, they come to question their faith. Some go through this phase as early as high school, but most face the crisis in college. If they do not handle it well, they can fall away from their inherited faith and wander spiritually for the rest of their life. On the other hand, if they overcome the period of crisis with creativity, their inherited faith roots itself firmly in their life and remains there.

In college, the Scriptures I had accepted as fact in my childhood became increasingly difficult to accept. The Bible seemed to be a book of myths, filled with exaggerated stories.

When I read the story of Jesus walking on water, I thought to myself, "What, was he a submarine, that he could go anywhere in water?" I figured that someone with poor eyesight might have hallucinated when what he actually saw was Jesus walking on a sand bar. The passage about fire coming down from heaven made me ask whether there was a furnace in heaven. I imagined this was someone describing lightning and thunder on a rainy day. Moses parting the Red Sea and God creating man from clay, these stories, too, seemed to be pure myth.

If we are going to accept a myth as our faith, I reasoned, why would we want to adopt a myth from the West?

Every nation has its myths. The only difference among myths is that they vary in content and depth. Imaginative myths provide mankind with inspiration. *The Odyssey* and the *Upanishad* are good examples.

The Korean people have a myth about how their country was founded. Hwan-in was a god. His son, Hwan-ung, wanted to live in the world of human beings. Hwan-in looked down on the land and thought that it was a good place for a people who would work for the benefit of others, so he sent down his son, Hwan-ung. Hwan-ung settled at the foot of Mount Taebaek and established a holy city. Along with his subjects, Wind, Rain, and Cloud, he ruled the world and exercised control over 360 components of human life, including agriculture, social organization, medicine, punishment, and good and evil. At that time, Bear Woman, the daughter of the earth, wanted to become a human being and marry. Thus, she prayed every day to be able to do so.

When Bear Woman eventually became human, Hwan-ung married her, and she bore him a son. They named the son Dan-gun. Dan-gun founded the city of Pyeongyang and called the nation Joseon. He ruled his people with the lofty ideal that man should live for the benefit of others, and thereby be highly regarded. Dan-gun ruled his nation for 1,500 years. He later became a mountain spirit, at the age of 1,980 years.

It occurred to me, isn't our myth superior to others? How could anyone compare the myth in the Bible with it? Doesn't ours embody a much deeper meaning and carry greater human appeal? In Hwan-in, Hwan-ung, and Dan-gun, we have the trinity of the Father, the Son, and the Holy Spirit. From it we can uncover the depth of humanity. The holy city on Mount Taebaek is the image of the kingdom of God and the birth of Dan-gun to the Bear Woman was comparable to the virgin birth of Jesus. I was convinced that if we needed a religion, we should create one of our own, rather than adopt Christianity. For me, however, it was not easy to turn my back on the church that I had known since childhood and I struggled with the conflict.

One summer day, during my sophomore year in college, I read a book entitled *Why I Am Not a Christian* by Bertrand Russell. This book helped me break out of the church mold. It enlightened me to what I considered the falsehood of Christianity, which the author laid out in detail, and to the harm that Christianity had brought to humankind throughout history.

I determined to abandon my Christian faith. I would unshackle myself from my religious adolescence and become a mature free man. I thought that burning the Bible would be a symbolic step to mark this milestone in my life. I threw my Bible into the stove and closed the door.

After a while, as the smell of the burning Bible permeated the room, my feelings pulled me in two directions. I felt a sense of freedom, as a man escaping from superstition, while at the same time I feared that something dreadful might happen to me for having burned a holy book.

I became an agnostic. I memorized a quote from Pyrrho, a Greek philosopher, and adopted it as my creed: "There is no God. If there is, it cannot be known. Even if it is known, it cannot be proven. Thus, there is no God."

My skepticism later turned to atheism, which in turn developed into pessimism, which eventually evolved into nihilism.

THERE WAS A CREMATORIUM near the Keimyung College campus. Looking out the window during class, I could see gray smoke coming out of the chimney of the crematorium. Sometimes, when the wind blew toward the school, a musty smell would come into the classroom.

One afternoon in spring, when classes were canceled, I left campus and headed for the crematorium. Rather, I should say that the crematorium pulled me toward it. Once there, after I spent some time observing families in the yard mourning their loved ones, I entered the furnace room. A "keep out" sign hung on the door. I had taken a pack of cigarettes to win my way into the mystical chamber.

"Excuse me. I'm doing field training. May I come in?"

"Field training? Training for what?"

"Philosophy training. We're studying how a body burns when it is cremated."

The stoker looked at me and then glanced at the cigarettes I was holding. As he reached for the cigarettes, he signaled me to go in. Inside, a most otherworldly scene unfolded. I watched a corpse being pulled into the fire and burned to a handful of ashes. With a solemn air and eyes half closed, I looked around, pretending to be an ascetic. I felt that

I was on my way to maturity and that I was close to the moment of learning the secret meaning of life and death. As I left the crematorium, I recited a quote from Buddha:

> What is life? A piece of cloud emerging.
> What is death? A piece of cloud disappearing.
> As a drifting cloud itself has no substance,
> So, too, is a man's life and death.

Life is an emerging cloud and death a disappearing cloud. Why struggle and worry?

What is learning? What is philosophy? It is said that they are for exploring truth, which will lead to an understanding of life. How could that be? They are but empty pursuits with no substance. I found myself losing enthusiasm for life, becoming more and more sarcastic and pessimistic.

It was around that time that I heard a story of a Japanese student. He had been admitted to the prestigious Tokyo University with the highest possible entrance exam score. In college, he was an excellent student and mastered all the books on Eastern and Western philosophy. In the autumn of his senior year, despite his success, he committed suicide by throwing himself over a waterfall. He had left a note in his shoe. It read, "Kant, what did he know?"

I understood the thoughts and feelings of the Japanese student all too well. I began to ponder the words I would leave behind, were I to jump into a waterfall: "Jesus, what did he believe in? Buddha, what did he see? Socrates, what did he know?"

I considered several possibilities, but nothing stood out as being grand enough. I put off thinking about my quote for posterity to consider which waterfall I should jump off. I came to realize that, unfortunately, there were no waterfalls in Korea high enough for what I wanted to do. There might be one on Mount Geumgang in North Korea, but that was out of the question because the Demilitarized Zone (DMZ) stood between the mountain and me.

A jump from the falls on Jeju Island would not be high enough. If I survived the fall with just broken legs, it would only create a lot of problems. I could go to Japan, but then there's a campaign going on encouraging people to use only Korean-made products. How could I possibly use a Japanese waterfall? No, I would need to use a Korean waterfall. I became amused by my chain of thought, which brought a grin to my face.

BEGINNING IN MY SECOND YEAR IN COLLEGE, things began to change for the better. The school had only 500 students, so there was a family-like atmosphere on campus. We were able to take classes from any professor, regardless of our field of study. I met some fine professors who tutored me privately. Whenever I visited their offices, they lent me books and helped me understand their disciplines. I discovered the true value of a college education and realized how fortunate I was to be able to receive one.

A young professor, by the name of Soh Heung-yeol, came to our school. He was fresh out of his Ph.D. program at the University of Michigan. He was a brilliant scholar with outstanding logic.

Professor Soh did not attempt to give us an understanding of philosophy through an accumulation of knowledge. He gave no passionate lectures, nor did he say anything worthy of being written down in our notebooks. Rather, his class was more a conversation, with the professor and the students exchanging ideas. In discussing the basics of philosophy, we reaped valuable fruit. Clear thinking, logical expression, aggressive critical spirit, respect for common sense, and creative imagination—these were the qualities we developed in Professor Soh's class.

Of all my classes, Professor Soh's logic class was the most beneficial. Every day we had to read three articles from the morning newspaper. Then we engaged in debate on what we had read. We discussed whether there were any flaws or weaknesses in the development of the stories and whether there were any discrepancies between the premises and the conclusions.

Once, on a logic test, he gave us an unusual task: "Write a guide to playing Korean chess for someone who is unfamiliar with the game."

We all worked diligently on it, but when we turned in our papers, Professor Soh said that the guides were too lengthy and told us to reduce them by half. We worked hard and managed to reduce them by half. That, he said, was still too long and that we needed to reduce them by half again, ensuring that the directions were readable and comprehensible to the unfamiliar player. He demanded clear, succinct wording. We tried everything we could to shorten them, while still keeping the meaning clear. Words cannot express the influence his training had on my life and that continues to this day. I was lucky to have had several mentors in college at a time when mentors were hard to come by. As time passes, I am even more grateful.

I have great pride in my alma mater. Some time later, when my 13-year-old son said he would go to Keimyung, I asked him why. He replied,

At graduation from Keimyung College, with Professor Soh Heung-yeol.

"You're proud of your college, so I'm sure it's a good school." I always tell young people, "Which college you attend is not important. The important thing is how you spend your time when you're there. You can enter any university and transform it into a top-notch institution, depending on the depth of knowledge and the breadth of insight you seek and acquire while you're there."

Halfway through my second year I came down with a health problem. I suffered from insomnia and developed gastritis, which I assumed had resulted from drugs I had relied on in high school to keep awake while studying for the college entrance exam.

Gastritis can be very distressing. For more than six months I was on a diet consisting exclusively of porridge. The diet was hard to cope with, and the little other food I managed to eat I only half digested. My illness worsened with time and none of the prescribed medicines worked. Finally, I decided to deal with it head-on. I took a blanket and traveled to the Unmun Temple in Cheongdo. I checked into one of the rooms at the temple and climbed the mountain behind it. I sat down on a large boulder with an unobstructed view of the temple. I was determined to have a showdown with the gastritis and overcome it by drinking only water from the stream.

I would call it my prayer on the mount, but since my body and mind were not in a normal state, my prayer could not have been very coherent.

"O God, Creator! You created my stomach, too. Please, restore my health by instilling harmony in my body. Must I perish from gastritis, when I have so much to do in this life? Grant me my health by lavishing my body with the energy of heaven and earth."

I went down to the stream for a drink of water whenever I got thirsty. When I grew tired, I would lean against a tree or sit on the boulder. I thought that I would rather die on the boulder than struggle to live without being able to eat anything. Three days later, as I awoke in the early morning, I found myself losing consciousness and my body going numb and cold.

My mind instinctively told me, "Ah! This is how a person dies!"

First, my feet and hands gradually turned cold. The chill spread to the rest of my body, except for my throbbing heart. Then the fear of death struck me. Desperate at what seemed the approach of death, I uttered a prayer.

"Please help me. I cannot end my life this way. Please give me another chance. I can't die from gastritis on this secluded mountain."

In the midst of my prayer, I sensed something strange happening. I could feel my body slowly warming and my energy returning. I was grateful for the sudden miracle.

Exuberantly, I ran down the mountain. It was as if I was flying, with my feet in the air. When I reached the town near Unmun Temple, I entered a Chinese restaurant, took a seat, and boldly placed my order.

"Please give me a double portion of *jjamppong*.*"

Oblivious to the fact that I was suffering from gastritis, I felt like I could digest a stone. After finishing off the noodle soup, I left to go to my home in Daegu. The *jjamppong* did not upset my stomach. My gastritis had been cured, and I slowly regained my health.

---

* Jjamppong is a spicy hot noodle soup with seafood and vegetables.

As a self-imposed regimen, I made it a routine to take a cold bath and go jogging every morning before dawn. I spent my winter break in the countryside, where I would go down to a nearby stream for my bath.

I bathed in the subfreezing temperatures of the biting winter mornings as a way to strengthen my body and mind. Often, a layer of ice had formed on the water, and I had to break it before jumping in. When people in the village saw me bathing in the stream, they thought I had gone insane. They pitied me because they thought that a man with great potential had lost his mind.

DURING MY SOPHOMORE YEAR, I fell madly in love. To my disappointment, it was only one-sided. The object of my affection was a younger sister of one of my professors. Not a second went by that I wasn't thinking of her, whether in class, walking on the street, or in my dreams.

I sent her a letter by certified mail every day for six months. On Saturdays, I sent two letters, to make up for Sundays. For material, I researched romantic poems by famous poets from both East and West—Wordsworth, Hesse, Rilke, and Kim So-wol. I sent poems because I thought they best reflected my heart.

In the middle of the night, I would pace back and forth in front of her house. On my way home, I would linger around the school gate, hoping to run into her. One rainy day, dripping wet, I walked past her house, singing a pop song:

>As I pass by her house, I yearn for her.
>Unaware that my feet had come to a complete halt.
>I start walking again at the thought that I might be spotted.
>I quickly walk away, but end up where I started.
>
>Again, today on a rainy autumn evening,
>I pass by her house, longingly.
>To forget the past
>I walk, counting the rain drops under the street light.

I was miserable, but at the same time I savored my melancholy. Then I discovered something I should not have. I learned that she was going on a trip to Gyeongju with a fellow who was notorious around campus as a playboy. I fell into a state of deep despair. When I tried to read a book, the words would not register. When I ate something, I could not taste it.

Of all people, why him? Why would an angel like her date such a jerk? It didn't make sense! When night fell, I wondered, O God, please protect her. Will she come back tonight? Or is she spending the night with him? He's a pro. In the darkness of the night, she will fall prey to the clutches of that beast. With his glib tongue and suave manner, he can easily get her, the way a sly wolf plays with an innocent rabbit.

Wildly conjuring up the scene in my mind, I couldn't calm down. I went up to the roof of the dormitory, looked down, and talked to myself. Shall I jump to forget this agony? No, I cannot end my life like this. She would have no way of knowing why I died.

I had to hold onto a post on the roof to combat my urge to jump. After taking a deep breath of the night air, I went down to my room, buried myself in the covers, and cried. A stream of tears rolled down my face. Ah, how can I communicate to her even a small fragment of this pure and impassioned heart of mine? Then, at the thought of her and that jerk walking hand in hand up the steps of Bulguk Temple in Gyeongju, a fire raged in my heart.

The next day, I sent her another letter. If I stopped writing, I was afraid that my existence would cease to have meaning.

Six months later, on a Saturday, she came to see me. I could hardly breathe as she stood in front of me. She opened her mouth and said, "Please stop writing to me."

She spat the words out quickly, turned, and went away. She did not even look back. At that, I fell into a fit of anguish, in which everything seemed meaningless. After some time, I came to my senses and realized that I had to put an end to the matter.

If I go on like this, I'll make a fool of myself. No, I already am a fool. There are more important things in this world than women and I refuse to ruin my life because of her. Let's end the letters and this desperate puerile yearning!

I did not go to class or to the cafeteria for several days. I bought a few bags of crackers and stayed home, living on only crackers and water. That was how I ended it.

TIME PASSED AND I WENT TO VISIT Bohyeon Buddhist Temple, near Daegu. I knelt before the head monk.

"Master, I have come to seek to understand Buddhism."

"How can I tell you the profound meaning of Buddhism in a few words? Where are you from, young man?"

"I'm a student majoring in philosophy at a local college. I had gone to church ever since I was a child, but one day it struck me that Christianity was superstition, so I left the church. Now I would like to study Buddhism."

"Good for you. I, too, was a Christian before I came to Buddhism. I was more than an ordinary believer. I'm sure you know the First Church downtown. I served there as an assistant pastor for ten years during the Japanese occupation. I know the Bible backward and forward."

"I am blessed to meet such a great person. I want to have you as my master. Please teach me."

"Since you look sincere and you are enthusiastic, I will help you as much as I can."

"Thank you. I know about Christianity because I learned it from childhood, but I know nothing about Buddhism. Please teach me, beginning with the basics."

"Comparing Buddhism to Christianity is like comparing college with elementary school. Comprehending the profound principles of Buddhism, one by one, is an endless process. You have now finished elementary school and are on your way to entering college. I will give you a book to read."

He gave me a Buddhist scripture entitled *Neung-eom*. It was about karma and all things in the universe. That night I read it. Three days later I went back to Bohyeon Temple. When I told the head monk that I had finished *Neung-eom*, he was pleased with my enthusiasm and said that I would make great progress. He then gave me another Buddhist scripture, *Geum-gang*, and told me to read it.

Geum-gang was much more difficult and profound than *Neung-eom*. There was a passage in it that I particularly liked, upon which I mulled extensively:

> Objects that have an appearance are vain.
> If, among the visible objects,

you can see something that does not have a form,
then you are seeing Buddha.

This passage conforms to Platonic Ideas. According to Plato, visible things are not real, but merely Archetypes. Behind the Archetypes of all temporal phenomena is an independent reality of Ideas or Forms. Plato's principle of looking beyond the Archetypes and seeking the world of Ideas is compatible with Buddhist belief.

Things such as lust, money, and status are transient and vain. If among visible things you see something neither transient nor visible, you are seeing Buddha.

I understood this passage to say that disciples of Buddha should seek the world of truth and resist succumbing to the temptions of the temporal world. This inspired me to seek the world of truth—Buddha.

I assembled Buddhist students from all the campuses in Daegu and organized an association of Buddhist college students. As the officer in charge of academics, I organized discussions about Buddhist scriptures, as well as seminars by scholarly monks. I was very zealous back then, considering that I was promoting these Buddhist undertakings at a college that had been established as a Christian foundation. I went around to temples in remote mountains to discipline myself and to meditate on the scriptures.

Even with time, however, my efforts to immerse myself in Buddhism went unrewarded, because I failed to grasp the world of Buddha, which for me remained vague and blurry.

As part of the Buddhist worship service, there is a time to recite the Four Vows that Buddhist disciples make to Buddha. They are similar to the Apostles' Creed.

First, one person recites a vow. Then, the congregation repeats it. The significance of the Buddhists' Four Vows is deep to the extent that it could be seen as the pinnacle of a man's religious pursuit:

No matter how many living beings there are,
I vow to save them.
No matter how many worries I have,
I vow to unshackle myself from them.
No matter how much I have to learn from Buddha,

I vow to learn it.
No matter how infinitely high the truth of Buddha is,
I vow to seek it.

I attended services diligently, reciting the Four Vows and reading the Buddhist scriptures, in a relentless pursuit to end my agony and achieve enlightenment, but my condition took an unexpected direction. In my attempt to extinguish the 108 human agonies and enter the state of nirvana, I fell prey to insomnia. I was unable to go to sleep until 3 or 4 o'clock in the morning and then could sleep only a couple of hours. The following day, all day long I would feel like I was floating on clouds.

Eventually, the death of the Venerable Hyo-bong, a high monk, led me to abandon any remaining interest I might have had in Buddhism. Hyo-bong had been a highly respected Buddhist leader. Before becoming a monk, he had enjoyed a successful career in law, becoming a judge during the Japanese occupation, a position rarely entrusted to Korean nationals at the time.

While serving as a judge, he sentenced to death a man convicted of murder and ordered his execution. Soon after the execution, the real murderer was arrested and brought before him. An innocent man had been put to death because of his sentence. Overcome with anguish, he gave up his post and went on a wandering journey. Having traveled to every corner of the country, he arrived at Mount Myohyang, where he shaved his head and took up Buddhism. In the years that followed, his devotion led him to the highest level of religious attainment, and he was ultimately characterized as a "living Buddha."

While on his deathbed, Hyo-bong said to one of the monks attending him.

"Today I am leaving on a journey."

"But you are not well. Where are going? Please stay and rest."

"No, I need to go today!"

"Please, Master. Please don't strain yourself."

Several hours following this conversation, at around noon, he passed away, sitting upright, as if meditating. The last word he uttered was "Nothing." My friends were thrilled with that word. Their admiration for him grew even deeper because they believed the last word of a great man was different from other words.

I was not convinced. Since childhood, I had had a propensity to question things. My training in philosophy at college had further sharpened my critical thinking. Whatever the word, I was in the habit of analyzing and critiquing its meaning. Thus, I pondered the word "Nothing" that the Venerable Hyo-bong had left behind and what he might have meant by it.

My religious pursuit was to seek something that exists, not something that does not exist. Then, why "nothing?" If it is "nothing" that I am after, then that's a problem. The reason that I wander, agonize, and doubt is because I exist. At least for me, problems occur because of the very fact that I exist. Why, then, "nothing?" Is it because he was at a level too lofty for a layman to reach? Will "nothing" be the word that I will utter when I die, after having attained a level as lofty as his?

I thought about it and made up my mind that I did not want to reach the level at which on my deathbed my final utterance would be only "Nothing."

Many young people, including myself, are toiling to seek something that is worthy enough to devote their lives to. How can we, then, teach them that life is hard, while you live, and when you die, it is nothing?

Jesus of Nazareth said it differently. Whether His word was true or not, at least His meaning was crystal clear:

> I am the truth and the way and the life. (John 14:6)

> I have come that they may have life, and have it
> to the full. (John 10:10)

> He who believes in me will live, even though he dies;
> and whoever lives and believes in me will never die.
> (John 11:25-26)

I felt that I needed something stronger and with more fire to it, something that was certain and that could ignite and consume my whole life. Looking back now on the word of the Venerable Hyo-bong, I might be able to understand it from a deeper level, but at the time it was difficult for me to comprehend. In addition, I was far from happy with Buddhism's outlook on history. I was especially uncomfortable with the idea of *samsara*, the indefinitely repeated cycles of birth, misery, and death caused by karma. I thought Buddhism's circular view of history was problematic for the Korean people, who historically had failed to fulfill their potential to achieve great things. Buddhism's circular theory that *samsara* is repeated endlessly relegates history to stagnation.

From that perspective, I see the Christian view as being much more progressive, providing a strong motive for building the Kingdom of God. If our nation was to overcome its stagnant history and move ahead, Christianity's forward-looking view would be much more desirable. After this turnaround in my thinking and belief, my visits to the temple became less frequent and eventually stopped. Despite my religious turmoil, I continued to study philosophy.

BEGINNING IN MY SOPHOMORE YEAR, I participated in the Annual National Philosophy Symposium. That year, I gave a presentation with the title "A Study on Platonic Ideas." The following year, my presentation was entitled, "A Study on Dialectical Materialism of Karl Marx," and in my senior year, I explored "The Philosophical Background of Einstein's Theory of Relativity."

People around me thought that I would someday become a philosophy professor. I took pride in having a goal to one day lead the Korean philosophy community and worked hard to achieve it. Because I was the first to enter the library in the morning and the last to leave in the evening, my fellow students gave me the sobriquet "library gatekeeper."

One morning, while in the library, absorbed in a book on metaphysics, a senior philosophy major, Hong Eung-pyo, approached me.

"Hey, Mr. Socrates, have you learned anything from studying your metaphysics?"

"No, but I haven't finished yet. I'm only coming up to the middle."

"That's not why I want to see you. I have something urgent and important to talk to you about. Meet me out on the lawn in front of the library."

Having said that, he strode away. I put down my book and followed him, wondering what was so important that he needed to talk to me about. When I reached the lawn in front of the library, he threw me a question, even before I had a chance to sit down.

"Kim Jin-hong, are you born again?" he asked.

"What? What do you mean?" I replied.

"Just what I said. Are you born again? I'm asking whether you believe in Jesus and are born again," he persisted.

"Hong, what kind of question is that? Is that what you call an important matter? I was busy studying. Did you have me come out here only to ask such an absurd question?"

Hong Eung-pyo presenting at a philosophy meeting, Kim Jin-hong sitting in front row, second from left in foreground.

"Yes, of course. Is there anything more urgent than this? No matter how much you study Kant, you won't find the answer there. Your study will only bring you more agony. You've already read a lot and it's about time you grew tired of it. The study of Kant is asking questions. He has no answers. Only Jesus has answers. Are you, too, like Kant, going to spend your life asking questions that have no answers?

"Studying metaphysics is like wandering in a forest with no way out. The deeper into it you get, the more you go astray. Judge for yourself. You're a smart fellow. The reason I said it was urgent for us to talk was because it's a matter of life and death for your soul. The most important thing for you now is to receive Jesus as Lord in your life and be born again."

He was trying to persuade me, but he was not succeeding. Not only did I feel sorry for him, I seriously questioned his intelligence. I thought it was deplorable that a student of metaphysics had failed to develop his thinking to any higher a level. From this exchange, I concluded that he was not qualified to discuss philosophy with me.

"This born-again stuff has nothing to do with me. Whether you go to heaven or somewhere else, that's your business. I have no desire to go anywhere where they take people of your standards. If I have to go to hell because I haven't been born again, I will go there like a man. How can one who has studied dialectics and metaphysics ask questions such as "Are you born again?" or "Are you saved?" If in heaven I have to live like a pig with no brains, I'd rather go to hell and live as a thinking Socrates," I argued.

"Those are noble words, but it's only a matter of time. The day will come when you'll know that I'm right. I'll pray for that day. You go ahead and study dialectics and metaphysics all you want. I'll talk to people who have ears to listen and tell them how to be born again. Let's meet after you have become much poorer than you are now. When you are malnourished, gaunt, and feeble from eating metaphysics, I'll give you again the bread of life that is filled with nutritious substance," he replied.

KEIMYUNG COLLEGE HAD A SCHOOL FESTIVAL every May, marking the school founding. During the festival, the May King and Queen would take part in a ceremony where the May King would put the crown on the May Queen. In electing the May King, each department would nominate a candidate. Then, in the presence of the entire student body, each candidate would give a 10-minute performance in a talent show, after which the winner was chosen by popular vote.

From my sophomore year until I graduated, each year I was elected May King. My secret was to make the students laugh during the talent show. Some people said they laughed so hard at my jokes that their stomachs still hurt the next day.

In my senior year, the whole country was in an agitated state because of massive demonstrations opposing the government's normalization of diplomatic ties with Japan. Demonstration fever was catching on quickly. Keimyung College went along with it.

To urge students to join the demonstrations, I was asked to make a speech at a student assembly. I was to use my talents to instigate. I accepted the request from my fellow students and made a speech before the student body in the auditorium. We then formed a phalanx and took to the streets. The police tried to stop us, becoming rough and provoking us. We responded by throwing rocks. One of the rocks broke the police chief's nose.

After the pushing and shoving, I and a few other leaders of the demonstration were arrested. I spent three nights in the Daegu jail and was released after being admonished by the police chief.

"It is admirable that you waged the street demonstration because you love our country, but as students, you need to study. That is good for you and good for the country. I am going to let you guys go. Now, go and study hard." That was my first jail experience.

It was a time when the motives of both the student demonstrators and the police trying to control them were pure. Later, students were led by experts in demonstrations. Things became nasty and violent, and the romanticism that had driven us vanished. Today Korea is a democratic country. I am pleased to say that the days of Molotov cocktails, tear gas, and violent demonstrations are behind us.

In any case, my college years were wonderful. I studied hard and played hard. I explored life completely and loved passionately.

6

A Maelstrom in Our Family

WHILE I WAS IN COLLEGE, MY FAMILY underwent a very difficult time. It was because of my brother. Four years my senior, he had been a fine young man, with good looks and a pleasant disposition. After returning from military service, however, he began acting strangely.

Sitting down to his meal, he would sniff his bowl of rice, glare at me furiously, and ask, "Did you poison my rice?"

"What? *Hyeongnim,** whatever are you saying? Why would I do such a thing?"

"Oh, yeah? Then you taste it first."

He would wait until I had eaten a spoonful of his rice before eating.

One time, in the middle of the night, he brought a knife from the kitchen and told me to stab our mother.

"Stab that woman. She's a devil in our home," he said.

"*Hyeongnim,* what in the world is going on with you?"

"Kill that woman or our whole family will perish."

This was extremely shocking for our family. Unaware of what was really taking place, everyone in the family started blaming one another. We had no idea how to cope with him. In despair, my mother stopped eating, and my younger brother, my sister, and I stayed away from home as much as possible.

Hyeongnim refers to an older brother.

Whenever there is a mental patient in a family, the illness spreads to everyone. The patient inflicts so much emotional harm on the other members that they too become deranged.

Once we figured out that our brother had a psychotic disorder, we all went out of our way to look after him, but we soon burned out.

Our alternative was to put him in a mental hospital, which we did, and we all worked part-time to cover the expense. A month after he was hospitalized, he showed signs of recovery. The doctors said that it would take five to six months of hospitalization to cure his illness, but our tight budget could not sustain it. We were forced to bring him home before he was cured. He seemed fine, at first, but three or four months later, he reverted to his psychotic state. We endured until we could tolerate it no longer. Then we took him back to the hospital. We repeated this routine of putting him in the hospital and taking him out three times. By the third time, we were emotionally thoroughly drained.

My younger brother once asked me, "Do you know of any rat poison that comes in white powder?"

"Why do you ask about rat poison?"

"Since Big Brother's medication is white powder, I figured that if I were to leave white-powder rat poison in his room, he'd take it thinking it was his medication."

"How can you possibly think of such a thing?" I asked.

"You know you feel the same way. Don't you wish that Big Brother would die? Why doesn't he do us a big favor and just kill himself? I would if I were him."

"We can't hope that. If anybody's going to commit suicide, it's going to be us. Big Brother has always been egotistical. He'd be the last person to commit suicide."

"Mother raised him wrong. She spoiled him by being too nice to him. She always treated him specially, just because he was the oldest and should have taken on Dad's responsibilities."

"Why do you blame Mother? Do you think she planned it this way? A mother's love is unconditional. Don't talk as if Mother is to blame for Big Brother's condition."

"Well, isn't she? Whenever there was fish on the table, he always got the middle, while we ended up eating the head and the tail. On New

Year's and Thanksgiving holidays, Mother would buy him new clothes, while we would wear hand-me-downs. That's how Big Brother came to be so selfish. You're right. If anybody's going to commit suicide, it's bound to be us. It would never be him. How I wish he'd end his life this very minute.... Anyway, because of him, our lives are going to be miserable from here on out."

Shortly after this conversation, my younger brother ran away from home. A senior in Gyeseong High School, he would otherwise have been busy studying for the college entrance exam. One day a letter arrived. It was from my younger brother. He had written it from a Marine training center. He wrote:

> *I've enlisted in the Marines and volunteered for combat duty in Vietnam. I'll send you my allowance to pay for Big Brother's medical expenses. I couldn't stand living at home and resenting him. I want to help, even if it costs me my education.*

My younger brother was deployed to the Blue Dragon Detachment. Not long afterward, another letter came, this one from the government and postmarked Vietnam. The letter said that my brother had gone into combat against the communists and that if he were to die in the field, a special compensatory allowance would be paid to the family. In the letter it said that my brother asked that we use the money to pay for his older brother's medical treatment.

Worried about her son, every day Mother prayed for him to come home safely. Meanwhile, I wrote to him, urging him to stay alive.

Fortunately, he did not die in Vietnam, returning with only a slight wound, but our brother did not recover as we had hoped. My younger brother had risked his life to pay his medical expenses, yet Big Brother's illness had grown worse.

Later he fell ill, showing signs of jaundice. His eyes turned a vivid yellow and his body began to swell. We took him to Dongsan Hospital in Daegu. When the doctor had examined him, he called me in. I listened to the prognosis.

"I'll be honest with you. Your brother has already received all the help modern medicine can provide. There's nothing else we can do. He has less than a week to live. It's too late now. Since you are on a tight budget, I suggest that you take him home and prepare for his funeral. Hospitalizing him will only run up a medical bill and can do him no good."

I thanked him and headed straight to the office to have brother discharged. I brought him home and made him comfortable in a sunlit room. Meanwhile, my sister, my younger brother, and I gathered in another room to talk.

"I feel sorry for Big Brother. He used to be so good-looking and was such a nice guy. It's a shame that the army did this to him. First we mistreated him and now jaundice is taking away his life. In a way, it's a good thing that our hardship is nearing an end. We'll have his funeral in a few days and then we can start living. We have to do our best to console Mother. After the funeral, let's make a fresh start. We have to stick together to get through this and make up for the loss."

We began to make arrangements for the funeral, filled with new hope. Mother, however, surprised us one morning by appearing with her suitcase in hand. "Children, I'll be gone for a couple of days. I'm going to my hometown."

"Big Brother will pass away soon. Why don't you wait until after the funeral?"

"No, there's something I need to do for him."

Two days later, my mother returned with a huge bundle on her head. Helping her put the bundle down, I asked, "What's this, Mother?"

"It's for your brother. I picked some herbs for him."

"You mean you went all the way to your hometown to get herbs?"

"How could I just sit there and watch him die?"

She had brought all sorts of leaves and herbal roots. The roots were mostly of mugwort, but also included motherwort, bellflower, *Codonopsis lanceolata* (a white fibrous root), and thistle. Determined to save her son, my mother had scoured the fields and mountains of her hometown to find these remedies.

After washing them, she put them in a big pot and filled it with water. She cooked it over a briquette fire for two days, during which time the liquid turned black. Taking the herbs out of the pot, she poured some of the liquid into a bowl and cooled it before giving it to Big Brother.

To our amazement, after drinking the potion three times, his jaundice completely went away. His yellowish eyes became normal, and his swelling went down. He soon regained his strength and sat up straight. We were crushed. Words cannot describe how discouraged we all felt.

I protested to my mother. "Mother, you've gone too far. Don't you think of anyone besides your oldest son? Can't you see how much we've suffered because of him? Your herbs have cured him of jaundice, and now we're left to go on putting up with his insanity. We've had all we can take. We're leaving home. You and brother can live here by yourselves."

At my strong protest, Mother was apologetic, but asked to be understood. "I know what you're saying, but you'll know how I feel when you grow up and have children of your own. You don't know what it's like to have to bury a child."

MY MOTHER'S DEVOTION CURED MY BROTHER of the jaundice, but his mental illness remained to torment us, as we feared would happen. Finally we decided to send him to Salvation Retreat, a Christian prayer house, a place that was said to miraculously cure mental patients. What appealed to us about the place above all was its low cost. It was only one-fifth of what a regular hospital would cost.

A couple of months after he was admitted, my mother and I paid him a visit. Seeing us with food and clothing in our hands, Big Brother broke down and cried. When we asked if anything was wrong, if he was sick, or if he was being poorly treated, he continued to cry. He appeared fearful as he glanced around. I had a hunch that something was not right. I pulled up his shirt. My mother and I were taken aback to see scars from whipping all around the upper part of his body. It looked as if a snake was coiled around him.

We found out later that the place made a routine of beating patients, claiming that it would drive out the evil spirits. They used an oak cane, shouting, "Out evil spirits." When a patient would cry out in pain, they would hit him again, admonishing, "Evil spirit, how dare you complain about your pain?"

When a patient fainted, frothing at the mouth, they would cry out "Hallelujah! The spirit has fled." They didn't recognize the patients as humans, but saw them only as bodies with evil spirits.

Mental illness is a disease and, like any other disease, it requires medical attention, where doctors diagnose the illness and treat it scientifically. Counseling and medication, as well as consolation and prayers by pastors, are all necessary components in curing it.

There are some extreme Christians in Korea who think that all diseases, from a cold to cancer, are brought on by evil spirits. They think that a powerful Christian pastor can take the place of a medical doctor and cure any illness by driving out the evil spirits. In practice, when this approach is taken, worship services become a pandemonium of ritual, with much shouting and moaning. We had no idea that we had put our big brother in such a place.

Seeing her son's scars, my mother's face flushed in horror, and she cried out.

"Oh, dear! My poor son!"

I looked at my mother and at my brother. "I'm sorry, *Hyeongnim*," I said. "It's all my fault. I had no idea what this place was about. Let's go home. If you're going to die, you're going to die at home. We can't have them beat you to death." When we brought him home, my little brother strongly protested.

"Why did you bring him home? You should have left him there, for better or worse."

"You wouldn't say that if you knew the story behind it. I had no choice."

I lifted brother's shirt and showed the marks on his body. Then I told them about the abuse he had been subjected to.

"How could I leave him at that dreadful place, knowing how he's being abused?"

How true it is that the bond among siblings in a poor family is ever so precious! My younger brother and my sister became solemn and said, "You did the right thing. We should have looked into that place before we sent *hyeongnim* there. He doesn't need to be beaten. It's bad enough just to be insane."

That marked a turning point in the way we felt toward our brother. The three of us agreed to show greater patience and make a greater effort to care for him.

Sister continued, "Poor Big Brother! Let's not leave him in the hands of strangers. We have to take care of him. It'll be hard, but we have to do it, for Mother's sake, too."

My younger brother, by then a college student, agreed. After coming home from the Marines, he had passed his high-school equivalency exam and had entered the School of Education at Gyeongbuk National University.

He quickly suggested, "That's right. We can rotate, taking care of him on a weekly basis. Whoever's in charge for a particular week will put everything else aside and work around the clock to care for him. That'll put Mother at ease, and we'll have no regrets later."

I chimed in, "That's a great idea. I'll take the first week. You take the second week, and sister can take the third."

Beginning that day, we put everything we had into caring for our brother. I took him to bathhouses, and we bathed together. I clipped his fingernails and toenails, ate snacks with him, we read poems together, and chatted our time away. Together we read the Bible and held hands in prayer. I also told him about current events and anything of interest. Meanwhile, I kept a detailed diary of my activities with him.

We followed through our plan for several months, faithfully caring for him. Around the fourth month, Big Brother began to show signs of recovery. I couldn't believe my ears when one day he said, "I feel like I'm getting better. The three of you have done enough for me. It's time I started earning a living."

"That's out of the question. You can't possibly work. You just stay home and work on getting healthy. What if you were to get stressed out and fall ill again? Don't worry about a thing. We're doing just fine as we are."

Laughter found its way into our home once again. Mother was in ecstasy. Tearfully, she exclaimed, "My wish has come true. Now that your brother is back to normal, I am free to join your father in heaven any day."

"Don't say that, Mother. There's nothing wrong with going to heaven, but you're in no hurry to get there. Now you should enjoy the life ahead of you."

THE JOY OF MY BROTHER'S MIRACULOUS RECOVERY quickly faded. He died of cirrhosis soon after regaining his mental health. The beatings and starvation he suffered at Salvation Retreat had apparently damaged his liver.

On the morning of the day he died, blood spewed from his mouth as he bent down to wash his face. Something extraordinary happened, however, a few minutes before he was taken. His face suddenly lit up with a mystical smile. It changed, as if he was deeply moved.

He spoke blissfully. "Today I am going to the Kingdom of Heaven. I have put you all through so much. I will go to Jesus and put in a good word for you, that he may keep you safe. I leave without repaying you for all you did for me in this world, but I will pay you back in heaven." Then, with a face flushed with joy, Big Brother asked, "Would you sing me a hymn?"

"Sure. Which one?"

"Would you sing 'Since Christ My Soul from Sin Set Free'?"

Our family sang the hymn together. Big Brother soon joined in to sing along with us:

Since Christ my soul from sin set free,
This world has been a Heaven to me;
And 'mid earth's sorrows and its woe,
'Tis Heaven my Jesus here to know.
Oh, hallelujah, yes, 'tis Heaven,
'Tis Heaven to know my sins forgiven;
On land or sea, what matters where?
Where Jesus is, 'tis Heaven there.

Once Heaven seemed a far-off place,
'Til Jesus showed His smiling face;
Now it's begun within my soul,
'Twill last while endless ages roll.
Oh, hallelujah, yes, 'tis Heaven,
'Tis Heaven to know my sins forgiven;
On land or sea, what matters where?
Where Jesus is, 'tis Heaven there.

What matters where on earth we dwell?
On mountain top or in the dell,

> In cottage or a mansion fair,
> Where Jesus is 'tis Heaven there.
> Oh, hallelujah, yes, 'tis Heaven,
> 'Tis Heaven to know my sins forgiven;
> On land or sea, what matters where?
> Where Jesus is, 'tis Heaven there.

As we sang the third verse, my brother looked toward the window and, smiling, held his hand out to us. Then he whispered, "Jesus is coming to take me." Those were his last words, as he closed his eyes.

My brother's death had a profound effect on me. It transformed my values and gave me a renewed sense of direction. It instilled in me a new conviction that perhaps death is not so bad after all. Relocating to heaven is more like moving from a run-down house to a luxurious villa. Life in this world should be devoted to serving people in the name of the Lord and when death takes us, we will rest with Jesus.

Whenever I face hardship in life, I remember my brother's final words about how he would ask Jesus to look after our family. Since then, throughout all of the hardship and agony I have experienced, I have always sensed his presence, clearing the road ahead and watching over me.

LATER, IN THE INITIAL STAGES OF STARTING UP a church in Namyang Bay, I was involved in a large-scale land reclamation project for the farming community. In the process of helping farmers, I incurred massive debt and was confronted with total failure. I was in a quandary, with local residents accusing me of theft. I finally concluded that I should leave. One night I packed my belongings and lay down to sleep, waiting for the dawn, when I would leave. In a dream that night, my brother appeared as vividly as ever.

"Little Brother, I know how you must feel, but don't leave. Jesus knows all about it."

"Is that right, Big Brother? You mean that Jesus really knows what I'm going through?"

"Of course, He does. He's watching you every step of the way and he's proud of you. Don't despair. Don't give up, because things'll get better in time."

"OK. Knowing that Jesus knows about my problems gives me strength to go on."

Awaking from the dream, I was overwhelmed with happiness. I headed straight to the church and knelt down to pray. I then went home and unpacked my bags. I would start anew.

Often, when I have found myself struggling in a sea of troubles, my brother has appeared to me. Now, whenever I am approaching a critical point, I have come to expect him to talk to me.

Mental illness is increasingly prevalent in modern society. Because of my experience with my brother's illness, whenever I encounter families with members who are mental patients, my heart goes out to the family first because I can empathize with the ordeal they are going through. I believe that mental illness is curable. As in the case of my brother, it can be treated with wholehearted devotion and earnestness in caring for the patient. Love is more potent than any medicine.

I have long dreamed of founding a mental hospital in memory of my brother. Not that I have a magical cure for mental illness, but I would like to set up a hospital that cares for and caters to the true needs of both patients and caregivers.

AS I GOT CLOSER TO GRADUATING FROM COLLEGE, I was confronted with a dilemma. I was undecided whether I should follow in the footsteps of Soren Kierkegaard or those of Nikolai Grundtvig. Kierkegaard was a thinker and philosopher who laid the groundwork for modern existentialism, while Grundtvig devoted his entire life to awakening the souls of the people of Denmark and infusing them with spirit and energy.

Reflecting on the contrasting lives of the two figures, I felt impelled to choose between them for my role model—should I follow the thinker or the activist?

Both had attended the University of Copenhagen at about the same time. Kierkegaard was a philosopher who had broken off an engagement to pursue philosophy in seclusion. He referred to himself as "a solitary pine on a mountaintop, so lonely that not even a bird comes by." The goal of his philosophy, according to Kierkegaard, was to discover how to stand naked before God. He wrote a number of books that to this day influence philosophical thought.

Grundtvig was a very different person. At the university, he majored in theology. After graduating, he prepared for ordination. In his qualifying sermon preached before examiners, he voiced criticism of the Danish clergy and urged them to repent. Not surprisingly, his message annoyed the ecclesiastical authorities, who later refused to ordain him. Grundtvig was soon banished to a remote island, where he developed a neurosis. His courage waned, his mind became enfeebled, and he almost became an invalid.

Confronting his crisis, he knelt before God. "Dear God, pour your grace upon me. Save me from this darkness," he cried out, as if his life depended upon it.

Then, one day, Grundtvig perceived the heavens opening, and God reaching out to lay His hand on Grundtvig's soul. Deeply touched by this spiritual experience, he wept, overwhelmed with gratitude. Having been healed through this experience, his sermons became more dynamic and full of vision and conviction. He preached passionately and infused the Danish people with the principle of three loves: love of God, love of land, and love of people.

Torn between whether I should follow the path of Kierkegaard or that of Grundtvig, I spent my last few months in college mulling over my future.

In November of my senior year I was awarded a full scholarship to a graduate school in the United States. My school would finance my education through to a doctoral degree.

When my name was posted on a bulletin board as the school's first scholarship student for overseas study, I became the envy of the campus. Going overseas to study was a rare opportunity in those years. I soon firmed up my plans to pursue a Ph.D. in the U.S., with the ultimate goal of returning to my alma mater to devote my life to teaching.

I was sitting at my desk one night, with some twenty philosophy textbooks in front of me, and thought to myself. Is what is written worth spending my whole life on? I sensed that something was missing. I felt that somewhere, deep within my soul, there remained an unquenched thirst. I couldn't help but feel that something was not right.

I graduated in the spring of 1966, in the midst of my philosophical ruminations. Upon graduating at the top of my class, I accepted a position as a teaching assistant at my university. The teaching assistantship would allow me time to apply to a graduate school in the U.S. I lectured in place of the professors of philosophy.

It was May. I was lecturing in an introductory course in philosophy, when a student raised his hand.

"Professor, I have a question."

"Yes?"

"What is truth?"

Now that I look back on it, that student's question served as an electric spark of sorts in my life's journey, although he may not have understood the depth of the question or the challenge it posed. In my unsuccessful search for an answer, I stood, hesitant for a while, stammering awkwardly before finally replying.

"Kant's first major work, *Critique of Pure Reason*, starts out by addressing the issue of truth. According to Kant, things can be true only when the concept of truth exists in our mind. Only when 'reality' coincides with the concept in our mind does it become true. Take this fountain pen, for example. When the concept of this fountain pen in my mind and the real object in my hand coincide, then that is the truth. This is part of what is called an *a priori* form of sensation...."

After I finished, I glanced at the student as if to check his response. He snorted and responded, "Professor, that's beside the point. I'm talking about the kind of truth I can live and die for. Who cares who Kant was or what he said? What does that have to do with me?"

I was aghast. The student had callously attacked one of the innermost blind spots of my mental realm. I figured that my only recourse would be honesty.

"I don't know such truth. I'm searching for it myself."

The student didn't back down. He continued.

"Well, Professor, you started today's lecture by saying that philosophy is a discipline in search of the truth, but since you yourself haven't discovered the truth, I don't see how you can possibly teach us. There isn't any need to go on with this. It's a waste of our time. Why don't you just call it a day and dismiss the class?"

The whole class burst into laughter. Embarrassed and bewildered, I fumbled my way through the remainder of the hour and, when the bell rang, I rushed out the door. In the privacy of my office, I sat in my chair and took a deep breath.

THE QUESTION POSED BY THE STUDENT was perfectly valid. How can I possibly teach something that I, myself, do not know? Isn't it the blind leading the blind? Indeed it is. Then what should I do? Shouldn't I hold off lecturing until I have achieved enlightenment, something for which I can live and die? As an assistant, I can get away without giving lectures, but what will happen after I become a professor? Shouldn't I first be equipped with a clear understanding of truth before I begin teaching?

In Buddhism, Prince Siddhartha renounced his royal title and became a wandering ascetic in search of a solution to the problems of death and human suffering. He achieved supreme enlightenment after seven years of spiritual discipline in the cold of snow-covered mountains. Only then did he devote his life to teaching his doctrines.

Jesus did likewise. Having worked as a carpenter in Galilee, Jesus began a public ministry as a teacher only after he was enlightened to the divine idea. In His first sermon, He declared, "The time has come. The kingdom of God is near. Repent and believe the good news!" (Mark 1:15)

What does He mean by "The time has come"? Does it mean that it is time for Him to teach? Does it mean that the time has come for people to listen? Or does it mean that it is time for God to reveal Himself to the people? Shouldn't I, like Buddha or Jesus, wait until I reach enlightenment and am convinced that the time has come, before I set about to teach others? What about other philosophy professors? Have they attained enlightenment? Probably not. Although the depth of their knowledge and the breadth of their understanding of humans may go far beyond mine, we are all probably in the same boat, in that we teach without knowing.

In most Korean philosophy courses, professors only repeat what they read in Western philosophy books. Dr. So-and-so's field of expertise is Kant, another Dr. So-and-so's expertise is Heidegger. They pore over books in their field, translate them, and write their dissertations on them. In academia, time brings authority. The great majority of professors speak, not from their own realization, but from their knowledge of Kant or Heidegger. Such teaching is likely to drive confused students deeper into a state of confusion.

What if I were to follow their footsteps? What would I teach when I lecture? What would I say to a student who asks, "What is truth?"

It was beyond me. Deep within my soul, a voice said, "This isn't for you. You have only one life to live."

After contemplating this matter for a long time, I came to a conclusion. I would try to lead my life so that in my later years I would be able to reflect on it and show myself and young people what truth is. Whether a barber or a farmer, whatever a person's work, if he can live by his own convictions and practice the values that he has acquired from life, isn't that a much better life? Isn't a laborer, who is able to sleep at night, better off than a neurotic professor?

The story of the great Buddhist monk Won-hyo came to mind. As a young man during the Silla Dynasy, seeking the truth, Won-hyo embarked on a journey to China to study Buddhism. One night, while on his journey, he stopped to rest at a small cottage. During the night, he was awakened by thirst. In the moonlit darkness, he groped for the water bottle and soon, to his delight, found a bowl full of water. He immediately gulped it down. It was as sweet as honey. When he awoke the next morning, he was stunned to see that the bowl was actually a skull and the water in it was liquid from a decaying body. At this realization, he immediately became nauseous and his stomach wrenched violently. He made himself vomit. Then it occurred to him:

> Where there is a will, truth is produced, but when the will is gone, truth no longer exists. Desire and lust come from one's heart, just as truth comes from one's mind. The liquid was sweet water because I thought it was, but I threw up in disgust this morning when I learned what it really was. Everything, including affliction and peace, comes from the mind. Hence, there is no need to search elsewhere. I will not continue my journey to China. Discipline is not in China, but within me.

Won-hyo returned to the Silla Kingdom and lived a secluded life in a cave to cultivate his spiritual discipline. He was then forty-five years old. He strove and reached the highest level of spiritual attainment.

I wanted to live like Won-hyo. To pursue philosophy genuinely, shouldn't I cultivate discipline from my innermost self, instead of going abroad to study? Shouldn't there be a modern-day Won-hyo?

Somewhere in this land, infused with spirits of our ancestors, should I not be able to find the meaning of life?

Arriving at this realization, I abandoned my original plan and decided to start from scratch. I would embark anew on my journey, from the very beginning, just as a person would shave his head to become a monk.

7

To Be, Or Not To Be

D URING MY SUMMER VACATION* from teaching, I raised
some money and headed for Seoul. There I took up peddling
ice bars in a hilly part of Malli-dong, behind Seoul Station.
Purchasing ice bars for 2.7 *won*, I sold them for 5 *won* each. I had to sell
about 300 ice bars to afford one meal. Many times I sat astride my icebox in front of the gate of Soui Elementary School, calling out, "Ice
bars—two for 10 *won*!"

With a straw hat pressed all the way down over my eyes, I looked
out through two holes I had punched in it. I had gotten this idea from
reading about Hideyoshi Toyotomi, a Japanese warrior and dictator
who had peddled needles in his youth and who was said to have observed
the world through pinholes in his hat. I wanted to see the world through
the holes in my straw hat.

My route started on top of a hill in Malli-dong. It then went down
to Seoul Station Plaza, on to Namdaemun (South Gate) Market, then
to Myeong-dong, today a well-known fashion district, and City Hall,
and back to the hilltop. I would do my route on foot, completing several
rounds during the day.

On clear days, I was able to sell enough ice bars to buy three meals
and a place to sleep for the night. When it was cloudy or when it rained,
sales diminished to where I could barely afford one decent meal. At that

---

*School year in Korea begins in March. There is a six-week mid-year break in
summer.

time Soui Elementary School gave out corn bread to the students as their daily snack. For children who ate it every day, the corn bread was nothing special. Students often brought their bread to me and asked to barter it for my ice bars. I gladly traded two ice bars for one piece of bread. For me, it was a good deal, because I was selling ice bars to be able to buy bread in any case. By the end of the day, my icebox would be full of bread.

I would take the bread home, which was a homeless shelter in Namdaemun, and dole it out to my fellow residents. Needless to say, this made me very popular. When in the evening I returned to the shelter, the residents flocked around me. They were lazy and incompetent, but their warmth and lack of guile made them likeable.

People also began to gather around me when I stopped at the front gate of the Soui Elementary School. All sorts of peddlers passed by, as I sat on my icebox—weary and desperate people in tattered clothes, peddling their goods. It was a moving display of the struggle of the impoverished. My heart felt for them in their determination to survive. I would always call them over to where I was seated.

"Ma'am, come sit and rest here in the shade. Here, have an ice bar."

Wary and suspicious, they approached me cautiously at first, but after getting to know me, they soon became more at ease. I eventually got to know all the peddlers in the area. It became routine for them to stop by, rest, have an ice bar, and chat with me. We talked about mundane matters, which for me were lessons in life that later I could put to good use.

One day, I had been sitting along the wall of the school calling out, "Ice bars—two for 10 *won!*" when I saw a young man pulling a cart up the hill. His cart was full of sundry goods, such as old clocks, rubber shoes, an array of other secondhand items, and bars of laundry and hand soap. With a towel, he wiped perspiration from his brow after every step.

During three seasons of the year, he would sell taffy, but because taffy could not stand the scorching summer heat, for several months of the year he earned his living by selling other items.

I sensed there was something different about him, but still I called out to him, just as I would to any other peddler.

"Hey there, fella! Why don't you take a break and come over and have an ice bar?"

He took me up on it, pulling his cart into the shade, and wiping his brow once again. "This heat's unbearable! Thanks for the ice bar, but I'll pay you for it."

"Don't mention it. It's on me. So, how's business? Summer can't be too good a time for secondhand dealers?"

"No, I barely make enough to get by."

Taking a bite of the ice bar, he tossed his towel over onto his cart. My eyes followed the towel, which landed on a copy of a foreign textbook that lay on the cart. As I read the title of the book, my eyes opened wide in amazement. It was by Heidegger, the German philosopher, and was entitled, *What is Metaphysics?*

At the unexpected sight of the familiar philosophy textbook, I asked, "Where did you get that book? Can I have it?" I figured that a philosophy book would be the last thing a secondhand dealer needed and that it was serving no purpose.

He stared at me in bewilderment. "How do you know what that is?" Meanwhile, my philosophy book, *Problems in Philosophy*, by Bertrand Russell, happened to be sitting on top of my icebox. When he saw my book, he was astonished.

"You're reading that?"

Without hesitating, we introduced ourselves to one another. He had been a philosophy major at Seoul National University and had taught German at a girls' high school. He soon resigned, having become discouraged trying to teach a bunch of disinterested students who routinely chatted or slept in class. He said that he was exploring the real world. He chuckled, talking about how he had abandoned teaching, whatever the future, to become a taffy peddler and practice philosophy.

When he stopped telling me about himself, I told him that I had given up trying to find truth in Western thinkers and that I was now seeking a deeper meaning in life by feeling the pulse of the common people.

Excited by our common interest, we went straightaway to have a drink. We could not have cared less about the possibility of someone stealing our things. It was more important for us to sit and talk. Sitting on wooden chairs in a grogshop, we filled each other's bowl with chalky *makgeoli** and discussed life and the world. We drank and talked until we were so drunk that our twisted tongues no longer allowed us to speak without slurring.

He elaborated pompously, "Confucius once said, enlightenment in the morning will let a person die content in the evening. I totally agree, because that's exactly how I feel. My words are the words of Confucius. If someone could tell me the reason for my existence, I would follow him all my life. If anybody could show me how I should live, the path of my existence, I would honor him as my master all of my life and become his servant, but my search has been in vain.

"I've concluded that there are only servants in the world, and no masters. I've searched for a master for an entire year, as I walked the maze of this city with this cart of mine, but to no avail. I've spent a lot of time in the search, but I've found no masters."

He burped the entire time he imparted his worldview, while I sat serious and solemn. He mirrored my very thoughts. I felt as if I was looking at my other self. After we parted company, I hoisted my icebox up onto my shoulder and set out to walk around Seoul Station Plaza, thinking about what he'd said.

"There are only servants, and no masters for them to follow.... I earnestly desire to dedicate my life's work to a master, but haven't been able to find one.... I've spent a lot of time in search of a master, but to no avail."

Then I heard a bell chiming from a nearby church. I followed the sound to a church not far from Seoul Station. Across the entrance was a placard with the words, "Spiritual Revival Night." Inside, praises, clapping, and prayers were in full swing. I went in and quietly took a seat in the back and prayed.

"Dear God! The truth that penetrates the universe! Through the speaker tonight, may you instill wisdom in me. Please reveal yourself through the pastor's message. I will become your servant, once I am convinced of your existence. If only I could know for sure that you exist, I would become your servant and dedicate my life to you."

Earnestly I prayed, as a thirsty fawn searches for a stream. Then I

---

*Makgeoli is a traditional fermented grain drink.

waited for the pastor to deliver his sermon.

That evening's message, however, was far too off the mark to give direction to a soul as lost as mine. The church was in the process of raising funds for the construction of a new building. The pastor's message was intended to convince the congregation that the more they gave to the building fund, the greater the blessings they would receive. He gave an explicit account of instances where such-and-such deacon and such-and-such elder had prospered in their business after offering a certain sum of money to the church's construction fund.

The congregation responded enthusiastically with "amen, amen," throughout the sermon. The speaker concluded by saying that if one gives up his assets and even goes so far as to sell his house to donate to the church, God will later bless him with a house ten times or one hundred times bigger than the original.

For me, the Lord's revelation was nowhere in sight. The only phenomenon that overcame me was incessant yawning. How can a person put down an offering for a church building without ever having met Jesus or even gotten a glimpse of His shadow? I grew increasingly agitated and walked out mumbling to myself, "Go on, collect your donations, erect your magnificent building!"

The church is a holy place where lost and desperate souls come to quench their thirst for truth and direction. The church should be instrumental in helping people meet the Savior. Only then will they become inspired to dedicate their lives to the Lord.

Churches have failed to carry out this role. Instead, they endeavor endlessly to drum up more respect for the pastor and more donations for more land and grander facilities. That approach has sent many disappointed souls back onto the streets. Some people, in their search for the "right path," fall into the trap of religious cults. Elsewhere, in many churches, the sole aim of those who remain is to receive blessings by obeying the pastors. I deplore churches made up of such mindless congregations.

AS I WALKED OUT OF THE CHURCH, I headed to Seojongsam, a red-light district, located in downtown Seoul. I entered the alley behind the Piccadilly Theater. Prostitutes with heavy makeup beckoned to passersby and reached out and took their hands.

A woman latched onto me aggressively, saying "Come and play with me." I followed her. She led me to a small room, where she started to distort her face in funny ways, and stare at me suggestively, asking, "You wanna to make it a full night or a short one?"

I stood there with a blank face, not knowing what she was talking about. I asked hesitantly, "What's a full night and what's a short one?"

"Aw, come on, don't tell me that this is your first time! You look like someone who's been around here before."

What has she taken me for? Do I look like a regular in Seojongsam? As far as I could figure out, she meant it neither as a compliment nor as an insult, but it bothered me, nevertheless. As I sat, saying nothing, she nudged me, "I guess you don't really know about these things. A short one is when you play for just a little while. A full night is when you sleep through the night. Why don't we make it a full night. I'll be happy to give you some extra fun."

"How much would a full night cost me?"

"It's still early. If we start now, it'll cost you 3,000 *won*."

I went through my pocket and emptied it, handing over to her everything I had, including the money I needed to replenish my stock of ice bars. It came out to be only two thousand and a few hundred *won*. She took it and started to undress. She moved quickly and casually, as if she were only taking off her shoes.

It was my first experience, so I had very little control. Before I knew, it was over. I was quickly overcome with regret, thinking that somehow, things weren't right. I knew that what I had experienced was not what it was supposed to be.

The prostitute pulled up her underwear and said teasingly, "You're a weak one," as she fixed her hair in front of the mirror. I had an overwhelming feeling of disgust and nausea.

I spoke with my eyes fixed on the calendar, evading her eyes, "Could you please go somewhere else to sleep?"

"What'sa matta? Ain't I your type?"

"It's not that. I just want to read for a while before going to sleep."

"OK. I'll come back early in the morning, then."

"No, really, don't bother. I've had enough."

Her face lit up as she slipped out the door. She beamed at the opportunity to still earn more money that night. Meanwhile, I lay down in an unsuccessful attempt to fall asleep. I tossed and turned. The damp bedding, the humidity from the floor, and the intrusion of human breathing sounds that came through the thin walls, unsettled me and made me nervous. I felt an intense animosity toward man kind in general. This isn't what intercourse between a man and a woman is supposed to be, I thought. How vain are the consequences of giving in to lust!

I got up to retrieve my Bible from under my bag. Clasping it between my palms, I knelt and prayed.

"Heavenly Father! If this Scripture is really from you, please guide me to your message as I open the Bible. May you enlighten my soul."

I closed my eyes and flipped open the Bible. I held my breath as I opened my eyes. It had opened at a blank insert that marked the separation between the Old Testament and the New.

I could expect no spiritual enlightenment from a blank page, I thought, so I closed the Bible and opened it once more. It opened to Jeremiah 20:1. "When the priest Pashur son of Immer, was chief officer in the temple of the Lord, heard Jeremiah prophesying these things."

It meant absolutely nothing to me, so I closed the Bible once again and opened it to yet another page. This time it opened to Romans 13:1. "Everyone must submit himself to the governing authorities, for there is no authority except that which God has established."

Disappointed, I closed the Bible and put it in my bag. I then curled up to sleep. At dawn, I awoke, hurried out of the room, and left.

With an empty stomach, I went to the ice bar distributor. It was customary for peddlers to pay for their stock in advance, as a precaution against someone fleeing with a full icebox. Because I had spent all my money the night before, I left my ID card and my bag with the ice bar distributor for security. I could then walk out with an icebox strapped across my shoulder. I walked my route, finally reaching the Soui Elementary School, where, once again, I sat down against the wall. It was business as usual for the next several days.

Then something dreadful happened. I began to have a burning sensation in my penis and in a few days noticed there was blood in my urine. Later, the blood became pus. Sapped of my energy, I became alarmed. I thought I must have contracted some terrible sexually transmitted disease and figured I was on my way to becoming an invalid. I had heard that a sexually transmitted disease would make me lose my hair. Then I would lose my memory and eventually go insane.

Plagued by this wave of petrifying thoughts, I went into a deep depression. I couldn't afford to go to a doctor. This is what I get for trying to be another grand monk, like Won-hyo, I thought, and regretted everything I had done.

I could picture myself falling down a mile-long cliff. I searched for a drugstore behind Seoul Station. A sign saying "Wonder Drug for Sexual Diseases" caught my eye from the window of one of the drugstores. I mustered courage to enter the store. When I described my symptoms to the pharmacist, he said nonchalantly, "It sounds like you have an inflammation of the urinary tract."

"What kind of a disease is that? Is it really awful?"

"They also call it urethritis. Don't worry about it. It's curable, if you treat it promptly. You'll have to take medicine for a week. It'll cost you 700 *won* per day. Would you like to start today?"

I was relieved to hear the pharmacist's diagnosis, but my problem didn't go away. How was I supposed to pay for treatment for an entire week? Seven times 700 *won* came to 4,900 *won*. Where could I raise that kind of money? It would be impossible to earn 700 *won* a day selling ice bars.

I left the pharmacy. The infection worsened every day, and I was dribbling bloody pus like a leaky fountain pen.

Meanwhile, I ran across university students who were starting their fall term, after summer break. Wistfully, I watched them, coming and going.

Should I go back to my teaching or should I follow the path of the truth seeker? Walking my route with my "leaky fountain pen," I pondered my future.

Toward mid-September I came to a conclusion that going back to college in my doubting state would serve no purpose because I would continue with my indecision. In Buddhism it is said that if one wishes to become enlightened, one needs to stand on a 100-foot pole and dare to take one step forward.

I needed to decide. Either I would end up failing or a new path would open for me. Having descended by choice to the lowest rung on society's ladder, I thought I might now find the truth I had been seeking. This thought reassured me and encouraged me to continue my quest.

MY IMMEDIATE NEED WAS FOR LIVING EXPENSES. When at the end of August, a cool breeze began to dampen the summer heat, I was soon out of the ice bar business. I needed to find another line of work, something that would generate enough money to pay for my treatment.

Wandering around Namdaemun Market, I stopped in front of a wholesale toy store. I bought a pinwheel, a whistle, a trumpet, a wooden flute, a top, and a jump rope and attached them to a pole. Carrying the pole on my shoulder, I trudged toward some residential areas. As I walked along the alleys, I blew the trumpet and drummed up the kids on the block.

I sat them in a big circle on a vacant lot and started to tell stories—world literary classics like *Treasure Island*, *Wuthering Heights*, *Daddy-Long-Legs*.... The children were excited and quickly became engrossed in my stories. As I approached the climax of my stories, I would pause, cough once or twice, and give my sales pitch.

"Kids! I need to earn a living. I need to eat so I can keep telling you stories. Here's what you do. Go talk to your mom, get whatever money you've saved, and buy one of these toys I have here. Then I'll pick up where we left off."

The naive children would do as I told them, whispering as they left, "Mister, please don't go anywhere while we're gone. You have to stay here until we come back, so you can tell us the rest of the story. OK?"

Some kids returned with their mom or older siblings, bought their toys, and listened to my stories before they returned home. Storytelling is like planting seeds on a fertile field. The craft of storytelling instills children with dreams and an imagination that will mold and shape creative minds of the future generation.

I envisioned this and attempted to take pride in my new venture with children. I enjoyed a brisk business in toy sales. It yielded enough to pay for my medicine, with some left over to buy noodles for my fellow residents at the shelter.

After the sunshine, however, comes the rain and after autumn came the winter wind. The children were off the streets. Although there were still a few who would come out, despite the biting cold weather, most were nowhere to be seen. My trumpeting, resonating through the streets, no longer drew them out of their houses. I knew it was time to change my line of work once again.

I NEXT BECAME A SALESMAN FOR JULIA COSMETICS. Because it involved door-to-door sales, the cold weather didn't matter. When I knocked on the doors of houses at around 10 o'clock in the morning, it was usually the housemaid who answered.

"Yes, what do you want?"

"I'm from Julia Cosmetics, ma'am."

"No, thanks. We don't need any cosmetics."

"I'm not a salesman. I'm in marketing, promoting a new line we've just developed. I'm not asking you to buy anything. All you need to do is sit and listen to what I have to say about our products."

"No, really. I'm not interested."

"I'm speaking in your interest, young lady. You really need to listen to this, if you want to look good. But…why do you have so many freckles and blemishes on your face? You'll damage your skin, if you don't attend to them."

"Oh! How insulting! What blemishes? Everyone tells me what a fine complexion I have!"

"Why would I lie to you? I see blemishes emerging on your skin. You'll see them, too, if you leave your face the way it is now. You need to take preventive action. This medicinal cream was developed for just that purpose. I'll simply tell you about the product and leave."

By that time, most housemaids would gladly invite me in. I would spread my entire display of cosmetics out on the floor. I would then suggest that they invite a friend or a neighbor in to join my presentation on the latest makeup techniques. At that, they would usually call the housemaid from next door.

I eagerly explained the ABC's of putting on makeup, starting from basic skin care to putting on foundation and finally the makeup itself. I explained how to match the color of the lipstick to one's outfit, as well as ways to flatter the shape and complexion of the face. I addressed them individually, starting with an analysis of their skin type and the shape of their face, followed by a recommended line of cosmetics for each one, concluding with words of caution for their skin care. For example, women with high cheekbones should cover them up through makeup, while emphasizing their lips. So and so should use a certain cream because she has dry skin, so on and so forth.

My consultation worked like a magnet and successfully influenced women to buy my products. They were charmed by my approach and before leaving I was often invited to eat a hefty meal.

Still, I had no intention of permanently working in cosmetics sales. The return of the spring breezes, after the long winter, stimulated my agitated mind. My life seemed too precious to be wasted on talking about skin care and lipstick. I decided to get out of cosmetics and try something else.

This time it would be magazines. There was a company named Production Headquarters that published a monthly magazine titled *Business and Management* or *Management and Information*—I forget the exact title. I became one of their salesmen. My job was to sell subscriptions to businesses, companies, and stores by showing them samples.

My first day on the job, I carried the stack of magazines in my bag and started at Cheonggye-cheon, visiting all the stores along the way. An entire assortment of hardware and furniture stores, in great numbers, lined the street. I entered every shop and delivered my spiel.

"You need to be well read in your field, if you wish to succeed. The key to management in the modern world rests on ease of mobility and access to information. Your first step should be to collect all the information you can from this magazine. That way, you'll keep abreast of the latest developments in your field."

I would then offer summaries of a few articles from the magazine. My tactic was successful in convincing store owners, as they eagerly bought their subscription, saying "I suppose I'll lose out to the competition if I don't read up on this stuff!"

In this way, I managed to secure thirty to forty subscribers a week. The marketing department soon recognized me as one of the company's top salesmen. As with other past moneymaking efforts, I was not going to make a career out of magazine sales and I left it after three months, turning to selling insurance. I found a job at Jeil Life Insurance Company's Yeongrak branch office.

I began work, but just as I warmed up into my routine as an

insurance salesman, I ran into trouble. I awoke one morning in my room at the homeless shelter to find that my bag had been stolen. During the night, someone had taken everything I owned, except for the clothes I was wearing the night before. By being generous at the shelter, buying noodles for everyone and lending them cigarette money, I must have conveyed the impression that I had a lot of money.

IRONICALLY, WITHIN ONE YEAR OF LEAVING HOME in search of something grand, I had lost everything I owned and was left with only the clothes on my back and the shoes on my feet. I dragged my weary body up to the summit of Mount Nam. Looking down on the city, I thought of Pascal and how he must have felt when he wrote in *Pensées*:

> It is good to grow weary from seeking good. That will eventually make you hopeful of attaining salvation from God.... Do you not know that the key that will unshackle you from misery does not lie within you? Searching there will prove to be in vain and will only show you that you have no truth or good within.
>
> Philosophers often claim to have learned the truth, but they have all stumbled. They have failed to discover the goodness you possess or the object of your search. How can they draw up a plan to save you from your misery when they are blind about the sources of misery? If you reach the Lord, know that it is not your nature that made it possible, but the Lord's grace that fell upon you.

Pascal was deeply moved one day when he was showered with God's blessings. He encountered God with all his heart and soul. Overwhelmed with happiness, he ended his wandering and anguish. Inspired by God's grace, which granted him salvation, he wrote:

> He was not the God of philosophers, nor of scientists, nor of mathematicians. He was the God of Abraham, the God of Isaac, the God of Jacob. When I sought the Lord, He hid from me, but when I knelt before Him, He embraced me. I praise you, Oh Lord!

But I was not able to meet Pascal's God. As much as I wanted to, I knew of no way to reach Him. Pascal said that when as a philosopher he had sought the Lord, God had hidden from him, but when he knelt down before Him as a child, God offered his hand in salvation.

I, too, wanted to submit to God, so I could put an end to my wandering and solitude. I wished to deny myself and kneel before Him. The question was, how? Should I go to a sanctuary and fast? Should I confess my sins to a priest? How did Pascal meet God? I would be willing to do whatever it took to experience the kind of ecstasy Pascal wrote about, if only I knew how.

I had a feeling that my search for the truth would be in vain. Then I remembered my mother and the God she worshipped. In my earliest recollections, I had always heard my mother's prayers around the house. In the early hours of the morning, she offered prayers for each of her children. When she prayed for me she would say, "Heavenly Father, I pray that you will make Jin-hong a pastor so he may serve you—that he may lead people to your path."

How I despised that prayer back then! Why would she want to make a pastor out of me? Why not a judge, a general, or even a president of a company? Of all things, why would she want me to live the hard life of a pastor?

After all my years of wandering, the son had come to think about his mother's prayer and the God he had worshipped so faithfully in his childhood. I longed to return to God, but didn't know how.

"LIMITING CIRCUMSTANCES" IS A TERM used in existentialist philosophy to refer to barriers in life that humans cannot overcome. For example, besides the obvious birth, aging, illness, and death, existentialists have identified four additional limiting circumstances—sin, solitude, struggle, and wandering.

Why is sin a limiting circumstance? It is impossible for humans to live without falling into sin. Just as humans breathe air, they sin as part of life.

Solitude is also a limiting circumstance. Why? Because solitude is unavoidable, as long as one lives. Friedrich Nietzsche once said, "Solitude is man's fate, so one might do well to come to love it. Do not evade solitude, but love it with your heart. Then, it will befriend you."

Nietzsche spoke of *Amor Fati,* which is the love of man's fate, or solitude. He himself loved it, saying, "Solitude is my home."

Existentialists also include struggle as a limiting circumstance. As long as we live, there is struggle.

Wandering and anguish constitute another limiting circumstance. We cannot escape them, like shadows that follow us all the days of our lives. The Book of John begins:

> In the beginning was the Word, and the Word was with God, and the Word was God. He was with God in the beginning. Through him all things were made; without him, nothing was made that has been made. (John 1:1-3)

One existentialist rephrased the above verses in the following words:

> In the beginning was wandering, and the wandering was with God and the wandering was God. Wandering was in the beginning with God, and all things were made through wandering. In the wandering was solitude, which is man's fundamental life. God, who agonizes while wandering, created man to tolerate the solitude. Hence man is a result of solitude. Therefore, solitude is man's companion.

In other words, man came into being with all the elements of sin, solitude, struggle, and wandering. No one ever came into being of his own volition. We are cast into this world without knowing. The existentialists say that existence is passive, referring to the fact that man's destiny confines him to this world. Under no circumstances can he transcend it to any other.

Once in this life, however, existentialists maintain that man has one chance, and only one chance, to find meaning by throwing himself into it entirely. For Karl Jaspers it was God; for Sartre, freedom; for Camus, action.

Camus said, "Humans are saved through deeds. Do not judge the morality of man's deeds. The action itself is beautiful. Be it a holy servant lecturing the congregation, a robber fleeing on a train, or two lovers in bed—actions themselves suffice, as they carry significance."

I pondered this. I, too, wished to hurl myself at something, but I knew not at what. To what end should I let my whole self be consumed? Sartre once gave an answer: "Modern man has a goal, but he does not know how to reach it."

I once knew of a God who I accepted wholeheartedly. It was the God my mother believed in without the slightest reservation. Yet, that God was at too great a distance from my troubled soul. I couldn't find the way to Him. He existed only in my mind, as a longing, a fleeting wind.

I DETERMINED TO RETURN HOME. I would end the life of a nomad and force myself to kneel down before my mother's God. I boarded the night train to Daegu. I couldn't afford a ticket, so I snuck on board. Unfortunately, I was soon caught and kicked off. The conductor smacked my face so hard that it felt as if he had burst my eardrum. I had to spend the night in the Daejeon Station, only halfway home. In the morning, I successfully snuck onto another train, arriving in Daegu a couple of hours later.

By the time I arrived home, I looked like a beggar in every way. Despite my long absence from home, it hadn't stopped my mother from continuing with her prayer, "May Jin-hong become a pastor." She asked me to go to church with her.

"Mother, how can I possibly go to church when I have no faith?"

"That's not how it works. Faith grows after you go to church. You don't need it before you go. You attend services. Leave it to God to instill faith in you. You don't have to worry about His end of the bargain. All you need to do is go."

"I understand what you're saying, but let me think about it."

"Please, do think about it, because life is too precious to be wasted. If you come before the Lord, I know that He will use you in a very special way."

As she spoke, she went to her closet and took out an army draft notice that had come for me.

"This came quite a while back, but I had no way to get it to you. I knew you'd always wanted to enlist, so I contacted some of your friends to track you down. If all you're going to do is wander about, you might as well join the army and do your service for the next three years."

While I should have been drafted at some point during my college years, my notice was delayed because I had led a student demonstration. Reading the notice, the reporting period had expired three days earlier.

With the notice in hand, I went to the Office of Military Manpower Administration. I explained the circumstances that had kept me from replying previously and urged them to accept me. They flatly rejected me, despite my persistence, saying it was their policy not to accept anyone after the end date of the reporting period.

I visited them again a few days later, only to find out that I had been transferred to the Army reserve pool. I have always felt it was unfortunate that I missed having an army experience.

8

An Earthquake, Shattering My Soul

K EIMYONG COLLEGE HAD BEEN looking for me to urge me
to return to school, but I had already decided against it. I had
concluded that studying philosophy would get me nowhere in
my effort to find answers to my questions about life.

I had a feeling that a day of understanding was approaching, a day
when I would come to some understanding of life, and that I would
then realize what I should devote my life to. I had no idea what form
the inevitable would take, whether it would fall on me from heaven,
surge from within me, or perhaps would be no more than something I
learn from others.

Although the day was at hand, I did not want to wait for it, sitting
in a library. Rather, I wanted my day of awakening to come when I was
involved in the lives of others, amidst the bustle of worldly activity, with
farmers working in their fields or with laborers at their work.

One day, when I returned home after my wandering, an American
missionary, Ku Ui-ryeong, who had taken an interest in me during my
college days, suggested that I go as an assistant pastor to a church in the
countryside.

"Mr. Kim, there is a small church in a rural area south of here, a
village called Mokdan. Why don't you go there and serve God's people?"

"Thank you, Pastor, for the suggestion, but how can I carry out
missionary work when even I'm not sure of my own faith?"

"You can. Pastors often awaken their religious faith while doing
His work, like teachers who learn by teaching. You may not now be

convinced of your faith, but I am sure you can deal with it because you were brought up in a religious home."

My mother was excited about Ku's suggestion. She must have thought that I had finally found a way to serve God. Concluding that I would continue my effort to find God while doing His work, I accepted the missionary's suggestion.

In the summer of 1967, I loaded my belongings in a jeep and traveled south to Mokdan. The church there was small and built on a hill. When I arrived, the door was open. I entered and knelt down, before unloading the jeep.

"I swear that I will be faithful to you for the rest of my life, if you call me from this pulpit." That day I started my work as an assistant pastor, at a salary of 3,000 *won* and a sack of rice per month. I spent more time doing village chores than church work. I helped farmers who were short of hands. In the beginning, the villagers were suspicious, but they soon changed their minds and came to trust me. Still, some church members disapproved of me.

"The new assistant pastor neglects his church work and helps farmers who are not even churchgoers. He's strange."

"Yes, he is. If he wants to help someone, he should help Christians. I don't understand him helping people who don't come to church."

I didn't mind what they said about me. I continued to work hard, helping the villagers. I tried to ingratiate myself particularly with the young men. I used my own money to buy a volleyball for them to practice with. I also organized a theater troupe for the young people of the village. I adapted the Book of Esther into a play for them to perform, and to that end took upon myself several jobs, including producer, director, and drama coach.

We rehearsed the play until late at night. This caused concern among the villagers and gave rise to gossip. Church members in particular expressed strong disapproval. Their concerns were on the order of, "What if the girls get pregnant, getting together with the young men until late the way they do? The church would have to shut down, if that happens." "The pastor should dedicate himself to spiritual matters." "If things go on like this, people will nickname our church the mating church or the fathering church."

Time passed and the play's opening day came. The church was

packed for the performance. The staff were concerned about the safety of the building because it was so shoddily constructed and there were so many people in it.

Unfortunately, our concerns translated into reality. Halfway through the play, the actors and the audience were swaying together, putting pressure on the structure. Before long we heard a great rumbling sound. The rumble was soon followed by yells and screams, which mixed with dust, as one of the church walls fell down.

I choked and prayed. "Lord Jesus! Please help the people emerge unscathed. I don't care if the building falls down, but please protect the people."

When the dust settled, I inspected the site and found that there were no casualties. We announced an indefinite postponement of the play and got to work repairing the fallen wall.

We were unable to stage the play later because church members, who had opposed it from the outset, blocked its performance. They said that the performance of a play diminished God's glory, adding that if I wanted to go ahead with the play, I should leave the church. The young people of the village were very disappointed.

I shifted my efforts from recreation to education. I divided the village into six sections and visited each section once a week, between Monday and Saturday. At around the time of day when farm families had finished supper, I made a bonfire and gathered the children to read them stories and teach them songs. After a series of songs, the grownups joined the children to listen to the stories.

I used readings from my school days as material for the stories. The children responded with noise and clapping when the stories got exciting. When the stories turned sad, they sighed and became heartbroken. Tears would well up in their eyes when the lead characters met with tragedy. Thanks to this activity, Sunday school was always well attended.

ONE MORNING, A YOUNG MAN FROM A CHURCH in a neighboring town came to see me. He introduced himself as the president of the church's youth club.

"Pastor, is it a sin for Christians to commit suicide?" he asked.

"Yes, it is a great sin, indeed. God holds human lives. People have no right to kill themselves. Before God, it is the same as committing murder."

"Is it also a sin to conduct a funeral for a person who has committed suicide?"

"Ah, that's a different issue. Someone must perform a funeral for anyone who is dead. It is not a question of sin. Why are you asking me these questions?"

"A teacher in our church killed herself by taking farm chemicals. She was only nineteen. The pastor is against conducting a funeral for her because her suicide was such a terrible sin. He also told us not to put our hands on her dead body because she took her own life, against the teaching of the Bible, and touching her dead body would also be to commit a sin. Her body has been left abandoned for four days. I've come to ask your advice."

"I don't understand. Your pastor may have a reason based on his religion for not conducting a funeral for her, but what about other people? People in rural towns usually take the tragedies of others to heart. Doesn't she have family?"

"It's planting season and everyone is busy. Otherwise, the villagers would have seen to her funeral. They are so tied up with their work that they can't make time for it. Also, people aren't very sympathetic toward her because her family drifted around before finally settling in our village. They comment flippantly that she picked the wrong time to die, and the church should concern itself with her funeral because she always attended church."

"What a shame. None of this was her doing. You say she was a good church member. You mentioned that she was a teacher. Where did she teach?"

"She taught children at Sunday school. She also was a member of the choir and never missed early morning prayers."

"Now I really do not understand. How could she have killed herself, being such a role model? She must have known that Christians don't have the right to take their own lives."

"It's a long story. Her father is a drunk and her mother has been mentally ill for years. She also has younger brothers and sisters to support. As the oldest daughter, she had a very hard life. She seems to have cracked under the pressure."

"That's a heartbreaking story. I will see to her funeral, but I need help. I'd like to ask some young men from the church to help me."

"Pastor, we'd like to help, but people say that we shouldn't because she killed herself."

"I'm not interested in that argument. Later, when I die and go to heaven, and God accuses me of arranging a funeral for someone who committed suicide, I will tell him that I was ignorant of the teaching of the Bible. Then I will confront him that he taught us to put a higher value on human life than on the Bible's teachings. I don't think that God will kick me out of heaven for it."

I went with the young man to the girl's house. A woman who seemed to be the girl's mother was in the living room, staring blankly. In another room, an old woman was sitting next to the body. The girl was covered from head to toe in a shabby blanket. We told the old woman that we had come from the church. She gave us a warm welcome.

"I was about to work out a way to bury her myself, if I didn't hear anything from the church." She clicked her tongue and continued to say, "Poor thing, she had a bad life and hasn't even gotten a proper burial."

Helped by the old woman, I washed and shrouded the body. The chemicals she had killed herself with had caused internal bleeding and a trail of blood went from her chin all the way down to her chest. Dead flies were stuck in her dried blood. I shooed away other flies, cleaned the blood off her with a wet towel, washed her hands and feet, and combed her hair. I went through her wardrobe and picked out the best of her clothes to put on her.

A Bible rolled off her chest onto the floor when I was changing her. I opened the Bible to find a picture of Jesus stuck in one of its pages. It moved me that she had held the Bible to her chest until the last moment of her life. I wished that she had held onto her life with as much persistence as she had held onto the Bible. Had she done so, she might have lived to see better days.

Looking into her face, I felt as if she were my sister. I felt a pang in my heart and tears filled my eyes. Dressing her, I fought back the tears. When I finished, I put the Bible back on her chest.

I put her body on a stretcher made from a burlap bag. Three young men from the church helped and together we carried the body to a mountain beyond the village. Two carried the front of the stretcher while the third and I carried the rear.

The body weighed more than I had counted on. Climbing the hill, I wondered whether a human body weighed more after death than before. The two young men in front had no difficulty climbing the hill because they were used to work and had a lot of energy, but I had to struggle.

"Hey, guys. Please slow down."

Following behind, I tried to catch my breath. Suddenly, I fell, and the stretcher slipped out of my hands. The body rolled off the stretcher, down and onto the road. I was too embarrassed to say anything, watching the body roll down the hill. I was sorry that on her way to be buried she should be treated with so little dignity. She had had such a hard life and, even in death, could not have a proper coffin and was now being carried on a stretcher. On top of that, she had to put up with a clumsy person like me, fumbling and letting her body fall and roll down.

The body stopped, stuck on a pine stump. I hurried down and held the body, consoling her and wishing she could hear.

"I'm sorry. I'm sorry I could not comfort even your dead body. Find peace in heaven, even though your life on earth was harsh. I'm sorry to let your body roll down the mountain," I said to her, as if she were alive, pushing back the hair on her forehead.

I carried her up the mountain in my arms and buried her in a sunny place. I did not put a mound over her grave, as is the custom for adults. I made her a level grave because the graves of children or the unmarried are flat. I broke down a pine tree to make a cross.

"Let's say a prayer," I said to the young men. Holding one another's hands, standing, we prayed.

"Jesus, please let our sister rest in heaven. We have been taught that people who commit suicide are not admitted to heaven, but Jesus, I believe there is no rule that is without exception. This girl deserves your pity. Please take pity on her, who grasped her Bible until the last moment of her life, and let her dwell in heaven. Please let us all see her later in heaven."

The young men, who had fought hard not to cry, now burst into tears. They slumped to the ground and cried out, calling her name.

"You should have told us your life was so bad. We didn't know, because you always seemed so cheerful and happy. How could you take your life like this?"

She had been a cheerful person, despite her wretched family life. I was waiting for the young men to stop crying, but they did not. I had to urge them to go down the mountain.

"You have cried enough. You should have helped her when she was alive," I admonished them. "Crying cannot change what has happened. The sun is setting. Let's go down now."

I came to her church at the bottom of the mountain, on the way to the village. It was Saturday and, as I passed, I heard the choir singing. I could hear the sound of laughter over the fence. The dead girl had been one of them as recently as last week. Now she was gone, but life seemed to be going on as usual for everyone else. The place was abuzz with their laughter and good cheer.

Her church had failed her. Any church that turns its back on suffering is not a church. Jesus said that He came into the world to heal the broken of spirit, but churches professing belief in Jesus too often have become the exclusive domain of the healthy and the able. Jesus remains outside the church's fence, while the people who have everything gather inside.

I went to the girl's house in the center of the village to tell her family where we had buried her. Entering the front yard of the house, I saw a man who seemed to be the girl's father, drunk on a mat, mumbling a tune. He was lying with his hands and feet spread wide. Rage surged from within me.

I cursed him, saying that living, as he did, in a liquor jug, he deserved to be taken by the devil. He was so drunk, even after his daughter had taken her life, that if I had told him where she was buried, he would not have understood me. Her mother was staring at a distant mountain and had left the door to the living room open. It seemed to be more sensible to tell her the whereabouts of her daughter's grave, even though she was obviously mentally unstable.

"Ma'am, I buried your daughter in a sunny place in the valley up the mountain. Why don't you go see it when you regain your senses? You cannot miss it because it is marked with a cross made from a pine tree."

After telling her this, I was about to turn around to go. Then she beckoned me over to her. Going near her, I asked, "Is there something you want to tell me?"

She pulled something from under the mat of the room. "Thank you, sir. Thank you for burying my daughter. Please take this and have a soda."

I took it to find that it was a faded 100-*won* note, folded many times. Taking it, I looked into the woman's eyes. They spoke of the grief of a hard life, of the sorrow and the pain. My heart broke. I could say nothing. I bit my lip, twitched with emotion, turned around, and left.

She had only been pretending that she knew nothing. She had known all along about her daughter, who could endure her life no longer and killed herself, and that no one would conduct a funeral for her, even though her body was decomposing, and that a pastor from a neighboring village had come to bury her daughter. Reading her mind, I felt her sorrow.

I came back to my reading room and put the money from her on my Bible. I could not stop my tears, thinking about the depth of the woman's pain. My feet ached and were swollen until the following morning.

DURING THE FARM OFF-SEASON, the young villagers would meet in the community center and gamble, often coming to blows. I came up with a plan to channel their energy into something constructive.

Late one evening, I paid a visit to the center with some bags of snacks. As I joined them at cards, they changed their bets from money to cigarettes. I persuaded them to change the bets once again, from cigarettes to the snacks I had brought. Playing the game, I chatted with them on a range of issues. I brought up a suggestion that we hold events such as volleyball games, a singing contest, and a *yut** tournament with their counterparts from other villages. I told them that playing cards was a waste of their time and that they should serve as models to change the overall atmosphere in the village.

At first, they seemed to think that the job was beyond their capability. I persisted with my suggestion and finally succeeded in getting them away from their card game long enough to come up with an action plan. After a round of discussions, we decided to set up a project

---

* *Yut* is a traditional game played with sticks on a mat.

committee to develop a plan. They carried out their first event successfully, which gave them confidence to work harder on other events. The
events were all successful and drew compliments from senior villagers.
Encouraged by this series of successes, the young men became proac-
tive in coming up with projects of their own. I no longer needed to
make suggestions.

The overall atmosphere of the village improved. Then a problem
arose. Some church members complained that I was playing cards with
the young men. Being conservative old-style churchgoers, they could
not accept how I practiced my ministry.

One night, asleep in my room, I awoke, sensing something moving about. A young woman I recognized was sitting quietly, close to me.
She attended church diligently, although her family was strongly opposed to her coming to church. I sat up. She offered me a dish of rice
cakes. The moon was up outside the window.

"You're not supposed to come to my room by yourself, and especially not so late at night. Thank you for the rice cakes. Leave them and
go, please. Others can easily misunderstand this sort of thing."

"Don't worry. Nobody saw me come." She said that since she trusted only me, she was giving herself up to me. Her voice was trembling.

My ministry was difficult enough as it was, and I certainly did not
need this. I realized then that it was time for me to leave Mokdan
Church. Coincidentally, I had just received an offer from Cheongsan
Church in Daegu and had decided to take it.

On the day I left Mokdan, not only church members, but all the
villagers came out to see me off. Many were crying. Thus ended my
first assignment. It was a priceless experience that I will never forget.

AT CHEONGSAN CHURCH, I was put in charge of the student group.
The atmosphere there was friendly and caring, thanks to the leadership
of the pastor, Shin Hu-sik.

In Daegu, I ran into Hong Eung-pyo, my senior in college who
had asked me whether I had been born again. He gave me a big welcome and took me to a coffee shop, where we sat and talked.

"I went to the college to ask after you the other day, but nobody
knew where you were. Our professors were worried about you. They
said that they had had great expectations of you, but that you had

suddenly disappeared. How're you getting on?"

"I left college because I saw no future for me there. For a while, I wandered from one place to another, but now I'm working as an assistant pastor."

"Do you remember the discussion we had some years ago?"

"Do you mean the one about being born again? Are you still asking me that?"

"Yes, I'm serious about it. Are you willing to listen to me, if I talk to you about it again?"

"Yes, I'll listen. Although I'm working as a pastor, I'm still confused about my faith. Please tell me anything you can that will give me faith and help me believe."

"I'm relieved to hear that. Are you busy these days?"

"Yes and no, but I can manage time for you."

"Great! What do you say that we get together once a week to read?"

"Why read? I've decided not to read another book until I find enlightenment."

"It's not a matter of reading or not reading books, but rather what you read. You must read books that help you find the enlightenment you're after."

"I'd go anywhere to find a book that would teach me such a valuable lesson, but so far I haven't found it."

"You know Romans, don't you? There's a book titled *Interpretation of the Epistle to the Romans* by a Japanese theologian, Kanzo Uchimura. It's different from the books by Western theologians. It has depth and insight. Why don't we meet to discuss it?"

I had no reason to turn him down. I accepted his proposal in hopes that studying with him would clear up my confusion. This was the beginning of my study of the Bible.

At first, I did not take it seriously, but I soon found myself pulled into it. I admired Paul's confidence in his faith, as demonstrated in his letter to the Romans, in which he wrote:

> I am not ashamed of the Gospel, because it is the power of God for the salvation of everyone who believes: first for the Jew, then for the Gentile. For in the Gospel a righteousness from God is revealed, a righteousness that is by faith

from first to last, just as it is written: "The righteous will live by faith." (Romans 1:16-17)

Reading this, I prayed to God, asking Him to give me a faith as certain as Paul's. I was ready to accept whatever thorny path lay ahead, once I gained confidence in my faith. Halfway through the reading, a part of Romans 3 caught my eye. I read it over many times. For me, it was the heart of biblical truth:

> ...for all have sinned and fall short of the glory of God, and are justified freely by his grace, through the redemption that came by Christ Jesus. God presented him as a sacrifice of atonement, through faith in his blood. He did this to demonstrate his justice, because in his forbearance he had left the sins committed beforehand unpunished— he did it to demonstrate his justice at the present time, so as to be just and the one who justifies those who have faith in Jesus. (Romans 3:23-26)

I examined the meaning of the verses by breaking the sentences down into short segments:

- Man falls short of the glory of God.
- Glory is given by God.
- The reason man falls short of God's glory is because man sins.
- That man falls short of the glory means that his relationship with God is severed.
- God wants to reconnect that severed relationship.
- The relationship between God and man is severed because man sins. Therefore, the relationship could be restored when man is redeemed from sin.
- God found a way to redeem man from sin.
- The way is through Jesus Christ.
- To achieve this, Jesus sacrificed himself and died bleeding.
- The man who sins should die bleeding for his sins, but Jesus died bleeding for him.
- God gave man the blessing of reclaiming human nature.

- What, then, is man supposed to do?
- He is to believe in what Jesus did.
- God decided to redeem man from sin after finding he believes in God.
- Why, then, did God resort to such a complicated process to forgive man's sins?
- Why did Jesus have to die bleeding?
- It is because God needed to manifest His righteousness on earth.
- It is because God's righteousness could be established only when a sinful man bled to death.
- Before Jesus bled to death, God had simply overlooked man's sins, to demonstrate His righteousness.
- After Jesus bled to death, God showed His righteousness by interrogating man about his sins.
- This satisfied two necessities. The first is that God is righteous. The second is that any man can be redeemed from sin, and his relationship with God restored, on condition that he believes in God.
- This restoration of the relationship will lead man to find the glory of God.

I fell deep into thought, reading every word. It made perfect logical sense, but I could not take it to heart. The more I read it, the more questions came to mind. Every question gave rise to still another.

One of those questions was what the word "sin" meant when it said that man sinned. I could not define the concept of "sin."

A second question was that I could not find a link between the act of Jesus bleeding to death and mankind's redemption from sin.

A third question was what the word "believe" refers to when people "believe" in Jesus bleeding for the good of mankind.

A fourth question was why God should manifest justice on earth. Why should God bother to establish justice on our planet, which He created? For whom should He show justice? Is it for Himself or for others? Who asked God to establish justice?

A fifth question concerned the nature of the relationship that is restored when man is redeemed from sin. What is the difference between God's relationship with man before and after redemption? After redemption, what will man be like?

The questions went on and on. The more I thought, the more questions I had, but I continued to study Paul's letter to the Romans. While engaged in this study, I found myself attracted more and more to Paul as a human being. I could not agree more with him when in Romans he expresses his despair: "What a wretched man I am! Who will rescue me from this body of death?" (Romans 7:24)

Reading this, I thought about the existentialist crying out for life. Nietzsche and Kierkegaard are often regarded as the founders of existentialism. Reading this part of Romans, however, I would say that it was actually Paul who founded existentialism. He can rightly be referred to as the warrior of religious faith, after undergoing soul-searching conflict.

In Romans 1:16 he writes: "…it is the power of God for the salvation of everyone who believes." In Romans 7:24 he finds himself asking who would rescue him from the body of death. It would seem that in his inner being he experienced conflicting feelings of despair and assurance.

I felt a common bond with Paul because the conflict he underwent had something in common with the questions I was asking. This gave rise to an expectation that if Paul could remain faithful throughout his life, there had to be something about God to which I could devote my life.

TIME PASSED. THE STUDY OF ROMANS, which started in the summer, continued into the autumn and then the winter. In the beginning, Hong Eung-pyo and I met only once a week, but after we got started, we met more often.

Kanzo Uchimura's book was a great help to me. His writing gave me a feeling different from the one I had gotten from Western theologians. Western academics were very good at developing their logic, but were short of insight. They could not appeal to my soul. In this sense, Kanzo's book stood out, and studying it increased my interest in studying the Bible.

Among Kanzo's other writings was *Kyuanroku*, a record of his search for peace. It is an autobiography that chronicles his search for peace through a period of wandering and agony.

Kanzo was born into a low-ranking samurai family in 1841. While in his teens, he was introduced to Christianity by an American missionary. Returning to Japan after studying theology in the U.S., Kanzo devoted himself wholly to God, the Bible, and the Japanese people.

He opposed war and Japanese imperialism and delivered speeches based on his conviction that Japan would be blessed and could contribute to world peace only if it avoided imitating the Western imperialists' way of dominating other countries. His speeches provoked outrage from the Japanese military, costing him his job. He then dedicated himself to teaching the Bible to young people, starting in a small room in Tokyo. He set for himself a lifetime objective of building a new Japan, based on the truth of the Bible.

His disciples became the backbone of postwar Japan. Three of his Bible students went on to become presidents of Tokyo University. The former Premier Masayoshi Ohira was also one of his students, as were the founding members of Japan's Socialist Party. In recognition of his contribution to Japanese society, Kanzo is identified as one of the twenty most influential leaders in building Japan over the past century.

On his deathbed, he asked that the following epitaph be inscribed on his tombstone:

> I FOR JAPAN
> JAPAN FOR THE WORLD
> THE WORLD FOR CHRIST
> AND ALL FOR GOD

I was moved by Kanzo's achievement in balancing his pledges between his country and Jesus and prayed, "Jesus, if you let me believe, please allow me to so believe that I can love both Jesus and my country. If you allow me to believe in this way, I will do everything I can to make the most of my life."

Others who were influenced by Kanzo's teaching were Kim Gyosin and Ham Seok-heon. As my admiration for Kanzo grew, I also became an avid reader of the works of Kim and Ham.

Through their writings, I realized that Christians should not limit their religious lives to the church, but should reach out to become involved in the lives of others.

Around that time, I had an experience that changed my life at its very core. On December 4, 1968, Hong brought a Mr. Choi to our Bible study session. The three of us read Ephesians. Coming to Ephesians 1:7, I felt as if I had been struck by lightning. I held my breath and continued reading: "In Him we have redemption through His blood, the forgiveness of sins, in accordance with the riches of God's grace."

"In Him," meaning "in Christ." I was overwhelmed by this phrase. What place is this "in Christ"? It is where God's love for man resides.

Bible study group with Hong, at the far left, and Kim Jin-hong, second from left in back.

God came to the world to look for His lost partners. We call Him Jesus Christ. Jesus, who descended to the world, deployed His love for man by suffering pain and bleeding to death. I will become one with God when I realize God's great love and throw myself at it. When I do that, I will be saved. It was like an earthquake, shattering my soul.

Where had I been searching for salvation? Where did I think I was searching? It had not been in Christ, but outside of Christ. I had been searching for the truth in philosophy and in humanism. I had always had a vague sense that philosophy would not provide me an answer, but I failed to realize that humanism would also be a dead end.

That night I could look inside myself. I had concentrated on finding answers outside of Christ and because of that could not discover how to be saved. Inside myself, I had experienced agony and uncertainty, agony and uncertainty rooted in sin.

To my amazement, Jesus removed the burden of sin from my shoulders. He loosened the grip of sin, which had dominated my soul, and let me savor the joy of being free from sin. All of a sudden, Christ loomed larger than the universe. I saw myself in His world. All the doubts and questions that had haunted me for so long disappeared at once, and Christ emerged before me as the answer.

I got down on my knees and vowed to myself that I would serve Him as my master for the rest of my life. As I knelt there, Jesus embraced me. I was transformed from being a son of the earth into being a son of heaven. A river of joy enveloped my heart. All of this happened between 11:00 p.m. and 1:00 a.m.

I read aloud 2 Corinthians 5:17. "Therefore, if anyone is in Christ, he is a new creation; the old has gone, the new has come!"

Overwhelmed by emotion, I stood up and sang Hymn 210, "Everything is Changed," in a loud voice, crying and clapping:

> Everything is changed since my sins were forgiven,
> Everything is changed since I knew the Lord;
> Now my feet are walking the pathway to heaven;
> All the guilty past now is under the blood.
>
> Everything is changed, praise the Lord!
> Now I am redeemed thro' the blood:
> Free from condemnation, God is my Salvation,
> Everything is changed, praise the Lord!

The sun that rose the next day was not the same sun I had always known. The wind that blew was not the same wind. A new sun and a new wind welcomed my rebirth. Everyone passing by looked happy, and God's love seemed to permeate every stone and every clump of grass.

WHAT HAPPENED ON THE NIGHT OF DECEMBER 4 determined the course of my life. It was then that I resolved to dedicate myself to the church and its people. To keep my resolve, I decided I should attend a seminary and study for the ministry. My mother was very pleased.

She had prayed for decades, asking God to let me serve Him, and now her prayers were being answered.

I was concerned about how she would get by while I was studying. I asked her about it. Her answer was simple. "Don't worry about me, my son. I have plans of my own. You just concentrate on your studies. I'm so pleased that you've decided to become a minister."

I took her at her word and in March 1969, enrolled in the Presbyterian College and Theological Seminary in Seoul. After studying for some months, I went to Daegu to visit my mother. To my embarrassment, she was working as a housemaid.

"What are you doing?" I asked. "I trusted you when you said you had plans of your own. Why are you working as a housemaid? This isn't right. I'll quit school and get a job and take care of you. I can't go on studying, letting you work as a housemaid."

She strongly opposed me. "What are you talking about? I'm fine. I'm filled with joy, even though I work like this. All jobs are equal. What's wrong with being a housemaid? Don't worry. I'm proud of you. The family for whom I work has three sons, but the three of them combined are not worth what you are worth alone. You continue your studies."

Working as a housemaid, she was confident of my future. She was sure that I would become an important person. When I was small, she had heaped praise on me even for small accomplishments.

"Well done, my son," she would say. "You are different from other kids because you are destined for greatness."

It was my mother's faith that I would one day become an important minister that kept her going. That same faith kept her full of joy, even as she worked as a housemaid.

9

Cheating by Day, Praying in Tongues by Night

THE PRESBYTERIAN COLLEGE AND Theological Seminary program was an elite three-year course that accepted only college graduates. As first-year students, my forty classmates were aflame with ambition to lead the nation's churches. The seminary was located on Mount Acha, a place where the Baekje king, Uija, had built a luxurious castle and lived an opulent life before losing his kingdom to the enemy. On one side of the mountain was the Walker Hill Hotel and on the other the seminary. In the evenings, we would go up the mountain and talk about our ambitions to become spiritual leaders of our fellow Christians and the backbone of the Korean church.

There were some odd fellows in my class. When praying, they would shake their bodies hard and speak loudly in tongues. I found this behavior unseemly, and even disturbing, because I had never had such an experience. Why should they make such a production out of prayer? The Bible teaches us to "pray in secret." I considered it unbiblical to pray so ostentatiously.

"Are you suffering from a stroke? Why are you shaking like that? What language are you babbling in? Why don't you speak Korean?" I would ask them.

"Mr. Kim, don't think like that. You need to have spiritual strength to practice a ministry in today's condemned age. Speaking in tongues is the best way to acquire spiritual power. Don't be so sarcastic."

"I'd rather speak to God in Korean," I responded. "If I can communicate with God in Korean perfectly well, why should I use some other language?"

One evening, a classmate and I were invited to visit a family. When we were about to leave, the family's one year-old baby started to cry hard. It had a high temperature and the baby's mother was at a loss for what to do. It occurred to me that the baby might have gotten an infection.

"Ma'am, you should probably take the baby to a hospital. Can I call you a taxi? The baby seems to be very sick. I think you should hurry."

My classmate intervened, saying, "Please, let me see your baby." Holding the baby to his chest, he started to pray in tongues. He soon finished his prayer, saying, "In the name of Jesus Christ, I tell the devil of disease to go away." At that, the baby stopped crying and its temperature returned to normal. I was stunned.

I felt so insignificant. While my classmate healed the baby with the gift of speaking in tongues, all I could do was ask whether I should call a taxi. That night I visited my classmate in his room.

"Please help me to pray in tongues," I said. "After seeing you heal the baby today, I realize that to practice my ministry, I need the gift of speaking in tongues."

"Now you admit the importance of speaking in tongues. That's a step in the right direction, but speaking in tongues is not an easy gift to acquire."

"Stop taunting me. I'll do whatever you say, however difficult it is. Please teach me."

"I'm not saying it's beyond your capability. What I'm saying is that you mustn't take it lightly. You need to put as much effort into it as you would put into uprooting a pine tree with your bare hands."

"What does speaking in tongues have to do with pine trees?" I asked.

"Your mind has to be prepared for it. I once knew a pastor in a rural church. He found it difficult to conduct his ministry because the members of his congregation could pray in tongues, while he could not. He prayed to God for the gift of speaking in tongues. He prayed hard, but received no answer. He began to feel anxious, so he took a blanket and went off to a mountain. Holding onto a pine tree on the side of the mountain, he prayed.

"Still, there was no answer. He persevered and continued to pray, shaking the pine tree harder and harder. He shook the tree with such force that by dawn the next day he had pulled it out by the roots. The momentum of the ground letting go of the tree sent the pastor down the slope and into a ravine. At that very moment, the pastor blurted out in tongues. I tell you this because it demonstrates how much effort you need to exert to achieve the gift of speaking in tongues."

What he said made sense, so I decided to expend the effort to achieve my goal. My problem was that I could not manage time to work on it because I had to study during the week and do church work on weekends. "I'll have to use the holidays to do it," I thought, and penciled in Children's Day, May 5, as my day of action.

"God, our Father, I pray with all my heart. To become a minister, I need the gift of speaking in tongues. I need to be able to serve with the healing power of speaking in tongues. On May 5, I will go to the mountain to pray. I will offer you prayer with sincerity equal to that of pulling up a pine tree. Please allow me to have the gift of speaking in tongues. I believe that you will do this for me."

On May 5, I left early in the morning to go to a prayer house on Mount Samgak, in Seoul. I arrived at the prayer house at around 10 a.m. I went to the rear of the house, where I found a flat rock beside a pine tree. I knelt down on the rock and began to pray, holding onto the tree with both hands.

"My Lord Jesus, I believe that here you will give me the gift of speaking in tongues. I will not budge from this spot until you give it to me. Please grant me this."

I started to pray, but it took only a few minutes before I realized that I had chosen the wrong place. I felt a sharp pain in my knees. I should have put a blanket or a flat cushion under my knees. It was from bravado that I had knelt on the rock on only a thin layer of leaves. The agony became unbearable, but I had already vowed to God that I would not move an inch until I received the gift of speaking in tongues. There was no turning back. I put up with excruciating pain to continue.

I thought, I have to endure this. If I endure the pain, God will take pity on me and give me the gift of tongues. I won't die from pain in my knees. I continued to suffer. A while later, I no longer felt the pain in my knees, but by this time I had developed pain in my waist. Still, I continued to pray. At around 3 o'clock that afternoon, I was so exhausted I could not speak. My mouth was dry and my sides were stiff, as if I had been beaten. There was still no sign that God had given me the gift of tongues. I kept praying. "My God, you are not going to give me the gift of tongues, are you?"

It was then that a verse from Romans struck me. "He who did not withhold his own Son, but gave him up for all of us, will he not with him also give us everything else?" (Romans 8:32)

I pondered this phrase and it occurred to me that I had been wrong to seek the gift of tongues. God had given me many things. Yet, instead of being grateful for all that He had given me, here I was seeking something that He had not. It was with unyielding faith that I had become God's son and was going to heaven, but I was still not satisfied. Watching my friend speak in tongues, I was envious and wanted to get the gift quickly. I might not have gotten everything that God has to offer, but from believing in Him I had life and faith in heaven. I have to go out into the world and pass this on to other people. I can always seek the gift of tongues and healing power later.

I pulled myself up from the ground and, because of the pain in my legs, hobbled to the express bus terminal in Dongdaemun (East Gate). People in the terminal were waiting for a bus bound for Busan. I removed my shoes, stood up on a chair, and launched into an impassioned sermon.

"Everyone, please listen. I would appreciate it if you would spare some time to listen to what I have to say. The expressway is the path to death, but Jesus Christ is the path to life. You will find life by believing in God. Now is the time. Now is the time for you to choose life."

I was so engrossed in my sermon that I failed to notice when a security guard approached me and grabbed me by the neck.

"What did you say, freak? The expressway is the path to death? Are you trying to chase away all our customers and put us out of business?"

"No, that's not what I mean, Teacher.* I'm sorry it came out that way. I only wanted to say that Jesus is life. It was a slip of the tongue."

*Because in the Confucian system teachers are honored, to indicate respect, people sometimes refer to others as "teacher."

"What did you call me? Teacher? I've never taught a student like you. You Christians are all words."

"I apologize. Please let go of my neck. You're choking me."

"OK. I'll let you go, but get out of here. If I see you in here again, I'll break your arm. You have a lot of nerve, standing in a bus terminal and saying that the expressway is the path to death."

With that, he threw me out. I should have been ashamed of myself, being run out that way, but I was not. On the contrary, I felt refreshed and happy.

Yes, this is what I have to do, I thought to myself. I must be thankful for the blessings I've already received. Before asking for more, I must spread God's Word. He even gave us His son. Why would He not freely give us His other blessings?

ALTHOUGH I HAD BEGUN SEMINARY LIFE full of ambition, as time passed, I grew pessimistic. My enthusiasm turned to disappointment as I came up against organized religious life.

The church had inherited Jesus' word and had been founded on truth. With time, truth became institutionalized and distorted in the name of religious principles. As the religious principles became stronger, they were imposed on people. The Gospel, which was meant to free the human spirit, now became a burdensome yoke. It seemed to me that seminaries were the epitome of all these problems.

I became disillusioned when I took my first exams. Many of my classmates cheated, which made me seriously question what was going on. How could they allow themselves to do such a vile thing, having pledged that they would take up the spiritual lead of their countrymen? Was I going to spend three years in a place inhabited by this kind of people? I was cast into doubt.

One evening, while on Mount Acha praying, one of my classmates, who had cheated on the exam during the day, shuddered while praying in tongues. I thought he was repenting for his wrongdoing. The next day, to my surprise, nothing had changed. He continued to cheat on his exams.

"What's going on?" I wondered. "By night he prays in tongues and by day he continues to cheat on his exams."

He cheated his way through to graduation. We ran into each other some years later. He was working as head minister in a church that had between three and four thousand members. I gave him a heartfelt greeting because twenty years had passed since we were in school together. He, however, had become so arrogant that he would not even greet me properly.

"Ahh, Pastor Kim. Long time no see. Hallelujah."

His voice croaked when he let out the word, "Hallelujah." It reminded me of his cheating on exams in college.

"Pastor Lee, what's become of your voice?" I asked. "Why do you sound like a frog croaking?"

"You haven't changed at all," he replied.

I left with a bitter taste in my mouth. The biggest enemy of religion is hypocrisy and self-deception. When hypocrisy settles into religion, the human spirit rots. Those whose spirit is rotten deceive themselves and heaven in the name of religion and eventually even come to deceive one another.

I became progressively disillusioned in the hypocritical environment of the seminary. It had not been easy for me to get there. I recalled all the anguish and pain I had experienced in arriving at Christianity. I had believed that all my questioning would end when I began my seminary studies, and thereafter a life of tranquility and peace would unfold. It was not to be. The seminary turned out to be no different from any other place.

After some months of thought, I decided to practice Jesus' love as an individual, not as a career pastor. I concluded that affectation and hypocrisy are bound to follow when a person accepts the label of "pastor." I should not be attached to anything, but rather would live with people who need me.

Kierkegaard said, "The goal of my philosophy is to discover how to stand naked before God." I wanted to live a fulfilling life. I wanted to strip myself of all vanity, including the title of pastor and affiliation with a denomination, and live a wholesome life as Jesus had done.

I vowed to live up to this resolution and left the seminary at the end of my first year. On the day our final exams were to begin, I packed my things and set off for Daegu. My classmates tried to get me to change my mind, but I was determined.

"You don't understand," I said to them. "I'm leaving. I'm not saying it's wrong for you to stay here. I only need to be true to myself. I can't live as a career clergyman. I want to live among the little people, like weeds in the streets. I want to cry, laugh, and agonize together with them. I'm sure that my master, Jesus, will be happy with me living that kind of a life. I'll stake my future on it. I don't want to be only a talking pastor. I want to be a disciple of Christ, experiencing Him and living His life."

I was married at the time. My wife and I had gotten married at the mid-year break during my first year at the seminary. The wedding was presided over by Elder Kim Yong-gi of the Canaan Farmer's School. We had no money for a honeymoon trip, so we went by train to Incheon and stayed our first night at an inn. The marriage ended badly, for which I have never been proud.

My wife and I had met when I was studying the Bible with Hong. She was a senior at Ewha Womans [sic] University, majoring in social work. Her family was wealthy and had three housemaids. We had strong feelings for each other after several meetings and later enrolled together in the seminary. Her family was furious with her for going out with me. They were against the marriage because they considered me a ne'er-do-well. They were so adamant in their disapproval that to be with me, she had no alternative but to follow me to the seminary, whereupon her family disowned her.

In hindsight, I now can say that we should not have gone against her parents' will when they so strongly opposed our marriage. I tell young people who plan to marry, "Parents love their children very much and want only the best for them. Unless you are absolutely sure, if your parents oppose your marriage, you should give it a second thought. Either that or you should wait until you can persuade them to give their approval. You will be able to use that time to confirm your love for each other." This advice is based on my own experience.

RETURNING TO DAEGU, I WANTED TO WORK among laborers. To do that, I needed to become one. I prepared a résumé that listed graduation from elementary school as my highest education level. I launched a job search and found work in an iron foundry.

I passed for an uneducated laborer because I did not look particularly refined. Seeing me, they did not question my résumé. It was the first time in my life that I was grateful for my appearance.

The foundry owner was considered a model Christian, serving as a deacon in a very conservative church. He had set up churches in many areas and had donated large amounts of money to them. He was also renowned as a respectable businessman.

I worked as a furnace tender, at 270 *won* a day. Shortly after starting the job, I sensed that something was not right. Whenever I brought up Christianity, I got a negative response from my coworkers. "Don't talk to me about Christians," they would say. "I'm sick of them."

At first, I did not know where this negative attitude was coming from, but the better I came to know the company, the more I understood why they felt the way they did. It was because church members held all the high positions in the company, while workers were paid ten percent less than their counterparts in other companies and were required to work an hour longer.

The worst part was that the staff all had to attend morning prayer service, although the thirty minutes taken for it was not included in their work hours. Coming to work early was a burden, but they had no alternative because the company called roll and any absence was factored into their pay.

Under these circumstances, it was natural that the workers had a negative attitude toward the church and had no reservation in cursing it. In their eyes, Jesus was a villain who deprived them of both their sleep and their rightful pay.

They would vent their resentment on leaving morning prayers, complaining "You're all a bunch of hypocritical sons-of-bitches. If I sent my kids to church, I'd be just like you."

It was clear that there was something else I had to take on before trying to teach the workers about Jesus. I had to change the situation that gave rise to their grievances. If I attempted to teach the workers about Jesus in that environment, I would only be inviting ridicule.

My plan got off to a slow start. I had chats with my unit coworkers during working hours and with workers in other units during the lunch hour or outside working hours.

"We have to work hard. At the same time, we have to demand that the company change unfair working conditions. To achieve this, we have to band together and form a union because individual demands will have no effect. Forming a union is neither complicated nor illegal. We can make a labor union that will benefit both the company and us. If we are satisfied, we'll be more productive."

The initial response from the workers was not encouraging. They said that they had already attempted to organize a labor union, but failed. Their attempts always trailed off with no result, other than costing some of their coworkers their jobs. I did not give in. With the passage of time, an increasing number of coworkers joined me. We started to put more and more time into meetings.

It was not long before the company, sensing something was afoot, began to investigate. A few workers were called in before I was finally ordered to report to the office. I was grilled with questions.

"I hear that you're instigating our workers. Why're you doing that? Are you crazy? You know that you'll be branded a communist, if you continue what you're doing. Stop it now and give me the names of the workers who are sympathetic to your cause. Then we will let you stay."

"Don't put what I've done in such a negative light. I don't like being called a communist. It's not right that this company forces workers to attend prayers and work under unfair conditions. I'm not saying that holding prayers is wrong. You can ask them to hold prayers after you pay them on a par with other companies and reduce their hours to those of other companies. It doesn't make sense that you force the workers to hold prayers in the mornings while they're struggling with lower pay and longer hours.

"I'm neither a labor movement organizer nor a troublemaker. I will step back, if the company promises to get two things right. One of them is to adjust the level of pay to that of other companies. The other is to cut back on working hours. If you need to extend the workday, workers should be paid overtime. Then you can ask your workers to attend prayers."

"What would you do if I said no?"

"I'd have to continue what I've been doing, but I, myself, cannot give you an answer on this. I need to talk with my coworkers about it."

"You're a hard-core communist. How long do you think you can continue with this? You're cocky, but the day will come when you'll get down on your knees to beg us to take you back."

"Yes, you're right. I'm cocky, but why can't a cocky person like me work at a cocky company like this?"

"Did you say work? You're mistaken if you think that this company is going to keep you on."

"We're beyond the point of no return. We're going to take action within the framework of the labor law. All I'm asking is that you stop treating us unfairly. As I see it, we can further one another's agenda within the law. Don't vilify the workers, please. Put yourself in their shoes. Do you think it makes sense to demand that workers pray every day while they're working longer hours for less pay? I'm a Christian, but I can't agree with company policy. I also ask you to treat me with respect. You'll regret it, if you continue treating me this way."

I got tough with them. Once I got started, there was no going back, but inside I wasn't convinced of my position. I had never been involved in anything like this and I was afraid I was losing control of things.

The following day, a man from management came around to me at work. He invited me to dinner. I turned down his proposal, saying that I had not done anything to merit a dinner invitation. If I had to, I said I could come to dinner with a few of my coworkers.

He grinned and said, "Don't be so hard on yourself, please. We just want to talk with you about how to settle this matter. We'll send the company car to pick you up after work. We'd like to hear what you have to say."

After he left, my coworkers became sarcastic, saying "Mr. Kim, you have a good chance of getting promoted. After you land a cushy job, don't forget about us."

I was uncomfortable. The company's going soft had put me in an awkward position. I did not appreciate my coworker's sarcastic reaction.

After work, I went out the front gate to find the company sedan waiting for me. I was treated to a big dinner at a fine restaurant. The senior manager I had met in the afternoon began by saying, "Sir, we had no idea who you were because you were hired here in disguise. Please accept our apology for failing to treat you properly. Forgive us, please, but you are partly responsible for what happened to you because you gave us the wrong information.

"I'm not interested in arguing about whose fault it is. I just want to say that a small company like ours is not suitable for reputable people like you. I suggest that for our mutual benefit, you find employment in a company where you can make the best use of your abilities. Here is a small token of our appreciation. We would like you to take it as an expression of gratitude for your service in our company."

At that, he attempted to stuff a thick envelope into my pocket. I could only assume that he had gone over my background and concluded that I could make trouble for the company. To avoid that, he wanted to buy me off and be rid of me.

"Thank you for your consideration," I said, returning his envelope. "I had my own reasons, when I came to work for your company. I've already become involved in things. I cannot stop halfway through. I'll let you know when it's time for me to go."

"Don't do this to us. We think we know what you are going to do at our company, but what good does it do any of us? I didn't want to say this, but we hired you on a contract basis. A contract worker has no employment security. The company can fire him at any time. We arranged this meeting because we, as Christians, want to resolve this issue for the benefit of everyone. If you don't accept our proposal, we'll have to resort to other means."

"I understand what you mean, but I've made up my mind. I'm not going to leave my job voluntarily. Of course, if I'm fired, I'll have no choice but to leave. I can't work in violation of the law. In the meantime, I'm going to do what I can to keep workers from being exploited."

"The terms you're using make me very uneasy. You say that workers are being exploited. Who's exploiting them? I thought I would hear that word only on Pyeongyang radio. Unless you're from Pyeongyang, you'd better watch your tongue. Anyway, we've made you the best offer we can. Now the ball is in your court. We're willing to help you. If you'd like to further your seminary studies, we can ask our boss to arrange a scholarship for you. If you'd like to start a church, we can suggest that the company help you."

"I understand the president likes churches. Pass my word on to him. He should stop exploiting workers and treat them as they deserve."

"Now you've gone too far. What makes you so confident? You have to listen to us. We're a force to be reckoned with around here. It'd be an easy matter to shut you up."

He became furious. I felt sorry for him, as he tried to regain his composure. "I apologize, if I've gone too far," I said, in a lower voice, "but please reconsider. Factories run by Christians are expected to pay more than those run by non-Christians, but your company pays workers ten percent less than others. Taking into consideration that workers put in longer hours, their wages are 20 percent lower than elsewhere. You say that the money saved is used to build churches. Do you think that's what God wants? You should pay workers what they deserve. It makes no sense that money saved from paying workers less is used to build churches, does it? God won't accept it, so you should stop it. Thank you for the dinner."

I was about to get up when he pulled me back down.

"Let me tell you this. I'm saying this because you're young enough to be my son. You have to take care of yourself. The world is not an easy place. No one's going to help you, if you continue this. You have to learn more about the world. Don't confuse religion with business. If you ran a company like a church, you wouldn't last three months.

"There's an old saying, 'Make money like a dog and spend it like a nobleman.' It's not a bad idea that the money saved from running the business is used for God's work, is it? You have to take the president's situation into consideration. Now, please accept this as an expression of our appreciation for your service and save yourself a lot of trouble. You may regard the time you worked with us as a lesson in how the world works."

"I apologize for being so persistent, but I'm not doing this for personal benefit. I wanted to be around workers so I could teach them about Jesus. Working with them at this company, I became sympathetic to their situation. My intention is only to help them. I became involved in this because I'm confident that this is what God wants me to do. I'm sure everything will be fine, once the company shows a little more consideration for the workers. Things have to change. They can't go on like this, and if nothing is done, problems are bound to erupt. Then it'll be too late to put things right."

The next day I continued in my effort to form a union. I selected a leader from each department and held a meeting with them in the furnace room. I told them to collect signatures from workers who wanted to sign up for the union. I set an agenda that required them to hold discussions on day-by-day progress and to draw up action plans after work. The company managers then became hostile. They persuaded or threatened the members of the union, one by one, not to contact other workers.

A week passed and I went on night shift. Working at night was exhausting. I was a lot more tired at night because I was not used to manual labor and had become stressed out. By the time I left work early in the morning, my legs were swollen and my eyes were spinning from standing in front of the furnace from seven in the evening until six the next morning. Walking along the street on my way home, I would be so dizzy that at times I had to stop and rest against a wall before continuing.

This was the first night shift I had worked since I began to organize the union. It was usually at about two a.m. that I found it most difficult to stay awake. Unable to shake off my sleepiness, I would go outside to get some fresh air.

There were two furnaces in my section. They called them furnaces, although actually they were more like stoves. I was responsible for the larger one and someone else was responsible for the smaller one. My job was to adjust the temperature on two pipes that channeled in air and oil, while picking half-finished products out of the furnace after they had heated up. The job was hard and dangerous because you could blow up the furnace if you got the mix wrong.

One night I came back from my fresh-air break to find the other member of the team away from his post. We were supposed to work in teams of two. When one member of the team was away, the other had to fill in. Becoming suspicious, I checked the two furnaces before noticing something strange on the side of the smaller furnace. I was checking the valve to see what was wrong when a blaze of fire leapt out at me with a thunderous noise. I was knocked unconscious. I do not know how much time passed, but in coming to I heard what sounded like faraway voices calling my name.

I opened my eyes to see seven or eight workers looking down at me. I inspected myself to see if I had sustained any injury. The hair on my forehead and my eyebrows had been singed, and I had a light burn on my face. Other than that, I seemed to be all right. The accident was reported to management, but no one came from the office to find out how I was.

I was in bad shape for some days after the accident. The burns on my face hurt and my body ached all over. I put ointment on the burn area and stayed home while my hair and eyebrows grew back.

Some days later, I received a registered letter from the company. It contained wages for the days I had worked and a dismissal slip. The excuse they gave for firing me was that I had been absent from work for a long period without giving notice. I had to acquiesce. I knew nothing about labor law and did not know where to go for expert advice. I felt ashamed and defeated and there was nothing I could do about it. My best had not been good enough to elicit support from the workers in whose interest I was working.

Thus came to an end my ambition to emulate Jesus, protesting a company owner's abuses and protecting workers' rights. I was now grounded, a defeated soldier.

A WHILE LATER, I FOUND WORK TEACHING BIBLE at the Gyeongsan Mennonite High School, near Daegu. I spent some months there before returning to the seminary in March 1971. It had been only one year since I had left, protesting that institutionalized religion had no vitality and that career churchmen were bound to become hypocritical.

When my classmates asked why I returned, I would say, "I tried to change things on my own, but I came to realize that if I want to bring about change, I needed an institutional system and an organization. Courage and enthusiasm alone are not enough. If the church has lost its vitality, then the thing to do is to breathe life back into it and change it for the better. I came back because I learned that if the church fails to perform its function, it is up to us to make it serve the Holy Spirit."

Returning to school, I matured and settled down. That summer, I had an experience that would define my life's work. It was the first experience that inspired me with the idea of establishing a church for the urban poor.

During summer vacation, I signed up for a training program for urban missionaries, sponsored by the Yonsei University Research Institute for Urban Issues. The Institute carried out research on living standards in urban slums and promoted missionary activity to educate slumdwellers.

Seven of us were assigned to a slum in Yeonhui-dong, under the direction of Pastor Shin Sang-gil.

The slum consisted of some 200 families, jammed into makeshift huts on the side of a hill. They were mostly former farm families who had come to the city to find work. The day we moved into one of the shacks, rain poured down, causing massive landslides. The mud washed out five houses and left the dead and injured in its wake.

Among the dead was a third-grade boy. His badly injured parents were taken to the hospital, while the child's body was left on the ground, in the hot summer sun, covered with only a burlap bag. Flies swarmed around the body, close to which lay an open math notebook, showing an assignment with a perfect score. Residents told us that there was no one to carry out a funeral for the dead child as the parents were hospitalized and the local government office was tied up with other things.

Pastor Shin assigned us to carry out the funeral, but he took all our money, saying that we were supposed to complete the mission without using our own money.

We learned from neighbors that the child's family had attended a church in an affluent area at the foot of the hill. We visited the church to seek help from the pastor.

"Some people in the village on the hill died in the landslides. One of them, a boy, attended this church with his family. His parents are in the hospital and his body is lying unattended. We want to bury him and would appreciate your help in funding it."

Going in, I had no question that the church would help us. Because of that, I was surprised when the pastor replied only half heartedly, "I'll talk with members of the church this Sunday and will let you know what they say."

"Pastor, today is Thursday. The child's body is decomposing. By Sunday it'll be too late. You may not know about the family, but the neighbors say they were members of this church. I would expect you to help us, even if they were not members of your church. This is not something that can wait until Sunday."

"I suppose that our church is expected to fund the whole cost of the funeral. I cannot make the decision on my own. I need to put it on the agenda and take it up with others."

"Pastor, I realize there is a process the church must follow before it can act, but we cannot wait. Why not fund the funeral first and make the decision later?"

"I have to go. I'm sorry that I cannot help you."

As he turned to flee back into his church, I felt like cursing him but decided against it, realizing that it would not look good for a seminarian to use abusive language. Still, his uncompromising attitude disturbed me. I thought the church was supposed to be more willing to help people.

I tried to convince myself that dressed in work clothes, perhaps we had given him the impression that we were out to swindle him. Still, I could not suppress my uneasiness.

Returning to the slum, we held a meeting beside the child's body.

"How can we conduct the funeral?"

"…"

We had no answer.

The meeting got us nowhere because there could be no funeral without money and we had none. At that point, a well-dressed man came up to us and asked, "Are you planning a funeral for the child?"

"Yes. We're talking about how to go about it."

"I see. I was told that the child's parents are in the hospital. Can I help? I'd like to do something, if possible."

Thinking that he was a good person, I stepped away to ask the women around us.

"Do you know who this man is?"

"Yes, he's a missionary from the Tiger Sect.*"

"What's the Tiger Sect?"

"It's a religion of people who every morning bow over a bowl of cold water in the direction of Japan, repeatedly invoking Nam-mu, a tiger cub, in prayer. That's why it's called the Nam-mu Tiger Sect. They

---

*Tiger Sect refers to Nam-Myoho-Renge-Gyo, a Japanese Buddhist sect. Nam-Myoho-Renge-Gyo sounds to Koreans like "Nam-mu horang-i sekki," which in Korean means "Nam-mu tiger cub." The religion calls on believers to chant daily "Nam-Myoho-Renge-Gyo" to purify their lives. Hence, people superstitiously came to identify the sect with "a tiger cub named Nam-mu."

say that people who join the sect are cured of disease after six months and get rich after three years."

I then realized that he was a missionary of a sect from Japan called Soka Gakkai (Society for the Creation of Value). I cut in on my fellow trainees who were talking with him, saying, "We were already proceeding with the child's funeral. We'll ask you to help us, if we need your help next time. Thank you very much for your interest."

I did not want him to take part in our work because I felt uneasy collaborating with a Japanese sect. He was incredulous.

"That's OK, but please let me contribute for the funeral. I believe you will accept my contribution in good faith."

At that, he gave us 5,000 *won* and left. Having seen what had happened, the residents told us, "They are good people, even though they believe in a Japanese religion. They do things the right way. We contacted the Christians many times, but no one has shown up here to help."

I felt my face going flush. We got together enough money for the funeral, having pawned a watch to come up with another 5,000 *won*.

Given a choice between a church that refused to help with the child's funeral, even after several requests, and the Soka Gakkai, which volunteered to contribute money for the funeral, it was obvious which the residents would follow. People are disposed to give their hearts to religions that care about their welfare and that have leaders who treat them with respect.

As a new religion, Soka Gakkai carried out its missionary work on the urban and rural poor. It claimed to have one million adherents. Its message was simple. Whoever memorizes their scriptures and believes will avoid disease, be blessed with prosperity, and live a long life.

Their personal approach to teaching was strict and effective. The trained members took up residence among the people and met with residents one by one, with testimonials of confession and success. They then met regionally, in groups, and invited attendees to tell about their experiences of having been cured of disease and of having gotten rich. They took advantage of the weakness of the poor and the sick to expand their membership. I was afraid that Christian churches would lose people to this sect, particularly in slum areas, if they continued to ignore the problems of the poor.

It was then that I began to pay much closer attention to the conditions of people living in slums. I spent time with them, read books about them, and studied them. Getting to know more about them, I wanted to do something for them.

10

Moving to Shantytown

I N THE EARLY 1970S, SEOUL HAD a population of approximately six million. There were some 185,000 illegally built shacks in the city, each shack sheltering an average of 2.2 households. Assuming that five people constituted one household, the 407,000 households represented more than two million people. One person out of every three was a slum resident.

Even in the center of Seoul, an agglomeration of shacks extended from Cheonggye-cheon to Jungrang-cheon and Ttukseom.

What influence did the church have on this destitute population? Virtually none. By comparison, Soka Gakkai, which had roots in shantytowns, was expanding its influence. That said, it was the shamans who exercised the greatest influence in shantytowns. Shamanism worked on the population at the subconscious level. The shaman flags flying everywhere in alleyways were testimony that their business was thriving.

I made a round of shacks to hear what residents thought of the church. Once, in chatting with a resident, he told me that previously he had gone to church but had stopped.

"Why did you stop going?" I asked.

"Going to church? It sounds good, and I know that I ought to go, but it costs money to go to church."

"Why do you say it costs money? The Bible says that rich or poor, all should come to be saved, and that Jesus came to the world for the poor and the weak."

"You don't live in the real world. The Bible may say that Jesus came to the world for the poor, but the church has no room for people like us."

What he said was true and an indictment of Korean churches. Talking with him, I realized that there should be a church for the poor, where they could rest their minds. This realization heartened me in making the rounds during the hot days of summer.

In those days there was a Christian pamphlet entitled *The Mind of Young Park*. Going down all of the alleys of Seoul's shantytowns, I passed out the pamphlet, chanting, "Let's be saved by believing in Jesus," "This shows you how to live a proper life. Please give this a good read and go to a church nearby."

Mine was the most primitive and elementary way of conducting missionary work. It also might be regarded as the easiest. Still, it was the best way I knew to reach people to get them to believe in Jesus.

I continued to pay visits to people living in shacks. One day I arrived in Cheonggye-cheon, a slum along a creek that ran through the center of Seoul and into the Han River. The name Cheonggye-cheon means "clean creek." It had been called that from long before because its water had run clear.

Now, however, the creek stank because it had become a major conduit for the city's sewage. Makeshift shacks had been erected along its banks. In the early '60s, an elevated highway was built over several miles of the river, beginning in downtown Seoul. The upper reaches of the creek, corresponding to the section where the elevated highway ran, were covered over and paved. Farther down, it was still an open sewer. About 60,000 people, in 12,000 households, lived on both sides of the creek in abominable conditions.

I started my rounds with houses at the end of the elevated highway and went along the creek's lower reaches, downstream from the rear gate of Hanyang University, where the worst of the shacks had been built. The area's administrative address was No. 74 Songjeong-dong, Seongdong-gu. Some 1,600 households were listed at this address.

My heart went out particularly to the people living in this area. There, I met a young man named Kim Jong-gil. He had a wife and three sons. Hearing that I wanted to work in the area, he gave me a big welcome. We hit it off from our first meeting, when he invited me to

Making my way around Cheonggye-cheon.

his house for dinner. We had a good talk. He had come from Jangheung, South Jeolla province, in the southwest of the country, and was one year my senior. He was self-sacrificing and religious and had a strong sense of justice.

Beginning the day I met Jong-gil, I paid a visit to every house at the Songjeong-dong address and distributed Christian leaflets. While going about my work, I observed how people lived.

ON AUGUST 6, 1971, AT AROUND TWO O'CLOCK in the afternoon, I happend onto one of the houses. I called out and asked whether anyone was about, but there was no answer. Through an open gate, I saw some shoes out front. I went in and looked around.

There, lying on the floor in a dimly lit room, was a boy of twelve or thirteen. I was shocked. He looked terrible. He was only skin and bones and had a distended stomach. Pus was streaming onto the floor from an open wound about a half inch below his navel. Maggots were swarming in the puddle of pus that had accumulated on the floor.

I was speechless. I could not turn and leave, pretending that I had not seen him. I entered the room and asked him, "What happened to you?"

He did not respond. Although he did not otherwise react, his eyes moved, so I knew he was alive. Seeing his condition gave me a sharp pain in my stomach. How could any human being fall to this miserable condition, much less a child? His eyes were hollow, as if the shadow of death had already settled upon him. I brushed the maggots away and mopped the floor.

If in this life there is a hell, this would be the closest thing to it. How could this happen? Who's fault is it that this boy has been abandoned? I thought, we are all guilty that he is suffering from this horrendous pain. Abandoning a child in hell, we, adults, are guilty of greed and selfishness. We are concerned only with ourselves and neglect our neighbors.

I decided to do everything I could to save the boy. I could not let him die. I prayed. "My Lord Jesus! I have to save him. I don't know how he came to this condition, but my Lord, you must know. If this boy is left to die, it is a death sentence on the collective human conscience. You know how to return this boy's life to him. I will put the best of my heart into bringing this boy back to life. Please help me."

After the prayer, I waited for someone to come. A couple of hours later, a woman in her mid-forties came in. She asked me haltingly, "Who are you?"

"I was in the area doing missionary work and came upon this boy. I was waiting for someone to come home. Are you his mother?"

"Yes, so what?"

"What happened to him?"

"He's my liability. He's killing me. I wish he were dead."

"How long has he been in this condition?"

"He's been sickly with a cold since he was five or six years old. He used to get better when he took aspirin, but beginning last year, that stopped working, and since then, his condition has only gotten worse."

"When was it that he first discharged pus?"

"About two months ago."

"Did you take him to a doctor?"

"A doctor? It's impossible for us here, barely surviving from day to day. I put disinfectant on him. I started going to Nam-mu Tiger Sect after learning that if I did, and if I believed in them, he'd recover. It's been nearly a year and nothing has happened. I think I'm thinking of quitting."

"Ma'am, let's work together to save him."

"I appreciate your consideration, but it's too late. I had hoped that I could take him to a doctor before he died, but I haven't been able to…."

"If you allow me, I'll take him to a hospital."

"Thank you, but I can't afford it, and I can't ask you to pay."

"No, I'd be happy to. I'm a student studying to become a minister. It's a minister's job to do this kind of thing. I know you'll let me do this. I'll come tomorrow morning and take him to the hospital."

"Thank you, but I won't blame you if you don't come. Don't go to any effort to keep your promise."

"No, I won't. I'm grateful that you'll let me."

The boy's name was Kim Hak-hyeong. He was 12 years old. That evening I returned to the dormitory at my seminary to collect money from my classmates. "I need money to save a child's life."

Being students of theology, they were different from other students. They did not hesitate to contribute. I did not go to class the next morning. Rather, I took a taxi to No. 74 Songjeong-dong. Arriving there, I prayed first, holding the boy's hands.

"My Lord, you said that you would not break a bruised reed or put out a smoldering wick. I believe that you will not let this boy die. We are of the same heart to save his life, aren't we? My Lord, you've been too hard on him. Why should this boy suffer for what grownups have done? I am praying from the deepest recesses of my heart. Please let him live. Please give him back his bright smile and twinkling eyes. I pray in the name of Jesus, who bled to death and was buried to save man from sin, pain, and weakness, and was resurrected. Amen!"

The boy's father came in just after the prayer. He was stocky and in his early fifties. We exchanged greetings and had a talk. "I came today to take your boy to a hospital. I found him the other day when I was making missionary rounds. I would appreciate it if you could manage the time to go with me."

"I'm grateful to you for your concern for my son, but as you see, I no longer regard him as my son. I don't want to burden you with this."

"No, you're wrong. One life is more precious than anything in this world. It's wrong to let a person die. You shouldn't think that the boy belongs only to you. He's not only your son, but a son of heaven and a son of this nation. He's my brother. I realize it may be too late to save him, but life is in God's hands. We've seen miracles. We have to do our best."

"Do you think I don't want to save him? We live from hand to mouth. We haven't been able to do anything to save him from his horrible condition. I know that if he dies like this, I'll live with a broken heart for the rest of my life. Several times a day, whenever I remove pus from his skinny body, I think of killing him to put him out of his misery. Then, out of frustration and anger, I drink."

"I understand. I have a taxi waiting for us outside. Please come with me. I'll pay for everything."

I got Hak-hyeong and his father to the taxi and went to the Central Medical Center. I asked them whether I could get a free medical checkup. They told me to follow procedures, starting at the City Children's Hospital near Sajik Park. I went to the Children's Hospital and asked them to process Hak-hyeong for a free medical checkup. They told me to get a "subsidy-beneficiary" paper. I had never heard of it, so I asked again.

"What's a subsidy-beneficiary paper?"

"You get it at your ward office."

"Will they give one to just anyone? What if they refuse to give it to me?"

The doctor grimaced and said curtly, "Then you'd better just go to a pharmacist."

I felt my insides churn at the doctor's attitude and barked at him sarcastically, "Damn it, you carry some weight around here. Cut us a break. Why do you have to be so snappy?"

The doctor shot me a sharp glance.

That day, I returned to Hak-hyeong's house empty-handed, having gone from one hospital to another, with Hak-hyeong suffering all along and gasping for breath. Failing to get him admitted, I felt bad for him and his father.

"I'm sorry that I dragged you around like this and that I failed you."

"No, you don't have to be. He's my son. I really appreciate your

143

hard work and I'm sorry for the effort and the expense you went to today."

"Don't mention it. I'm fine. I'm just sorry that we accomplished so little. Do you know what a subsidy-beneficiary paper is?"

"No, not really, but it may be a document from the ward office saying that I'm a beneficiary of a flour subsidy."

"That could be it. Can you go to the office to check it out?"

"I'll go there straightaway and ask them to give me one, if there is such a thing."

"Great. I'll come back tomorrow. They said that the paper would get us a free medical checkup. We'll go back to the hospital in the morning."

I returned to the dormitory. That evening I went up Mount Acha. I knelt and prayed to Jesus that He clear the way to get Hak-hyeong medical treatment. I finished my prayer feeling confident that everything would go well the next day.

The next morning I went to Hak-hyeong's house. His father had gotten the subsidy-beneficiary paper and was waiting for me. The three of us went again to the Children's Hospital. Entering the hospital, I regretted the manner in which I had spoken to the doctor the day before, but there was nothing I could do about it.

I went to the same doctor, pretending that nothing had happened. Without saying a word, I handed him the paper. He accepted it, called in one of his staff and told him to take us through the process. This all happened very quickly. I imagined that he was afraid of being subjected to further abuse.

Hak-hyeong had to have his spine x-rayed. We were then told to take him home and return three days later for the results. Three days later, we returned and learned that he was diagnosed with consumption and a spinal infection. According to the x-ray, three of his vertebrae had disappeared and two others were half-disintegrated. The doctor told us that the tuberculosis virus had affected his spine, adding that he could not understand how he had been left untreated in that condition. Holding Hak-hyeong's hands as he lay in bed, I asked the doctor what we could do to treat him.

"It's too late to do anything. He requires major surgery, which would cost a fortune. It's very complicated to remove damaged vertebrae and replace them with artificial ones. It's also very difficult."

"Is there any way other than surgery?"

"His condition is too serious to try other approaches. There might be a way, however, that could stop the condition from getting any worse."

"What would he be like if his condition did not deteriorate?"

"He'd be hunchbacked, but that'd be the best-case scenario. His condition is so serious that we'll be lucky to save his life."

Although the doctor was pessimistic, I was confident that Hak-hyeong would neither die nor be hunchbacked. I had faith that after man did his best, God would take care of the rest.

I asked the doctor to prescribe medicine for Hak-hyeong for a few months and took him home.

"Hak-hyeong, you heard the doctor, didn't you? Your condition was caused by a TB virus that infected your spine. Your vertebrae have been damaged, so beginning today you have to take medication. The doctor said that medicines alone cannot cure your condition so we need to pray. God will help us, if we pray to Him. Do you know how to pray?"

"No, I've never prayed before."

"Do you know how to read?"

"Yes, I can read."

"Fine. I'll write down what you should say when you pray. Read it aloud when you eat your meals and when you take your medicine. Praying is not difficult. You talk to Jesus the same way you talk to your father. You just say, 'Jesus please help me recover. I would like to play with my friends.' In your prayer you say what's on your mind. I'm sure that Jesus will listen to you."

I wrote a prayer in his notebook.

"My Lord Jesus, I want to get well. Please help me. Like my friends, I would like to go out to play. If you help me recover, I will work for you to help others who are suffering. I believe that I am going to get better after taking this medicine."

Hak-hyeong was a good patient. He never missed taking his medicine after a meal and always prayed after taking it. After ten days, he started to show improvement. His eyes regained their vigor, his pus stopped, and his appetite improved.

145

We were greatly encouraged. After twenty days, his complexion improved. The progress he was making gave his parents hope. As a consequence, they put more of their time and effort into helping him.

One afternoon, after finishing my classes at the seminary, I went to Hak-hyeong's house, where I found his mother praying. What she was saying was strange. She was rubbing her hands while she prayed over a bowl of cold water on a table in the corner of the room.

"I'm begging you to cure my Hak-hyeong so he can live long. I'm begging you," she said as she prayed. I asked her what she was doing.

"I'm praying," she replied.

"No, that's not how you pray."

"I have never said a proper prayer so I'm just doing it my way."

"I see. And what's the water for?"

"Praying with nothing in front of me felt like something was missing."

"If you think you need something, I'll give you a Bible that you can use instead of a bowl of water. You kept saying that you are begging. You may say that when you pray to a shaman spirit, but when you pray to Jesus, you say, 'My Lord Jesus, I pray to you. Please let my son, Hak-hyeong, have his health back.' You end your prayers with, 'I pray in the name of Jesus.' "

After I taught Hak-hyeong's mother how to pray, she prayed over the Bible. Hak-hyeong also prayed before every meal. I asked my classmates at the seminary to pray for him and took him some medicine to help his digestion, having heard that his TB medication could cause indigestion. I also gave him vitamins and calcium supplements. I put all my heart and effort into helping him recover.

His condition improved every day. One day he asked me, "Can I stop the medicine now? I feel much better."

"No, Jesus helps those who take their medicine and pray. He is not happy with people who pray only, without taking their medicine, because it's like wanting to have a free ride."

I knew that he was sick of taking medicine because the amount that he had to take every day was formidable.

Watching Hak-hyeong recover, I felt that I had accomplished something. After some time, his condition had improved to such a degree that he could sit up with no help.

The doctor said, however, that further improvement could hardly be expected unless he had surgery. The surgery would cost at least three million *won*. After the surgery, he would have to stay in bed for almost a year. His father sighed, saying that he could not pay 300,000 *won*, much less 3 million *won*.

I did not give up. Believing that there must be a way, I asked around to arrange surgery for him. It was then that I met Pastor Min, a Baptist missionary from the United States. I told him about Hak-hyeong. He promised that he would find a way to arrange for his surgery at the Baptist Hospital in Busan.

A few days later, he told me that he had arranged free surgery for the child at the hospital. Full of joy, we went down to Busan.

The hospital suggested that he wait until he regained his strength, before they undertook the surgery. Returning home, we worked together to improve his condition, but a miracle was already under way. We had simply overlooked it.

After visiting Busan, Hak-hyeong's health improved considerably and he could go outside to play. I was nervous as I watched him run around because I recalled the x-rays that showed his damaged vertebrae. I was concerned that his spine would collapse. I asked him to move carefully, but his response was naively childlike.

"I'm fine!"

On a visit to the slum, I was frightened to learn that Hak-hyeong had been wrestling with his friends. I called him and asked, "Are you crazy? How could you put your back under so much strain? Your body can't take it."

"I'm fine. Really, I'm fine."

I could not believe what he was saying. His mother and I took him to the Children's Hospital. After examining him, the doctor told me, "He's cured. You did a great job."

I was stunned.

"But you told me a while back that without surgery we'd be lucky to save his life. Now you're saying he's cured? I can't believe it."

"Yes, I know I said that then, but now it's a different story. Medical opinion is based on scientific evidence."

"You must have it wrong. Maybe you're looking at someone else's x-rays."

"Impossible. You're the first outpatient to come in today so there is no way we could have someone else's x-rays. If you are still in doubt about the result, you can go to another hospital and get a second opinion."

He said this curtly and called in the next patient. I had been snubbed, but felt no anger. Hak-hyeong had been cured and that was all that mattered. His remaining vertebrae had healed and fused, leaving him with a slight stoop, but nothing serious.

Hak-hyeong's mother and I were happy beyond words. Holding my hands, Hak-hyeong's mother thanked me, again and again.

Leaving the hospital, I used every cent in my pocket to buy fruit and snacks. I returned to the shantytown and gathered all the children I could to have a party.

"Kids, Jesus has cured our Hak-hyeong. We're going to have a party to celebrate. Please come."

After that, older people in the town would say to each other when they saw me in the street, "He's the teacher who cured Hak-hyeong. Let's ask him to build us a church. A church will be good for the children's education."

Young married women also would say to me, "When are you going to build us a church? My husband and I have decided to attend, once it's built."

This made me think. Maybe Jesus was commanding me to build a church here and look after these people.

The question developed into an assurance, which I translated into action. This was the foundation for Hwalbin Church. Thus, I began my career doing missionary work among the urban poor. Hak-hyeong was more precious to me than anyone. He helped me sort out my mission in life.

THE 1,600 HOUSEHOLDS LIVING AT NO. 74 Songjeong-dong had left unprofitable farms to come to Seoul. They arrived with no particular plan, thinking perhaps that they could make a living as porters, delivering goods. All of the delivery jobs had been lost to motorized vans, however, and the displaced farmers were unemployed and impoverished. Failing to find work, they would gather to gamble or drink, even during the day. Families would eke out an existence with money the wives or children earned working in small shops or factories.

Walking along the embankment, I indulged in a reverie. If Jesus were to come to Seoul, where would He go first? He would not go to fashionable downtown areas. I was sure that first He would visit smelly Cheonggye-cheon. He would walk along this embankment and say, "Everyone here, suffering from a heavy burden! Come to me. I will throw a feast where you may rest." He would then provide people with food enough to fill their stomachs.

I continued to let my imagination run. If I were to build a church here and live with these people, Jesus would come by. He would say, "Good work, Jin-hong. You're doing my job for me. I would like to invite you over for dinner." I found this thought comforting. Yes, I will build a church here and live with these people. I will commit my life to missionary work for the poor. It is God's will.

Having decided, I talked to some of my close classmates. Their reactions to my plan to build a church in the Cheonggye-cheon slum and live there varied. Some suggested that I should think more about what I would do after graduating from the seminary. Others said they did not think that missionary work among the poor would be productive, and that I should concentrate my work on college students or intellectuals, to deliver God's word in an efficient way and further spread the Gospel. Still others suggested that I continue to study to become a scholar and contribute to the development of the Korean church.

Some of them, however, encouraged me, saying, "It's the right decision. Missionary work among the poor has always been neglected by the Korean church. You will be a pioneer."

Once, on reading Isaiah, one passage made a strong impression on me. In it I felt that I had found my reason for committing to missionary work with the poor:

> The Spirit of the Sovereign LORD is on me, because the LORD has anointed me to preach good news to the poor. He has sent me to bind up the brokenhearted, to proclaim freedom for the captives and release from darkness for the prisoners, to proclaim the year of the LORD's favor and the day of vengeance of our God, to comfort all who mourn,... (Isaiah 61:1-2)

149

The Spirit of the Lord is upon me. Why is He upon me? He is upon me to order me on a mission, to preach the Gospel to the poor. How can it be done? I must go into the slums to heal the brokenhearted and proclaim liberty to the captives of poverty and disease. It is to deliver news of hope and to comfort them. It is to live among them to share their sorrows and their joys and to alleviate their suffering. I felt in my heart that God had ordered me to commit my life to this work.

When I told one of my classmates my intention, he asked, "Have you found financial support for your work?"

"I hadn't thought about it," I replied.

"It's not the kind of thing that you can simply throw yourself into with only your passion. You can go into it only after you are assured of support from a big church or a wealthy contributor. If you have to give up halfway through, it'd be better not to start."

His advice made good sense. I thought about it and prayed for three days before coming to a conclusion. The conclusion was simple, but important, and it became a principle that I have lived by during the three decades since. I would be a servant to Jesus, from beginning to end. A servant gives all of his heart and effort to his master and the master looks after all the servant's needs. I would commit myself to carry out Jesus' work, and Jesus would provide whatever I needed.

When I was young, I lived at my grandparents' house in a remote rural town. My grandfather had three servants working on his farm. I recalled how my grandmother managed them. In the mornings, the servants reported for work. She acknowledged them by nodding and later in the day she sent lunch to them.

Sometimes she would have me take them their meals as they worked in the field. The servants had only to work and left everything else, their shelter, meals, and clothes, to the care of their master. This memory of my early days inspired me with how I should prepare myself to serve Jesus.

In undertaking this work, my concern should be whether it is doing Jesus' work, not whether it has the financial support of some contributors. If Jesus does not respond in time, it would be for one of two reasons. It would either be because the work is not truthful to Jesus' will or because Jesus is not the Lord. The latter reason is out of the question so I need only to ask whether the work I have planned is in accordance with His will. I did not need to wait for an answer to this question because I had found it in Isaiah. I decided to take the bull by the horns.

Having made up my mind, I went to the Cheonggye-cheon shantytown whenever I could manage the time. Visiting every alley, I thought about my plan. What should I do before building a church? I wondered, if I started a church, what principles should I apply in running it? What kind of a church should it be? I decided that I needed to get to know the residents so they would invite me to build a church.

As a first step, I gave a party in a vacant lot for people over the age of sixty. I gave everyone a bowl of cooked rice with soup and a pack of cigarettes. I also prepared *makgeoli*, in an effort to cheer them up. When they were in a good mood, I introduced myself and made a speech, saying that I would like their help in building a church in the area.

Hak-hyeong's father, Kim In-ok, also spoke. He said, "This is the man who cured my son's back. He was sent from heaven. He will never lead us in the wrong direction so let's follow him. If you agree with me, please let me hear your applause." The people clapped; the mood became cheerful; everyone was happy.

People who attended the party became my supporters and encouraged other people to join in. They were very enthusiastic in persuading others.

They said, "He's the man who cured Hak-hyeong's back. He can be trusted. He has good manners and respects his seniors. We're going to ask him to build a church in our town. Think about it. A church will help educate our grandchildren. The basics of Confucianism we learned in our school days are virtually the same as the teachings of the church. Their teachings are all good. Let's support him."

After winning over the older people, I began to work on the children. With my pockets full of candies, I went throughout the town to meet children. I passed out the candies and asked the children to call their friends because I was going to tell some stories. Soon about 200 children gathered and I told them a story. When I finished, I introduced myself and told them that I was going to build a church. After that, whenever I visited the area, I always had a big following of children.

"When are you going to open the church, Teacher?" they would ask.

Getting acquainted with the children resulted in getting to know their parents. Their parents would ask me, "Are you the teacher who's going to build a church? Our children are waiting for it to open because they're looking forward to hearing more stories."

After the elderly people and the children, I shifted my focus to the young men in the town. I visited and introduced myself to those who were well-known, whether for good reasons or for bad. I told them about the work that I would like to do in the town and asked for their cooperation. Outwardly, they looked tough, but they had a soft spot in their heart, which I appealed to. Most of them responded positively, saying they would help me in any way they could.

As expected, there were some who responded negatively. "Jesus Teacher, I wish you luck. It's fine by me, as long as you provide the booze."

I did not mind their response, telling them, "Thank you. I'll serve you anything you want, if only you believe in Jesus."

The last obstacle for me to tackle was to persuade my wife. By that time we had a son, Dong-hyeok, so I reckoned it would not be easy to persuade her to move to a slum. My wife was not cut out for slum life, and I was not sure that she would be able to adjust to it. Another concern I had was Dong-hyeok's health. Unsure of any of this, I gathered my courage to talk to my wife about my plan to move to the slum to work and start a church. To my surprise, she went along with my plan.

"I'm ready to move with you, as long as it is Jesus' will and yours."

"Thank you for your support, but I'm afraid that I may be asking you and Dong-hyeok to make too great a sacrifice."

"It doesn't make sense that you should live in the slum while we remain outside."

"That's my dilemma. If I had decided to do this before we married, it would have been simple. I could have just moved in by myself."

"Don't think that way. Dong-hyeok and I can participate in Jesus' work too, so don't think of it as a sacrifice."

After agreeing on the move, we decided to spend all of our savings, 300,000 *won*, for the good of the slum. Using 145,000 *won*, we purchased a shack and started to rework the interior. Two rooms were set aside for the church and one room as our residence. Hak-hyeong's father, Kim In-ok, took care of purchasing the house and Kim Jong-gil, who encouraged me when I first came to Cheonggye-cheon, took charge of reworking the interior.

While the work was in progress, a volunteer, Kim Young-jun, joined us. He had been my student when I taught at Gyeongsan Mennonite High School in Daegu. Having heard about my missionary plan, he volunteered to work with me. He was competent, sincere, and meticulous. With four of us on the job, we were able to speed up our work to open the church.

Kim In-ok went around the town, spreading word that I was going to open a church. He applied himself to the task with such commitment and sincerity that some people suspected he was being paid for it.

In-ok had a history of fighting. During Korea's fight for liberation from Japan, he was one of a group of partisan fighters, operating in Manchuria. After liberation, he was involved in political activities, before being reduced to living in the slum. He was athletic and had a strong sense of justice. Telling me his experience with the church when he was young, he cautioned me to be discreet.

His story was that after the Korean War, he had worked for his church and was faithful to his religious upbringing. At that time the church was receiving a lot of relief goods from the U.S. Whenever a shipment of goods came in, the pastor would pick the best for his family and would have In-ok deliver them. In-ok thought this was wrong and asked the pastor to stop. The pastor rebuked him for not showing proper respect for God's servant. In-ok quit his job and left the church altogether, disillusioned by the pastor's attitude.

After leaving the church, he drifted away from religion. He wandered around, gambling and drinking before finally settling in the slum. He thought the pastor was partly responsible for what he had become. Therefore, he advised me, if I wanted to continue my missionary work, I had to abandon all my selfish impulses. Leaders who indulged in selfishness were bound not only to tread the wrong path, but also to corrupt others.

Taking his advice to heart, I resolved to keep myself clear of material things and hold "honest poverty" as my credo. As time passed, I found myself becoming more involved in the mission for the poor, and it became more rewarding. I was grateful to God that I had been given an opportunity to devote myself to such work.

In their 100-year history, the Korean Protestant churches had achieved substantial growth, but a problem had been brewing within. Christianity, which in its early stages was a grassroots religion, spread and increasingly came to be associated with the middle and upper classes. The poor—the laborers and the farmers—who in the 1970s constituted the majority in our society, became alienated from the church.

Many residents of the slum had once attended church, but had stopped. They said that they felt out of place in church. The atmosphere and environment of the church were so elegant and upscale that they were uncomfortable when they went to church after working on construction sites or in factories all week. Overwhelmed by what they saw around them, they left the church.

Their experiences made me explore my thoughts deeply. The church should reach out to the hearts of the poor, not only for the sake of the poor, but for its own survival. I do not understand the mentality of church leaders who spend massive amounts of money on the construction of church buildings. God's religion is concerned with people's lives, not with buildings. The church should reform itself to take center stage in the lives of the people, leading them in the direction of Christianity. To this end, the church should invest in people, not in material things. The church should take an interest in the quality of people's lives, not their numbers. The church should make its way into the hearts of the people before rising high or expanding far.

WE PROCEEDED WITH OUR WORK, STEP BY STEP, to build a church in Cheonggye-cheon shantytown. We finally got to the point where we had to decide on a name for the church. Finding a name that not only corresponded to our theological and ideological foundation, but also to the image of a church in a slum, was not an easy task.

We decided to hold a competition. The person who suggested the winning name would receive a 20-pound sack of flour as a prize. We put notices up all over town. The competition had an ulterior motive, which was to attract residents' interest and participation. It was a huge success. A number of names were suggested. Anyone who proposed a name was asked to stand up and explain the name's meaning to the audience.

On the day of the selection, many residents gathered to listen to the candidates' explanations. The entries were put to a vote and the name "Hwalbin" was chosen.

The winner explained, "Everyone! You all know the Hwalbin band in the Story of Hong Gil-dong, do you not? I came up with the name because I wanted the church to inherit the band's tradition. The chief of the Hwalbin band, Hong Gil-dong, was a thief, but he was no ordinary thief. He was a Robin Hood. He stole grain that was rotting in the sheds of the rich and distributed it to the poor. I'm not suggesting that we become thieves. I'm suggesting that we build a church that practices God's love and becomes a beacon of hope for the poor."

The people cheered him on, shouting, "Yes, go on." He continued with his impassioned speech.

"I'm sure you remember that in the story the Hwallbin band stole grain from the Haein Temple to give to the starving people. They also stole from corrupt officials to give to the powerless. The Haein Temple had taken advantage of its religious privileges to accumulate great wealth and then it charged high-interest rates on money it lent to poor farmers. In Seoul, there are many churches that are today's equivalent of the Haein Temple. We need a church that can play the role of the Hwalbin band, namely a Hwalbin Church. I therefore urge that we build a church in the tradition of the Hwalbin band and give the name Hwalbin to the church."

He received the biggest applause and a majority of the votes. He was awarded the sack of flour.

After the name for the church was selected, we endeavored to teach the religious dimension of the name "Hwalbin." Since first appearing in the story of Hong Gil-dong, the name Hwalbin coursed through the veins of people in eras of suffering. During the Japanese occupation, farmers in the south forged a resistance movement that excluded upper-class Koreans. They adopted the name Hwalbin for their organization. Hwalbin Church resolved to establish a church faithful to the teachings of the Bible, embodying this tradition and practicing Jesus' love.

Christianity is a religion that promises to save the souls of people who believe in Jesus and lead them to heaven after they die. Without this promise, Christianity would find little acceptance. But going to heaven is not everything. Christians should not be denied a decent life while on earth. People will not be satisfied with a promise of heaven after death, if they must endure poverty and wretchedness in this world. Hwalbin Church would help people overcome their poverty and live a good life, as if they were in heaven.

As a beginning, I held prayer meetings. We prayed that Hwalbin Church would become instrumental in correcting economic and social injustice and political oppression. We prayed that Jesus, who had saved us, should save our society.

WE SCHEDULED A FOUNDING SERVICE for the first week of October, after completing renovations. We felt the timing was perfect, as October 3, 1971, a Sunday, was National Foundation Day, which added significance to the event.

At that time, the Seoul city government had a policy. Shacks that had been illegally built would be allowed to stand, but they could not be repaired or remodeled in any way, even when the roofs leaked and doors fell off their hinges.

We had spent two weeks repairing the interior of the shack to be able to use it as a church. That amount of activity was bound to get the attention of the city's demolition crew. With our work as the pretext, the demolition crew showed up on September 2 and tore down the building. I was overwhelmed.

Watching the building come down, I prayed, "Lord Jesus! Please give me courage to start again. I am going to face many difficulties along the way before establishing this church. Please give me strength not to give up before I even get started."

The church building had been razed, but the incident brought residents together. My missionary efforts were paying off. The residents volunteered to restore the building. They worked day and night for us to be able to celebrate the founding of the church as scheduled and were on track to succeed. We were about to put the finishing touches on the building when a corner wall gave out. We had been in such a hurry that we did not wait long enough for the concrete to dry.

We rebuilt the corner. My hands were bleeding and my shoulders swollen from carrying bags of sand and shoveling. I was so deprived of sleep that I dozed off anywhere I could find a place to sit down. Late into the night of October 2, we put up the roof frame and the interior walls. The building was sufficiently complete to hold a service as planned.

At 3 p.m. on October 3, 1971, Hwalbin Church held its inaugural service. There was no glass in the windows frames and the floor was clay covered with a straw mat, but we were all excited. Two wooden boxes covered with white paper served as the pulpit.

Standing next to the Hwalbin Church bell tower.

During the service, I read Isaiah 61:1-4 and spoke about the reason for establishing Hwalbin Church. In my sermon, I enunciated the five principles on which the church was founded. Thirty years have passed since then, but I still remember the principles:

> *First, the church, whose master is Jesus, was born out of a mission to liberate the poor, the oppressed, and the deprived. The Korean church could not have grown to what it is in the span of only one hundred years, without having put down roots among the dispossessed in its founding years.*
>
> *Since then, the Korean church has become the province of the upper classes, alienating the poor, who constitute the majority of the population. The Korean church will be subjected to the judgement of history, if it continues to turn a deaf ear to the outcries of the underprivileged, serving only the*

interests of the conventional and the well-to-do.

Jesus' Gospel favors no class and does not discriminate. The Gospel was sent to save and bless everyone, including the wealthy and the educated. The Bible, however, repeatedly expresses a concern for the poor. We, Hwalbin Church, take our first step today, undertaking a mission to spread the Gospel to the poor, following the Bible's teaching.

Second, the Korean church has failed to contribute to the community and has distanced itself from the community. A church should be at the center of a society spiritually, socially, culturally, and sometimes even politically, and should work to heal physical, moral, and social ills. Hwalbin Church will serve the community and lead its development.

Third, the essence of Jesus' teachings and truth lies in "being saved by faith" and "living by love." The faith that saves us will be demonstrated outwardly in the form of love. One of the prime purposes of the church is to practice love, but today's church has substituted love for ritual and dogma.

To reform the Korean church, Hwalbin Church is committed practicing love. This role is clearly defined in the Gospel of John. Faith is dead when it falls short of practicing love. Hwalbin Church members will become role models in the practice of love.

Fourth, the church undertakes missionary work that is suited to the people, the society, and the community to which it belongs. The Korean church is dominated by the theology of Western missionaries, their methods, and church organization. The Gospel is the absolute truth, transcending place and time. Theology and approaches to missionary work to teach the Gospel, however, must be able to evolve and respond to changes in society.

In Korea, this does not happen. Hwalbin Church will create a theology, a church organization, and an approach to missionary work suited to the nature and disposition of the Korean people. It will draw up strategies to spread the Gospel, and put action into words.

Fifth, one of the missions that any church, anywhere,

must carry out is to speak out for and work for social justice. Inheriting the tradition of the Old Testament prophets, Christianity in Korea has a history written in the blood of its martyrs, who died in pursuit of social equality, political freedom, and truth.

In neglecting its tradition and mission and by indulging in indolence and corruption, the church will not only be stripped of its role, but will lead to a breakdown of society. Two thousand years of church and world history teach us this lesson.

On National Foundation Day, we declared these five principles for the establishment of Hwalbin Church and dedicated ourselves to live by them.

11

Nobody Said It'd Be Easy

T O CARRY OUT THE FOUNDING mission of Hwalbin Church, I had to diagnose the problems of the community. I began by identifying problems, both personal and societal, affecting residents' lives.

I visited their homes and, by talking with them, tried to open their minds. This approach helped me build trust and get closer to them. Based on this trust, I went about my missionary work. I called this process "Operation DDT" or "Door-to-Door Tackle Operation."

I compared my efforts to deal with the shantytown residents' problems to a soccer game. I tried to arm myself mentally with the level of readiness that soccer players have when they go into a game, having to "tackle" their opponents. The other part of the name, "door-to-door," comes from how I approached people, knocking on the doors of their houses, one by one. DDT is also the name of the chemical used to kill vermin in agriculture. The name of our operation carried the message that I wanted to rid the slumdwellers of troubles and problems the way farmers fight harmful insects, using DDT.

Along with the DDT Operation, I coined another term, "TLC Therapy" or "Tender Loving Care Therapy." This meant that we would exercise TLC to cure the pains and heal the wounds of slumdwellers.

Many of the people living in the slum had been denied love and recognition in society. They suffered from "love deficiency." Everyone is aware of the problems caused by vitamin deficiency, but people little understand the problems that result from love deficiency. For shantytown residents, this was a lifetime condition. Victims, however, can be cured when others lavish love and care on them.

TLC Therapy was used by Jesus. He said, "I have come not for the healthy. I have descended to bind up the broken heart." Jesus indeed worked to mend broken souls. Truthful to His spirit, the church should devote itself to taking care of such souls, anywhere and at any time.

In the Bible there is the story of an adulteress who was brought to Jesus in something of a setup. The people who accused her asked Jesus, "What do you have to say about this woman, Jesus?"

If Jesus had told them to forgive her, they would have accused him of violating Moses' law. If, on the other hand, he had said they should kill her, as the law required, then they would have accused him of being a hypocrite. Having detected their ulterior motive in asking him, Jesus wrote something on the ground and then said to them, "If any one of you is without sin, let him be the first to throw a stone at her." (John 8:7)

Hearing this, the people dropped the stones that they had picked up to throw at the woman and went away. The story does not say what Jesus wrote on the ground, but I suppose it was a wrongdoing for each of the people there.

After the people left, Jesus asked the woman, "Woman, where are they? Has no one condemned you?"

"No one, sir."

"Then neither do I condemn you," Jesus declared. "Go now and leave your life of sin."

Thereupon, the woman became free of physical desire and escaped from death.

Whenever I recall this story, I picture Jesus' eyes gazing at the woman. What did his eyes look like? Understanding the frailty and vile nature of people, and having pity on their insincerity, Jesus must have had eyes with power to rejuvenate. Looking into His eyes, surely, people were moved by their depth and found courage to start their lives anew.

I believe that Jesus used TLC Therapy to mend shattered spirits. This is what gave me the idea to visit families in their homes.

The shacks in shantytown did not have their own walls and gates, but butted up against one another, sharing common walls. The front door usually opened onto a kitchen, which led to the only other room in the house.

Six or seven family members would live in a single room of 100 to 135 square feet. The shacks were alike in that their condition was invariably substandard, with leaky roofs, dangerous charcoal briquette heating, excessive humidity, and bad ventilation.

The problems of slumdwellers broke down into three categories. First were those problems they could manage on their own. Second were problems that needed some help from the church. Last came the problems that could not be solved without outside intervention, wheth-

Visiting a family at No. 74 Songjeong-dong, Seongdong-gu.

er by the church or someone else, because they were beyond an individual's capacity to cope.

I began by taking on the problems in the first category. Once they were resolved, I went to work on those in the second category. Finally, the missionary team of Hwalbin Church set about dealing with the third-category problems.

THE THIRD SUNDAY AFTER THE ESTABLISHMENT of Hwalbin Church, about halfway through the service, a *soju* bottle shattered against the church's exterior wall. Six men, reeking of alcohol, charged into the church. The leader of the gang lashed out with a threatening gesture, "Why are you singing and raising such a racket? You were supposed to have reported to me before opening a church."

The church members held their breath. Kim Jong-gil, who had once been in a gang and was not a stranger to confrontation, stepped forward and shouted at them, "Who do you think you're talking to, you idiot?"

I held him back and treated the men courteously. After some squabbling, the leader said, "OK, we're finished here for now. They know their place." He left first, followed by his cronies.

Late that evening, I took a bottle of *soju* and some dried squid and went to the gang leader's house. He was sleeping, but I asked his family to wake him. I sat face to face with him. From my experience, I knew that men like him were naive. Drinking *soju* together and eating squid, we had a good talk. I spoke frankly with him about how I had gone through a period of wondering and agony before finding Jesus, how Jesus wanted to help him, and what had brought me to this shantytown.

Hearing my story, he knelt down. "From now on, I will treat you like my older brother," he said. "I think you'll accept me as your brother. If Jesus is such a great man, I'll believe in him."

I replied, "Thank you, my brother. I'm so happy to hear this from you. Just imagine, then, how happy Jesus will be."

After our conversation, he took out a razor. He wanted to write his resolution in blood, marking the start of his new life, taking Jesus and me as his brothers. I held him back, telling him that it was not necessary to go that far. When it came to bleeding, I said, Jesus had already bled enough for both of us. I persuaded him not to cut himself, saying that it was sufficient to have made the resolution.

Having decided against the blood ceremony, he still wanted to write down his resolution. Half out of curiosity about what he would write, I encouraged him. He wrote his resolution on a cigarette wrapper:

RESOLUTION

I swear that I am going to respect Jesus as my lifetime boss from now on.

M. K. Kim
October 1971

163

I returned home with his resolution in hand. The next Sunday came. As the 11 a.m. service was about to begin, he still had not arrived. I was disappointed. Offering a prayer, I heard some bustling footsteps. After the prayer, I looked up to see Mr. Resolution and his band seated at the rear of the room.

The church fell silent, everyone fearing that the gang might have come to disrupt the service again. Some people who were sitting near them were about to move to another location. I asked them to stay seated where they were and invited the men to take seats in the front row. They came to the front and sat quietly.

After the service, I asked him and his band to introduce themselves to the congregation. He seemed to be shy, before speaking. "We went astray, but now we've come back. Please accept us. We are ready to work hard."

We welcomed them with a round of applause.

THE NEXT DAY I WENT TO THE POOREST SECTION of the shantytown, Section 9, and launched my DDT Operation. The first house I visited was Mr. Nam's. Mr. Nam, who was 56, had moved to Seoul from a farming area. He had attended middle school during the Japanese colonial period. His wife had been a member of a performing troupe. They had three daughters, ages 8, 4, and 1.

Mr. Nam had supported his family by working as a day laborer at construction sites before collapsing from overwork and malnutrition. His left side was paralyzed. His wife then supported the family, selling chewing gum. Carrying her youngest daughter across her back, she went about to theaters and coffee shops selling her gum. They barely survived on a daily income of between 100 and 200 *won*. On rainy or snowy days, their income would shrink to between 30 and 40 *won*.

The Nam family could afford only one briquette of charcoal each day to warm their room and one small bag of rice or noodles to eat. On days when their income was less, they bought a pack of flour, which was less expensive than rice. They managed to survive at a minimum standard for 80 *won* per day, one briquette of charcoal for 20 *won* and a pack of flour for 60 *won*.

The room was dark and fusty, with no ventilation. Suffering from colds, the three girls coughed incessantly. I sat with the couple and went over their problems.

Their first problem was about getting medical treatment for Mr. Nam. Their second problem was to find work for his wife that could provide steadier and better income than selling gum. Their third problem was to treat an eye infection that affected the youngest daughter. Fourth was to install a vent and a window in the room. Fifth was to enroll the oldest daughter in school. Finally, the sixth was to have their expired ID cards renewed.

Beginning the next day, I set out to take on the problems one after the other. In the meantime, they became church members and their lives got better. Mr. Nam's health improved considerably. He eventually managed to get a regular income by selling discards, although what he earned was sufficient only for pocket money.

One day I called the couple in and asked, "What can I do to help you become financially independent? I'll do my best to help, if you tell me."

"Thank you very much for your consideration. We're so grateful to you. We've decided to work hard to earn a decent living."

"That's great. I'm glad to hear that you've set that goal for yourself. I'm sure you'll achieve it, if you stick to it. What can I do to help?"

"If you insist, we think that we'd be able to make a living, if we had a handcart, which would allow us to sell food on the street."

"That's a good idea. How much would a secondhand cart cost?"

"To get one in working order would cost around 7,000 *won*."

"Fine, I'll lend you that amount. You needn't pay interest on it, but I would like you to return the principal."

"Yes, of course. There's no question about it. May lightning strike me dead if I don't pay it back, and I'd pay any interest you ask. But don't worry, you'll get back your principal."

I went to downtown Seoul straightaway to see one of my friends. I asked him to lend me 10,000 *won* interest free. He lent me the money from his salary. Handing the money over to Mr. Nam, I said, "Mr. Nam, I've borrowed 10,000 *won* from a friend. You say that a cart would cost 7,000 *won*, but I know that you need extra money to start your business. When do you think you can pay me back?"

"Two months should give me plenty of time."

"I'll give you three. I know that you'll keep your word."

I gave him the money. After some time, to my dismay, I saw no sign that he had bought a cart. Uncomfortable about it, I asked him what was going on. He said he was buying other things he needed first because he figured he could buy the cart later. I had no reason not to believe him.

A while later, late one night, returning home from Section 9, I found a woman on a corner with a baby on her back. It was early winter, but already cold enough that the ground was icy. The baby on her back was crying.

Getting closer, I saw that it was Mrs. Nam. She was very drunk, lying on the freezing ground. I pulled her up. Her voice was slurred when she spoke, "Get off me, you. Do you want me?"

I had a terrible time getting her home. At her house, I found her husband so drunk that he had lost control of his tongue. He squinted at me.

"Hi, Jesus Teacher," he said. "I'm sorry. I've sinned again." At that, he vomited. I said nothing and went home. I felt helpless.

Two days later, Mr. Nam's neighbor came to ask me whether I knew that Mr. Nam and his family had moved away. He had sold his hut for 17,000 *won* and left that morning at dawn.

I was heartbroken. I was not concerned about the money. Rather, I was concerned about what would become of them. Moving would not help them find a way to make a living. Why did they feel they had to flee? I felt partly responsible for their having left and hoped they would not have an even more difficult life in the future.

JUST BEYOND MR. NAM'S HOUSE WAS MR. CHOI'S. At the age of 33, Choi had come to Seoul in pursuit of a better life, having been a farmer in South Gyeongsang province, where he had graduated from an agricultural high school. The first time I visited his house, his oldest son, Byong-gyu, was home alone. He gave me his family's background.

His father was out of work and his mother had walked out on them because she could no longer take her husband's beatings. Three children, including Byong-gyu, and their 86-year-old grandmother lived in the house. This was not the first time his mother had run away. She had done the same some years before, but had returned home with some money she had earned. Her husband welcomed her back, and she stayed for a while. When the money ran out, her husband went back to his old ways of getting drunk and beating her. She had not been heard from since she left the second time.

Byong-gyu said that they wished their alcoholic father were dead and that their mother would come back to live with them. Byong-gyu's grandmother was taking care of the house, but she was too old and weak to manage everything. The grandmother was involved with the Soka Gakkai. She prayed every day that God would make her son go on the wagon and his family become wealthy.

Byong-gyu also said that what he and the family disliked most about their situation was going hungry. Through the winter they had eaten only flour paste soup and they were fed up with it. His uncle came once in a while to give them money to help with expenses and, from time to time, their neighbors would give them money.

Some days later I met Byong-gyu's father. He was kind and ostensibly gentle, but he had a serious drinking problem. When he drank, he became a different person. After that, I tried many times to persuade him to stop drinking. I told him to begin a new life. I visited him every day for ten days before one day he burst into tears.

"Mr. Kim. Thank you for your interest in someone like me. You're a good person. I'm going to do everything I can to break my drinking habit."

He fought a hard battle. When he wanted a drink, he asked his son to tie his hands to help him fight off temptation. He finally overcame his habit and got back to work.

His family would be happy again, if his wife came back. I visited everywhere I could think of where she might be staying. I thought that if I found her, I would be able to persuade her that her husband was a changed man. I would tell her that her mother-in-law was ill and her children in tears, awaiting her return, but I found no trace of her. I went to their home and offered a prayer at their grandmother's bedside, with everyone holding hands.

"Lord, please make our mother return. Please let her know that our father does not drink any more. Also tell her that our grandmother is so ill that her days are numbered, and please tell her how much we miss her."

The children wept as we prayed. I, too, became emotional. I took comfort in knowing that Byong-gyu's father had stopped drinking and felt I had achieved something, seeing him leave behind frustration and despondency and recover courage and hope.

BEYOND MR. CHOI'S HOUSE WAS MR. LEE'S. He and his family of six lived in a hut that was held up by three wooden poles. It was more of a teepee than a house. To support his family, Lee, at age 68, read people's fortunes, sitting on a mat on a street corner.

Dwellings in the Cheonggye-cheon slum.

His wife had attended a Catholic church before becoming a member of Soka Gakkai. She had changed her religion because of her sick son, Won-seop. Won-seop, then 26, had worked at construction sites before contracting an undiagnosed illness. When I met him, he had been bedridden for more than eighteen months and was extremely gaunt. I asked him whether he had been to a hospital. He said that he had been to a public health office and an x-ray had confirmed that he didn't have TB. The office would not treat him because it was only supposed to accept tuberculosis patients. Since then he had not visited a hospital.

He hissed when he coughed and his face became distorted. He lacked the energy to sit upright. There was nothing for him to do but wait for death.

When I suggested that I would arrange an appointment with a doctor, Won-seop drew 300 *won* from his pillow. He wanted to pay for the visit. He had collected the money, little by little, in anticipation of going to a hospital. My heart ached to think how desperately he wanted to go to a hospital.

He seemed to have little chance for recovery. I left the house saying that I would make an appointment for him and return as soon as possible. Returning to Hwalbin Church, I prayed to God that He find a way for Won-seop to recover.

I was having lunch, after my prayer, when I heard a shout from the corner of the alley, "Here comes the demolition crew!"

The term "demolition crew" had a shock effect on the people of shantytown. The whole town suddenly became tense and agitated, with people running all about. I jumped to my feet and went outside, where I found a demolition van parked on the embankment of the Cheonggyecheon. A group of ten crewmen was heading for one of the houses.

Slum residents have unmitigated animosity toward the demolition crew. They called the vans "the vehicles of the King of Hell" and the demolition crew "Hell's Messengers."

Apprehensive about whose house was going to be knocked down, people watched the men closely. That day seven houses were to be demolished. The first house was that of an old woman who lived alone. The crew approached her house and began to tear it down. Screaming at them in rage, the old woman tugged at the men as they hammered on her house.

"You bastard! You'll tear down my house over my dead body, " she shouted, but her scream went unheeded. The demolition was already under way. Having exhausted all other means to dissuade them from their work, she came out with a kitchen knife, threatening to kill the crew foreman. They simply took it away from her. Then she watched as the roof canvas was ripped off, which was in apparent retaliation for her attempt to stop them. When house owners did not resist or physically block them, the demolition crew would leave building materials such as roof canvas and building planks as little damaged as possible so they could be reused. Whenever owners resisted or swore at them, they would destroy everything.

Having lost her knife, the old women fell on the ground and cried.

"You bastards. You shits. I hope generations of your descendants all live to carry on your devil's work."

In the meantime, the demolition crew had already moved on to their second target, the house of a disabled veteran. Watching the crew knocking down his house, he grabbed a pole and wielded it, shouting. "There is no law in the world that allows the demolition of a house without notice, you SOBs. I regret I didn't die in the war."

He fought with the pole as ferociously as he had fought on the front line, but, like the old woman, he was no match for the demolition crew. They took away his pole, knocked him down, and kicked him.

As far as regulations were concerned, a notice was supposed to be issued several days before houses were demolished, to give occupants time to prepare. This did not always happen and the veteran's house was one such instance.

At the third house to be demolished, a woman sat in the middle of the room crying, holding her baby.

As the house was being knocked down, debris fell all around her, some of it landing on her stooped shoulders, which covered and protected her baby. The woman refused to leave until the demolition had stopped.

Other than the obvious injustice of the demolition itself, there was a practical reason for people to protect their dwellings. They wanted to protect the heating system that was beneath the floor. At their worst, the men would dig up the floors, heating system and all. People could rebuild a house on the same site, as long as the heating system was still intact, even though the frame of the house might be gone.

These people were from the lowest stratum of society. I pitied them, as they struggled to make a life for themselves and their families. I wished I could help. Fortunately for her, thanks to her heroic effort, the woman holding the baby was able to preserve her floor. The crewmen left after only poking some holes in it, leaving the heating system little damaged.

The last house to be demolished that day was the most pitiful. A woman lived there who was about to go into labor. She pleaded with the demolition crew to give her a few days because her baby was due. Rejecting her plea flatly, the foreman ordered his men to get on with the job. Sitting in the middle of the room with a blank expression, she seemed to feel her labor beginning, her body wincing intermittently.

Watching, I turned around to wipe my tears. My patience exhausted, I approached the foreman to complain.

"I know you have to do this because it's your job. Even so, this is going too far. You cannot treat a woman who is about to have a baby like this. This is inhumane. You must know how badly this will affect both the woman and the baby."

The foreman took his cigarette out of his mouth. "I know this is wrong. I didn't want to come here today, but I was ordered to. A high-ranking official is supposed to be going to the Walker Hill Hotel. The order was that we should get rid of all shacks that can be seen from the main streets leading to Walker Hill. Those that were demolished today are the ones whose roofs could be seen. We have no power to defy the order. We have to report the demolition with photographs. I don't know you, but you look like someone who has had a proper education. Please do not let the people rebuild their huts overnight so the roofs can be seen tomorrow. Let them set up something to provide shelter. I'll pretend I didn't see it."

I went back to the church. My wife said, "Let's bring the expectant mother over to our room. The baby does not deserve to come into the world exposed to the elements. We can sleep on the church floor."

I agreed with her, and we put the mother-to-be in a cart to bring her to the church. She repeatedly thanked us, but still seemed to be ill at ease. We left the woman alone in the room and arranged a bed for ourselves on the floor of the church.

After dinner that night, we went around to the houses that had been demolished. We gave everyone food and bedding and proposed that those who could not pitch a tent come over to the church for the night. Everyone turned us down, saying that they would stay at their old houses and put up with the cold, even though the shacks had all been pulled down. These people were strong survivors, like weeds along the roadside.

That night my wife and I stayed up late, talking. She said, "Watching the demolition today was awful. It's terrible to see how differently people live. At one end of the bridge, people live in luxurious houses and high-rise apartments, while at the other end people endure such abominable conditions. I'm afraid that what we're doing here may end up serving no purpose. It hasn't been easy for me to adjust to this life. Although I often want to get out of this place, to live a normal life among normal people, I can't because of your commitment to your work. Having gone through so much, at least I now better understand Jesus' love for the poor."

THE NEXT DAY, I HAD TO GO OUT TO FIND a way to treat Won-seop. My efforts took me to the Christian Medical Missionary Association. The Association, which was located in downtown Jongno, promised they would treat him if I brought him in.

Excited, I set off for shantytown. On my way back, it occurred to me that I had no way to transport Won-seop, who was already extremely frail, all the way downtown. The bus was not an option and a taxi would not have room enough to carry a patient. I thought that a jeep, popular among foreign missionaries, would be just the thing.

I visited Mr. Brown of the Australian Christian Mission to ask for help.

"Mr. Brown, I have a patient who lives in our shantytown. I have to get him to the hospital. May I use your car?"

"Do you think it'll do? I can let you use it, but I won't be able to drive you because I have a meeting tomorrow. You'll have to get some-one to drive it."

Encouraged by his words, I returned to shantytown to deliver the good news to Won-seop's family. There I learned that he had already drawn his last breath. I felt completely washed out. Won-seop's mother was crying.

"My poor boy! You should have held on for just one more day so you could go to the hospital."

His father despaired at the thought that he had sinned so much that he was now being punished, watching his son die before his very eyes. Won-seop's thin face had turned blue. I closed his eyes and prayed. During my prayer, his family all knelt with their heads down— the father who read fortunes for other people, the mother who attend-ed the Soka Gakkai, and his younger sister who was a member of Hwalbin Church.

"My Lord Jesus, please bless this young man. He lived a sorrow-filled life in this world. Please let him rest in heaven and allow this family to have new life. Give them your blessing and allow them to enjoy a happy life."

After the prayer, I tried to talk with the family about the funeral. I felt a commitment to his funeral, after my efforts to cure him had failed, but the family would say nothing. At long last, the father muttered, "We want to bury him tomorrow...." After that, they sat in silence because they couldn't afford funeral expenses.

I gathered the people in the community and we discussed the matter. For a funeral to be conducted, we needed to attend to three things. First, we needed a death certificate, issued by a doctor. A certificate was necessary to get burial approval from the ward office. Second, the body had to be washed and shrouded and we needed a coffin. And third, we had to call to arrange for a funeral coach to transport the body to a crematorium.

We divided the tasks. Hwalbin Church would take charge of getting the death certificate. The residents would wash and shroud the body and buy a coffin. Finally, the family said they would arrange for the funeral coach.

I set out to go about getting the death certificate. I could have gotten it from the hospital, if Won-seop had been treated there. There was no evidence to support the claim that he had died of a disease. The only document pertaining to his illness was from the public health office, which showed only that he did not have tuberculosis. The only option was to have a doctor come to the house to confirm his death. That, I discovered, would cost 50,000 *won*.

I was helpless. Everyone was relying on Hwalbin Church to take care of the death certificate, but I had no money to call a doctor and the funeral could not proceed without it. I went back to the church and knelt down on the straw mat to pray.

After my prayer, I went to the Christian Medical Missionary Association, where I met with the administrator, a Mr. Kim. He referred me to a Dr. Lee at the Ewha University Hospital. I went to visit Dr. Lee. His refusal was so abrupt that it dazed me. Still, I could not back off.

Pleading and begging, I followed at Dr. Lee's heels for four hours. I waited, standing in front of the door when he went to the men's room. I followed him and stood in front of the door after he entered the operating room to perform surgery. I waited standing right beside him when he had lunch. Finally, he relented and gave me the death certificate, but only on the promise that I would get out of his sight.

I was sorry for what I was doing, but I did not have the luxury of obeying the rules of etiquette or exhibiting good manners. Receiving the certificate, I bowed deeply and left the doctor in peace. Residents were waiting for me, confident that I would not come home empty-handed.

The death certificate wiped away the clouds of concern that were on the relatives' faces. I sent someone to the ward office to apply for burial approval. We also started making the coffin. We learned that making a coffin with recycled wood would cost about 1,500 *won*, whereas a new one would cost at least 3,500. After a round of discussion, we decided to go with recycled wood. We raised 4,000 *won* for the purpose. We agreed that after paying for the coffin, we would use the remainder of the money for other things.

A while later, with the coffin ready, we received burial approval from the ward office. The only task remaining was to call a coach to transport the body to the crematorium. The obstacle here, too, proved to be money. We needed at least 13,000 *won*, but had only 6,000. I went to a missionary by the name of Min because I recalled him driving a car that was longer in the back than regular sedans. I had no time to exchange proper greetings, but went directly to the point of my visit.

"I need to use your car tomorrow," I told him.

"Why do you need it?" he asked.

"I need to transport a body to a crematorium."

"Can you carry a body in a passenger car?"

"Cars are made for people. I figure, just because a person is dead doesn't mean he should not be allowed to go in a car. I'd have asked people to carry it, if the crematorium were nearby, but the nearest one is too far away to walk. I need your help because we can't afford a coach."

He looked at me for a moment and then promised to send a car at one o'clock the following afternoon. Buoyed by this promise, I returned to shantytown.

The next day, a car arrived to carry the body. It was red, and too gaudy for such a purpose, but we used it anyway. After a simple service, we headed for the crematorium. The cremation was surprisingly cheap; the entire process cost only 50 *won*. It was one of a few things in those days that the city government managed to get right.

EARLY THE NEXT MORNING, while I was having breakfast, a young man came to ask my advice. He told me his story.

"My name is Park. I'm from a village in South Gyeongsang province. Although on my birth certificate my last name is recorded as Park, the fact of the matter is that a Mr. Choi is my real father. I was born as a result of an affair my mother had with him. He was a friend of my mother's then husband, whose name was Park.

"After I was born, Choi told Park that he was my father and that he had come to take his son. Park became furious. He told Choi that what he was saying was impossible and they came to blows. The story got around the village and they both became laughing stock. Park did not send me to Choi, but growing up I had to put up with a lot of physical and verbal abuse from him. He used to hit me on the head, saying I wasn't his son. My life got worse as I grew older and began to bear a resemblance to Choi.

"This caused endless feuding between Park and my mother. At the time, I didn't know why or how I could be the cause of their arguments. After growing up, I moved out of the house, but I couldn't shake off the thought that my blood was dirty. That thought affected my behavior. There was no way I could lead a decent life because I was born dirty. I was destined to live dirty, and therefore didn't need to straighten myself out. This thought led me to lose all self-control."

At this point, he asked, "Do you believe that a person like me, who was born dirty, can get his life right? I envy people like you, who are born with clean blood."

"I understand why you regard yourself as dirty, but there is no such thing as dirty blood or clean blood. The problem is that you think your blood is dirty. I have a solution for you."

"What's that?"

"Change your blood."

"Change my blood? You know, I've thought seriously about that, but I heard from a doctor that a man can't live after getting more than one-third of his blood replaced at a time. There's no point changing my blood, if I die in the process."

"No, I don't mean that. I suggest that you replace your blood with Jesus' blood. People who believe in Jesus are said to receive new blood. The blood you received from your parents is destined for doom, but

Jesus' blood is salvation."

"You mean that by believing in Jesus I can change my blood? I've never heard of such a thing. If I believe in Jesus, my father's blood will leave my body and will be replaced with the blood of Jesus. I like that idea. I'd like to learn more. I'll come see you again."

After that he attended services regularly. He was eventually baptized. After the ceremony, he told me, "Pastor, my blood has been replaced with Jesus' blood. I'm grateful for all that you've taught me."

Watching him transform himself, I witnessed the magic of spiritual power. Who but Jesus could have done that?

AROUND THAT TIME, my own family fell on hard times. We had spent all the money we had gotten together to move to shantytown. The day of reckoning came earlier than we expected because we had financed everything ourselves, without outside help, making over a house to be used as the church, and helping ill and hungry people.

I felt frustrated when slum residents came to me to borrow money. They would put on a broad smile, even though they knew me only in passing. Embarrassed, I would ask them, "Do I look like I have money?" They responded boldly.

"Look, Mr. Kim. You're not as good as your word. When you came to my house the other night you said you were willing to help me. I need money, so I thought you'd help. I only want to borrow it."

Hearing this, I had no choice. To let them save face, I would lend them part of the money they requested. Although they insisted that it was a loan, no one ever paid me back.

Of all of the difficult tasks in life, helping the poor has to be one of the most difficult. In many cases, even after doing your best, you end up being criticized.

Once, on a routine visit to one of the houses on my rounds, I found a family hungry and with no food. I waited until near midnight to take them a package of flour, afraid that a handout from me might hurt their pride and cause some conflict with other people who were in the same situation. They welcomed me as if I were an angel from heaven. There were tears in their eyes and the kids jumped up and down with joy. I returned home with a happy heart.

About a week later, the lady of the house visited me at the church.

"Sir, we're out," she said.

I wondered what she was talking about.

"What are you out of?" I asked.

"My goodness, you've forgotten. We've run out of the flour you gave us the other night."

I then recalled that she was from the family I had visited to give the flour to. "Is that so?"

"I'm sorry to say this, but we need another bag. Someday we'll pay you back."

I was irritated. They had been given a package of flour. After that, they should have tried to earn their own living by collecting rags, paper, empty bottles, or whatever. They had not even tried, and now, having run out of flour, they were back, with their hands out for more charity. I disguised my feelings and gave them another package of flour.

The problem with giving out food is the effect the handout has on people's attitude. When the church helps once or twice, people are grateful. After they are helped four or five times, however, they lose their sense of gratitude and develop a different mindset. They come to think that the church is somehow obligated to help them and that they have a right to it.

Once I noticed this change of attitude in people I had helped, I felt betrayed. At that point, I would lose interest in them as people, but it did not stop there. When they sensed this change in me, they became dissatisfied with whatever they were given. Then they would pick arguments and cause trouble and eventually develop animosity toward me. I was caught in a dilemma. I wanted to help the poor, but did not know how to go about it.

One Sunday during service, a woman stood outside the church, shouting and swearing at me.

"Hwalbin Church, or whatever you call yourself, stop swindling people! You get money from the poor and divide the church take among yourselves, after giving out only a pittance to the rest of us. You should repent. I'll get to heaven ten times faster than any of you."

I stopped my sermon and looked out the window to see a woman to whom I had given flour four times before. After the fourth package, I refused her request for more, saying, "Ma'am, you've had enough. You should be ashamed of yourself. How can you expect the church to go on supporting you? How can you expect us to extend help only to you? There are a lot of other people who need our help."

Now she was shouting and swearing for the entire world to hear. I wanted to ignore her, but the young church members were furious.

"How could anyone be so shameless? Let's go out and throw her into the creek."

They moved to go out. I tried to hold them back, but they were determined to confront her.

"Pastor, she should wise up. If we let her get away with this, she'll come back again. We have to teach her a lesson."

They did not dare beat her. Instead, they pushed her backward. She fell on her back. When she got up, she was clutching her side.

"My side, my side," she growled. "You broke my ribs. Take me to the hospital, you bastards."

"Ma'am, if you're hurt, let's go to a hospital and have you x-rayed. You can talk to a doctor," I suggested.

"No, it's a waste of time. Just give me the money it'd cost."

This kind of nonsense was routine. With every experience, I became more skeptical about what I was doing. Finally, I concluded that missionary work in the slum should not be simply to provide help. I should not simply provide food to the hungry and medicine to the sick, so I redirected my missionary work.

"Hwalbin Church will change the way it helps people. From now on it will lend money only to people who want to start a business or undergo training to get a technician's license, if they are unemployed and lack technical skills." I spread my message in the slum.

Hearing this, a resident came up to me.

"Please trust me. Lend me enough money to get a cart and a few boxes of apples. With that I'll show you that I can get on my feet."

After the church arranged for the money, I made sure he knew that we expected him to repay the principal. He assured me he would.

"Certainly. How could I not pay you back? This is a lot of money. I swear you'll get it back."

Taking him at his word, I visited one of my college friends.

"I believe you'd like to participate in God's work as a Christian. I need your help. I will not ask you to donate money, because I know you earn only a monthly salary. Could you lend me money for a few months? I can't guarantee that I'll pay you interest, but I assure you that I'll repay the principal. I need the money to help a poor person start a business to make a living."

"I've heard that you're working for a good cause," he answered. "Our friends call you the conscience of the church. You say that you want to borrow money to help poor residents start businesses. I have to say, I'm not optimistic about your chances for success."

"I think that this is my calling, even though I may be destined to fail. I know of no way better than this to help these people," I told him.

"OK. I'll lend you the money anyway. I hope that everything works out the way you want it to."

After collecting money from friends and relatives, I called the man who had asked for the loan.

"I'll give you the money today to start your business. As I told you, I don't want any interest, but I'd like to make sure that you pay me back the principal. This money is neither mine nor the church's. I borrowed it from friends and relatives, after assuring them that I'd pay them back."

"No question about it. You can bet your life on it," he assured me.

"You don't have to go that far. Please just keep your word."

"Don't worry. Everybody here knows how trustworthy I am."

As with others, I had him sign an IOU, thinking that would oblige him to do as he promised. The standard IOU read simply:

IOU

I, _____, borrowed _____ from Hwalbin Church and promise to repay it on ____.

Signature: _____, *1972*

_____

To begin, he bought a secondhand cart and ten boxes of apples. Having heard his story, a number of people came to apply for loans.

One man said that he wanted to peddle secondhand items, if only he had seed money to buy a bicycle and some cash for expenses. Another man applied for a loan to study molding technology so he could get a job abroad. We screened people carefully and supported them as best we could. After they started their businesses, I often visited them to encourage them.

Later, as the date on which the apple peddler had promised to pay was approaching, a resident came to me.

"Pastor, do you know that the man you lent the money to, to start an apple business, has moved away?"

"No, I don't think he has. I saw him on the street yesterday, selling his apples."

"You're a sucker. He got his rent deposit back yesterday and moved away. You got ripped off. You should have given me the money instead of him."

If he left because he did not have the money to pay me back, he could have asked me to extend the deadline. The more this experience repeated itself, the more I came to doubt what I was doing. I was coming to the conclusion that I could achieve neither of my two goals—economic independence for people in the slum or my religious mission. But then, nobody said it'd be easy.

12

What Is God's World?

AROUND THIS TIME, SAUL ALINSKY, an American social reformer, visited our shantytown, having been recommended by the National Church Cooperatives (NCC). He introduced himself as a people's movement activist. He had been involved in the Community Organization Movement in Chicago and had made something of a name for himself.

After looking around Cheonggye-cheon, he asked me to gather church activity leaders for a meeting. When we came together, he spoke to us.

"This place is hell. This slum is the only one of its kind on earth. What are you doing about it? You have to agitate, organize, and demonstrate. Occupy City Hall. It'll get you apartments. Become a major nuisance. Push your way into rich people's houses. Make trouble. It'll earn you a housing project for the poor. Power is in the people."

His speech impressed me very much. Yes, that was it, I thought. That was the way to spread the Gospel. In my missionary work, I had provided flour, lent money, and bought medicine, but it had done little good. In fact, it had had a negative effect on attitudes. That approach no longer worked, I thought. The Gospel of Jesus is ever true, but the way to put it across has to change with time and age. I saw Alinsky's approach as appropriate for our people. I considered it a fifth Gospel, which should come between the books of John and Acts.

I would adopt Alinsky's approach to missionary work, to encourage people to band together and confront their problems. I studied his theory, and Pastors Park Hyeong-gyu and Cho Seung-hyeok and Professor Moon Dong-hwan helped me learn his philosophy.

Professor Moon also introduced me to the work of Paulo Freire, a Brazilian educator. Widely known for his book *Pedagogy of the Oppressed*, Freire worked to abolish illiteracy in Brazil. Living with farmers, he campaigned for them to learn to read. As they learned, they also got an education. His student-farmers then staged demonstrations to claim their rights. Ultimately, the Brazilian government banished him from Brazil.

I was so impressed with Freire's theory and his activist approach that I decided to practice it in the Cheonggye-cheon slum. I first set out to organize the slumdwellers. The Hwalbin Church building became a center for action. I prepared posters and put them up on the walls:

> *Alone Fall, United Rise.*

> *Die Standing Rather Than Live On Your Knees.*

On either side of the pulpit, I put up two posters with verses from the Bible:

> *I have come to bring fire on the earth, and how I wish it were already kindled! (Luke 12:49)*

> *Take heart! I have overcome the world. (John 16:33)*

As for organizing residents, I divided the 11,000 households into four sectors of approximately 3,000 households each. One church was set up for each group, the churches thereafter becoming the center of local activities. Hwalbin Church, the coordinating office, served one sector, while branches in Dapsimni, Yongdap-dong, and Majang-dong served the other sectors.

I organized the Cheonggye-cheon Shantytown Residents Society. The residents gathered at the church to elect a chairman, deputy chairman, and secretary-general. Under the Residents Society, we established five committees, each assigned to deal with specific matters in their sector.

The five committees worked in the areas of resident education, health management, income generation, cooperatives, and volunteer services. As activities got on track, the churches and their communities bustled with vitality. The churches became community centers and residents began to go to them more regularly.

Things went so well that I regretted not having taken a more activist approach earlier. Four or five months into the program, however,

Standing in front of the coordinating office of Hwalbin Church.

problems began to surface. Latent antagonisms caused the Residents Society to divide into two groups, the mainstream and the opposition. This division resulted in squabbles between the leaders of the two factions. The atmosphere in the community became tense, which negatively affected the church. In the end, people held the church responsible for the situation.

One resident said, "Our town had enough problems, even before Hwalbin Church came here. They only made matters worse. I wish the church would go away and take the troublemakers with them."

Concerned about the changing atmosphere, I convened a meeting of some thirty leaders of the Society.

"What's going on?" I began. "I'm embarrassed to hear that you people are involved in partisan squabbles. Now that we're all here together, let's get everything out in the open."

A member of the opposition came forward. "I'm going to come right out and tell it like it is. Those guys are crooks. They drink and gamble with church money. Our town won't be livable until they leave."

The mainstream members became furious. The chairman of the Residents Society responded on behalf of the mainstream group.

"What are you saying? Are you saying that I've taken someone's money? Did you see me?"

"Yes, I did. Where does the money come from that you drink with?"

"I drink with my own money. Do you think I drink with other people's money?"

"You don't have any money."

"So you're saying that you saw me take money. You're after the wrong guy," he said angrily, and then ran out of the church. Assuming that he had gone outside to calm down, I asked people to avoid using insulting language. At that point, the man who had run out came back, wielding a kitchen knife. Startled by this, I told the men to take away his knife before he hurt someone.

He pulled up his shirt and bellowed, his eyes filled with rage. "OK, you say you saw me take money. Then let's have a look inside my stomach and see if we can find it. If I took any, it'll be in here somewhere."

At that, he slit his stomach open, like a Japanese samurai committing *seppuku*. Blood spurted everywhere. He screamed in agony, gritting his teeth.

"Now, look for yourself. Do you see any money?"

Frightened by all this, I held onto the man and told someone to call a taxi. A few people ran out to get a taxi while I got a sheet from the other room and wound it around his stomach to stop the bleeding. We took him outside and along the bank of the Cheonggye-cheon. A taxi came and took him to Hanyang University Hospital.

Luckily, his rash act did not kill him, but that was not the end of it. He was supposed to stay in the hospital. Concluding that he had slit his stomach to show his innocence, residents collected money for him, out of sympathy.

With that money, he would sneak out of the hospital and go drinking. He would return to the hospital drunk, stagger around, babbling tunes, and scratching at his wound with his filthy hands. He frightened the nurses. "You can't do that. If you scratch your wound, you'll infect it," a nurse told him.

"Shut your mouth, girl. It's my life, not yours." He climbed into bed, still scratching. It was bound to become infected, and indeed it did. Not long afterward, he died from the infection. His death had a profound effect on me and on the community.

After shrouding and washing him, I had his body cremated. I brought a bag with his ashes to the church, put it under the pulpit and knelt to pray. I prayed all night. "God, was it wrong of me to come here? Should I leave? Am I qualified to do missionary work in the slum? I came here to help people find a better life, and now one of them is dead. How can I continue my work? Do you want me to leave and give up everything I've started?"

In despair and frustration, I repeated this prayer over and over. On the fourth day of prayer, I recalled a passage in Matthew. I was at a crossroads. I felt I might be undergoing the same test as Jesus in the desert: "Then Jesus was led by the spirit into the desert to be tempted by the devil. After fasting forty days and forty nights, he was hungry. The tempter came to him and said, 'If you are the Son of God, tell these stones to become bread.' Jesus answered, 'It is written: Man does not live on bread alone, but on every word that comes from the mouth of God.'" (Matthew 4:1-4)

I came to a realization. I had started my missionary work for the poor with a flawed objective. Reflecting on Jesus' words, I realized I was supposed to be serving up the word of God. Instead, I had forgone God's word to give people bread. As a result, I ended up going nowhere, failing to deliver either bread or the word.

Bread is necessary, but God should come first. If a human being is given only bread, he is stripped of humanity. That morning, I thought hard and went over my activities in the slum, one by one. Instead of giving up my work, I would change its direction and put greater emphasis on fundamentals. I would build an economy of bread on a foundation of God's word. Thus, I got off to a new start.

THERE CAME A POINT AT WHICH MY SAVINGS were exhausted. We had taken all of our money when we went to live in the slum. When it was gone, we were destitute.

I recorded in my diary how desperate life in the slum can be:

November 26, 1971. Sunny

It has been 50 days since I held a service to celebrate the found-ing of Hwalbin Church. I did not go to morning prayer today because I was hungry from having had no dinner last night. Lying under my blanket, I sang hymns, and thought how I could overcome this crisis. Our financial end came far earlier than I had expected and I have no idea what to do. We are managing on only flour.

My son, Dong-hyeok, complained that his stomach hurt be-cause he was hungry. His innocent comment made us laugh. I feel sorry for my wife, who has endured so well. She is brave to man-age a smile, even when she goes without meals. I am very sorry for her. She has never had to live in such conditions.

By eight in the morning, I felt dizzy. I now know why people say that hunger is so hard to put up with. I need to set up a long-term plan to get money to live on. Was it wrong of me to turn down external help and finance my work myself? Someone called me "Don Quixote" and said that I would not last long.

Hwalbin Church was founded on a new concept. I therefore have to build it step by step, even though I am destined to go through hard times along the way. If God is happy with Hwalbin Church, He will clear the path.

Back to reality, however, I am now hungry and the hunger is hard to endure. I need to eat something. My wife brought me a bowl of powdered milk. It made me feel a little better. Only now are we coming to grips with hunger. I don't understand how for so long people here have taken hunger for granted without looking for a way out of it.

How do they endure the pain? Do they accept it as their fate? I have seen people lying on floors, not complaining, not demand-ing, and not resisting. Suffering as I have seen them suffer, I find the pain harder to bear than I thought. Why can they not pull them-selves out of their life of hunger?

Is it because they are used to it, or is it because of the social system? Is it from bad policies? Are they victims of the social structure, or is it because of their own incompetence, laziness, or corruption? After falling into the slum, why can they not escape from it? Their mindset may be partly responsible. I have heard that they have a mindset that leads them to a life of poverty, but that cannot be.

Even I find myself incapable of thinking about the future, now that I am hungry. Incompetence and lethargy are the result of poverty, not the cause. I have to extricate myself and my family from this hunger, if we are to help others.

I will be able to lecture on escaping poverty only when I find a way to struggle clear of it myself. How can I do that? Get a job? Start a business? Collect money? I have no idea where to begin.

I need to find a way out for these people. In this sense, going outside for help, such as support from a big church or by becoming a teacher, are not real options. Only when I can find a way that they can follow will they have no excuse for their lack of diligence, saying, "You can do it because you're different from us. Having lived in poverty for a long time and with no education, we're not up to it."

Most of the residents are from farming areas and came to Seoul with no plan. With no skills or special talents, they can engage only in labor. What can they do? Is there anything that I can do with them? Yes, there is. We can pick rubbish. By picking rubbish, I will rise above this situation.

That Sunday, because of my hunger, I could not deliver a proper sermon. Making an effort to lead the service, I stood at the pulpit, having had only water for several days. I felt dizzy and nauseous.

Struggling to keep myself from falling over, I read from the Bible and was about to begin my sermon. I looked out over the congregation, only to see their faces blurred, taking on the appearance of bowls of rice. Thinking to myself that I needed to eat before I could preside at services, I spotted Choi, who had been working as a rubbish picker, looking up at me.

Seeing him reminded me of the diary I had been keeping. I decided to have a chat with him after the service. I managed to finish the service and spoke with him.

"Can I go out with you to pick rubbish?"

"You're going to pick rubbish?"

"Yes, I'd like to."

"You must be kidding."

"No, I'm not. As you know, Hwalbin Church is founded on the spirit of self-reliance. For me to speak to residents about self-reliance, the church has to demonstrate that it is self-reliant. So far, self-reliance has only been an ideal. The truth is that the collection from the church amounts to only two or three hundred *won* per week. I need to make a living, too. After pondering it for a long time, I thought that perhaps picking rubbish would be ideal. You aren't going to turn me down now, are you?"

"I know what you're saying, but how can a person like you go out and pick rubbish? That's for poor people like me."

"What are you talking about? You didn't hear my sermon. Jobs don't discriminate between the rich and the poor. Living here, I've learned that the lowest form of life is the person who leaves his family to starve. The person who lives off help from others is only slightly better. The spirit of self-reliance is a treasure worth guarding. I'm going to make my living by picking rubbish. Do you know what I'm trying to say?"

"Yes, I do. You inspire me. Good! Let's work at it together."

Thus, I launched my career as a rubbish picker. One of the reasons I chose rubbish picking was that it did not require a big investment to get started. With a 900 *won* investment in a basket and 40 *won* in a clamper, I could begin right away. For the time being, I would share a cart with Choi.

Next day, I borrowed 4,000 *won* from my classmates at the seminary. I bought a sack of flour and put the remaining 3,000 *won* in a closet. I would invest it later in my rubbish-picking business.

At dawn the following day, I went out with Choi. We had to be out before garbage trucks came by because afterward there would be nothing left to pick over. Walking the quiet streets, I asked Choi, "How much can I expect to earn if I work hard?"

"It's all up to you. You can earn from one to two thousand *won* a day, if you only go after stuff that's abandoned, but as high as five to six thousand *won* if you sneak stuff that's unattended."

"What's the difference between abandoned and unattended?"

"Are you serious? Use your head. Unattended stuff is stuff that's left around people's houses. Abandoned stuff is stuff that's discarded in trash containers. You can earn good money, if you pick up stuff that's unattended. Otherwise, you have to settle for pennies."

An actor playing Kim Jin-hong in the film
version of his life is dressed as a rubbish picker.

"You mean you take stuff that belongs to people?"

"Yes. You've just started doing this kind of work, so I can see why you're asking these questions. Understand, however, you can't make a living just by picking rubbish. They say that even a saint needs to follow the worldly way of doing things. I'm sure you're going to think differently about this job after working at it a while."

"I'll let you know in a month. For now, I'll concentrate on picking up stuff that's been abandoned."

"Fine by me. Follow me and I'll show you what to do. There are three kinds of paper. The first is brown paper. That's paper that's used for making flour bags, cement bags, and cardboard boxes. That's the best kind of paper and sells for the highest price. The second kind of paper is newspaper. The third we call five-color paper, which sells for the lowest price. When you pick rubbish, you don't take just anything. You have to be selective and take stuff that you can sell. Not all rubbish is good rubbish."

On my first day on the job, following Choi around, I learned how to deal with different kinds of rubbish and the jargon of the trade. Picking rubbish turned out not to be as bad as I had imagined.

THAT NIGHT, AT AROUND ELEVEN O'CLOCK, a young man on his way home from work, was beaten and robbed of his month's pay by thugs from the shantytown. He was crying and had a bloody nose. I took him to the church and, while cleaning him up, asked what had happened.

After his father died, he was the sole provider for his mother and two sisters. His mother was barely able to walk, having suffered a heart attack from the shock of his father's death. When he said he lost 5,300 won, I gave him 3,000 won that I had in my drawer.

Thugs often robbed young workers, particularly on payday. Even worse, they would sexually assault girls, but residents would pretend not to hear their cries for help.

There was one such incident when a girl's cries for help were so loud that I hurried toward her with a flashlight. I intentionally raised my voice, shouting, "We're coming." A distance away, I came upon three young men staring up at me from the embankment.

As I approached, one of them shouted, "Who the hell are you guys? You wanna die? I'll cut you open."

Waving the flashlight up and down, I shouted. "Hold on, we're coming."

Getting closer, I could see one of the three turn around to walk away. He told his friends, "I don't feel like doing this." The other two followed reluctantly, one of them pulling up his trousers.

I ran down the embankment to find a girl of about twenty, crying. I felt sorry for her and did not dare flash the light on her. I lowered the flashlight to around her feet.

"Are you OK?"

She turned around and ran off into the dark, without saying a word.

I realized that I needed to organize a town watch team to protect the community. The people of the shantytown were often victims of robbery because the police did not come around. I thought that perhaps the church could take up the role of the police.

THE NEXT DAY, ON MY WAY TO PICK RUBBISH, I had no money to buy a basket. My wife gave me 1,000 *won*. Surprised, I asked her where she had gotten the money.

"I was saving it for an emergency."

"You had this money when we had no food?"

"I couldn't spend it on food because that would be just consuming. This is different. This is an investment that'll pay off."

Leaving the house, I saw a woman with a baby on her back, looking at us from a distance. I approached her, thinking that she must have a reason for coming around so early in the morning.

"Ma'am, do you have business with the church? I'm the pastor here."

The woman stood silently, with her head down. I realized she had a problem and asked my wife to have a talk with her. The woman's voice was barely audible.

"My husband got drunk and assaulted another man. Now he's in jail. I'm going to my mother's because I'm about to have a baby. My husband still has two months left on his sentence."

At this point, she fell silent again.

Sensing what she wanted to say next, my wife asked whether she needed money to go to her mother's house. She nodded. My wife asked where her mother lived and what the fare was. She mentioned a distant town and said that it would cost her 700 *won*.

"Then you'll need 1,000 *won* because you'll have to eat along the way."

Saying this, she turned to me and told me to give the woman the 1,000 *won* she had given me. The woman said nothing. Her eyes filled with tears. She took the money, turned around, and walked off.

With no basket, I met Choi and learned more about picking rubbish. As midday drew closer, and we began to get hungry, Choi picked up some rice that had been left in a plastic bag in front of a wealthy person's house. At the next house, he picked some drumsticks out of the garbage.

"Why are you taking chicken legs out of the garbage?" I asked.

"I'll have them for lunch. Why? Are you saying this food's too dirty to eat? I'm not going to eat them as they are. I'll boil them first, so there won't be any problem. You won't catch on to this business until you rid yourself of the prejudice that rubbish is dirty. I'm sure you'll get over it in a few days."

Arriving at where he had left his cart, he made a fire with some branches and went over to a nearby residential area to get more food. Returning, he mixed the rice with some *gimchi* and bean paste he'd collected and put them on the fire, along with the chicken legs. He offered me some of his lunch.

I turned it down because I could not bring myself to eat it. Choi began to wolf it down. Watching him, at first my stomach rebelled, but soon I joined him. I persuaded myself that in my line of work, I couldn't be choosy about what I ate.

Choi listed for me the benefits of being a rubbish picker. A rubbish picker can get everything he needs from the rubbish. It's his supply yard. Ashtrays, floor covering, pots, bedding, gas stoves—you name it. They all come from the rubbish. Eating lunch, he went down the list enthusiastically. In fact, he said his house was furnished with stuff he had picked out of people's trash.

Choi's romantic rationalization of his life as a rubbish picker impressed upon me man's need for dignity, that regardless of what a person may have to do to survive, it's possible to regard it in a positive light.

THAT AFTERNOON, RETURNING HOME, I found that one of my friends had sent me 3,000 *won*. The money came with a letter saying that he hoped that my hard work for a good cause would bear fruit. My wife and I agreed that it had been the right thing to give the money to the woman that morning. The 1,000 *won* we had given her had come back threefold. That night I fell asleep straightaway.

In the middle of the night, a noise woke me up, and I found someone shining a flashlight on me. I pulled up myself upright and was confronted by one of our neighbors. He was holding a knife under my nose. The knife was small and the blade was covered with rust. I could not help but smile at how unprofessionally the man was going about it.

"Hey, why are you doing this? What kind of a knife is that? It is so dull that I doubt that it could cut hot butter."

"Pastor! I heard that you pastors turn your cheek when you get slapped. I was gambling and ran out of money. I need to borrow some from you. I'll pay you back later."

"You came to borrow money and you're holding a knife on me? If I didn't know better, I'd say you were holding me up."

He put the knife back in his pocket and begged me. "I know I'm crazy. I gambled away the money my son earned working all month and I can't go home until I get it back. There's no way I can go home empty-handed. Please lend me some money."

"How much did you lose? How much do you need to make up for?"

"I'd be grateful for anything you could afford."

I don't know why, but I felt I had to help him. I gave him the 3,000 *won* that my friend had sent me.

"I'm not giving you this money to finance your gambling. This is to make up for your son's pay."

I could see he was not happy with the amount, but he thanked me and left. Early the next morning my wife woke me up to say that I had a visitor. It was the man who had come for money the night before. His visit made me uneasy, but he insisted upon coming in. I took him into the church.

Before he sat down, he grabbed my hands. "Pastor Kim, forgive me for my behavior last night."

With my hands awkwardly caught between his, I replied, "Don't mention it." I wondered whether the money had helped.

With his eyes half-closed, he pulled a large roll of money out of his pocket. It looked as if he had made a killing with the 3,000 *won*.

He counted 3,000 *won* out of the wad and gave it to me. "Here's the money I owe you."

Then he became serious, saying, "Pastor Kim, I'd also like to make a donation. Do you accept this kind of money?"

I felt uncomfortable about accepting a donation of money earned from gambling, but I did not feel I could turn it down either. "What happened?" I asked. "You seem to have won a lot for just one day. Tell me about it."

"Until yesterday, in my ten years of gambling I had never lost more than a little money. Never have I had such bad luck as I had last night. I lost everything I had. I came to you because I had nowhere to go. The church money was very lucky and turned my fortune around. I won everything back, and it was all thanks to Jesus. I'd like to donate some to the church. The rest I'll give to my wife. I'm washing my hands of gambling from now on. I'd like to believe in Jesus. Please show me how."

"Thank you," I replied, "but you don't have to make a donation. Why don't you give it all to your wife?"

"No, I'm serious," he said, showing no sign of backing down. "Please take this."

Giving in to his persistence, I told him to put the donation in the church collection box, just as any of our church members would do. He seemed to be bothered by this, but soon went to the collection box at the entrance and put in his donation.

Opening the collection box, following the next Sunday service, I found 7,000 *won*. If he felt he could donate such a large sum, he must have won a considerable amount.

EVERY DAY, AFTER EARLY MORNING PRAYERS, I would go out to pick rubbish, coming home at two or three o'clock in the afternoon.

Then I usually followed a routine of visiting the sick, counseling, chatting with people, mediating quarrels, and so on. I was always busy and got to have some influence in the town, such that people would come to me when they were involved in disputes.

Slumdwellers were often involved in quarrels. Their quarrels were sometimes fatal, with one person stabbing another. When a quarrel ended in a fatality, someone would contact the church. The young men in the slum had no fear of going to jail after being involved in such incidents. On the contrary, they would boast of their exploits, referring to themselves as "beneficiaries of a government scholarship."

Winter was particularly harsh in the slums. From spring through autumn, men could work at construction sites and women could peddle things. During the long winter, however, there were no jobs. Construction came to a halt because cement would freeze and peddling was impossible because people closed their doors tightly to keep out the cold. Kiosk businesses in the street also suffered because everyone was always in a hurry to get out of the cold.

Winter in the slums is cruel. When cold weather set in, some people would commit petty crimes to land in jail so they would not have to worry about food and a warm place to sleep. They would spend the winter in jail and be released in the spring.

One day, after finishing my rubbish picking, I came back to a big commotion in the shantytown. Guessing that something must have happened, I asked whether there had been an accident.

"Of sorts," was the reply. "There's been a fight. We've been here several times to fetch you. It's a good thing you're back."

They took me to where the fight had been. Spectators packed the area. The people made way for me as I passed through the crowd to the house. A church member caught me by the sleeve, "Pastor, it's dangerous in there. One man stabbed another and is threatening to stab anyone who goes near. Don't go in now. Give him time to calm down."

"What happened to the man who was stabbed? Was he taken to a hospital?"

"No. The fellow with the knife is standing in the doorway, keeping everyone out. No one knows if the other guy is dead or alive."

It was then that a rumble came from inside of the house, followed by a scream. "Please help me. He's going to kill me."

Then there was silence. I could not wait until the situation sorted itself out. The man wielding the knife was the vilest man in town. His cruelty was unrivaled. Perhaps the victim could be saved, I thought. There was no time to waste.

Previously, the man with the knife had stripped his wife, dragged her out of the house, and beat her in front of everyone. After that, she killed herself by taking poison, leaving behind a young daughter. Watching his wife throwing up blood after taking the poison, he was said to have shouted, "Die, bitch." He seemed to be possessed by an evil spirit.

I went inside to calm him down. I found the victim slumped on the floor, while his assailant stood over him with a kitchen knife in his hand. The victim was breathing heavily, his hands clasped over his stomach. Blood was oozing out from around his hand. I asked a young man nearby to call a taxi and went inside. I was afraid, but I put on the bravest face I could. Someone called from behind.

"The pastor's going in. Let's go in with him and get this guy."

I waved my hands to dissuade them. The devil-man inside took up a defensive position. I looked into his eyes. They were full of anger. Looking at him, I saw the face of evil.

I was so fearful that I prayed to myself. "Lord, please have pity on this vicious man." I pictured Jesus' eyes and how they would have appeared when He saw the woman who had committed adultery. I told myself that those were the eyes the man needed to see. Putting an expression on my face indicating that I understood him, I said to him, "You're angry, but you have to stop punishing yourself and others because of your anger."

Then I turned my head to look at the victim. The devil-man's eyes followed mine. I took the opportunity to move closer to him. He did not change his position.

I felt that I needed to say something, but nothing came to mind. Smiling at him, I stepped closer and held out my hands. He turned the point of the knife downward. I held my hands out further. He handed me the knife and ran out.

I called two young men to come inside and help me remove the victim, who was complaining about the pain. I told them to take him out to where they could get a taxi. Fortunately, the man's condition was not life-threatening.

The devil-man's adventure that day ended without further casualties, but it was not long before he was at the center of another violent encounter, one that had a worse outcome.

He was drinking in a bar when a young man passing by inadvertently kicked some charcoal ashes onto his clothes. Seeing this, the devil-man shouted at the young man, "You wanna die? What are you doing, kicking ashes on me?"

The young man, who also lived in the slum, was not a stranger to violence and was only too willing to take up the challenge. He shouted back, "What are you yelling about? Chill out!"

Furious with his retort, the devil-man grabbed a knife from the kitchen, ran at the young man, and plunged the knife into his stomach before anyone could stop him. The young man died where he fell. For that, the devil-man would later be sentenced to twenty years in prison.

I pitied the people in the shantytown, many of whom had no respect for their fellow man and little understanding of how to get along in society. They would pick a fight for any reason. I felt that if only they tried to understand one another better and worked together, they could achieve something constructive.

THE MEMBERSHIP OF HWALBIN CHURCH continued to grow, while I made a living, such as it was, picking rubbish. In the community, I continued with Operation DDT and TLC Therapy. Failing to find space to sit down in the church during services, some people would pray standing at the rear. Others gave up attending services, for want of space. To expand the church, I knocked down the walls of our adjacent living room.

December was upon us, and the church held a party to celebrate its first Christmas. The children cheered everyone up with songs and dances and young men performed a play. The play, which I had written, was about residents joining hands to defeat the demolition crew. The theme guaranteed the play's success.

When the actors played a scene of people defeating the demolition crew, the audience stamped their feet and clapped their hands. I hit on the theme of the demolition crew because I wanted to tell a story related to something from the lives of the people. I learned a lot from watching their enthusiastic response to the performance.

Just as God descended upon the world because he loved human beings, sinful though they were, the church should love and live with the people in the slum, who were living with grief, hunger, pain, and abandonment. Missionary work begins with sharing their pain.

The ceremony of our first Christmas became a celebration for the entire town. Swept up in the spirit, a shop owner distributed free snacks and a bar put a pot of *makgeoli* out in the public area so anyone who wanted could have a drink.

I learned that my mission in the slum should not be simply to build a church and hold services. I became excited about the future of Hwalbin Church, sensing an energy source in the people that would pull them out of poverty-ridden fatalism.

After the Christmas party, the atmosphere of the town changed. Children, who used to sing adult pop songs such as "I Like Women Better," were now singing wholesome songs, such as "Good Children Get Up Early" and "Amazing Grace," which they learned in church. The number of fights diminished and mothers began to exercise some control in scolding their children. Most of the members of the Soka Gakkai were now turning to Hwalbin Church.

Religion should teach people to put value on life. I respect any religion that does this, but I did not like the Soka Gakkai because it deceived people. It made people believe that it could heal the sick and would bring prosperity. It took advantage of the weakness and ignorance of the poor. Marx pointed out that "Religion…is the opiate of the masses." The Soka Gakkai was an example of how religion can exercise power over people. There are leaders in the Christian community who are not very different from the Soka Gakkai. Any church or faith that does not attempt to bring out humanity in people or contribute to improving their living conditions or enhancing their sense of self-respect is not a church of Jesus Christ.

The last day of 1971 arrived. Church members gathered in the church an hour before midnight. Hwalbin families held a fellowship rally, beginning at 11:30. We were full of joy, although we had to substitute cheaper wheat flour for rice flour to make traditional dishes to celebrate the New Year.

I addressed the congregation. "What is God's world? It is a world of love. God's world does not require money. It requires love and that there be no shantytown or demolition crew. God's world is where humans are treated like humans and get along with one another. We, the Hwalbin Church family, may not be rich, but we belong to God's world. Anyone who practices love in Jesus can live in God's world."

After the service, we had our New Year's dishes and we all sang. A singing contest and a traditional Korean chess match followed. Everyone was happy. As we played together, we felt the hard times of the past year drain from our bodies.

We would do our best to serve Jesus in the Cheonggye-cheon slum in 1972. Then everyone went home.

PART TWO

Exodus from Seoul

13

Strive and Succeed

T HE NEW YEAR BROUGHT TROUBLE. At its opening, we received a letter from the mayor's office, giving us notice that our church building was condemned to be demolished. It read:

NOTICE

Because the *Hwalbin Church building* is an illegal structure, you are required to remove it by the specified date. Should you fail to comply with this order, the building will be forcibly demolished.

Office of Mayor
January 2, 1972

Although the building was illegal when it was put up, it had subsequently been licensed by City Hall, which issued a certificate to that effect.

Squatters' makeshift houses began to appear in Seoul in the late 1950s. This situation was aggravated over the years by series of political events that resulted in large sections of the city being transformed into slums. Driven out of rural areas by the successive failures of the government's farm policy, many people had migrated to the city and built huts on any vacant land they could find.

Against this background, the Seoul municipal government decided to legalize houses that had been built illegally before 1970, but declared a crackdown on structures built without permits afterward. The building that served as home for Hwalbin Church dated back to 1962, and was among those grandfathered under the policy.

Out of the blue, and without explanation, Seoul City Hall had condemned our building. I was determined to find out why they had gone back on their word and contacted some people I knew who had connections in the Seongdong-gu* township office. I later discovered there were two reasons for their decision:

First, the bureaucrats thought that the church's name sounded suspicious and that we were involved in provocative activities. They reasoned that the church should be punished for attracting many slum area residents. The concern was that if the church's activities went unchecked, it could later become a source of serious trouble.

Second, the township office received a report that during the previous Christmas season Hwalbin Church had staged a controversial play in which slum residents ganged up on a demolition crew and ran them off the property. The authorities were angry that the church had staged a play that was of other than a religious nature, believing it could pit citizens against civil servants. They concluded that the church was a rebellious force that might at some future time challenge their policy with regard to slum dwellings.

The response of the township office to the situation was to demolish the church building. After thinking about how to cope with their move, I brought the issue to a forum of slum residents. I showed the notice to the congregation during one of our nightly services in the church. As I expected, they were outraged and called for immediate action.

---

*A *gu* is equivalent to a township.

One angry resident said, "Why is our church being singled out?"

Another said, "I'd like to know what their real intentions are."

"We should unite and do something about it," others shouted.

One elderly man, however, tried to calm them down. He said, "Please, listen. I don't think we have to get tough about this yet. It might be better if we were to first write to the authorities, asking them to hold off on taking action. Then perhaps we should send representatives to the township office and City Hall to explain our situation. Should they ignore our plea and move to tear down our building, then a showdown might be unavoidable."

A chorus of approval followed. No one voiced disagreement.

At the time, owners of makeshift homes were not allowed to make any improvements on their dwellings, even when deadly carbon monoxide escaped from a heating unit and seeped into the living area.* Whenever any repairs were carried out, the houses involved faced immediate summary demolition.

City Hall would leave most illegal dwellings alone, but they would not tolerate any repair or refurbishment.

The roofs of most of the shacks were frail and leaked when it rained. They were constructed in such a way that every year seven or eight slum residents died because of carbon monoxide leaks. Many children suffered from bronchitis, pneumonia, and skin diseases because of the moisture inside the shacks. To achieve even minimum comfort and safety, slum residents had no choice but to repair their roofs, put in heaters, and ventilate their rooms, even though their action would bring the demolition crew down upon them.

These crews were vigilant in spotting the slightest change, including repairs that were carried out without even the neighbors knowing about them. Rumor had it that authorities had informants in the community to report any repairs. Needless to say, people in the slum were extremely resentful and defiant toward the authorities. The community was, in fact, one big time bomb, waiting for a spark to set it off.

It was late in 1971 when a high-ranking official from City Hall

---

*The heating system in inexpensive Korean homes was fueled by molded coal briquettes. When first lit, briquettes give off carbon monoxide that, if not ventilated, could kill anyone in the closed space.

came through, riding in a car, lecturing slumdwellers, mostly women, on their civic responsibility. "Why do you build here and live in houses that are built without permits? Democratic citizens have an obligation to respect the law."

The women, who had been anticipating help from the official, became furious.

"You son of a bitch. You like to talk about law, eh? You tell us to get permits. You sound like someone who was born with a permit. Hey, people! Anyone born with a permit should have special balls, too. C'mon, let's find out," one woman said, rushing toward him.

Dwellings in the Cheonggye-cheon slum.

Others joined her in attacking him. "Why not? Take off his pants!"

The official was horrified and struggled to free himself as the women started to unbuckle his belt and remove his pants. The women would not let him go and he lost his composure. Only with the help of his assistant, his driver, and a community leader was he able to extricate himself from the mob and flee. He was so terrified that, in his haste, he left one of his shoes behind.

The women brought the shoe to the church and said, "Pastor Kim, this shoe belongs to that fellow who was born with a permit. You keep it for us. If he comes back to get his shoe, tell him next time he won't get off so easy."

It was shortly after this episode that we received notice that the church would be torn down. It was not surprising that the people were enraged by the notice, since at one time or another everyone in the slum had been threatened by the demolition crew. They wanted release for their pent-up wrath and fought back.

At a community meeting, five representatives were selected to deal with the problem. They drew up a petition, gathered hundreds of signatures, and sent it to the mayor's office and to the office of the Seongdong-gu township chief. The petition read:

> Hwalbin Church has contributed greatly to the education, health, and youth guidance for slum residents in the Seong-dong-gu area. The church building is not only a church, but a community center and a symbol of hope for some sixteen hundred households. Therefore, we, the residents, request that the notice, issued by the Seoul city government for the demolition of the church, be withdrawn.

Days passed after the petition was sent, but we heard nothing. Because there had been no response from the authorities, we breathed a sigh of relief, thinking that the petition had exerted an influence on them. As we were to find out before long, however, we were wrong.

IN THE SLUM, A WOMAN DIED. She was the first casualty that year that was a direct result of the city's demolition campaign. It was tragic.

The woman was twenty-nine years old, the mother of three young children, and had long suffered from tuberculosis. I had gotten to know her the previous fall, when I was visiting households in the slum as part of the DDT Operation.

Her husband, Park, until recently had been a bus driver, but had lost his driver's license because of reckless driving. She told me that it would require money for her husband to get back his license, and that was something they didn't have.

Park was always drunk. I told him to get a grip on himself, come to his senses, and stop drinking. "Wouldn't you rather pay for your wife's medicine or get your license back?" I asked, but he always said that it was not he but his friends who were paying for the drinks.

I knew that Park, himself, was not worth feeling sorry for, but I felt compelled to see to the welfare of his sick wife and three small children. I could not turn my back on the family. Beginning with our first meeting, I had worked to bring her back to health. Almost every day, I stopped by to give her streptomycin shots and have her take medicines for her TB. She started to recover and I was feeling a sense of relief, thinking that she might get well by the following spring.

Trouble started, however, when to keep her warm, we repaired her heating system. Immediately afterward, on a cold day, we paid the price for trying to keep the winter at bay, by watching the house being torn down. A few days later, she received a summons.

It was standard practice to send such a notice after an illegal building was demolished. Then, in a summary proceeding, fines were levied against the wrongdoer. In this case, Park, as head of the household, did not appear for the hearing, and a warrant was issued for him to be brought in. When the police showed up to take him in, he was not home. Instead, they arrested his wife.

While they were taking her away, the police told the children, "Find your father and tell him to report to the police station. Otherwise, your mother can't come home."

The next morning, she returned home, exhausted. She was barely able to crawl back and collapsed on her doorstep, having spent the night in a cold cell. She did not recover. A few days later, she died, suffering from high fever and delirium. She did not close her eyes, even in death, as though she was so worried about her three children that she refused to leave.

As I performed her funeral, I felt uncontrollable helplessness. It was difficult to acknowledge that I was of no help to these poor people when that was how I had defined my mission. On my way home from the Byeokje Crematorium, I headed for the Han River Bridge with all that remained of her, a handful of ashes. I let the white powder drop through my fingers into the river below and murmured, "You don't belong here in Seoul. This place is too dirty…filthy for good people like you. Go and rest in the great ocean, where there are no demolition crews or detention cells. Be happy there. The deep warm ocean will comfort you and console your tired soul."

Wiping away the tears, I pledged to myself, we should build a society free from this kind of tragedy. I did not know it at the time, but this was a pledge that I would make many times over, during the years that followed.

BEGINNING THAT DAY, I WAGED A CAMPAIGN to fight tuberculosis. TB was the most prevalent disease in the slum. Many of the people suffering from TB were unable to work. This was a loss, not only for the individuals and their families, but also for the nation.

With the aid of the Korean Tuberculosis Association, we called in a mobile TB clinic. Everyone in the sixteen hundred households in the slum was x-rayed and tested. As a result of these tests, we identified two hundred sixty-three people who had TB.

Personal health record cards were prepared and updated at Hwalbin Church to monitor their medical treatment. I encouraged the patients individually to get medical help at the public health office, taking advantage of free treatment programs available to them.

A problem developed when after several visits for treatment, patients refused to return to the health offices. For TB patients, it was important that they continued their treatment. Once they stopped it, they could not be cured with the same medication because they would have developed a resistance to it. As a practical matter, discontinuing their medication meant death for TB patients.

I sat down with each of them to persuade them to continue their treatment and asked why they were refusing to return to the clinic.

"I'm not going back there. I'd rather die than go back."

"Why? Why not go and get your treatment? It's free."

"It's because they don't treat us like human beings."

"Just put up with them for another six months and you'll be cured. Ignore them. Your consumption is being treated. That's the important thing."

"No. I'd rather go without treatment. I'll never go back there. Ever."

"What do they do there that makes you so upset?"

"Go and see for yourself. You'll see what I mean."

Pride is all that slumdwellers have to live for. Mistreatment at the public health office must have hurt their pride. I decided to find out for myself what was driving them away. I went to the office, along with a few patients.

After registering and waiting an hour, one of the patients was called in. When he approached a nurse, she asked, "Did you bring your phlegm?"

"Phlegm? I don't know what that is."

"You were told last time to collect and to bring in your phlegm."

"No. I don't know anything about it. You never told me that."

"Well, you heard me now. Bring in your phlegm."

"Can't I collect it now?"

"I don't care. Just do it."

Then she shut the door in the patient's face. I started to understand why the patients were so reluctant to come here. If all two hundred sixty-three patients were going to receive medication, something needed to be done quickly to improve relations between the health office and the patients. I knocked on the door, went in, and talked to the nurse.

"You just told the patient to collect phlegm. Could you be more specific as what you want him to do?"

"Are you a patient?"

"No. I'm a friend of his."

"What do you want? I just told him what to do. Come on. We're busy here. I don't need to show you the door, do I?" Then she turned away. "Next patient!" she shouted out the window. She didn't even bother to look up at me.

I found her response insolent and flew off the handle. "Damn it! All I asked was that you make yourself clear!"

She raised her voice. "Don't you swear at me. What are you trying to prove?"

"Who do you think you're yelling at, girl?" I lifted my arm, as if I were going to hit her.

She burst into tears and fled. Shortly afterward, several men in white gowns appeared, ready for a fight.

"Who's making trouble here?" a burley orderly bellowed.

"It was that man in the blue jacket. He's the one," the nurse said, pointing at me.

Glaring at me, the man shouted, "What's all this business with the nurse?"

"He said I was rude," the nurse chimed in, sarcastically.

Before I could say anything, the guy slapped me across the face. The slum residents quickly closed in around him. Noticing the uneasiness of the crowd, he called out for the police.

One of our people approached me and asked, "Should we fight them? This is as good a time as any."

"No. Let's go home. We'll come back tomorrow with more people. Call everyone out."

When I stepped out, the residents followed me, some breathing heavily with resentment. One of the women started to weep softly, saying that it was because of them that I had been hit. Some of the men complained about not having fought back.

"That's OK, ma'am. Something good will come of today's incident," I said, comforting the woman who was sobbing.

As soon as we returned, we got in touch with all the TB patients who hadn't accompanied us.

We told them, "Be at Hwalbin Church at nine tomorrow morning. We're all going to visit the health office together. We're going to get the treatment we need. Everyone who can is asked to participate."

That evening, five patient representatives worked out an action plan. At nine the next morning, more than one hundred fifty patients came to the church. We trooped over to the health office together and pushed our way into every door we could find. While people in the office were trying to figure out what was happening, the orderly who had struck me the day before approached us and shouted, "People, people. What's the problem? What do you want? Who's in charge here?"

"No one person is in charge. We're just a bunch of people with diseased lungs. How could we have a representative? We all represent ourselves. We've heard that you guys sell off all the expensive drugs meant for us and leave us with only the cheap ones. No wonder you're so fat," one of the men stepped out and shouted, poking one of the orderlies in the stomach with his finger.

Meanwhile, the police arrived, but no one paid any attention to them. The police approached and said, "Let's have quiet here. Now, what's the matter? Anyone who's unruly will be taken in and charged."

At that remark, the people roared with laughter, some even clapping. "He says he's going to bust us. Tonight we'll sleep in comfort."

The police blew their whistles. "Quiet, please. Now let's hear from your representatives." The five representatives moved forward, as planned.

These five people, the health office's staff, and the police entered a room, closing the door behind them. The rest of us waited for them to come out, chatting with one another. After a while, one of the patient representatives came out and said to me, "They said they will apologize for hitting you yesterday and that a nurse will be assigned to our community. The office also agreed to visit our community every week to administer treatment. What should we do?"

"Come on. What are representatives for? You decide. Why are you asking me?"

"Well. That's true, but we should consult with you. We honor your opinion."

I realized then that they had little confidence in themselves and were unable to manage their problems alone. They needed to be trained to trust their own judgment.

"Tell them to forget about the apology. That's not necessary. Ask them to provide second-stage drugs to the patients who have not recovered with the first-stage drugs. They've already said that they can't do that because they don't have the money, but ask them anyway. The rest is up to you."

He went back inside. A little later the door opened again. With a satisfied look on his face, the representative addressed the crowd. "The office has promised to come every Thursday to Hwalbin Church and provide us with medical treatment. They will also try to provide second-stage drugs, as soon as they secure the funding for it."

On the way home, one of the patients said, "Today, for the first time since I was diagnosed with TB, I have reason to smile—the first time. I never imagined that I would see the day. It was worth living for. We wouldn't have seen it, if we had died early."

Another patient added, "That's right. We need to take better care of ourselves."

ON THE MORNING OF FEBRUARY 27, a police officer came to see me. From what he said, I was accused of building illegal shelters and had to go with him to the district station. I told him I would go after I finished what I was doing, but he insisted that I go immediately.

I had no choice but to accompany him. With a worried look on her face, my wife asked when I would be back. I answered, "Soon. They'll let me go," as if it was a matter of no consequence. When I was about to leave, my wife stuffed 3,000 *won* into my pocket, just in case. My neighbor, Park, was also arrested for repairing his house illegally. From the local police station, Park and I were handed over to the Dong-bu Police Station and then to a summary court at Ttukseom.

We were put in a holding cell that looked like a cage at the zoo. Some two hundred men were already there. We were tired and hungry. People were being held on different charges, some for building illegal shelters, some for traffic violations, some for urinating near a police station, some for gambling, and others on a variety of petty charges.

At two o'clock, we were taken to a courtroom and told to sit on benches in front of the judge, where we were ordered to keep our heads down. The police kept shouting, "Put your heads down."

I thought it was absurd. Why should we put our heads down? Why should we all look down before the judge? People should be brought to justice, if they have committed a crime, and that should be that, but what does it have to do with looking down? It is no doubt a human rights violation to have people keep their heads down, even before they are put on trial. This practice is a legacy from the Japanese colonial period and ought to be abandoned.

With these thoughts, I looked around to see who was entering the room. As soon as I lifted my head, an officer yelled out with a voice that overwhelmed me.

"Hey, YOU! Keep your head down!"

I stared at him for a while, but soon did as I was told. If I had not looked down, he would have gone on yelling until I did. I felt sorry for him, in his foolishness.

The judge finally showed up. He was about my age. After calling up the first fifteen cases, he cleared his throat and began his questioning.

"Do you admit to having staged a mass protest on a certain day?" he asked a defendant.

"Yes."

"Didn't you know that staging a mass protest was against law?"

"In fact, we did know."

211

"Why, then, did you do it, if you knew that it was illegal?"

"We are small shopkeepers who rent stalls in the market. We were protesting because the head of the Merchants Organization swindled us out of our money. He refuses to give it back."

"Then settle the issue according to law. Our society is based on the rule of law. You cannot conduct yourself in a way that goes beyond the framework of the law."

"Of course. At first, that was exactly what we tried to do—make him pay according to law, but the law was never on our side. We had no choice but to take action, whether legal or illegal."

"What do you mean by 'the law was never on your side'? The law doesn't take sides. It only rules."

"That's not true. The Merchants Organization head ignored all of our demands. Instead, he threatened us. He thinks he can get away with it because he's backed by politicians. We couldn't fight him that way, so we took collective action!"

"What do you mean, backed by politicians?"

"Backed by a certain lawmaker. He has influence even over the police. The police say they can't do anything, although they're aware of how unfairly we've been treated. They say his connections go all the way up to the Blue House.*"

"Nonsense! The National Assembly and the Blue House are distinguished national institutions that respect the law. There is no way they could be involved in anything like this. Be careful what you say. Anyway, you violated the law in a law-abiding country. It is only right that you accept your punishment."

"We violated the law? I can't believe this! Why should we be punished, when the real criminal is out there enjoying his freedom?"

"Keep quiet!" The judge stopped them from speaking and flipped through the documents before him. He was about to make his ruling.

From the exchange, I saw the entire picture. The head of the Merchants Organization had taken advantage of some small shopkeepers. When the shopkeepers discovered the scheme and complained, the man bribed officials so he could get away with it. Knowing who was

---

*The Blue House is the equivalent of the White House in the U.S. and is so named for its blue roof. The term is synonymous with the executive branch of government.

behind him, the police were reluctant to act on the case, although they knew what was going on. Mentioning politicians and the Blue House might just have been a bluff. He might have known an assistant to someone in the legislature. It is difficult to believe that the government and the National Assembly would be involved in such a petty incident. What kind of a nation would that make us?

The shopkeepers appeared to have barged into the man's house and created a scene, knowing that they could not fight him by confronting him or by bringing the matter to court. Perhaps they threw around a few chairs or a telephone. The man was probably glad to have an excuse to call in the police. To keep his job, the police chief would have sent his men to arrest the shopkeepers. He knew about the man's misdeeds, but that was not important. That was how the shopkeepers wound up in court.

I could see that Hwalbin Church had a lot of work to do. We had an obligation to protect the rights and interests of the less privileged who work hard to scrape together a living.

A few minutes later, the judge rendered his decision. Some of the shopkeepers were released, some fined 3,000 *won*, and some detained for fifteen days. For a moment, I felt sorry for the judge. Being bright enough to pass the bar exam, he surely had grasped the situation, but rather than bring justice down upon the true culprit, he penalized the shopkeepers. His was not a good position to be in.

I myself had once studied to go to law school. I even had my goal written on a banner that read "Congratulations on your acceptance to Seoul National University School of Law." If I had been accepted, would I be doing what he's doing now? I asked myself. I was thankful that I had decided not to go to law school.

The judged called out my name, "Kim Jin-hong." I stood up.

Without so much as looking at me, he began to ask me questions.

"Did you build a house illegally?

"Not exactly a house, but…"

"Never mind. You are hereby ordered to pay a fine in the amount of 2,500 *won*."

The judge had finished his ruling before I could speak and had begun calling out the next offender on the list. I returned to the waiting room. There, people ordered to pay fines were released, once they had made their payment. Those who could not afford to pay were sent to jail, where their fine was amortized at the rate of 500 *won* for every night they remained in custody.

Fortunately, I could pay my fine because my wife had given me 3,000 *won* before I was arrested. My neighbor, Park, however, had only 1,000 *won* and could not pay his 2,500-*won* fine. He was upset because he had something urgent he had to take care of.

I asked him by how much he was short and lent him what he needed. He was reluctant to take it, but I insisted. He was concerned about my health because I would have to spend a cold night in jail.

"I'll be fine. Don't worry. I actually think it'll be a good experience," I told him.

Park paid his fine and was released.

On his way out, he said, "Thanks a lot. I'll pay you back as soon as I can. I'll see to it that you get out soon."

After Park left, I noticed a young man with a Seoul National University badge on his chest. He looked depressed.

"Are you an SNU student? What's your major?"

"Electrical engineering."

"Why are you here?"

"I was playing cards at a friend's house. The loser was supposed to go buy a pack of cigarettes and I lost. It was two in the morning, but I went out to get the cigarettes anyway and was picked up for curfew* violation."

"What's your fine?"

"2,000 *won*."

"Don't you have the money?"

"No. The money to buy the cigarettes and some change I had in my pocket add up to only 800 *won*. That's all I have."

"Why don't I lend you twelve hundred? Then you can go out and send the money to my address."

After I gave him the 1,200 *won*, he, too, was released. He was very thankful. Later I heard someone calling my name.

"Pastor Kim Jin-hong! Pastor Kim Jin-hong!"

Listening carefully, I discovered that it was coming from outside a

---

*Korea had a midnight-to-6 a.m. curfew that lasted from 1945 to 1981.

window, high up near the waiting-room ceiling.

"This is Pastor Kim Jin-hong. Who's that?" I replied, wondering who it could be.

Then a rock was thrown in, with bills wrapped around it. I picked it up and found three 500-*won* notes attached to it. It was from Park. He was quick in paying his debt because he sincerely wanted to get me out. I was moved, but I had already given 1,200 *won* to the SNU student and thus was still short. With Park's contribution, I had only 1,800 *won* and there were still 700 *won* between me and freedom.

A while later, I was taken in a jail van to the Dongbu Police Station. At the station, we were herded into a basement room. Six cells, all occupied, surrounded a briquette stove in an open area in the center. The inmates watched us, the "newcomers," as we were brought in.

Our group was comprised of four people. The guard on duty lined us up and scrutinized us. Comparing me to the photo on my record card, he addressed me.

"You're a pastor? You don't look like a pastor. I know, you're one of those phonies, aren't you? Those swindlers, pretending to be pastors. You squeeze money out of people by making them believe you're a pastor, huh? This is no place for a real pastor."

The crowd in the detention cells burst into laughter at his remark. "Maybe he's Park Tae-seon, the notorious cult leader," one inmate jeered. There was another burst of laughter.

The guard shouted, "Hey, knock it off!" glaring in the direction from which the comment had come.

The guard then made us stand up and sit down again several times. Out of step, I would be sitting down when others were standing up and vice versa. He came over to me and booted me in the shin. I fell to the ground, holding my leg in pain. Other inmates were laughing again.

"Why aren't you doing what I say? Do you think this is a church? Do I look like I'm teaching you to do exercises?" The guard yelled out, snarling at me, like a cat about to pounce on a mouse.

That was enough to agitate me. I had to teach him a lesson. Calmly, I looked at him and said, "You son of a bitch! Who the hell do you think you are? Yeah, you, big shot. Come on. Do you want your ass handed to you?"

The guard recoiled a bit when I confronted him aggressively, looking him straight in the eye. He seemed to be worried that he had picked on the wrong guy.

He pretended not to hear me and ordered us to take off our socks and turn in all personal belongings. In my pocket I had my ID card, a small Bible, and 1,800 *won*. We were told to leave our belongings with them and that we would get them back when we were released. Everybody's attention seemed to be directed to my 1,800 *won*.

A feeble man in his thirties and I were assigned to Cell No. 6. The self-styled "cell chief" told me to sit in a corner. He seemed to have absolute power, at least within the cell. He started to ask us some questions.

"Hey buddy, got any fags?"

"Fags? What are fags?"

"You really don't know? That's cigarettes."

"I don't smoke."

"Oh, yeah. You're a Christian."

He turned away from me, as if he had no interest in Christians. Supper arrived. It consisted of only barley, a coarse grain, in an old aluminum bowl, and some pickled radish. A pair of chopsticks was thrust in on top of the half-filled bowl. Because I had not had a proper lunch, I actually enjoyed it. Then the cell chief whispered in my ear, in a very friendly way.

"You know, you can order dinner from outside, if you have the money. I know, let's order two and share."

"No. This is fine."

"Don't be a cheapskate."

He was making the suggestion with my 1,800 *won* in mind. He seemed disappointed that I was not interested.

During supper, the other newcomer in our cell coughed heavily. Soon, an office clerk came in and asked whether he should accept medicine for an inmate named such-and-such. The man's wife was trying to deliver his medication.

The guard who had kicked me earlier turned him down. "No," he barked. "By the way, what kind of medicine?"

"PAS and something else."

"Instead of bringing him medicine, tell her to bring money for his fine."

"She says she can't afford the fine right now, but at least she'd like to give him his medicine."

As soon as I heard the word PAS, I knew that the man was a TB patient. The clerk seemed to be sympathetic to the wife, who had pleaded for his help, but he soon gave up trying because the guard insisted upon going by the book. Meanwhile, the man was coughing himself into a fit and seemed to be in serious condition.

The guard asked him, "Are you sick? How sick are you, to have your wife deliver you medicine?"

"I have consumption."

The word consumption stirred up a furor. The cell chief was the first to complain.

"What! You're telling me that I've been sharing a cell with a guy with TB? I won't stand for it! It's bad enough I have to be here, and you put me with a lung patient! He can't stay here. Get him out of here!"

Others in the cell were also complaining, saying that consumption is contagious.

"You, quiet in there. If you want red-carpet treatment, go stay at a hotel. You deserve to be with a TB patient. Maybe then you'll stop scamming people," a guard yelled.

The cell chief must have gotten sent up for fraud. He became sullen for a moment, but soon started hollering at the man with consumption.

"Hey you, numbnuts, get your ass over in the corner and make yourself small. How can a corpse like you walk into a place like this? Look at you. And you manage to find a woman who'll go to bed with you, while me, a strong, good-looking guy, go without."

Then, crouched in the corner, the TB patient started to cough again. An inmate sitting next to him was being hard on him, telling him to turn his head away when he coughed. With his head turned toward the wall, he continued coughing.

I felt sorry for him. I was sorry that he was ill, and it broke my heart to see him treated so cruelly by other inmates.

"This man has to take his medicine," I said. "The TB virus becomes inactive and is not contagious when a person is under medication."

"Hey there, deranged pastor! Then you sleep with him," the cell chief snarled.

I thought he was being too hard and said, "You're going too far. Do you plan to be in here for the rest of your life? If not, and if you want to live long, you'd better be careful and watch what you're saying."

He grumbled and turned away. Then I turned to the patient and asked, "You're in bad shape. How long are you in for?"

"Actually, I was fined 2,500 *won*."

"For what?"

"For building an illegal shelter."

"Did you build it by yourself?"

"Not really. I bought it for 30,000 *won*, but then a warning was issued. The house was demolished, I was taken to the police station and here I am."

He moaned and said he was not sure he could survive the jail, considering his condition. From what I knew, for a patient in his condition, sleeping on cold floors can be deadly. I was reminded of Mrs. Park, who had died after spending a night in a cold detention cell.

One way or another, I had to get him released. I prayed to the Lord for mercy. "Lord, this poor fellow needs your help to return home. I have 1,800 *won* and I need another seven hundred to get him out of here. Guide me and help me, so he can come up with the 700 *won*."

I prayed in earnest. After my prayer, I took a deep breath and called over the guard.

"This man's a TB patient and he doesn't look good. He won't survive a night here in this cold. Is there any way to let him go?" I asked.

"He's free to go, as soon as he pays his fine."

"He needs 2,500 *won*. I have eighteen hundred, so we're seven hundred short. There must be a way."

"We can't let him go, if he's even a penny short. That's the rule. I'm sorry, but I have to go by the rules."

While I was talking to the guard, the cell chief nudged my side. He wanted me to forget about the sick man and order dumplings for the inmates. I listened and said nothing.

A moment later, a man with a commanding appearance walked into the room. The guard, at attention, saluted him. He seemed to be the police chief. It occurred to me that perhaps he was influential enough to turn the situation around and help out with the money. I decided to give it a try and spoke up.

"Officer! Would you at least ask the chief if this fellow can be sent home? We can't have him spending the night here."

The guard hesitated. Noticing our conversation, the police chief asked, "Is something wrong?"

The guard replied, "A fellow with TB came in today. According to this guy, it's too dangerous for him to sleep here tonight. He insists that he wants to pay the guy's fine."

"He's a generous man. I think we'd better take him up on it."

"Except he doesn't have enough money."

The senior officer thought for a moment and then turned to me, "Is this guy a friend of yours?"

"No. I just met him here today."

"Then why do you want to pay his fine?"

"Because I'm healthy and he's not. I believe he's in critical condition. He won't survive here."

Then the chief asked the TB patient.

"How much were you fined?"

"2,500 *won.*"

"From twenty-five hundred, the man wants to give you eighteen hundred, so you'll be out in two days."

"…"

When the patient said nothing, I stepped in.

"I don't mind staying here because I'm healthy and I can put up with it, but it's different for this man. One night in here can kill him."

"OK. I'll chip in a thousand. Let's get him out of here together!"

I felt a tremendous sense of relief. The patient thanked me, just before he was released.

"I don't know how to thank you enough. If you give me your address, I promise, I'll pay you back."

"No. There's no need. Someone else gave me the money, so don't worry about paying me back. I'll pray that you recover soon and live a happy life."

He bid me farewell, his eyes full of tears. I was deeply moved to see him leave, wiping his eyes.

After the patient left the cell, everybody was quiet. No one swore anymore. No one exchanged jokes. There was total silence.

A while later, a young man sitting beside me asked, "You said you're a pastor?"

"Actually, I'm only studying to be a pastor. Why do you ask?"

"Because I think I want to start going to church."

He said he had gone to church until middle school, but stopped after factious squabbling broke out in the church he was attending.

"By the way, what church do you belong to?" he asked.

"We call it Hwalbin Church."

"No. I mean which denomination…Presbyterian, Catholic, Methodist? Whose side are you on?"

"None. We're all on the Lord's side."

"The Lord's side…. I like that. If I get out of here, I want to go to Hwalbin Church, on the Lord's side."

"I'm glad to hear you say that. Why don't we keep in touch when we get out of here? By the way, why are you in here?"

"It's nothing to be proud of, but I'll tell you about it. After finishing middle school, I came to Seoul and opened a small shop. Until then, all I did was pick fights with people, but I was willing to change my ways. I was doing OK, at least until I started gambling. One day I got caught and you know the story from there."

While I was talking to him, the guard bellowed out, "Hey you, Pastor, shut up, would you?"

I recoiled, knowing that silence is rule number one in the jail, but then someone from the next cell came to my defense.

"Hey, guard. Cut the guy some slack. Show some respect. I mean, he's a pastor. Don't think you can treat him like one of us hoodlums."

"That's right. Give him a break. It's bad enough that you kicked him so hard, so lighten up," said the cell chief.

Then suddenly, there was a general stir in the other cells. Noticing unusual tension, the guard strolled around and started to tell the inmates to be quiet, but in a softer tone.

"Shut up. Be quiet, everyone!"

Then he lit up a cigarette and walked around to check out each cell. When he reached our cell, the cell chief said what others had wanted to say all along. "C'mon, be a sport. Give us a hit on that."

"You sure are impudent. OK, but only today."

The guard gave out one cigarette to each cell. This time, all the inmates' faces lit up. Everybody took turns taking a quick drag on the cigarette. It was offered to me, but I declined.

"Now, get to sleep," said the guard, after everyone had finished smoking. Lying down on the cell floor with nothing but a sheet as a blanket, I felt the cold seep into my bones. I tried hard to go to sleep. Other people managed not only to sleep, but to sleep so well that they snored.

When I was about to fall asleep, I heard a steel door unlocking and people talking. Then a voice called my name.

"Pastor Kim Jin-hong. You can go now. Someone from your family is here for you," said the guard, politely. He almost sounded like a different person.

"Did you say I can go? Just like that?"

I felt sorry for my cellmates, now that I was going home. I felt like I was betraying them. I did not want to wake everybody up. I tried to leave quietly, but I didn't get away with it. The cell chief was awake and congratulated me on getting out. The man who had insisted that I order dumplings with my 1,800 *won* was not to be seen. I was looking at a different man, a sober, earnest man.

"I'm sorry I have to go and leave you all here. We'll meet again, if it's meant to be."

"You're going to be a great success, Pastor," he added, as I turned away; whatever he meant by that.

After gathering up my personal belongings, I made my exit through the steel door. The night-duty guard followed me out the door and apologized. "Pastor Kim. Forgive my rudeness. I know it was wrong, but being with the inmates, sometimes I'm forced to say and do certain things."

"I understand. I really do, but you need to change. They aren't bad people. Be more gentle with them."

"Yes, you're right. I'll try, but it's easier said than done. Good-bye. I hope you never set foot in here again. Like I said, this is no place for you."

Going down the stairs in the station, I felt a sharp pain in my shin where he'd kicked me.

Ha Seong-sam, a college student attending Saemunan Church, was outside waiting for me. He had visited the slum and had heard about me from my wife. When I arrived home, my wife was happy to see me. Our son, Dong-hyeok, was sound asleep. Lying down in my room, warm and comfortable, there was nothing more I could wish for. After the jail cell, it felt like heaven on earth.

14

Nowhere to Go But Up

THE NEXT MORNING I ALLOWED MYSELF the luxury of sleeping in. Then, in the afternoon, I took a walk around the neighborhood. When I turned a corner, I saw six or seven young men in a group, hanging out. I approached them and said, "Hey, guys. Young people should be working. Why are you standing around doing nothing? By working you stay healthy."

"We know," one of them said, "but we don't have jobs. If we did, we wouldn't be here."

"In that case, do you want me to find you work?"

"If you can, yes, indeed. We'll owe you a lot, if you can do it."

"No, no. You'll owe me nothing. All I ask is that you work hard. Be in front of the church at six tomorrow morning. I'll take you to your new job."

"You're not kidding, are you? Guys, did you hear that? We're going to have a job. That's what you said, isn't it?"

"Yes.... Just do as I say."

A little past six the next morning, four of them were waiting in front of the church.

"Are you guys ready to work?" I asked, to which they all answered, "Yes." There they stood, all dressed up in suits and ties, with polished shoes and their hair neatly combed.

"Why're you all dressed up?" I asked.

"Well, we want to make a good impression on the boss. After all, it's our first day on the job. We went to a lot of trouble to get this together, but we managed. How do you like it?"

"Workers should dress like workers. Why the neckties? Go home and get out of those clothes. Put on something comfortable, and wear sneakers. You don't look like people who are ready to work."

Dejected, the men went home and returned in work clothes. Then I took them to where they were going to work, near the racetrack. Handing each a basket and a pair of tongs, I said, "These set me back 940 *won*. Pay me back later, when you get paid, OK?"

"What? You want us to pick rubbish?"

"Exactly. We're all going to be rubbish pickers. Why do you have that look on your face?"

"You're wrong if you think we're going to pick rubbish. We're not going to do that. If we had known before, we wouldn't even have come. We're wasting our time."

"What's wrong with you?"

"What's wrong with us? It's you who's got it wrong! You said you'd get us a decent job. You didn't say anything about picking rubbish."

"And you think picking rubbish isn't a decent job? If that's what you think, you're mistaken. You don't realize what an important role rubbish pickers play. Korea is a small country, crawling with people. Pine trees, a few barrels of coal, and gravel are all we have in the way of natural resources. Given these circumstances, you should be able to figure out how important it is to recycle even a scrap of paper. When we reuse resources, it's the same as if we were producing new ones. You'll be doing something important for the country.

"Also, wasting your time just hanging out only destroys you, physically and mentally. As a rubbish picker, you become a resource-producing patriot who is healthy in mind and body. Try it with me for just ten days. If after that, you don't want to stay, you're free to go. I won't say a word, but for the next ten days, try to like what you're doing. If I can do it, you can too."

Reluctantly, one of them spoke up. "C'mon, guys. Let's give it a shot. They say a guy should try anything once. Picking rubbish is honest work. We have nothing to lose."

When he hoisted the basket onto his shoulder, the others went along. I gave them advice on how to make the job a little easier, but I also tried to change their attitude about what they were doing. After working our way through back alleys all morning, we stopped by a Chinese restaurant for lunch. I ordered a little more than I ordinarily would, since I figured they'd be hungry after working all morning.

"Picking rubbish.... This isn't so bad. Actually, it's better than I expected," one of them said.

"I'm glad to hear that. I think you're starting to get the hang of it. How about you other guys? What do you think?"

"Yeah, it beats hanging out doing nothing. You know, Pastor, doing nothing isn't as easy as people think."

"Good. Having something to do is, in fact, very important. It's good to see that you're catching on. You must be starving. Come on, dig in."

In no time, they became pros at the art of picking rubbish and soon they were encouraging other jobless young men to join in. At first, it was only one or two who took part, but as time went by, nearly a dozen others came along.

As more people came on board, I saw we were going to need some rules. Every morning, before starting out for the day, I would shout a slogan, "We may be at the bottom, but we're aiming for the top!" I would have them repeat it. They shook their fists in the air as they shouted.

Then they went off in all directions to do their day's work, each to his own workplace. By workplace I mean the various districts of Junggok-dong and from Ttukseom to Walker Hill, and by work I mean going through trash cans. After work, we sat around in a mobile tent pub, drank *soju*, and had a good talk.

I emphasized that our lives were not trash, although we spent our days rummaging through society's refuse. I reminded them that we must keep our hopes up and that was why every morning we shouted our slogan.

It comforted them that although we might be living in poverty, we must contribute to making the world a place where every human being can live a life of dignity, where we are all able to help others, and where everyone is treated equally. Our after-work talks went on and on, and always over a bottle of *soju*.

These sessions motivated the young men to work harder. I named them the "Hwalbin Development Volunteers." Then I had them set aside one-tenth of their income. I explained to them, "Christians give

225

something called a tithe. They save one-tenth of their income and give it to the church, to be used for the Lord's work. Like Christians, I suggest you tithe, but your tithe won't go to the church. Rather, we'll select a treasurer who'll collect one-tenth from everyone every day.

"We'll use the money to help the needy in our community. It'll be used to cure people who are ill, but cannot afford a doctor. It'll be used for scholarships for bright students who cannot afford to go to school. It'll be used to help those who cannot get technical training because they don't have the money. I won't get involved in deciding where the money will be spent. That'll be up to you. You manage it. My job is to advise." I asked them how that sounded to them.

"Great!" was their reply.

When it came to actually using the accumulated fund, however, if I may call it that, it wasn't as easy as it sounded. Giving, we learned, takes practice. Once, we received word that a pregnant woman was ill and unconscious due to toxemia. Someone suggested that we should use the fund to help her. Everyone agreed except one. He insisted that we not use the fund until we had collected a considerable amount. He added that if we kept taking money out of the fund, we'd never achieve anything major and meaningful. We decided to do it anyway. Then I proposed that the one who had disagreed be the one to go to her to help.

"I know it's a nuisance, but I'd like you to take care of this matter. If she is left untreated for a few more days, she could die. I'd like you to take her to the hospital, even if it means that you miss a day's work."

"What! You want me to do that? No way! In my entire life, I have never taken even my own wife to a hospital, so why would I take some other man's wife? It's out of the question."

"What's out of the question? What's so difficult about helping people in need? You can't live life caring only about things that concern you. Helping her will eventually help you. Trust me."

"If taking her to a hospital is such a good thing, let someone else do it. Why me?"

"Why not you? Now give me an answer, are you going or aren't you?"

He hesitated for a while and finally agreed, "OK, I'll do it."

"That's what I wanted to hear. Don't think that I'm unfair for asking you to do it. I know that you'll thank me later."

The next morning, instead of going to work, he took the woman to the hospital. She was diagnosed and hospitalized. In the evening, the man came to see me.

"I went with the woman to the hospital today."

"So tell me, after all, was it unfair that I asked you to help her?"

"No, not at all. Next time, count me in. I want to do it."

"What happened? You weren't happy about it yesterday."

"No, I wasn't, but I've changed. I realize that helping someone is good. I was proud of myself for doing it. I felt like I had a life. I want to be in charge of these things. Please let me."

As I had expected, he enjoyed the experience. Always, donors, more than recipients, gain in the process of their act. Unfortunately, many people do not recognize this simple truth and try to live only for themselves. Most young people in the slum are rough and are always distracted. There isn't a better way to heal their distorted and antagonistic personality than to give them a chance to help others. By reaching out, they experience the joy of serving others and develop a sense of self-worth.

AFTER THAT, THE HWALBIN DEVELOPMENT VOLUNTEERS initiated a variety of activities, beginning with assisting TB patients. TB patients are usually malnourished and suffer from a damaged stomach from their strong medication. They catch TB because they are poor, and with TB, they become poorer.

The volunteers piled up coal briquettes on a vacant lot in the slum and gave them out to TB patients who could not support themselves. We provided free vitamins, as well. We prepared warm and nutritious soup so patients who wanted could have it whenever they asked.

One morning, while working, I became dizzy and nearly passed out. I kept myself from falling over only by holding onto the pushcart. I was perspiring all over. I knew I couldn't go on working, so I went home early.

On my way home, I saw my son, Dong-hyeok, gazing intently into a neighbor's house. I went up to him, curious as to what he was looking at, and saw the neighbors eating rice.

It was chilly out, but they had left the door open, perhaps to allow carbon monoxide to dissipate. I called to him. He rushed into my arms and said, "Daddy, I want rice too."

All winter, we had not been able to afford rice and ate noodle soup instead. It was only natural that he wanted rice. That night, my wife and I talked about our son's health.

"Dong-hyeok hasn't looked good lately. He sweats and coughs a lot when he sleeps. I'm worried about him," my wife said.

"That's not good," I said.

"You've never been a responsible family member. Dong-hyeok has had to live without a father and I without a husband."

"What are you saying?"

"All you're interested in is this slum and the people who live here. You're so busy with them, you never pay any attention to us."

"It's true, I've been busy, but you can't say that I don't care about you. Of course, I do. You're my family."

"I don't know. I really don't know. You say you do, but you don't act like it. For me it's no problem, but it's too much for our son. I won't stand for it. It's insane."

"I understand how you feel, but the other kids in the slum are doing just fine. Why wouldn't Dong-hyeok be fine?"

"They're different. You can't compare him to the other kids here."

"How is he different from them?"

"He's just different. Dong-hyeok has been raised differently. He's been brought up in what you call 'bourgeois' circumstances. He can't live this kind of life."

Every time I thought of my family, I felt frustrated. My wife was right. It was too much for them, but what could I do? I was between a rock and a hard place.

My wife was becoming more annoyed and our son was growing weaker by the day. Our room was too cold and damp for a child and he wasn't getting proper nutrition. He became so weak that sometimes he mumbled in his sleep, whining and coughing. I was anxious, while my wife protested by maintaining silence.

One day, my mother-in-law came to visit us and was devastated to see how her daughter had been living.

"Jin-hong, is this the only way you can practice your religion? Do all Christians live like you?"

"I don't know what to say. I'm sorry."

"If you want to live like this, that's fine, but I can't allow my daughter and my grandson to go on living here. I'm taking them home with me today."

"How can we be separated? We're family. We have to stick together in difficult times. That's what families are for."

"You're out of your mind. You talk about family when you can't even support them. I hate to see my daughter like this. I'll leave for now, but you'd better make sure that from now on you take better care of them. As you say, they're YOUR family."

She left, exasperated. The next day, I took Dong-hyeok to a hospital for a checkup. The doctor said he would have to be tested for TB, which was what I was afraid of.

In the slum, TB is the greatest threat of all. I didn't know how I would handle it, if he was found to have TB. The results of the test would be available in forty-eight hours. As soon as I returned home, I went to the church and prayed.

Later I was told that my son had TB. On her way home, after picking up a three-month supply of medication, my wife said something she had wanted to say for a long time.

"We can't go on like this. I'm taking Dong-hyeok to my mother's so he can get treatment. While we're there, take some time to think about us. You'll have to make up your mind. It's either us or your work, your family or the slum. Make up your mind."

"You're threatening me, my dear?" I asked.

"I'm not joking. I mean it."

"I guess I'd better take it seriously."

"You might say you can't give this up, but I think differently. I don't think God wants you to do His work by sacrificing your family. He wouldn't be happy with that."

A few days later, I saw my family off to Daegu at the Express Bus Terminal. On my way home, I went to a public bath, where I weighed myself. Before, I had weighed around 120 pounds, but now I weighed only 105 pounds. I was emaciated, considering my 5'6" height. It bothered me. I kept thinking of my wife's remark, that I had to make a choice between my family and the slum. I had nowhere to go except to the church.

"My Lord Jesus. Guide me in your way. Give me wisdom so I don't have to choose between my mission and my family, between my ideal and my reality. Help me, Lord…" I prayed.

BEFORE I WAS DONE, I HEARD SOMEONE CALLING frantically, "Pastor, Pastor." Outside were three women in their work uniforms. They had been working in greenhouses and were still carrying their tools.

"What's wrong?"

"Pastor, thank God you're here. Hun's mother* is in trouble. We think she might die. You have to come help her."

"Tell me, why do you say she might die?"

"She insisted on coming to work, even though she's been ill a lot lately. Today at work she fainted. We took her home and came as fast as we could."

I followed the women to Hun's house. Hun lived in Songjeong-dong, which was about a mile away. Since the previous fall, Songjeong had been virtually at war with demolition crews trying to tear down shelters. The Seoul city administration wanted to clear the whole area to build a sewage treatment facility. With nowhere else to go, the residents resisted being displaced.

In particular, it was the women who staged the most aggressive protests. Theirs were very unusual protests. Dozens of women would charge the demolition crew at full tilt, holding their children out in front of them. The crew were concerned that the children would get hurt.

"You sons-of-bitches, get out of here and never come back!" cried the women.

They were like kamikaze pilots. Aghast, the demolition crew foreman shouted out to his men, "The kids! Stay away from them!"

The demolition crew were forced to retreat. There were nearly fifty such protests. The residents were as persistent as the demolition crew. In the end, some two hundred shanties were torn down and the residents left homeless.

Twenty or so of the two hundred households returned to build tent

---

* In Korea the custom is to refer to a mother not by her own name but by the name of a child, if the speaker knows the child's name. If the speaker does not know a child's name, a mother is commonly referred to as "Baby's mother" or "Child's mother."

shelters and stay on. One of these was Hun's family. Hun's father died while working at a subway construction site. He was supposed to wear his hard hat while working underground. One day he had taken it off to rest and was struck by a rock that had become dislodged from the ceiling of the tunnel and came down on his head. He died of a concussion, but his family was not fully compensated because he had violated safety regulations.

After his death, Hun's family could not make ends meet. The family, comprised of Hun's grandmother, two sisters still in elementary school, five-year-old Hun, and his mother, barely scraped by. Their only income was from the grandmother, who sold goods in the marketplace, and Hun's mother, who worked in a greenhouse, tending vegetables. Hun's mother was already ill and weak, but her health deteriorated when, unconcerned for her own welfare, she pushed herself to the limit to support her family.

"Are you saying she's ill?" I now asked them.

"I'm afraid she's in a serious condition. When she works, she complains of nausea and dizziness. Her stomach seems to be a little swollen too," one of them said.

"That sounds familiar. If you ask me, she's not sick at all."

"You know about this ailment?"

"Yes, of course. She's pregnant. Nausea, dizziness…what else could it be but morning sickness."

"What? You must be joking. How could she be pregnant, when she doesn't have a husband?"

"Why not? Actually, we live in a world where widows can become pregnant. I mean, that happens quite a lot. Even single women have babies these days. She might just be reluctant to tell us."

"No, her financial situation is very bad. She has no time for men. She's too busy working to feed her family."

"You can be busy making a living, but that doesn't mean you can't have babies. They are two different things."

"I'd bet money on it. She can't be pregnant. She's ill. That's all."

"Well, I'll take her to the hospital for a checkup. We'll find out what the problem is."

A few days later, on a rainy day, I took Hun's mother to a hospital. While we were on a bus, I looked at her swollen abdomen and said, "If the doctor says you're pregnant, if that's what it is, you have to respect the baby's life. If you think you cannot raise the baby on your own, we'll all take turns looking after it."

"Why don't we just wait until I see a doctor."

She was calm and steady, as she whispered those words. Contrary to her appearance, she was truly a strong woman. In the end, after undergoing several tests, she was found not to be pregnant. Saying she had a tumor in her womb, the doctor rebuked me, assuming I was her husband.

"How could you have let her suffer for so long? You should have brought her in much earlier. She must have been in excruciating pain for the tumor to have grown this big."

"If it's a tumor, would she be all right after surgery?"

"Yes. You're lucky that she doesn't have a cancer. It's just a tumor, so she'll be fit and healthy after surgery. I suggest that you make your decision fast and have surgery as soon as possible."

"Thank you, doctor.... Surgery.... Well, I guess that'd be quite expensive."

Returning from the hospital, I put all my energy into seeking ways to secure enough money for Hun's mother's surgery. On Sunday, everyone who was present at church prayed for her health and asked God for guidance in financing her surgery.

Things happen, however, even when we're not prepared. Hun's mother went back to work, where again she fainted. No one could blame her. She had no choice. One way or another, she needed to feed her family.

She had to squat to work and that must have triggered the fainting. It was fortunate that people were around and managed to come to me as soon as they did. Upon hearing the news, I ran to Hun's house. I raised the straw matting that was used as a front door and walked in. There I saw three children, sobbing beside their sick mother.

Their room was nearly roofless, with the sky visible through the beams. There was no heat. In one corner of the room, two apple boxes held some clothes. They had little in the way of kitchen equipment and cooked over a kerosene burner. I was upset to see that people had to live that way. The woman's face was swollen and she was in a lot of pain. Sitting down next to her, I asked, "You seem to be in a bad way. Could you describe your pain?"

"It feels as if I have a large rock in my stomach. I can hardly breathe and sometimes I feel like I'm going to faint."

"I'll call a taxi. Why don't you get ready to go to the hospital."

While walking to get a taxi, I figured there was some chance the hospital would not admit her, because she did not have money to pay for surgery, but I also thought that she might be able to receive free treatment, if she presented a certificate issued by the ward office stating that she was living on a government subsidy.

Entrance to a slum residence.

I hurried to the ward office and explained the woman's situation to the chief. To my frustration, the ward chief refused to issue the certificate on the grounds that she was living in an illegal dwelling. I repeatedly asked for mercy, but he refused to listen.

Feeling helpless, I returned to Hun's house by taxi. While I was helping Hun's mother into the cab, a group of housewives stepped forward and handed me 3,000 *won.* Like Hun's mother, they did menial work.

One of them told me, "Pastor Kim, you have to save her, at any cost. We believe in you. This isn't much, but we want her to have it as an expression of our affection for her. We hope it'll help."

Upon arriving at the Central Medical Center on Euljiro Avenue in central Seoul, I first ran to the emergency room, assuming that the hospital, as a state-run medical facility, would not turn away a patient on the grounds that she did not have enough money.

After examining her, a surgeon said that unless she was operated on within 24 hours, there was little chance she would survive. He told me to have her admitted to the hospital right away. Then I went to the administrative office to go through the necessary procedure. For her to be admitted, hospital staff told me I would have to deposit enough money to cover the costs. I gave them all the money in my pocket and pleaded for help.

"This is all I have right now. People living in our community are poor so it's impossible to get money together so quickly. We would like to pay on a monthly basis, after she's operated on."

"What are you talking about? Are you saying that you want credit? Do you think a hospital takes installment payments? She'll be admitted to the hospital only after you come up with the money."

I protested. "As you know, she's in critical condition. I'll pay the bill. I swear it on my name."

The clerk looked at me as if my integrity was poor collateral. "No, that won't do. Step aside. Who's next?" he responded coldly.

I kept trying to convince him, but without success. He and his colleagues soon started chatting among themselves, paying no attention to me. Hun's mother had become increasingly pale and was breathing heavily. In desperation, I approached the hospital staff again and begged for mercy, only to be turned away one more time.

Finally, I could no longer contain my rage.

"You bastards. Don't you have any sympathy for this poor woman? Have you no feelings? She's dying and you're talking about money. Money, money, money. You sons-of-bitches! I'd like to blow you all to bits."

Perplexed, they looked at me as if I was out of my mind. I walked out of the hospital, carrying Hun's mother on my back.

I told myself, "Someday I'll make you pay the price, you bastards," but I had no way to hurt them. The threat was only an expression of my frustration.

I hailed a taxi and put her into it. We drove to Severance Hospital in Sinchon. Severance Hospital was run by foreign missionaries. I thought they would surely accept Hun's mother, destitute though she was, but my expectation proved unfounded. I explained to the administrative staff.

"I couldn't get her admitted to the Central Medical Center because I have no money. I am a church pastor." I asked them to admit her quickly. Attempting to capitalize on my faith and integrity, I promised to pay the hospital bill later.

"She needs emergency surgery. I was told that unless she's operated on within 24 hours, she won't survive. Please, please admit her now," I begged.

The staff were short in their response. "We have no confidence in the integrity of pastors these days. When they're in trouble, they always promise, but later they don't come through."

"But, please. This woman is in critical condition. I beg you, show her some mercy."

"We're not a charity hospital. You'll have to deposit the money, before we can accept her."

I looked nervously at my patient, whose face was turning white. I heaved her onto my back again and made my way to Seoul National University Hospital, but they refused to treat her there, as well. As a last resort, I made my way to the Ewha University Hospital in Dongdaemun. There, too, they told us we had to pay a deposit first.

For sure, the one in need in this case was the patient, not the hospital. In this vast city of Seoul there were any number of hospitals and thousands of doctors, but Hun's mother could not get treatment anywhere.

We had been riding in taxis, going from hospital to hospital all day, and I didn't have a coin left in my pocket. I had not eaten lunch and was ravenously hungry. With Hun's mother still on my back, I went to the bus stop in front of Dongdaemun Stadium. I boarded a bus going to Ttukseom and pleaded my case with the conductor.

"I'm very sorry, Miss," I said. "I've been going all over Seoul trying to find a hospital to treat this woman and have no money left. Could you let us ride for free?"

"It's rush hour. Do you really expect me to let you on the bus for free, with a patient on your back, at such a busy time? You should wait until after rush hour."

There was nothing to do but walk, but when I thought of walking from Dongdaemun to the Cheonggye-cheon shantytown, it seemed like a journey of a hundred miles. Reciting Bible verses and words of solace to Hun's mother, I set out walking.

"What can we do? There is nowhere in all of Seoul that will take us. Not the public hospitals, not the Christian hospitals, not the university hospitals—not one will take you as a patient. Let's go home and pray and tomorrow morning we can start again."

It was late autumn and darkness came quickly. We were near Seongdong Fire Station when I felt my strength give out. To make matters worse, Hun's mother kept leaning back. Thinking she might have fallen asleep, I tried to shake her awake and said, "Hold on tighter. I can't walk if you keep pulling back like that. Stay close and hold on tightly."

I shifted her to a better position, but not long after she started pulling back again, this time to the side. I found myself leaning sideways as well. She did it again and I shifted her back into position, but when it happened once again, I found myself getting angry.

"Please try to understand. You're not riding in a car or on a donkey. You have to help me out, instead of making it more difficult," I complained, but I immediately regretted what I'd said. Her plight was so miserable and I didn't have the heart to be annoyed with her. Instead, I grew annoyed with myself. I felt useless, having spent the whole day going from hospital to hospital, only to return home without success.

I said to Hun's mother, "I'm sorry I snapped at you. Whatever happens, we have to stick together and help each other, but if you want to go to sleep, lean against me."

She still would not cooperate, however. Whenever I shifted her into a better position, we would go no more than a few steps before she would be pulling back again. I finally blew up and let go of her. She fell to the ground with a loud thud on the concrete drive of the fire station. When I heard her fall, I grumbled,

"Haven't you been listening. I'm not your husband and I'm not your brother. You have to help me out...."

As I stood there complaining, fighting back my anger, I turned around to look at her and a strange feeling came over me. She lay motionless on the ground. Worried, I moved closer. She was dead.

EVERYTHING BEFORE MY EYES WENT BLANK. My body went limp. I collapsed on the ground next to her body and cried out, "No! No!

No! This can't happen. You can't die like this. You have to fight for your life. How could you die like this? What about your children? You have to go on fighting. Don't you realize how unjust this is? You're too young to die. You have to live!"

I lifted her body. Already it was growing stiff. I realized then that when she was falling backward and sideways on my back, she was already dead.

Strangely enough, that night no one was out on the street. For a long time I sat there holding her hand. After a while, the chill in her body passed on to me. I was cold, hungry, sad, and angry. I wanted to pour gasoline over the entire city and set it ablaze. I felt anger rising in me and said to myself, "This stinking world! May it crumble and fall!"

I stood up, shook my fists at the sky, and said, "Jesus? Who needs you? Savior! Ha! What kind of a savior are you? What kind of a savior would let this good woman die on my back after spending the whole day shuttling back and forth? Who needs a savior who is so weak and unreliable? How can we trust you? I'm going to the church to tear down the sign. I'm going to go out and take revenge on the world."

Blind with anger, I was unable to think rationally and found it hard to control myself. As soon as I got back to the neighborhood, I would tear down the church sign. I vowed that I would spend the rest of my life turning the world upside down.

I did not have the strength to carry Hun's mother's body again, but neither could I leave her there. In the end, I took hold of her clothes and started dragging her. Alternately dragging and heaving her, I passed Hanyang University and started to cross Seongdong Bridge, which led to Ttukseom. I was so tired that in the middle of the bridge my knees gave out and I collapsed. I leaned her body against the rails and sat down. It was now very dark and cars with their headlights on were whizzing past.

I had been sitting there for a while when I felt someone approaching. I looked up and turned around, but there was no one there. It was unlikely that anyone would be standing in the middle of the bridge at that hour, but as soon as I dropped my head again, I heard a voice. It was the soft voice of someone very close.

"Jin-hong. Do you know who died on your back today? It was me, Jesus, who died on the cross."

I was so startled that I almost stopped breathing. I looked around. Of course, there was no one there, only absolute silence. I felt a pain in my heart and started to cry. I rose and knelt beside the body. Kissing the back of her hand, I said, "Jesus, I understand now. I understand that you died on my back today. I was wrong."

I rose and took out my Bible and went under the streetlight. I found Psalm 57 and read verses seven and eight:

> My heart is steadfast, O God,
>   My heart is steadfast;
>   I will sing and make music.
> Awake, my soul!
>   Awake, harp and lyre!
>   I will awaken the dawn.

I read it three times. This was the poem that David recited when he was at the lowest point in his life. It was when his enemy, Saul, was hunting him down and he had to flee. In all of Israel there was nowhere for him to hide.

He escaped to a secluded part of the border region, where he hid in the Adullam Cave, without food or water. When news that David was hiding in the cave spread from village to village, people started to gather. They had dreams, but with no way to make them come true. The event is described in 1 Samuel:

> David left Gath and escaped to the cave of Adullam. When his brothers and his father's household heard about it, they went down to him there. All those who were in distress or in debt or discontented gathered around him, and he became their leader. About four hundred men were with him. (1 Samuel 22:1-2)

The people gathered at the cave were only a ragtag bunch, but they were entrusted with the founding of David's kingdom. They had been transformed by their vision of the future. That vision gave them the power to overcome their hardships.

Stuck in despair, they held onto their dream, the vision of

awakening Israel from the darkness. Before they came to this vision, they were a band of misfits, but were transformed when given a mission to accomplish. They became missionaries, armed with the task of awakening the people from a dark past to the light of a new day. In accomplishing their task, they changed history.

I prayed, thinking about David and the Adullam Cave, about the four hundred people who gathered there, and that they were, indeed, the dawn of Israel.

"My dear Lord. I know what I must do. I know the road I must take. I understand my mission. I will awaken the dawn in this age of darkness. I have understood your will as you died there on my back and I vow that I will devote my life to bringing light to this land."

I took the body in my arms and returned to the neighborhood. During the night, the old women of the neighborhood took apart the lining of a blanket to make burial clothes. We dressed Hun's mother and the next morning took her body to be cremated. Before going to the crematorium at Byeokje, we stopped off at the local ward office to get permission to bury the body.

I remembered the last time I was there, when it had been impossible to obtain a certificate to save her life. We had been refused outright, but this time, when I asked for a death certificate, it was an easy matter. It is the way of the world for people to be hard on the living and generous with the dead.

AFTER THE BODY WAS CREMATED, I took the ashes and made my way to the Han River Bridge. As I spread the ashes over the river, I muttered, "Hun's mother. You are now on your way to the land of Jesus, where there are no shanty houses and where no one who will come to demolish your home. May you find rest there.

"When you meet Jesus, take hold of his clothes and cry your heart out. You died without being able to cry when you wanted to. In heaven, hold Jesus and cry all you want. Don't worry about your children. The church will take care of them. You can see them later in heaven. Until then, rest comfortably in the arms of Jesus."

Finally, I took the cloth in which the ashes had been wrapped, threw it into the river, and, praying, turned away.

"Jesus, please make me an instrument of your will. May such a sad

239

thing as this never happen again in our country. Please guide me so I can devote myself to leading our nation out of darkness. Please use the churches of Korea as a way to bring the light of the spirit to this land."

On the way back to the neighborhood, I bought some hot buns for her children. Though his mother was dead, Hun looked happy as he ate the buns. Their grandmother stood by, choking back her cries and wiping the tears from her eyes. Of the twenty or so families living in the neighborhood, no one said a word. Only one person spoke. It was an old woman. Taking no notice of me, she glared at heaven and said, "I curse this rotten world! I wish it would go up in flames."

I dragged my tired body to my room and collapsed. I wanted to sleep and never wake up again. I fell asleep reciting from Revelation:

> Then I saw a new heaven and a new earth, for the first heaven and the first earth had passed away, and there was no longer any sea. I saw the Holy City, the New Jerusalem, coming down out of heaven from God, prepared as a bride beautifully dressed for her husband. And I heard a loud voice from the throne saying, "Now the dwelling of God is with men, and he will live with them. They will be his people, and God himself will be with them and be their God. He will wipe every tear from their eyes. There will be no more death or mourning or crying or pain, for the old order of things has passed away." (Revelation 21:1-5)

At dawn the next day I put on my shoes and went outside. Breathing in the fresh morning air, I started running. As I ran, I shouted out, "My heart is steadfast! I will awaken the dawn! My mission is clear. I will be the one to awaken the dawn."

15

Even the Worm Resists When Trod Upon

ONE NIGHT MRS. IM CAME TO VISIT ME. I had taken a sack of flour to her house two weeks earlier. "I'm so sorry, Pastor. I'm ashamed to say it, but I've come to ask for more flour."

I decided that I had an obligation to help her, not with charity, but with counseling. Otherwise, it was just a matter of time before she would be back with her hand outstretched. It would be much better to motivate her to help herself.

I told her, "I've been thinking about something. Would you ask your husband to come see me?"

"You want me to send my husband to you?" she asked.

"Yes. I'd like to discuss something with Mr. Im."

She went home. A couple of hours elapsed and Mr. Im did not come. The Ims had asked for my help and that could not be ignored, so I went to their home.

Mr. Im was in his room. When he saw me he looked embarrassed and started bowing. His manner struck me as being overly servile. Irritated, I walked into the room and sat down.

Praying at the back of my mind, I thought, I harmed these people by giving them a sack of flour. It harmed their character, just as if it had been rat poison. Mr. Im is servile to me because he has taken my charity and therefore cannot deal with me as an equal. By accepting charity, they abandoned the only thing they had left—pride.

I realized that how I handled this situation would form the

foundation of my missionary work with the poor. I thought I should make an example of this case and begin again.

The Ims, I decided, should be treated with the utmost sincerity and honesty. It would do no good to resort to stopgap measures or become sentimentally sympathetic. The only thing I could do was go straight to the root of the problem.

"Mr. Im, your wife came to me a while back and told me you had nothing to eat. Now she has come to ask for my help again. To be honest, I'm annoyed. The flour I gave you last time was bought with money I earned by picking rubbish. I helped you, while I, myself, went hungry.

"I'm telling you this because today you've taught me a very important lesson. I've been in this neighborhood for more than six months now and I've observed that people around here are very lazy. That's why you live without hope. In nearly every home, as long as there's something to eat on the table today, no one bothers to work for tomorrow.

"There's no way to escape poverty, as long as people think that way. Receiving charity from others is not a solution. It only postpones the inevitable. You should look for a solution on your own. You can escape poverty only if you decide to do something about your poverty and your destiny."

I made a great effort to get my message across. Mr. Im listened quietly. When I finished, he sat silently for a long while. Then he spoke, "Everything you say is true. We are lazy. Able-bodied men lie around at home living off the little bits of money their kids bring in. We know that. We're not completely shameless. We think to ourselves, 'I gotta do something,' 'I can't go on like this,' and as we think about it, days go by. It's like trying to move a cripple. We think, but we can't seem to take action. I'm ashamed to listen to you tell me this. I wasn't always like this...."

I was grateful that Im bore me no ill will for what I had said. I felt that he could be helped and asked for his cooperation. "I want to ask you something. Do you think you can get up the courage to go out and find work? Whether the work is paid or not, whether the pay is good or bad, just going to work will itself be a good example for the people in the neighborhood."

"I'd go tomorrow, if I could, but where would I find work? Do you have any ideas? If there's something I can do, I'll do the best I can."

"Good. What kind of work do you think you can handle? Do you have any skills? What about a trade or manual labor?"

"I don't have any particular skills. When I first came to the city, I worked with a junk dealer. That's something I think I could do."

"What do you need to start that kind of work?"

"Well, the good thing about it is you don't need anything in particular. You put on some shoes and put a little money in your pocket and go round buying up used stuff cheaply. Then you sell it for a profit. For example, you buy old clocks, irons, and electronics from people who don't want them and sell them to people who do. Or you can take the stuff to a secondhand dealer."

It sounded like a good idea to me. I found myself thinking, if Im becomes a junk dealer, I can follow him around and learn some of the tricks of the trade. We decided to become partners, my money and his skill.

THAT DAY MARKED A CHANGE IN MY MISSIONARY EFFORTS toward the poor. I tried to help the people help themselves by pooling their strength and getting organized. I went around the neighborhood, trying to convince people to find work.

"Let's band together and help one another!"

"Alone you failed, but together we can succeed!"

I tried to persuade everyone I met. I visited the drink houses and I joined in card games. Wherever people gathered, I went and talked to them, from morning to night. At first, people were not interested. They were against the idea. They avoided me, saying that there was little hope for them, but there were a few who liked the idea. Initially, however, some rumors circulated.

"That pastor at Hwalbin Church, he buys people drinks while he's trying to get them to believe in Jesus."

"He's suspicious."

Although I knew of the rumors, I kept silent. Time is the best answer to gossip and, sure enough, with the passage of time, the rumors diminished and more people began to come around to my way of thinking.

The obvious place to start was to strengthen activities of an already existing organization, the Cheonggye-cheon Shantytown Residents

Society. I tried to activate its five committees. Learning from my experience working with the residents' problems, I reorganized the committees into five new teams, responsible for resident education, health management, cooperatives, income generation, and volunteer services. A committee chief and a general manager were appointed for each team of seven to nine members.

The committee chiefs were good honest men living in the area, and the managers were young people from the church who were willing to serve. With its organization in place, each committee began to pursue its own projects.

The resident education committee began a variety of programs, including classes for children, night classes for youths, a youth lecture series, education for mothers, a social group, and lectures on the government's *Saemaeul* (New Village) Movement.

The health committee began health services for babies and small children, prenatal care for mothers-to-be, prevention and cure of tuberculosis, family planning, general health, and dental treatment.

The income-generation committee started a job information service, job training, and bringing in work that could be done in the home. Later, when the employment section and the self-support section were added, the income-generation committee became the most important of the committees.

The cooperatives committee established a credit union and a consumers' union. Filled with ambition and dreams, the committee then moved on to establish a production cooperative. In poor neighborhoods, the credit union plays an important role. One of the psychological ills of the poor is the inability to save and plan for the future. People spend what money they have and, when it's gone, they go hungry.

I don't know where they suddenly got the money, but one day one of the families in the church bought 25 pounds of beef and cooked up a feast of *bulgogi*, a seasoned grilled beef dish. The smell went through the whole neighborhood. With their noses tantalized by the smell, one by one people commented, "Damn it! Do you think we've never tasted meat before? What are you trying to do by sending these smells through the neighborhood. It feels like I have worms in my stomach, I can't stand it…."

Having gotten her neighbors' attention with the smell, the woman of the house dished the meat onto plates and sent it around to people. A festive mood soon took over. The son in the family came to my home. Carrying a plate, he said, "Pastor, my mother said to bring this to you. Please take it. Let us know if you would like some more." I thanked him and asked what the occasion was, whether there was something to celebrate at his house. He didn't answer, but I let it pass and enjoyed the meal anyway.

A few days later, the mother came to see me. "I'm so sorry, Pastor, but could you lend us some of rice?"

I shook my head in disbelief. Earlier, her family had been celebrating with a feast of meat and today they have no rice.

I asked her, "Did someone steal your rice? The other day you treated the neighborhood to a feast. Why are you here borrowing rice today?"

"Oh, that. We came into some money for the first time in ages and figured we might as well spend it."

The poor have no sense of priorities. When they get money, they spend it without considering putting it away for the future. To preach to these people, it's not enough to tell them to believe in Jesus and to come to church. For missionary work to succeed in such a neighborhood, you have to help the people find some purpose in life, help them save, and get them to help each other with a community spirit.

In this respect, a credit union is very effective. In the slums, loan sharks lend money at thirty percent. The credit union is the perfect organization to counter them. For democracy to work, human rights and freedom must be backed by economics. In a state of absolute poverty, democracy and human rights are only empty slogans.

Finally, the volunteer-services committee, made up of youths from the area, was a special group in charge of looking after the roads, cleaning, sanitation, funerals, crime prevention, fire fighting, and other civic activities.

As each committee got under way and became busy with its various projects, the mood in the neighborhood began to change.

In a neighborhood where previously fighting had gone on from morning to night, brawls became less common. People who had spent their days drinking and playing cards began to look for work at the Residents Society. Youths who had terrorized the neighborhood as thugs were now members of the volunteer-services committee and stayed out late at night guarding the formerly crime-ridden alleys of the town. Most of them had been to jail or prison three or four times, one of them having gone to jail thirteen times. If you sat down and talked to them, it was soon clear enough that they were not terrible people. They had potential to become contributing members of society.

Among them was one young man whose specialty was grabbing handbags and raping women. He had attacked a number of young women in the slum area.

"Why do you defile those women. It's dangerous. If it's sex you want, you can always go to a brothel."

"Oh, I don't do it for the sex."

"Then why? What does it do for you?"

"I have nothing better to do. Life is so frustrating, and after I did it a few times, it became a habit. I'm young and my hormones are active. Although the world seems large and interesting, there doesn't seem to be anything for me to do, and that bothers me."

"If you have nothing to do, come out with me and pick rubbish."

"We'll see. I've been hitting on those poor factory girls, but lately I've been feeling guilty about it. Rather than go on hurting them, I'm gonna get me a rich bitch and make a haul, just one last time."

Not long afterward, I heard that he'd been dragged into the police station. It seems his plan to get "a rich bitch" had gone awry. If I had gotten a hold of him earlier, I might have made something of him, but I was too late.

The churches in Korea hold themselves up as being squeaky clean. Rough souls such as these, untempered by social responsibilities, find it hard to approach the church. There are times when such people do seek out the church, intending to start anew, but when they come into contact with it, they are intimidated by the atmosphere and cannot open their minds. Out of guilt, they become rougher and harder than ever. Thus, the church is always filled with model citizens, while the hard cases cannot find their way in.

ONE DAY, A MEDICAL STUDENT from Seoul National University came to the shantytown. His name was Kim Sang-hyeon. He was filled with a desire to help the poor and seemed to have been chosen by God particularly for this work. Sang-hyeon and I went from house to house, treating the sick, talking to them and consoling them. Although Sang-hyeon was only a student, his treatment and the medicines he prescribed worked wonders. He became famous around the neighborhood.

A crippled woman lived in our area. Her husband had been a policeman. They had two children, ages two and four. After the birth of the last child, she suffered severe bleeding and had been crippled ever since. She would push herself around on the floor with her hands, doing housework and trying to look after the children. Her situation was pathetic and we wanted to cure her.

Kim Sang-hyeon (left), a medical student, and Kim Jong-gil, in front of Hwalbin Church.

First, we took her to a hospital to get a proper diagnosis. After taking a few x-rays and looking them over, the doctor told us that he could not treat her. We asked whether there was anything at all that could be done for her.

"Well, if she had a lot of money, a way might be found, but in her condition and under her circumstances, she has no chance of getting well."

After hearing the doctor's words, we returned home. En route, I asked Sang-hyeon, "The doctor says it's impossible, but can't we find a way? After all, the doctor isn't God."

"Medicine is science. What can't be done, can't be done."

"We can't just give up. I'll pray and you try to find a medical cure."

"I don't know. I doubt that I can come up with anything. Perhaps I should pray, too."

"No, I'll do the praying. You just tend to the medicine. The doctor has already said it's hopeless, so we have nothing to lose. We may as well try. Give her something, anything."

247

Sang-hyeon made up a medicine of digestives mixed with vitamins. He put them in a big bag and told the woman to take them three times a day.

I told her, "This is not a disease you can fix with medicine alone. As you take the medicine, you must also pray. It is neither the doctor nor the medicine that will cure you, but God. Whenever you take this medicine, say a prayer."

Sang-hyeon and I took the woman's hands and prayed. After that, every day I prayed for her, visiting her often to encourage her.

It was not long before she was able to get up on her feet. At first, she used her hands to push herself up onto her knees. Soon she took one step, then she took two, and finally she was able to walk properly.

After the woman's miraculous recovery, Sang-hyeon and Hwalbin Church gained some recognition. Rumors spread that we had the power to heal the lame. We thought it was a good thing, but soon found ourselves in an awkward and difficult position.

Hearing the rumors, the disabled came to seek us out. One person even came in a taxi from far away. I was caught by surprise and had the embarrassing task of turning everyone away.

Through Sang-hyeon's efforts, we put together a medical team comprised of students of medicine, pharmacy, dentistry, and nursing. We called them the Songjeong Medical Service Team and every Saturday they provided free medical and dental treatment to local residents. Their services were generally effective and many people were cured. Some people who could not be cured at the bigger hospitals were cured by the medicine prescribed by our team.

ONCE THE HEALTH PROJECT WAS UNDER WAY, we worked to educate people. In the slums, poverty is more a mental problem than a material one. Of course, economic and social elements are important, but the most important factors are psychological. As such, the best approach to a problem was usually to find a way to change people's mindset, to awaken their consciousness through education.

We had to convince residents that they should strive to overcome their poverty and lead a constructive life. That would be the foundation for a healthy mind and would eventually help build a democratic society. To make this happen, we had to train people to improve their skills and use them to achieve a goal.

We devised an education program that took all these considerations into account and worked in stages to implement it.

On April 6, 1972, we opened the Baedal Academy, our social education center, as part of our education project. Our first program consisted of middle-school night classes for 56 of the local children. After that we instituted a number of other programs.

On April 15, we selected a number of young people, in their twenties, to take six hours of training per week in a six-month leadership course.

Three times a week, we held classes on childcare, health, culture, cooking, and technical skills for housewives, as a way to help them get part-time work they could do at home.

Three times a week there were classes for children in painting, singing, and recreation. These programs infused the neighborhood with new vitality.

Soon, however, we ran into a major problem. The church building was torn down by the township office's demolition crew. It came in a surprise attack. At around 9:30 a.m. on April 24, I was making house calls in the neighborhood when a child, out of breath, ran up to me.

Children gathered in front of the Baedal Academy.

"Pastor, they're tearing down the church!"

I asked him why, but all he could say was that demolition crewmen had come in droves and were now hard at work. I ran to the church, but the work was already under way. The demolition men had parked two trucks on the Cheonggye-cheon banks and were moving quickly.

People began to gather. The young men grew angry and people began to swear. My rubbish-picking partner, Choi Il-jin, came over to me and said, "Pastor, this is too much. Why don't we fight?"

"I don't know," I said. "Let me think." Before he heard my answer, Choi had already gone to gather a gang and they were preparing to do battle with the demolition crew.

I hesitated. It was as if the Seongdong-gu township office had realized there might be an uproar from the community and had decided to preempt it with an early morning surprise attack, sending along three times as many crewmen as usual. Public employees begin work at nine and the fact that demolition work had already begun at half past attested to their concern.

When the demolition work was half finished, the mood among the residents became menacing. They appeared one by one carrying wooden clubs and steel pipes. One of them gave out a fierce yell.

"Hey, you bastards! I'm going to enjoy this. Start saying your prayers because you're going to need them."

The demolition crew had anticipated things would get violent and were ready for us. They had recruited some thugs who were known to be ruthless and handy with their fists. Stones were already being thrown in the direction of the demolition crew who, as if driven by anger, began to tear down the building with vicious energy.

I thought hard. What should I do? Should I leave the residents alone, all worked up as they are, or should I try to stop them? Should I try to deal rationally with the demolition crew or just sit it out and let it happen? Which is the better way? After weighing everything in my mind, I came to a decision. I decided to calm people down and let the church be torn down. We could build a new church and the process of demolition and reconstruction would put our efforts for community development to the test. It would also be a good opportunity to raise consciousness among the residents.

I called together some of the leaders and spoke to them.

"I have a plan. Could you please quiet people down?"

"What? I don't understand. We can't just let them tear the church down. It's not that easy to get people worked up like this."

"No. Listen to me. If this gets violent, everything will go wrong. It's better if we just put up with it. Please listen to me and do as I ask."

They didn't look happy about it, but they gave in to my request. They wended their way through the crowd saying, "The pastor wants us to cool down, so hold back. Hold still." The people dropped their stones and stepped back, but the swearing got worse.

Finally, the roof caved in. Watching the church being torn down, the church I had worked so hard to put up, gave me stomach spasms. but I didn't let my feelings show and stepped back. I watched the scene from under the eaves of a neighboring house.

When the demolition crew had finished, Kim Jong-gil, a deacon and head of the volunteer-services committee climbed to the top of the rubble with a shovel in his hand. He raised the shovel high and shouted, "The building has been torn down, but that doesn't mean Hwalbin Church has been destroyed. Victory is ours!"

I waved at him to come down. One of the youths came to me and said, "Pastor. We have something on the demolition crew. A guy was in the medical-equipment room and put something in his pocket. When Choi saw him and complained, they assaulted him. We're not going to take this. When they go to get on their trucks, we'll give them what they deserve!"

"No, you mustn't. Just let it go."

"Don't worry. We'll make sure they don't blame you."

He ran around yelling and telling the young men to gather on the bank. The demolition crew was heading up the hill. The swearing started again and the young men started moving around. In a panic, I went toward them and pleaded with them.

"Guys, guys! Calm down. Do you want to ruin the feast before it starts? Please don't do anything!"

They listened to me and stood still. When the crew had left in their trucks, I went to the home of one of the church members. I went into an empty room, pulled the blanket over my head, and tried to sleep. I slept soundly and the next morning headed for where the church had been. Some people from the neighborhood were already there having a meeting.

One of them got up and said, "Hwalbin Church is our benefactor and our shelter. The fate of the church is our responsibility. It's the same as if our own homes had been demolished. We will unite and rebuild the church."

THEN AND THERE THE LOCALS ORGANIZED the Hwalbin Church reconstruction committee and set up teams for collecting funds, for organizing work crews, and for managing public relations. They prepared a public notice, informing the neighborhood of the project, and circulated a petition to request permission to rebuild the church. The petition would later be sent to Seoul City Hall. Everything went ahead without my involvement. Then they went around getting signatures for the petition and collecting money for construction.

Those in charge of rebuilding the church discussed the plans and design and how to get materials. The reconstruction committee took the lead and secured the consensus of the residents, fixing the work schedule. It was gratifying to see and deep down I was almost grateful to the authorities for having torn down the church.

Copies of a petition with 560 signatures were delivered to the Seoul mayor and Seongdong-gu township office. Members of the reconstruction committee had gone from house to house collecting signatures. They believed in the cause and said they were prepared to fight and go to prison, if the petition was rejected. It was agreed among the residents that if a satisfactory answer was not forthcoming by May 2, they would go en masse to City Hall.

That night the members of Hwalbin Church called a meeting. They held a long and heated discussion. The hard-liners were ready to storm the township office the next day and tear it down. Their view was that the demolition crew had come unjustifiably and had torn down our church so they would do the same.

The moderates said we should give the authorities a deadline for responding, with the idea in mind that we would take action if City Hall failed to approve our plan to rebuild the church. An even more conciliatory group said that it was a success just to have all the residents come out and take an active part in the rebuilding project and that we should just support them.

After a lengthy debate, they asked my opinion. I told them that since residents had sent a petition to the Seoul mayor, they, the church members, should follow it up with a stronger-worded one. At the same time, church members needed to continue to support the activities of the residents who had initiated the rebuilding campaign. Everybody should participate in the project, not as church members, but as residents of the community.

As the news spread that Hwalbin Church had been demolished, support came from many quarters. City Hall and the township office were hounded with complaints and newspapers soon picked up the story.

In a few days, we had collected enough money to erect a new building. The 1,600 families had contributed a minimum of one hundred *won* and one day's work each, enabling the project to go ahead.

May 2, the deadline set by the residents for a response from City Hall, was fast approaching. They discussed what to do next, if permission to rebuild the church was not forthcoming. The committee prepared a list of people who would participate in a demonstration, in case it came to that.

A petition was drawn up by members of the church and sent to City Hall. The petition read:

> We salute the mayor who works hard for the nation's development and the Saemaeul Movement. It is to our regret that we find ourselves, the congregation of Hwalbin Church, with no option but to send this petition.
>
> On April 24, the Seongdong-gu township office came and with no justification tore down our church. We would like to know if this was a simple administrative error or a deliberate act of persecution of our missionary work.
>
> In regard to this matter, we have already sought the support of the National Council of Churches in Korea (KNCC) and news organizations and have lodged a formal complaint with the head of the township office, who we believe is responsible for this action. We now request full compensation for the loss of the building.

The building was erected seven years ago and was registered as legal structure No. 24-24622. Notwithstanding its registration, dated September 2, 1971, the building was targeted for demolition. In January 1972, when the demolition notification was issued, the local residents sent a petition for the notice to be retracted, citing that the building had been registered and that the church played an important role in the neighborhood. No answer to that letter was received and, in February, Pastor Kim Jin-hong was taken into custody, relative to the matter, and was locked up overnight.

In spite of all this, on April 24, the demolition crew came, pulled down the church sign, and began their work. Moreover, when one of the residents, Choi Il-jin, caught one of the demolition crewmen putting something in his pocket and protested, he was beaten by five or six of the men. The members of the church and the residents are very upset about this incident.

In keeping with the Saemaeul Movement, pursued by the government of President Park Jeong-hui, our church has undertaken many projects to encourage the youth, educate the people, improve the health of the residents, and improve life in the neighborhood in general (details in attached appendix).

We have received no help from the government for any of our work. On the contrary, we have had many threats to tear down our church building and have even seen our pastor locked up. We, members of the church, can no longer just watch without taking action. The General Assembly of the Presbyterian Church of Korea agrees that these actions are a direct challenge to the church and against the interests of the Saemaeul Movement and has pledged to work with us. We are of one mind and hope to see this issue resolved.

If we do not soon receive an acceptable explanation for the actions taken and a reply regarding measures to rebuild the church, we and five hundred members of the church will call on the mayor directly.

April 27, 1972
Members of Hwalbin Church

ON THE AFTERNOON OF MAY 1, I was contacted by the chief of Seong-dong-gu township office, who said he wanted to see me.

"We don't need to meet," I told him. "The people own the church. Meet with them. Are you and I both not here to serve the people? If you have something to say, say it to the residents. And don't talk to them sitting in your office. Come out here to the site."

The next day, a jeep came from the township office. I approached the scene and listened. I heard one of the residents say, "You can't treat us any way you like, just because you think we're powerless. If we spread rumors that you are a great man, you can become mayor, but if we denounce you as an impotent public official, they will strip you of your post as chief of Seongdong-gu township."

I was surprised at this logical argument. The residents were usually mild-mannered, but now, armed with a purpose and in a mood for action, they had changed. Noticing this change in them, I saw the potential for realizing democracy in our country.

In the afternoon, members of the reconstruction committee sought me out and said that the township office wanted me to pay them a visit.

"Their attitude seems sincere," I said. "Perhaps it'd be a good idea to drop by, but do I really need to go? You can go and take care of things on your own."

"Do you really think so, Pastor? They keep telling us that we have to bring you along."

"Well, that's their side of things, but the reconstruction committee is an independent group and it'd be better if you acted without me."

"The township office says that we may be independent, but you're the one controlling us, so they think it's no use talking to us without you. They say that if you don't agree, then it's all over."

"I don't like that. The authorities always think people are being controlled by someone. They can't go on thinking that."

"We know what you mean, but at this stage it'd be better if you came with us."

"If that's what you really think, then I'll go. Let's see what happens."

I accompanied the representatives to the Seongdong-gu township office. The head of the ward office was there when we arrived. He told us that the township chief was out, but the deputy chief would see us. He said the deputy chief was in charge of civil petitions, in any case. We sat in the deputy chief's office, drinking tea. As the talk went back and forth, I said nothing.

The residents talked about the demolition and claimed that the city had to recognize that the land belonged to the church and had to grant permission for the church to be rebuilt. They also said that in compensation for the demolition, the authorities should supply the materials for the reconstruction. The deputy chief talked about the difficulties of doing as they asked, from an administrative point of view, and said that the demolition of the church was not done in bad faith, but according to statutes governing unauthorized buildings.

The resident representatives responded, "We aren't here to talk about the law. We want justice. The city has to give us permission to rebuild and supply us with the materials. If we get the materials, the work will be done by the residents." The deputy chief, however, told us that that was impossible.

The discussion was not going smoothly and the residents began to raise their voices and get up from their seats.

"Forget it, if all you can say is 'It can't be done.' We have our own ideas. Haven't you ever heard, even a worm resists when trod upon?"

Being the deputy township chief, he was a skillful negotiator. He tried to calm them down and, when they had taken their seats again, came up with a compromise.

"If that's what you really think, let's not argue. Let's negotiate and see if we can't come to some agreement. If you really are united in this project of rebuilding the church, instead of putting up a proper building, why don't you set up a tent instead? We will buy you the tent."

"If we can put up a tent, we can also put up a building. You don't have to give us a tent. We can do that much on our own. We've collected money and will build a church with a proper roof."

"Don't do that. Try to understand our situation. They say you should check whether the mouse has a hole to escape from before chasing it. We have to solve this problem in a way that suits both parties."

I had been sitting quietly, but the deputy chief addressed the next words to me.

"I think you'll have to help us out here, Pastor. Please accept our compromise."

"I don't know. I don't think I need to put in my two cents. They have come as representatives of the residents and they'll have to solve the problem for themselves."

Then the head of the ward office came up with an idea.

"Well, then, why don't you have the residents build the church, but roof it with the tent material that the township office supplies."

At this the deputy chief said nothing. His silence was taken for agreement. The residents looked at me. I nodded and said, "I think that's a good idea, one that saves face for everyone. The residents get to build a real building and the township office comes off as having given permission only for a tent."

Then, with an acceptance from the head of the reconstruction committee, the matter was resolved.

"If that's your position, we accept the compromise."

The deputy chief said he would send the tent within the next three days. The residents promised to put up the building and use the tent for the roof. The deputy chief pretended not to hear that and spoke to me. "Pastor, if there's ever another problem, let's talk about it and try to find a solution before it gets out of hand."

"I'd like that, too."

As soon as we returned to the neighborhood, a resident's meeting was held so that those who had gone to the township office could report what had transpired. The residents applauded them for their effort. Then everyone began to discuss the construction.

The next day, work began in earnest. Workers were organized into groups and everything progressed smoothly. We found all the workers we needed among the residents, including carpenters, plasterers, bricklayers, and painters, all of whom put in their day's work. Those who were not able to work donated money.

We finished the building on May 22 and held a ceremony to dedicate the new church.

To celebrate the dedication, Kim Sang-hyeon recruited the services of the Seoul National University Medical College string ensemble. Thanks to them, the church festivity turned into a party for the whole neighborhood.

ONCE THE CHURCH WAS REBUILT, the programs that had been interrupted were started up again. I worked hard, as an expression of my appreciation to the residents for the spirit of participation and service they had shown in the church's reconstruction.

I gathered 110 young people from the area and formed the Self-Support Association. The members were mostly delinquents and ex-convicts. The purpose of the group was to help them help themselves by motivating them and putting them to work.

The following is a mission statement of the Association:

THE OBJECTIVE OF THE ASSOCIATION: The people of the 1,600 households of No. 74 Songjeong-dong, on the downstream part of Cheonggye-cheon, are mostly from rural areas and have been living in distressed circumstances, due to extreme poverty, disease, ignorance, and despair.

For us, reality is cruel. With no foundation on which to build, we have lived in despair, with 70 percent of us unemployed and addicted to alcohol and gambling. Having no way to relieve our suppressed anger, we have often turned to violence and many of us now live branded as ex-convicts.

We now realize that we cannot allow ourselves to be alienated any further from the human race and believe that only we can find the way out of our distress. For this reason, we have risen up and united to find a way to support ourselves. The road will be paved with pain, sweat, and blood, but rather than live with bowed heads, we have chosen to die standing up. We have decided to take our fate into our own hands.

In the past, we felt defeated and alone, but now we are united and intent on overcoming our adversity. As we take this action, we believe that a new life will open up before us. The Bible says that God helps those who help themselves. We believe this truly.

June 9, 1972
Shantytown Residents of Songjeong-dong

The members of the Self-Support Association developed a fresh outlook on life and participated in a variety of activities, such as rubbish picking, collecting secondhand goods, junk recycling, and food processing. They worked hard for success.

Next we formed the Association for the Unemployed. High unemployment and a general attitude of desperation were the stark reality of the slum. People lived a self-destructive lifestyle, playing cards, drinking, and brawling.

I went around and met the men, all heads of households in their 30s and 40s, one by one, and organized them as a group. I made plans to lead them in a new direction, through cooperative activity. On the strength of their cooperation, bit by bit, opportunities for employment opened for them.

Those who gained work through the Association for the Unemployed donated 5 percent of their earnings to the group. The accumulated funds were used for health care for their families and grants to the men who remained unemployed.

16

Stopping by Woods on a Snowy Evening

ONE YEAR HAD PASSED SINCE I had moved to Cheonggy-cheon. I was satisfied with what I had accomplished in that time. When I first arrived in the community, I was a stranger. After twelve months, I was supported in my missionary activities by the congregation of Hwalbin Church and the Residents Society. Their support gave me confidence that if things kept going as they were, I would eventually be able to achieve something worthwhile.

Contrary to appearances, serious problems were brewing for me of which was wholly unaware. The first problem occurred in the church. Members of Hwalbin Church had had little experience in church affairs because most of them had begun their religious life in the slum. Thus, few of the members were capable of efficiently handling the administration of the church. The most sensitive of these problems was that no one knew anything about church finances and how to manage them.

In the beginning, donations by the congregation amounted to only four or five hundred *won* per week. This sum increased as the membership grew and the church became the center of people's religious life.

I put a man in charge of church finances who was, by all appearances, honest and competent. He made a living by going around collecting used items that he would then fix up and sell. During the first several months, he seemed to be managing church affairs relatively well, but as time went by, his financial reports became less regular. Whenever the church needed money to buy something, he would say there was none.

I finally examined the account books and discovered that he had been embezzling money. I confronted him with it. When asked how he could steal God's money, he proffered an absurd explanation. "You spend the church's money. Why shouldn't I?"

I was overwhelmed by his lack of guilt. I took the account books from him and never saw him again. I had lost both the church's money and a believer.

This incident led us to select a financial officer by election. We chose a man by the name of Choi. He was a construction crew foreman, although in the slum he was regarded more as a construction contractor. Shortly after he took over the church's financial affairs, rumors began to circulate that he, too, was misappropriating funds.

I took the matter up with him.

"Mr. Choi," I said, "there's a rumor going around that makes me wonder whether the church's financial affairs are being properly managed. Could you please put the account books in order and make a report to the congregation this Sunday? As soon as they are ready, I would like to go over them with you."

I met Mr. Choi on Saturday and asked if I could see the books. At first he hesitated, but then said he would work on them and bring them to my house that evening. He failed to show up, although he did come to church the next day. While I was delivering the sermon, he sprang up from his seat and shouted.

"Everyone, listen to me. I want to use this service to speak out. Pastor Kim is a thief. Don't be fooled by him. He's a hypocrite. He says one thing and does another. While delivering his sermons, he speaks of love, but in reality, he has been siphoning off the church's money. I don't say this without evidence. I'll show it to anyone who wants to know the truth."

At that, he pointed at me, saying, "Pastor Kim. Stop telling us lies. Come down from the pulpit right now." I was taken aback by his accusation. There was a commotion among the congregation.

One worshiper said, "This guy is surely out of his mind. Get him out of here."

Another person, however, shouted, "Why all the racket? Let's listen to what he has to say. He says he can produce evidence. Let him do it."

At that, the church became as noisy as a marketplace.

I spoke up, "Everyone, be quiet. Please, be quiet!" but my plea was to no avail. In an effort to calm down the congregation, I started singing a hymn. At first, only a few people joined me in singing, then others joined in.

While singing, I was searching for a way to cope with the incident. I hit upon the old saying, "Give a man enough rope and he'll hang himself." Thus, I made up my mind to let Choi speak, instead of trying to keep him quiet. Immediately, when the chorus wound up, I said, "Mr. Choi, speak up if you like. Take whatever time you need to say what you want to say in a logical manner..."

One young man stood up before I had completed my remarks and said, "Pastor, I think that a mad man like this one should be flogged. He should be beaten until his eyes pop out."

Another chimed in. "I agree. He seems to have a death wish. Perhaps he has lived too long."

Again I tried to calm people down. "Everyone, I must disagree. We are one family and everyone should be given a chance to speak out. Let Mr. Choi explain. Wait and see what evidence he produces."

Choi became perplexed by my remarks. He apparently believed that his attack on me would result in my preventing him from speaking, or I would counterattack in some way. He was at a loss because I was allowing him to speak. Standing, he mumbled, "If I say what I know, you will be kicked out of this community, so for now I'll keep quiet. If any of you wants to know the real story, I will meet with you in person."

At that, he stormed out of the church. I continued my sermon. After the service, we held a meeting where we took up Choi's allegations. Unexpectedly on my part, the congregation was split in two groups, with a considerable number of people coming to Choi's defense.

One of his accusers said, "Choi must be a mad man. He's accusing the Pastor because his embezzlement of church funds is about to be exposed. I don't think that he should be left to get away with this."

Another person spoke on behalf of Choi, however, saying, "It's not right that we condemn Mr. Choi in a kangaroo court. He would not have made his accusation, if he had no evidence. The truth should be brought to light. When the church building was under construction, donations poured in, but we have seen nothing."

It was all but impossible to conduct the discussion in an orderly way, with the congregation being so split. If the wrangling continued, it looked as if the argument would deteriorate. It was then that I realized how a church begins to come apart. I announced that open debate would take place at the evening service, with Mr. Choi present, and I urged his supporters to bring him to the church without fail.

That evening, Mr. Choi didn't show up. He gave the income and expense accounts to another church member who had gone to his house and who then delivered them to the church. Choi was quoted as saying that he could not believe in God under the direction of an unscrupulous fellow like me.

To the congregation, I shouted, "Everyone, please listen. As the books are now with us, I suggest that several people be selected to look into the matter, while at the same time putting everything in order."

Most of the congregation agreed. By the time we finished, a team of five people had been selected and was assigned the task of examining the books. Several days later, the team announced the results of their investigation, indicating how much of the church's funds Mr. Choi had misappropriated. The misappropriation was recorded as a deficit, following much discussion.

The episode was put to rest and Kim Yong-jun, who was now considered the most dependable of the church members, was named the church's new financial officer.

UNFORTUNATE THINGS SEEM TO HAPPEN IN SERIES. Money was also misappropriated from the income-generation committee. They had planned to engage in a variety of activities, including food preparation, recycling of used goods, and part-time work for women, to raise funds.

For food preparation, people cut up dried pollack, which they packaged and sold to drink houses. The rubbish pickers collected cast-off items and recycled them as reusable products. For part-time work for women, committee members would collect sewing materials from clothing factories in Pyeonghwa Market and deliver them to housewives in the slum, to be sewn and returned.

To help finance these projects, I borrowed 500,000 *won* from my sister, an elementary-school teacher living in Gwangju. She said she did not need interest on the money, but asked me to be sure to pay it back, saying that she had saved it from her small salary.

I distributed the money to the manager of each business unit, all of them agreeing that the principal would be repaid within six months. I thought that I would be able to return the money to my sister within 10 months, at the latest. As it turned out, however, I was miserably out of touch with reality. Trouble developed just a few days after the money was distributed. There was a rumor that the business fund was being squandered by several men. Rather than believe the rumors, I chastised the people who passed on such gossip.

I told them, "You can't improve your lot if you have so little faith in others. Believe in your fellow man the way you believe in God."

One person replied, "Pastor, you'll find out soon enough. You'll get yourself in trouble, if you put that much confidence in everyone."

About three weeks later, I called in the business project managers. I asked about their work progress and details of how they were spending the money. Strangely enough, they said little. After dispersing the group, I met with them individually. They all responded that they had spent the money they controlled to meet their own financial obligations or on living expenses.

I felt betrayed and could not stand to be with them. It served no purpose to argue about money that was already spent. I called them together and said in disgust, "I don't want to make a speech. As you are aware, we are Hwalbin comrades who, united by faith, are trying to overcome poverty and, in the process, build a legend. Our belief and integrity, as well as our future, can't be measured by a few hundred thousand *won*. I will repay the money that I borrowed from my sister. Let's say publicly that I recovered all the money from you and we'll leave this incident behind. We'll put our cooperative projects aside for a while and, for now, try to focus on our own livelihoods. I don't think we're ready to undertake projects like these just yet."

This incident shocked me greatly. Unable to trust either residents or church members, I was losing my confidence in carrying out any projects.

ONE DAY, AS I WAS ABOUT TO LEAVE THE CHURCH to resume my rubbish picking, a U.S. military jeep pulled up ahead of me and stopped. The vehicle was pulling a trailer full of canned beef.

An American soldier got out of the vehicle and told me that at the pleading of a missionary he had brought canned beef for malnourished children of the slum area. Dozens of children were already surrounding the jeep, anxious to devour the food. I was not comfortable with the idea of the community accepting canned beef from a foreign solider.

One unfortunate legacy of the Korean War was the nuisance of relief goods. When the war was under way, vast amounts of relief items came from the U.S. and reached every remote village of Korea. I was very much concerned that Korea, as a nation, would develop a habit of depending on others.

Korean Christian organizations perhaps received relief goods in greater volume than other organizations in Korea. As a result, these organizations developed a relief mentality and came to measure their success in terms of how much they received. This attitude had to be corrected to foster long-term self-sufficiency not only for individuals but for the nation as a whole.

In this case, it would be difficult to reject the canned beef because it had been brought by a well-meaning American solider who was not aware of any of these issues. Still, it would have been impossible to accept the aid unconditionally. Doing so would have had a negative effect on the children, who were only too willing to gobble it up. Compounding the difficulty of the situation, there was not enough to satisfy the needs of all the children.

After some hesitation, I told the soldier, "Thank you, but no. We have to stand on our own two feet. Please take the cans away. I'm very sorry, and thank you for your concern."

The soldier tensed up immediately and asked, "What are you saying?" He then examined my facial expression. I repeated my words in a reassuring voice. He left, having understood what I meant.

The children watched as the jeep drove out of sight. When it was gone, they stood staring into the distance, gripped by a sense of loss and reluctance. I hurried to go about picking rubbish, unable to face their disappointment.

I HAD TEAMED UP WITH A 23-YEAR-OLD RUBBISH PICKER named Jong-cheol. We went about our work by first putting our cart in an alley near where we were working. We then went about collecting paper and cans,

265

putting them in our baskets, which we dumped in the cart. We repeated this until we had filled the cart to overflowing. We then moved our cart to the salvage center, where we sorted, weighed, and were paid for our day's work. One day, while sorting our day's take, Jong-cheol grabbed his stomach and began to sweat profusely. When I asked him what the problem was, he groaned painfully.

"Is it bearable?"

"No, it feels as if something is clawing at my insides."

Shaken, I stopped a taxi and took him to the emergency room at Hanyang University Hospital. We were sent to the radiology department. There they told us that we would have to pay before they could see him. The cost of an x-ray was quite expensive and I did not have enough money. I begged for mercy.

"This man is in serious condition. Please x-ray him now. I'll go home and bring the money, but he shouldn't have to wait."

A clerk in the accounting department turned me down. I returned to the x-ray room and shouted, "I can't pay the entire bill right now. Please x-ray and examine him. I promise that I'll bring money from home as quickly as possible."

The x-ray room staff turned me down flatly, saying that hospital rules did not allow for credit. Exasperated, I had Jong-cheol lie down on a bench in front of the cashier windows.

"You stay put here until I come back with the money."

"Return quickly. Otherwise, I know I'll die," he said.

"Nonsense. Do you believe a person could die so easily? You won't die. Just hold on."

I ran back to the slum, leaving behind Jong-cheol, who was breathing heavily because of the severe pain. It was difficult to borrow money from anyone in the daytime. Anyone with any money was at work and only children and laggards were hanging around the neighborhood. Visiting several homes, I managed to borrow some money and hurried back to the hospital.

Hanyang University Hospital was located in a hilly area, so I had a hard time climbing the steps leading up to the hospital. I was away nearly three hours.

When I arrived at the emergency room, Jong-cheol was still on the bench. His breathing was labored, his shoulders moving up and down.

Concerned, I knelt beside him and pleaded with him, "Jong-cheol! Please wake up! Jong-cheol! I came running. You must wake up!"

He was looking at me in such a way that I did not know for sure whether he recognized me. Fearing the worst, I softly slapped his cheek several times, saying, "Jong-cheol! It's me. It's me. I got the money. You can get your x-ray. Wake up!"

Then, looking distant, he arose and spat out, "Money! Money! Money for medicine! Money for medicine!" He then collapsed and died.

I could hardly suppress my anger, as I watched him die. I said to myself that the hospital would not go unpunished because it had let a young man die for such a paltry sum. I wanted to bring the rubbish pickers to destroy the place.

I slipped out of the hospital. Running, I thought, I'll rally the rubbish pickers. I'll tell them that Jong-cheol had died because Hanyang University Hospital refused to treat him. I don't think the hospital should go unpunished. I'll have some of the rubbish pickers break the kneecaps of the hospital director, while others break the windows, starting with those at the entrance. Others will smash the windows of the administration offices and the x-ray room. They'll trash the place completely, and I'll take full responsibility for their actions.

The rubbish pickers, who hold grievances and resentment, would welcome the chance to gang up on the hospital and tear it apart. They would say, "Gladly. What fun. You stand back. We'll show them what we're made of."

I stopped near the rubbish-picking center in Ttukseom, out of breath. Would Jesus be pleased with what I want to do? How would Jesus feel, if I let the guys trash the hospital and beat up the director?

I was not sure he would approve. I thought that instead of praising me, Jesus would chastise me.

Suddenly, I wavered. What should I do? Should I follow through on my plan, or do I stop here? After much hesitation, I returned to the church. Inside, I knelt and prayed.

"Jesus! In dealing with this rotten world, please let me become a builder, not a destroyer! Jesus! Let me dedicate myself to healing our wretched world, instead of cursing it."

After taking a deep breath, I returned to the hospital to see to Jong-cheol's body.

IN THE EVENING OF THE DAY Jong-cheol's funeral was held, someone told me that the shaman's daughter was gravely ill and that she urgently needed care. A while before, the girl, 15, had given birth. No one knew who the father was.

I went to her, trying to figure out what might be wrong with her. When I saw her, she looked as if she could not survive the night. It was as though death's dark shadow had already come over her.

I wondered whether the slum was not some kind of United Nations for all manner of sickness. It seemed that it was plagued by every disease known to man. The girl appeared to be suffering from a skin disease, but her overall condition was beyond description. Wherever her

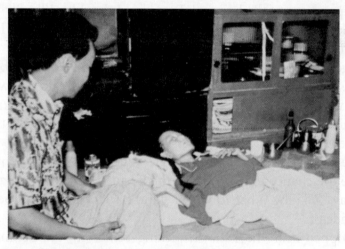

Attending the shaman's daughter in her home.

skin had been in contact with the floor, it had concave sores that discharged a fluid.

I angrily asked her mother, "How has she come to be condemned to this miserable condition?"

"She began to show sore spots after giving birth, but I paid no attention to them. Since then the sores have grown larger."

"Why have you kept her sickness a secret?" I asked.

"Why should I volunteer to make public the illness of the girl who gave birth to a bastard?"

"You should at least have tried to care for her."

I felt like hitting the mother. I asked the girl to roll over on her stomach to see her back. The skin on her back was decomposing, as maggots ate away at her flesh, exposing her backbone.

I shuddered. The girl wore an expression of resignation, as if she had already experienced enough pain to last a lifetime. I took pity on her and wanted to talk to her with my heart, not my voice.

Dear girl, why are you forced to suffer such terrible pain? You are not at an age when you really need a man. How did this happen? I could not pray for her to survive. Rather, I prayed that she die in peace. "God. Please let this girl die as quickly as possible. Do not let her suffer more pain. Let her die peacefully. I pray in the name of Jesus. Amen."

I prayed loudly while holding her hands. Her eyes were wet with tears. She began to cry. The mother deserved punishment, I thought, but the innocent daughter was suffering all of the consequences.

Before getting married, her mother had been a hospital nurse. She was a happy housewife, until her husband became paralyzed because of a traffic accident. She deserted her disabled husband, who was confined to his room, and with her children had moved around, before settling down in the Cheonggye-cheon slum.

Supported by his relatives, the husband managed to get along and searched desperately for his wife and children. He heard that they were living in the Cheonggye-cheon shantytown. First, his relatives found out where they were. Then, the next day, they brought the disabled man to the house where his runaway wife and children were living.

The man crawled to the house and pounded on the door with his forehead, unable to use his paralyzed hands. He then cried out his children's names. His wife was shocked by the sudden appearance of her husband. She quickly locked the door, telling her children not to open it.

She then shouted at him, "You cripple! What on earth has brought you here? I have enough trouble feeding my children. Should I struggle to feed you as well? Go away! Get out of here!"

Weeping, the children pleaded that their father be let in, but the mother would not listen. She would not change her mind, because she had since taken a new husband, ten years her junior. She had no use for a creaky old model, now that she was happy with a strong new one.

According to her neighbors, the woman and her young lover

engaged in nightly "wrestling bouts," making a lot of noise, which made it difficult for them to sleep. Most houses in the shantytown were separated by thin wooden walls, so it was nearly impossible for a person not to know what was happening in the house next door. The neighbors were concerned about the emotional effect the noisy couple would have on the children.

The former husband waited outside for two days, begging for her to change her mind. His children fed him. Two days later, his relatives came back to the house to check on what had happened. They were upset to see that the man had been left outside. In disgust, they cursed her.

One said, "You are worse than a beast. You must be a demon disguised as a human. I want to see what end you come to."

Six weeks later, there was a rumor that the woman was on her death-bed, having been stricken by some disease. Many people believed that the woman's illness was the result of her husband's vendetta. Eventually, she recovered. This was the woman standing before me.

After prayers, church members talked about the woman often. They recounted how as soon as the girl's mother recovered from her illness, she became a shaman. While she was suffering from a high fever, she said God had sent her a sign and that she was invited to heaven, having been inspired by a "magical spirit."

She boasted that she could predict the future and performed exorcisms for shantytown residents. The shaman limped, presumably because of the result of her illness.

It was around this same time that her daughter was stricken. People said that the baby's father was her mother's lover and that the man had forced the girl to have sex with him while her mother was out. They said that the man had raped her again, just a few days after she gave birth, which resulted in an infection. Of course, these were only rumors, but I wanted to know what the man was really like.

When I visited the shaman's home the second time, the man was in the girl's room. He looked dull-witted. I wanted to curse him for his behavior, but I restrained myself. He was smoking in the presence of someone who was ill, which forced me to confront him.

"How dare you smoke with a sick person in the room? Put out that cigarette right now. You have no common sense."

In response to my angry voice and my glare, he grudgingly complied. He looked around for a place to put the cigarette and, not finding any, left the room. I told the girl's mother that her daughter needed to be hospitalized. She hinted that it would be useless for her to be hospitalized because she had no chance of survival.

"I just want her to die in a clean place."

The mother nodded, turning away from me, cowed by my stern manner. I took the girl by taxi to the Southern Municipal Hospital. During the ride, I held her hands and prayed.

"Lord. I pray that you exert yourself to make a hospital room available to this girl. I don't want to let this poor soul take her last breath in a dirty and dimly lit room. I plead that there be a room with a clean bed, a white sheet, and a comfortable pillow, even if it is small."

The Southern Municipal Hospital said they had no vacancies, but that even if they did, it would be pointless to admit her. They explained that there was little chance that she could survive. I pleaded with a doctor, whom I knew from before.

"I sincerely ask you to prepare a bed. I want this poor girl to pass away in peace."

The doctor appeared to be touched by my plea and promised to do what he could to find a room for her. After waiting three hours in a corridor, a room was finally found for the girl. I told her mother to stay with her and returned home.

In the evening, rain began to pour. As I listened to the heavy rain falling on the roof, I was unable to sleep. I became restless at the thought that I could be of no help to the girl.

THE FOLLOWING DAY, after presiding over the early morning service, Choi and I went out to pick rubbish. I promised myself that I would call on the girl at the hospital, after picking up two bags of discards early in the morning. To reach the rubbish-picking center behind Ttukseom Racetrack, we had to walk along the Cheonggye-cheon embankment and cross a wide road that lead to Walker Hill.

At dawn, as we were about to cross the road, I saw a bundle on the ground under a streetlight. Believing that someone had lost it in the night, I said, "Choi, do you see that bundle over there, under that streetlight? Go see what it is. If there are any valuables, we have to return them to their owner."

Examining the bundle, Choi exclaimed, "Ah hah! It's money, money! We've struck it rich!

Throwing off his bag, he dashed away with the wad of money in his hand. Puzzled, I shouted after him, "Calm down, man. Where are you going?" but he wouldn't listen.

After chasing after him, a short distance, I walked to the work site, picked a cartful of material, and then went to the hospital.

On my way, I bought a rose, a packet of candies, and some orange juice, but when I got to the room where I'd left the shaman's daughter, another patient was occupying it. A nurse told me that the girl had died in the early hours of the morning and had been moved to a mortuary.

I went to where they had taken her body. It was covered with a white sheet. I put the rose and candies by her side. Outside, it was raining again. The next day the rain continued. Her body was cremated at Byeokje Crematorium. As I left the crematorium, taking a pouch containing her ashes, I felt empty and worn-out. The whole world was gray. If felt as though the wind was blowing through a big hole that had been made in my stomach.

The more I thought about the girl's death, the more I pitied her. Why did she have to pass on to the other world, after undergoing so much hardship in this world? The wind carried the girl's bitter cries and every plant I stepped on was filled with her troubled soul. I arrived at the Han River Bridge with the pouch.

I spoke as I scattered her ashes over the water flowing below the bridge. "Make your way to the big Pacific Ocean. Several of our neighbors have already gone before you. Go and live in the same neighborhood. You lived here for only fifteen short years. I hope you can live longer there. Live there until Jesus comes to us. Let's all live together in heaven, when Jesus comes."

After throwing her ashes and the pouch in the water, I went downtown. Amid the driving rain, I felt cut off from the world. I wanted to go off to heaven as well. Walking slowly, I recited *Stopping by Woods on a Snowy Evening* by Robert Frost. It was one of my favorites:

> Whose woods these are I think I know.
> His house is in the village though;

He will not see me stopping here
To watch his woods fill up with snow.

My little horse must think it queer
To stop without a farmhouse near
Between the woods and frozen lake
The darkest evening of the year.

He gives his harness bells a shake
To ask if there is some mistake.
The only other sound's the sweep
Of easy wind and downy flake.

The woods are lovely, dark, and deep,
But I I have promises to keep,
And miles to go before I sleep,
And miles to go before I sleep.

The woods in the poem symbolize death. It is "lovely, dark, and deep." I wished that the girl could enter such a dimension. Although the world of death may be lovely, dark, and deep, it is not a world that is open to anyone at anytime. Before death, a person is obliged to deliver on a promise and tread a certain path.

While walking over the Han River Bridge, I pondered the promise I should keep and the path I should thread, before I die. I prayed, "Lord! I pray that you give me strength to keep the promise I have made with you. Let me have the courage to travel the bumpy road that lies before me. Lord! Come to earth soon and put an end to this world of grief. I pray in the name of Jesus. Amen."

The next day, I went out to the rubbish-picking site, but Choi was nowhere to be seen. I asked other rubbish pickers of his whereabouts, but they were equally curious as to his disappearance.

Then someone said, "Haven't you heard?"

"Heard what? Is it good or bad?"

"I'm not sure. It may or may not be good for Choi. The man had a windfall, but it looks as if he's in trouble now because of it."

"What do you mean?"

"Money seems to have affected his mind."

"What are you talking about?"

"I was told that yesterday he went drinking all day, spending money like water. After getting drunk, he left the drink house, leaving his money behind. Later he returned and tore the drink house apart in an attempt to get it back. The owner called the police and they arrested him. After leaving the police station, the man was beside himself, mumbling to himself, 'My money. Where has my money gone?' It's such a pity. It seems that he squandered all his money on booze."

After that incident, Choi was always in trouble with the law, getting in and out of jail. I always thought that money held magical powers. It was especially true for Choi. The money had plunged him into hell.

Money spells disaster for anyone who is not prepared to use it wisely. It is useful to us only when we work to earn it. Choi put himself on the road to ruin because he had come into money in an immoral way.

17

Until Their Tears Turn to Laughter

TIME PASSED IN THE CHEONGGYE-CHEON slums. It was the summer of 1973. The Baedal Academy, our social education center, was doing well under the direction of Suh Jong-mun, a student of Korean literature at Seoul National University. Che Jeong-gu, a political science student at SNU, had come to live in the slum to take charge of a youth guidance project. Che also became a rubbish picker, a move that earned him the respect of residents.

Some sociology majors from Ewha University operated the Pear Blossom Kindergarten. It was such a success that complaints and pleas started coming in from neighboring areas. Why were their neighborhoods being ignored? they asked. Could the students not come and operate a kindergarten for them, too? As a result, students of early childhood education, from Sookmyung University, started a kindergarten in a neighboring area. It was called Rose Kindergarten, and was expertly led by a student named Shin Myeong-ja. She later married Che Jeong-gu.

Although my missionary work in the slums progressed, my health was deteriorating. I was unable to do anything for any length of time, and my ability to concentrate dropped dramatically. I perspired in my sleep and after giving a 20-minute sermon I was so weak I had to hold onto something for support. I was still hungry after eating and still tired after resting.

I went to the hospital and was diagnosed with chronic fatigue. There was no medicine for it. The only cure was to do nothing but rest for an entire year. I was told that if I kept going as I was, I would end up an invalid.

My wishes were simple. I wanted to go away somewhere, eat as much meat, and sleep as much as I wanted, but life in the slum was far too harsh for such a wish to ever come true. I could find no escape and, like a hamster on a treadmill, I kept going round and round and round.

One hot day, I had my rubbish picker's basket around my neck and was digging through a rubbish bin when I suddenly became dizzy. I leaned against the wall, but was barely able to stay on my feet. The sky spun and a chill went through me. I abandoned my cart and my basket and went home to lie down.

I had a high fever that lasted ten days. It was the middle of summer, but still I lay with a blanket over my head, shivering from cold. As my body weakened, so did my mind. Could I keep going? If not, would it really be possible to stop? Then I remembered my commitment, which I made when I first came to work in the slum.

"I come here on the orders of Jesus Christ. I am alive, but, if necessary, I am prepared to die."

It was a pledge I had made to myself to work hard. Now that it looked as if I would have to leave, those words had become a trap. I could hear the taunts of my friends, if I left now. "Kim Jin-hong. You said you were prepared to leave the slum feet first. What are you doing here alive and well?" Then what could I say? Could I say I had gotten sick and there was no avoiding it?

Friends aside, what would I tell Jesus, who had given me the mission to do God's work in the slum? He wouldn't forgive me, if I said, "Lord, I am sorry. I tried, but my body couldn't take it. I couldn't help it, I had to leave." I was afraid Jesus would be disappointed with me. I was sure He would say something on the order of, "When I was your age, I died on the cross for you. There's nothing wrong with you. Stop complaining."

I decided that succeed or fail, I would have to keep going. My committment did not last long, however. All my thoughts were painful. I thought of my wife, her face pale, and how she had gone back to her parents; my son, who had tuberculosis; myself, now weighing less than 110 pounds; the patients in the area; the unemployed; the drunkards; the demolition crew. All these images came to haunt me and I felt it would not be long before I collapsed.

If, in doing God's work, I overexerted myself and collapsed, wouldn't that be defeating the purpose? I felt that perhaps the wisest thing for me to do was to quit. Going ten days without food, the first thing I wanted to do when the fever abated was to eat, but there was no food in the house. Until I could go out and pick rubbish to earn a little money, I would just have to go hungry. I had no choice. Although I managed to put on my shoes, I could hardly walk, let alone drag my pushcart.

I went back to my room to lie down. If I kept up my missionary work, it seemed I would lose not only my health, but my family as well. Without my health, I could not do God's work and my efforts in the slum would come to naught. I would stop now, go back to the seminary, and come back to help the poor after I had regained my strength.

My only question was, exactly how was I supposed to stop? Could I just disappear? No, I couldn't do that. I would have to find someone to carry on my work, but who would take it up? Would I be able to find anyone who was as big a fool as I had been? Perhaps I could organize a self-governing body for the residents.

As I lay there, I agonized over the solution, but nothing came to mind. I fell asleep and had a dream. In it, I was preaching, when a fire started at the door. The fire spread through the church. I tried to escape, but all the doors were locked from the outside and there was no way out. I went from door to door, trying frantically to open them, when I awoke. It was a strange dream to have at this time in my life.

I usually did not place much significance on dreams and fantasies, but to have had such a dream at such a time, I could not help but take it seriously. A fire had broken out in the church, but I could not escape. What did it mean? Did it mean I could not escape from Hwalbin Church? Was I making too much of an absurd dream?

The more I thought about it, the more I convinced myself that the dream meant something. While I sat there trying to figure it out, I became hungry and stepped outside. I was intending to get something to eat at the house of a church member, but as I went from house to house, no one was home. By the time I returned to my room, I had arrived at a decision. If I kept on like this, I would have a nervous breakdown, so I made up my mind to leave the slum.

I WENT OUTSIDE AND TOOK DOWN the Hwalbin Church sign. I had put it up two years earlier with my own hands. As I took it down, my heart was beating so rapidly that it nearly made my hands tremble. For a moment, my mind wavered, but I told myself once again that it was for the best. It was a step toward something bigger and better.

I rationalized that surrender could be a strategic move. I took the sign inside and placed it in a corner, facing the wall. Then I started packing. I was weak from hunger and packing seemed to take forever. I spent several hours getting my things together. Then I opened the door and went outside to get a truck to move my things.

For some reason, there were 30 or 40 children playing in the churchyard. They came and crowded around me. "Pastor, where are you going? Tell us a story."

They were used to me telling them stories at Sunday school. I brushed them away and said, "Please, children, go and play."

I could not very well leave while children were playing there. I decided to go back inside and wait until they had gone. After a couple of hours, I went outside again, but they had not left. Instead, more children had come to join them. I went inside again and waited another hour, but later, when I went back outside, they were still there.

After going back and forth several times, I wondered why on that day, of all days, the children were hanging around so long. My conscience would not allow me to pack and leave in front of them. I would have to wait until night.

By then, it was three in the afternoon. It was summer and it would be a long time before dark, so I decided to take one last walk around the neighborhood. As I walked through the alleys, I thought back on all the things that had happened over the past two years.

Reminiscing, I began to feel guilty. These people live beside the stinking waters of Cheonggye-cheon Creek because they have nowhere else to go, whereas I had other options and had already packed my bags. Was I doing something wrong? Who cared if I got sick or was called a fool? Shouldn't I persevere?

The longer I agonized over my decision, the weaker I was becoming and the closer I was to having a breakdown. Finally, I got tough with myself. I had packed my bags. I would go. I would not wait until dark. I would go to the church and leave straightaway.

I turned the corner and the church came into view. The house on the corner next to the church was all shut up, but children's shoes were scattered in front of the door. Five children, ranging in age from three to thirteen, lived here. The father had gotten drunk and punched someone and was now in jail and the mother was trying as best as she could to keep the family together.

It seemed strange for the house to be all shut up on a hot summer afternoon. I stopped in front of it and knocked on the door. "Hello. Can I come in? I've come from the church," I said, as I opened the door. Entering, I saw all five of the children lying in a row on the floor. I was startled and asked, "What happened? Are you sick? Why are you lying down in the middle of the day?"

I went over to them and felt their foreheads. They did not have a fever, but still they were lying there, totally exhausted, as if seriously ill.

"What's wrong? Are you sick?"

The oldest boy, a thirteen-year-old, sat up and said, "We're hungry. Mom went out to work three days ago and hasn't come back, so we don't

Telling stories to children in Cheonggye-cheon.

279

have anything to eat."

While the father was in jail, the mother earned money by selling snacks from a street stall. She had found a spot on a side street of Cheonggye-cheon 6-ga* and was out there every day, rain or shine.

The family lived hand-to-mouth and since their mother had not returned, the five of them had gone without eating. While the oldest boy was talking to me, the other four had slowly risen and were wiping tears from their eyes.

As I looked at them, I felt my body crumble and a pain in my chest. I became dizzy as I watched the children cry, exhausted from hunger and waiting. I sat quietly as I let the truth sink in. These children had gone hungry for three days and were crying and calling for their mother.

Then I caught sight of the youngest child, the three-year-old, wiping his tears with the back of his hand and wailing for his mother. As I stared at him, I got a big shock. It was a shock that I will not forget as long as I live. Superimposed on the face of the child was the face of Jesus, staring intently at me before disappearing. It was for only two or three seconds.

In that brief moment, when my eyes met the eyes of my Savior, my heart felt as if it was aflame and I burst into tears. I suddenly knew. Jesus, who had loved me enough to die for me, did not want me to leave this neighborhood. He wanted me to stay here with these children and wipe tears from their eyes. I thought of God wiping tears from people's eyes, as is written in Revelation:

> For the lamb at the center of the throne will be their shep-
> herd; he will lead them to springs of living water. And God
> will wipe away every tear from their eyes. (Revelation 7:17)

I sat there and stammered to myself. "Yes, Jesus, I know. I will go back to the church and put the sign back up. I will unpack my bags and stay." I told the children to wait for me and went back to the church. First, I put the Hwalbin Church sign back up. Then I unpacked my bags and went to the store. I got some noodles on credit and returned

------

*A *ga* refers to a section of a street.

to the children. I cooked the noodles for them and we ate together.

"Now that you've eaten, let's go and look for your mother. Let's pray that we find her and that she'll be able to come home with you."

We sat and held hands and prayed. Then we left the house. The oldest boy said he knew where his mother's stall was and led the way. As we were leaving the neighborhood, we ran into the postman, who said he had a registered letter for me and asked for my seal. I signed for it with my thumbprint instead and opened the envelope.

Inside was a money order for 5,000 *won* with a note saying, "Please use this for a good cause." There was no name or return address. This 5,000 *won* gave me strength and I became confident that we would find the children's mother. The quest did not seem entirely hopeless. From my experience in the slum, I had a hunch about where the mother might be.

At the time, the police had been cracking down on unlicensed street stalls. They regularly arrested the vendors and fined them. Those who could not pay their fines had to spend time in jail. Under the circumstances, this seemed to be a plausible explanation for her absence.

When we reached the location, somewhere between Euljiro 5-ga and Cheonggye-cheon 6-ga, neither the mother nor the stall was to be found. I went to a nearby cigarette kiosk to inquire.

"Excuse me. By any chance, do you know what happened to the woman who had a stall here? She hasn't been home for three days and her children have come to look for her."

"The police are being very strict these days. A lot of the stall vendors haven't been showing up."

"But she hasn't been home for three days!"

"Well, there was a crackdown a few days ago. Do you think she might have been taken in? I suggest you ask at the police box."

When cracking down on street stalls, the police would close off the exits to the area, round the people up, and subject them to summary trials.

I took the children to the local police box. They told me that, yes, a few people had been taken in during a crackdown a few days earlier, had been tried, sentenced, and handed over to the jailer.

We went to the police station and there, in the lockup, we found the children's mother. She was in handcuffs. At her trial, she had been fined 12,000 *won*, but she was short 6,000 *won* and was doing time to pay off the rest. Anyone who did not have the money to pay their fine could stay in jail instead, at the rate of 500 *won* per day. She would have had to remain in jail for 12 days.

From the moment she was brought in, she had pleaded her case with the officer in charge, petitioning him with tears.

"If I spend 12 days in here, my children will starve. There's a church in the neighborhood. If you contact the church, the people there will look after them. Please contact them for me."

"If you give us the phone number, we'll make the call."

"There aren't any phones in our neighborhood."

"Then how do you expect us to contact them? Do you expect us to go running errands for you?"

Every time a different officer came on duty, she pleaded again, but no one was prepared to contact a church in a neighborhood that did not even have a telephone.

By the time we found her, she had spent three days in jail, worrying herself sick over her children. When she saw us, she burst into tears.

"Ahh! You poor children! You've been starving, haven't you? It's not your fault you were born to such parents. Oh! What's the point of living like this? We'd be better off dead."

She bashed her head against the bars and wept. I could not hold back my tears, as I tried to comfort her.

"Please stop crying, please. Let's get you out of here. Take heart. Your children are fine," I said.

"Thank you. How will I ever repay your kindness?"

Then I knelt down on the concrete floor of Dongdaemun Police Station and said a prayer of thanks.

"Thank you, Lord. When things got tough, and I thought of moving on, you showed me through the tears of these starving children where I belong. When I packed my bags to leave, you showed me through the anguish of a mother with hungry children where I must live and die.

"Lord Jesus, I have no money, talent, or power, but there is one thing I can do. I will stay where I am until the tears of the hungry children turn to laughter. I will stay until the anguish of parents who cannot feed and educate their children turns to a song of praise."

I went out and cashed my 5,000-*won* money order. I returned to the police station, paid off the fine, and reunited the mother with her children.

THAT NIGHT, THE FATIGUE OF THE PAST FEW DAYS washed over me. I passed up dinner and fell asleep in my clothes. In the middle of the night, I was awoken by a noise from outside. I lay there listening, trying to figure out what was going on. Someone was on the roof making a racket. I went outside to have a look.

Chung, the president of the church youth group, was very drunk, standing on the roof and shouting. With one hand, he held a bottle of *soju*, with the other he shook his fist at the sky, calling out, "God! Come down here. Come and have a drink!"

I was amazed, but perhaps I should not have been. When I first met Chung, he went by the nickname "the liquor monster." Word was that whenever he had something to drink, he turned into a monster, a monster so violent that he would try to butt and knock the teeth out of anyone who came in sight. Nearly all of the little money he earned from picking rubbish went to repairing his victims' broken teeth.

I had felt particularly sorry for him and paid him a lot of attention. When we went out picking rubbish together, I tried to instruct him on how to live a better life. He quit smoking and drinking and became a good, hard-working person. I baptized him and, even though he was still a bachelor, he was made a church deacon. I wanted to teach him well so he could become one of the pillars of Hwalbin Church. Now, it was as if all my effort was going down the drain.

I looked up at the roof and said, "Hey! What's going on up there? Come down this minute. Hurry up, now."

He looked down at me. "Oh, here's our sham pastor. Come on up, Pastor. The three of us can have a drink together, the sham Trinity: sham God, sham pastor, and sham deacon."

The "liquor monster" was in fine form. His words were fast and fluid, as if he was showing off his skill as an orator. I told him to be quiet and get off the roof. He started to make his way down. I was worried he might slip.

"Be careful," I said. "You don't want to fall and break your neck. Careful."

The roof of the shanty that served as the church was not much of a roof at all. It was so low, I could almost touch it. I walked over to the edge of the roof and raised my arms to help Chung down. When he was close to the edge, the alcohol in his stomach turned and, looking down, he vomited. Standing under him, he doused me in vomit. The disgusting smell covered my face and my body. Exasperated, I said, "Chung! What kind of baptism is this?"

Despite my state, I could not let go of Chung's hand for fear he might fall. I had no choice but to wait until he was safe on the ground. Then I made a beeline for the water pump and washed myself off, over and over again. Regardless of how much I scrubbed, I couldn't get rid of the stench.

It was dawn when Chung, who had slept off his drunk, came to see me, shamefaced. I was still angry and had not been able to sleep.

"I'm sorry about last night, Pastor," he said. "I didn't make a fool of myself or do anything seriously wrong, did I?"

"What do you mean, did you do anything wrong? You're amazing," I told him.

"If I did anything bad, it was the alcohol, not me. Please forgive me. I'll make sure it doesn't happen again."

"OK. OK. Try not to let it happen again, but let me know next time you're planning to go up on the roof. That way I can at least get a ladder ready for you."

It is a difficult thing for a person to change his nature. I had pinned so much hope on Chung that naturally I was disappointed to see him go back to his old ways.

THAT DAY I DID NOT GO OUT TO PICK RUBBISH. Rather, I made visits to church families. I was about to go to sleep when Mrs. Won came to see me. Her clothes and hair were in disarray and there was a large bruise on her face. She spewed out a stream of bitter complaints.

"We're ruined, and it's your fault."

"Excuse me?" I asked. "It's my fault that you're ruined?"

"That's right. That's what I said. It's all your fault."

Mrs. Won's husband had had a serious case of tuberculosis and also exhibited symptoms of epilepsy. When I first came to Cheonggye-cheon and saw him, he often spat blood and rolled around on the ground in epileptic fits. When the fit would subside, he would go out and yell loudly, as if to release his frustration, his face covered in blood.

The women and children of the neighborhood would run away in fright. That was when I came across him and started to treat him. After that, I went to his house every day. I gave him injections of streptomycin and got him to take other medicines. To treat his epilepsy, I got in touch with a charity organization that specialized in caring for epileptics and from them procured medicines for him.

My efforts were rewarded in seeing Won's tuberculosis noticeably improve and his fits of epilepsy reduced to only one or two a month. With his health improved, Won went back to work selling taffy. Every morning he would pass by the church with his taffy cart and hand a piece of taffy to my son. After a while, he stopped passing by and I began to wonder why. My son, thinking of the taffy, often asked me, "Has the taffy man moved away?"

From Mrs. Won's behavior, I was concerned that something bad might have happened to Won.

"Mrs. Won, calm down. What are you saying? I don't know what you're talking about."

"Calm down, you say. Maybe you can be calm, but I can't. If you had left my husband alone, he'd be dead by now. But no, you had to go and cure him and make him strong again so he could go back to beating me. What am I going to do? The kids and I'd be better off without him, but you just had to meddle. Now he's back to being mean again. I can't stand it any more."

She was half crying, half babbling. What was I to do? Why was life so full of problems?

I told Mrs. Won to go inside and went off to look for her husband. Their "house" was nothing more than a tepee-shaped hut on the banks of Cheonggye-cheon Creek. As I approached it, I saw that the children were outside, while Won was inside, shouting at the top of his voice. I lifted the straw mat door and went inside.

"Hey, Jesus man! Come in and sit down. Let's have a drink," he said when he saw me.

It was upsetting to see him in this state. I could not help thinking of how hard I had worked to help him through the past year, getting him to take his medicine, giving him injections, and even getting children to catch frogs for him because they were supposed to help him recover his strength. Seeing how he used his regained vitality to drink and to beat his wife and to make his children stand outside, shivering in the cold, I was speechless.

As he offered me a cup of *soju*, I realized that I had made a big mistake. I had treated the body, but the disease of the mind had gotten worse. I grabbed the bottle and the cup from Won and said, "Don't do this. If you continue this way, the disease will get worse and you'll die."

I returned home with an ache in my heart and an emptiness in my soul. I mumbled to myself, "Everything is going wrong, with Won, myself, the neighborhood, the church. Everything is going wrong with the whole world." I would have to find out why this was happening, I thought. I would have to discover the root of the problem and begin to fix things from there. All the way home, I wondered where, exactly, things had started going wrong.

Not long after this incident, Won's wife and oldest daughter disappeared. Won's health grew worse and the oldest boy, an 11-year-old, was forced to drop out of school and go to work in a factory. The two hundred thirty *won* that he earned daily barely kept them from starving. I went to see Won many times and urged him to start over again, but he had already crossed over into insanity. With bloodshot eyes, all he could do was curse his runaway wife.

Looking at Won, I thought to myself, this is the life of a man falling apart. He has thrown himself into a living hell and now is dying there. Who said human life is precious? Here in the slum, life is cheaper than spit.

Won made me realize my limits. There was nothing I could do for him, other than stand aside and watch him destroy himself.

I SPENT THE NEXT FEW DAYS THINKING. I tortured myself, saying I had to start over. I wrestled with myself, thinking of the verses in Genesis where Jacob meets and wrestles with God by the river.

What do I want to accomplish here in the slum? What can I do? Relief and salvation of the poor? Salvation for whom? How? I was at an impasse.

The limits of what I could do became all too clear. I could not sit by and watch, but I had no power to be of any real help. I could not solve the problems, but neither could I ignore them.

I give food to a family that is hungry and they became servile. I lend money to someone wanting to gain independence and he disappears without a trace. Because the individuals fail, I set up organizations, but then the organizations fail. I help a sick man recover and he uses his renewed strength to abuse his wife. I put my trust in someone, giving him responsibility for the financial affairs of the church, only to lose both the church's money and the person.

I use all my energy organizing funerals and literally carrying sick patients from hospital to hospital. The problems are legion and over-whelming—lung ailments, sexually transmitted diseases, skin diseases, malnutrition, unemployment, child labor, hunger, abuse, snow, brawl-ing, alcoholism, winter chill, summer heat, gas inhalation, dank living areas, foul odors, garbage and sewage, demolition crews, theft, rape, laziness, inertia, corruption....

Does Jesus have the power to deal with all these problems? If he does, then why does he just look on? Why does he keep silent? If Jesus keeps silent, what, then, am I supposed to do?

My abilities are far too limited, I thought. Close to zero, in fact. I thought about my situation, and in the end arrived at one undeniable truth—that God was my master. He sent His son, Jesus, to earth to save us. There was no doubt that God had saved me from emptiness, confusion, and meaninglessness. This fact, every cell of my body knew to be certain and gave rise to the following confession, which came forth from my soul:

> I believe, therefore I exist.
> I believe that God has saved me, therefore I exist.
> I believe that Jesus loves me and, with that faith,
>   that I in turn love the poor, therefore I exist.
> I love the poor, not only in words,
>   but through my actions, therefore I exist.

I reached this conclusion:

> I act and show love according to my belief.
> Therefore, I continue to work in the slum.

Having renewed my committment to my work, I still had my doubts. Why had everything gone wrong? I began to think that the problem was within me and that there was something wrong in my attitude toward my work. I opened my Bible and read from Matthew, attempting to find the answer to what I was doing wrong. In the Sermon on the Mount, I read:

> So do not worry, saying, 'What shall we eat?' or 'What shall we drink?' or 'What shall we wear?'... But seek first his kingdom and his righteousness and all these things will be given to you as well. (Matthew 6:31-33)

As I read, I realized that in my work I had confused my priorities. As far as missionary work in the slum was concerned, some things must come before others. The one thing that must precede all others was to "seek his kingdom and his righteousness," but I had been engrossed in the questions of what to eat, drink, and wear. The entire foundation of my work had been misguided.

For the hungry family, I had been quick to hand out flour, but I had been remiss in not passing on God's word. I had been busy trying to help people increase their income, but I had neglected to lead their souls to salvation. I had been obsessed with improving their physical and social condition, but I had failed to lead them toward Jesus and show them how to find strength in Him.

Every time I carried out a funeral, I felt that something was missing. In my efforts to heal the sick, I had never taken the time to talk to them about the value of life or the meaning of death. I had not concerned myself with the salvation of their souls. Those whose bodily diseases were healed were still sick at heart, and those who could not be healed passed away without first freeing their souls from their earthly sorrows. The same went for those who had gone hungry through lack of work. Even if they managed to find work and escape from hunger, the problems lodged within them remained and only grew worse with the passage of time.

One family I knew was a good example. In poverty, they were happy, the mother and father being one another's best friend and support. I managed to find work for them and their lives improved materially. Then, the father began drinking and coming home late at night. The couple began to fight, quietly at first, but their rows got louder until it was all-out war.

One day, there was a loud crash and the woman was heard screaming, "Kill me." The children cried with fright.

The day finally came when the woman walked out, leaving the children behind. While the father was in a drunken stupor, the baby boy, who was just beginning to crawl, fell from the threshold of the kitchen onto the coal briquette heater. As I carried the baby to the hospital, I regretted the day I had found work for his father.

I HAD BEEN WORKING UNDER THE LOFTY BANNER of saving the poor from poverty, but I had neglected the most important part of my work. I had failed to lead them, one by one, to the life and truth of Jesus. I prayed for forgiveness and made a new resolution:

> From this day forth, my missionary work with Hwalbin Church will be a balance between "substance and means," "the Word of God and the bread of life," and "the food of heaven and the food of the earth." I will pour all my energy into bringing the people of the slum to serve God as lord and master, and through guidance of the Holy Spirit they will rise up from their own faith and determination as people of God.

To turn this resolution into action, the first thing I did was to start an evangelical mission. I sought to spread the good news in the area more effectively by training church members, identifying and defining mission strategies, and improving members' outreach ability, with the eventual goal of developing the community.

I set a time limit of one month and selected ten volunteers from among church members for ten days of training. Over the next twenty days, these ten people were to go out and spread the Gospel in their designated areas.

Our evangelical mission was unique. It was not a series of door-to-door visits, where we urged the residents to "Believe in Jesus and have eternal life." Rather, the basis of our mission was the DDT Operation that had been the focus of Hwalbin Church from the very beginning.

That is, we concentrated on getting to know families, identifying their problems, and trying as hard as we could to solve them.

We defined the purpose of the mission as follows:

Since its inaugural service on October 3, 1971, Hwalbin Church has done its best to become involved in the activities of the people in this area and has reaped some positive results. To preach the Gospel through volunteer service and community development, the church has carried out a variety of activities designed to educate the residents, improve their lives, and organize them into groups in which they now actively participate.

On reflection, however, we must not forget that all activities of the church must focus on spreading the good news of Jesus Christ. In our experience so far, we have learned that the poverty of the slum is not an economic problem, but a spiritual one. It is also a kind of physical disease. This disease called poverty can be cured only by finding Jesus Christ. Finding God is the short cut to finding true humanity.

This point is the focus of Hwalbin Church's evangelical mission. A church must have a strategy and motive for evangelical work in the neighborhood in which it works. A church in which the Holy Spirit resides will always grow in influence and will breathe vitality into the neighborhood. The spirit of Jesus Christ must be conveyed to the heart of every person. We believe that God will be with us in our efforts.

Hwalbin Church
Kim Jin-hong

Over the next month we saw some encouraging results, which both gratified and surprised the members of the mission team.

One night, at mission headquarters they heard that gambling was taking place in one of the houses in the neighborhood. One of the members, who in the past had been a heavy gambler, went to the house. Though it had not been long since he himself had left gambling behind, he tried to persuade his former gambling friends to stop.

"You know what a wasteful life I led when I spent my days

shuffling and dealing cards, like you're doing now. You know how my wife and children suffered. Look at me now. As you can see, my life is much more fulfilling. You guys should stop wasting your time with cards and get close to God. You can save your hungry families."

Moved by his earnest plea and his testimony, the men gathered up their cards. Their game turned into a prayer session. When he returned, he brought the cards with him.

IN THE AUTUMN OF 1973, one of the DDT mission members brought to mission headquarters a young man by the name of Park. He was in the last stages of tuberculosis and was reduced to skin and bones. He was in his thirties and had been a shaman. He said his disease was the result of his unhealthy lifestyle as a shaman.

I realized that he was a man with a strong religious yearning and talked to him about Jesus. Wracked by disease and remorse, the word of God took root in his heart and he became much happier, spending his days praying, reading the Bible, and singing hymns.

We tried to cure his tuberculosis, but it was so far along that we were told primary medicines would be of no use. We would have to use advanced medicines, but those were expensive. We were all too poor to be of any help. We had no way to come up with money, but were given hope when we were told that it was possible for a person to get the medicine if he was admitted to the municipal tuberculosis clinic.

I accompanied him on the long journey to the clinic, but when we got there we were told the clinic was full and Park could not be admitted. They did tell us there was a way, however. If we could come up with 30,000 *won*, they would find room for him. Though the clinic was, in principle, free, with demand so far outstripping the hospital's capacity, it was not uncommon for patients to be admitted through underhanded transactions. We came away disappointed.

Park always said that when he recovered he would study theology and assist me in my work. That day never came. On his deathbed, he asked me to sing a hymn. When I asked which one he would like to hear, without hesitation he answered, "Amazing Grace."

Amazing grace! how sweet the sound!
That saved a wretch like me!

> I once was lost, but now am found;
> Was blind, but now I see.

While he listened to us sing the hymn quietly, with a faint smile on his face, he drew his last breath and went to his final rest in peace.

Quickly, Park's wife went into the kitchen and came back with her finger all bloody. She dropped blood into the mouth of her dead husband, but the blood spilled out of his mouth onto the floor. It seems she believed an old tale that if you drop blood into the mouth at the moment of death, the dead person will come back to life. Heedless to this desperate expression of his wife's love, Park's body was already beginning to stiffen.

As I washed the body and prepared it for burial, I noticed that his face had a look of contentment. To be able to die happy is a blessing, I thought. Death is the threshold to a world of eternal rest. It is the threshold that leads from this painful world and the peaceful afterlife. Death is a blessing bestowed on those who are ready.

As had become my custom, I took the body to Byeokje Crematorium to be cremated. Then I took the bag of ashes and, with Park's wife, went to the Han River Bridge. Leaning on the rail of the bridge, I spread the ashes over the water flowing below.

There I renewed my pledge to build a world where nobody died because they could not afford medicine. I would help bring about a world where the sick did not go without treatment simply because they had no money.

Still on the bridge, I thought that just as in war soldiers crossed this river, one day soldiers of peace would cross it too. These soldiers would be armed not with tanks and guns, but with love, justice, truth, and a spirit of service. These rifleless armies would bring about a revolution. Hwalbin Church would operate as a base to prepare for the revolution of Jesus. This I vowed as I left the bridge.

I awoke at dawn the next morning. I washed myself with cold water and read the Psalm that I had read when Hoon's mother died at my side.

> My heart is steadfast, O God,
> My heart is steadfast;

I will sing and make music.
Awake, my soul!
Awake harp and lyre!
I will awaken the dawn.

As I read this verse, I prayed and meditated. I had taken on the task of torch bearer as my life's work. I dedicated my life to bringing light to the people of this land, who were living in darkness, and awaken the Korean churches from slumber. I would let them know that the dawn was approaching.

I pledged that I would be a guiding light for the 60,000 people of the Cheonggye-cheon slum, whose souls were oppressed with poverty, disease, anger, and pain. I would also awaken to reality the wealthy, content in their expensive residences, unaware of the sufferings of the poor.

I rang the bell outside our church.

Ding dong. Ding dong.

Lights appeared in windows. The neighborhood began to greet the new day.

18

I Will Awaken the Dawn

AS PART OF ITS ANNIVERSARY celebration, in October 1973, the Seoul-based Christian Broadcasting Station (CBS) announced a cash prize for the most outstanding essay of Christian experience. I do not remember how much the prize came to, but I do recall that at the time it was considered a large sum. Needing money, I decided to enter the contest.

While enduring the physical and emotional agony of life in the slum, as a form of therapy I had developed a habit of recording my daily experiences. From the beginning, I had kept a written record. By this time, it filled several notebooks and I asked some of my friends to read them over. Encouraged by their reception, I took my diaries, checked into an inn, and spent a week writing my story.

I was 32 years old at the time. I submitted an 800-page essay, assuming I would win the prize. As it turned out, I did not win, so I retrieved my manuscript from CBS, took it home, and put it on a shelf in the prayer room adjacent to the main chamber of the church. In January 1974, I was arrested and imprisoned for political activities.

Not long afterward, Pastor Motoyuki Nomura, from Japan, visited Hwalbin Church. He had heard of my arrest and had come to Korea to gather information to rally support in Japan to bring pressure on the Korean government to secure my release.

During his visit, he learned about my manuscript and asked whether he could take it. Because he was a supporter of Hwalbin Church, church members gave it over to him. Not knowing Korean,

Pastor Nomura was not able to read it. He realized that because of my status as a political prisoner, if security forces learned that he was carrying my manuscript, they would confiscate it. To avoid that, he went to Jungang Market and bought enough sheets of dried seaweed to disguise the manuscript, which he inserted between the leaves. This way he was able to smuggle it past the authorities.

A meeting with key members of Hwalbin Church, including Che Jeong-gu, second from left, and Pastor Nomura, standing. Kim Jin-hong is seated center front, wearing glasses.

Back in Japan, he had the manuscript translated into Japanese and published under the title I had given it, *I Will Awaken the Dawn.* That was its first publication. It became a bestseller and, thanks to support from Japanese readers, I was finally able to overcome financial difficulties that I had been experiencing. The publication of my book was a godsend to me in my missionary work and for that I have always been greatly indebted to Pastor Nomura.

Quite unexpectedly, however, trouble developed after the book was printed. North Korean authorities bought 1,000 copies and distributed them to local officials in rural areas. The book graphically recorded the harsh living conditions of slumdwellers in Seoul and included photographs. As such, North Korea regarded the book as propaganda to publicize the hardships faced by South Koreans.

My subsequent blacklisting as a political prisoner kept the book from being published in Korea until 1982. The book has now been re-printed nearly one hundred times in Korean, and has been published in English, Russian, Chinese, and Arabic versions. The book was also the subject of a television drama and was later made into a full-length film. Although my story attracted a lot of attention from the media, I attach more importance to the fact that it may have been a help to restless youth. I have always thought it ironic that a book that was originally rejected by the CBS later generated so much attention, both at home and abroad.

The Korean-language version of *I Will Awaken the Dawn* records my experiences from college days through late 1973. It does not contain accounts of my work after 1974, my political incarceration, or activi-ties on behalf of farmers, because it was printed in 1982, when the country was still under military rule. Many readers later asked when a new edition would be coming out. I had always wanted to produce an expanded version, but that plan had to be set aside.

Beginning in 1997, I finally published my story in serial form in a monthly current-affairs magazine. The series was entitled *Exodus from Seoul* and ran for two years.

IN THE FALL OF 1973, THE DOMESTIC POLITICAL SCENE began to show signs of unrest. The government's so-called *Yusin,* or Reform, political system, engineered by President Park Jeong-hui to extend his rule, began to crack under strong opposition from various sectors of society. Students and religious leaders staged rallies and issued manifestoes denouncing the president. University professors also took a stand, col-lecting signatures of people against the *Yusin* political system.

While carrying out missionary work for the destitute in the slum, I developed an understanding of the importance of politics on the lives of common people. My experience showed me that even though indi-viduals may be honest and morally upright, they are doomed to suffer, if the moral standards or the political system of their society are flawed or if their political leaders lack moral stature or a proper sense of their authority.

Che Jeong-gu, a political science student from Seoul National University, moved into the slum to work with me after having been expelled for his involvement in anti-government protests. Another frequent visitor to the slum was Suh Gyeong-seok. He had led anti-dictatorship protests among Christian circles. It was largely through him and Che that I became aware of a wide range of problems in our society. I read the Bible diligently and used it as the foundation for my interpretation of the reality confronting us, with the result that I began to look more critically at domestic politics.

I added my signature to an anti-*Yusin* movement that was started by young Christian leaders in November 1973. I also took part in other anti-government activities, joining the Urban Industrial Mission, led by Pastor Park Hyeong-gyu.

On January 8, 1974, I was taken aback as I read the evening newspapers. It was reported that President Park had declared what were referred to as Emergency Measures numbers 1 and 2, banning the public from conducting debate, spreading news, or holding assemblies concerning constitutional amendments. The promulgation of these measures shocked me, and I could not help but think that the government was taking us into a dark chapter in our nation's history. Exactly ten days after their promulgation, I was taken to jail.

KOREA'S POLITICAL INSTABILITY, which had begun to surface in mid-1973, reached a crescendo toward the end of the year. Koreans from all social sectors, led by people from academic and religious circles, sought to express their grievances against the *Yusin* political system, invariably demanding an overhaul of the *Yusin* Constitution.

What had begun as sporadic protests grew into a national movement, igniting a campaign to collect one million signatures for constitutional change. Led by a number of well-known social figures, including Chang Jun-ha and Baek Gi-wan, the signature-collection drive drew enthusiastic support from the masses. It was these developments that led President Park Jeong-hui to issue the emergency measures.

The seven points of Emergency Measure No. 1 read:

I, the President of the Republic of Korea, by virtue of the authority vested in me by Article 53 of the Constitution, and upon deliberation by the State Council, hereby proclaim Emergency Measure No. 1, as follows:

ARTICLE 1. It shall be prohibited for any person to deny, oppose, misrepresent, or defame the Constitution of the Republic of Korea.

ARTICLE 2. It shall be prohibited for any person to assert, introduce, propose, or petition for revision or repeal of the Constitution of the Republic of Korea.

ARTICLE 3. It shall be prohibited for any person to fabricate or disseminate false rumors.

ARTICLE 4. It shall be prohibited for any person to advocate, instigate, or propagate any act or acts that are prohibited in Articles 1 through 3 of this emergency measure, or communicate such act or acts to others through broadcasting, reporting, or publishing, or by any other means.

ARTICLE 5. Any person who violates any provision of this emergency measure and any person who defames this emergency measure shall be subjected to arrest, detention, search, or seizure, without warrant therefore, and shall be punished by imprisonment for not more than 15 years. Suspension of civil rights may be concurrently imposed.

ARTICLE 6. Any person who violates any provision of this emergency measure shall be tried and sentenced in the emergency court martial.

ARTICLE 7. This measure shall take effect as of 1700 hours January 8, 1974.

The government also issued Emergency Measure No. 2, which called for the establishment of an emergency court martial to punish anyone found guilty of violating Emergency Measure No. 1 and other presidential decrees.

At the time, I was involved with the Urban Industrial Mission. I had a hectic schedule and little time to participate in politics. Nevertheless, reviewing Emergency Measure No. 1, I realized that it would set back the cause of democracy in Korea. What worried me the most, however, was not the constitutional amendments or the structural flaws of the political system. I was more concerned with the infringement of the freedom of expression and freedom of assembly, both vital components of democracy. To me, these were fundamental rights, bestowed by God upon the human race.

I am of the view that human rights guaranteed by God are above any rights derived from the law. As a consequence, human rights are not a political issue, but a religious matter and should not be encroached upon. Emergency Measure No. 1 constituted a serious infringement of human rights because it banned the signature-collection campaign for constitutional change.

The domestic political situation had deteriorated because of serious conflicts between those who defended the *Yusin* political system and those who opposed it. Revision of the *Yusin* Constitution would be required to revamp the *Yusin* political system and restore democracy to Korea. Constitutional amendments required motions from either the executive branch or the National Assembly, as the first step, but neither would move on them.

Consequently, the only way to achieve this goal was for the public to petition the National Assembly for constitutional change. The constitution contained provisions that a petition to amend the constitution would be entertained if it carried one million signatures. With this in mind, opposition forces launched a signature drive.

The campaign attracted enthusiastic support from the public, a development that forced the government into a corner. Their response was Emergency Measure No. 1, which was issued just as the drive was drawing to a successful close.

Using tanks to counter the people's campaign was tantamount to aiming guns at the Lord. This barbarous approach could take place in a fascist state under a Hitler or a Mussolini, but how could Korea tolerate such abuse of political power?

We should rise up! Churches and their members should lead the protest! These thoughts flashed through my mind as I leafed through the evening papers. Opportunely, I received a visitor, Pastor Lee Hae-hak of the Seongnam Jumin Church, a strong advocate of social justice. We needed little discussion to agree to spearhead public protests against the government and talked well into the night about a variety of issues.

Our conclusion was that the situation was such that neither

students nor civilians should lead the protest movement. Rather, the church should assume the leadership. Because clergymen are prepared to sacrifice themselves for missionary work, we believed that there was no difference between our service in a designated area or being incarcerated. We decided to enlist clergymen for the protest movement and quickly moved in that direction.

BEGINNING THE FOLLOWING DAY, we contacted a number of senior members of the Christian community to ask for their support and participation. Many clergymen, however, counseled caution, noting that Emergency Measure No. 1 represented a formidable threat.

What disappointed us most was the response of one particular respected religious leader. In the past, he had strongly urged Korea's Christian circles to work for greater social justice and broaden their participation in politics. He was widely regarded among Korean clergy as a man of impressive academic achievement and high moral standards. Pastor Lee and I had contacted many religious leaders to invite their participation in the first rally, but no one would make a commitment. Worse yet, we failed to enlist the support of a senior pastor who could deliver a sermon at the rally.

We paid him a visit and, as we were being led into his study, he talked grandly about current issues and noted that it was "…high time Christians shed blood." We were jubilant and briefed him on our plan for a rally, soliciting his participation. We asked him, "Professor, there are many young Christians who would gladly take the lead in this event, but we are short of pastors who can deliver sermons. Would you deliver a sermon at the rally?"

We were disappointed by his response. The professor said softly, "Well, now is the time to put your safety ahead of anything else. If you fight this regime, it'll be like trying to break a rock with eggs. You should keep a low profile, until they lose their steam."

He had been transformed into a completely different person. Only moments before he had called for Christian blood for political reform. His attitude underlined the weakness of Korea's Christian leadership. Members of the Korean clergy have always shown a lack of courage in difficult times, while saying the opposite when times are good. We say, "They have a big mouth, but small arms and legs."

Leaving his home, I shouted back at him, "You son of a bitch!"

Pastor Lee looked away, as if he did not hear me. It was the professor who had said, "Words should be matched by action." We abandoned our plan to enlist senior clergy in our movement. Instead, we decided to go ahead with the rally with the participation of young churchmen only. We would call the rally a prayer meeting and issue a release stating our purpose in religious terms.

Among those who accepted invitations to attend the gathering were the Pastors In Myeong-jin of Yeongdeungpo Industrial Mission, Hong Gil-bok of Sinchon Daehyeon Church, Im Sin-yeong of Gyeong-dong Central Church, and Park Chang-bin of the Urban Research Institute at Yonsei University. They all came under the Presbyterian Church of Korea.

Other participants from the Presbyterian Church included Pastor Kwon Ho-gyeong and Pastors Park Yun-su and Lee Gyu-sang, as well as Pastor Lee Hae-hak, who was already involved. From the Methodist Church, Pastors Kim Dong-wan and Kim Gyeong-rak promised to attend. As a group, we committed ourselves to accomplish the mission of a messiah to guide the political future of the nation, moving it back on course toward democracy.

We would hold the rally at the office of the National Council of Churches in Korea (KNCC) on January 17, as "a prayer session by Korean clergymen." We did not apply for approval for the gathering from the Council because we were concerned that details of our plan would be leaked.

Preparations got under way smoothly, with specific responsibilities assigned to particular individuals. Overall responsibility for the preparations rested with me and with Pastor Lee Hae-hak, who served as deputy representative. Pastor Kim Dong-wan was selected as representative of the Methodist Church. Pastor Lee Gyu-sang was in charge of the media and Pastor In Myeong-jin was assigned to deal with problems after the rally. We agreed to have 33 clergymen participate in the rally, symbolic of the 33 intellectuals who in 1919 signed a declaration of independence against the Japanese occupation of Korea.

THE "KOREAN CLERGY PRAYER MEETING ON CURRENT ISSUES" was held at the KNCC beginning at 10 a.m., January 17, 1974. It was officiated by

Pastor Kim Gyeong-rak of the Methodist Church. Pastor Kim Gwan-seok, secretary-general of KNCC, offered a prayer, while Pastor Kim Gyeong-rak delivered a sermon. Later, Pastor Lee Hae-hak read a statement that Pastor Hong Gil-bok and I had written. It read:

> *Honoring the glorious order of the Lord, the master of history, we, all members of Korean Christian churches, are determined to become martyrs and declare our religious intentions as follows:*
>
> *1. The present emergency measures must be abolished immediately, because they make a mockery of the will of the people.*
> *2. Debate on constitutional change must be conducted freely, according to public opinion.*
> *3. The government must do away with its Yusin structure and restore democratic order in Korea.*

All participants in the prayer meeting were convinced that their prayers would be answered and were not concerned with their physical safety. At about 11 a.m., six people, I including, were arrested, while being interviewed by reporters and distributing copies of our statement.

We were initially taken to Dongdaemun Police Station, but at around 2 p.m. the same day were herded into the headquarters of the then Korean Central Intelligence Agency (KCIA), at the foot of Mount Nam. At 11 p.m. on January 19, after spending two days at the KCIA, we were taken to Seodaemun Prison. We were each assigned a cell. I was put into Cell No. 6, on the bottom level of Building 9.

My name was taken away as soon as I entered prison. In its place I was assigned a four-digit number, 2012. I had no way of knowing then, but I would not know freedom again for thirteen months.

From the prison, I was taken to KCIA for interrogation. A black sedan picked me up at 9 o'clock every evening. I would sit between two agents in the back seat, as we drove past City Hall and through Sajik Tunnel. Taken to a basement room on the first day, their first question took me aback.

"Kim Jin-hong, when were you last in Pyeongyang?"

I replied with astonishment.

"How could Daegu guy know how to get to Pyeongyang?"

"You must have undergone training as a spy in Pyeongyang, considering what you've done. Do you know what Pyeongyang broadcasts say about you?"

They showed me a transcript they said was from a North Korean radio broadcast. It was absurd and palpably bogus. "We send enthusiastic support to Comrade Kim Jin-hong and other revolutionary fighters who are staging a heroic struggle for national liberation. We know that the day of national liberation is approaching by virtue of your revolutionary struggle."

Returning the document to the KCIA agent, I said, "Who would have thought that I would become a hero of the revolution?"

This was an extremely difficult time for me. In the beginning, I was forced to stay awake round the clock, answering questions. It became particularly difficult to stay awake in the early hours of the morning. The interrogation dragged on for two months and was extremely painful. I thought it would never end.

The KCIA investigated me thoroughly. Agents traced my activities at ten-minute intervals for the period from when the emergency measures were announced on January 8 until the time of my arrest. Because my memory sometimes failed me, I often had to modify my earlier testimony, while at the same time keeping the participation of others involved secret. I was subjected to the most severe questioning because I was considered the instigator of the rally.

Fifty-three people were implicated in the incident, either directly or indirectly. It would have been impossible for my testimony to match everyone else's. Whenever our answers conflicted, I was questioned again.

The endless, repetitive questioning reminded me of Prometheus, from Greek mythology. According to the myth, Prometheus was sympathetic toward mankind, which had been living without fire. Consequently, he stole fire from the gods and gave it to man, for which Zeus chained him to a rock and sent an eagle to devour his liver, which grew back daily. I thought I was being punished like Prometheus, in my case, however, for trying to awaken the people to the importance of democracy.

In handcuffs, every morning I would be returned to Seodaemun

Prison, half asleep. I would fall onto my bed and be out the moment my head hit the pillow.

After a short sleep, the iron door would creak open and a guard would shout, "Number 2012, front and center!" Before I was fully awake, I was handcuffed again and taken to the interrogation chamber. Upon entering, an interrogator shouted at me.

"Kim Jin-hong. Why are you hiding the truth, causing trouble for both of us? We should wind this up as quickly as possible, don't you agree?"

"What are you talking about? You've wrenched everything from my guts. Is there anything left untouched in me?"

"We know that seven people gathered at X o'clock, X day, X month, but you say six people were there. How can you explain this discrepancy? Pretending to be innocent, you are actually telling lies. Why are you causing us so much trouble?

"Doctor Kim said you called on him at around ten in the morning, but you said it was at about 4 p.m. Your lies are bound to be brought to light. Let me have some rest. Although you have gotten some sleep, I haven't been home for a week. You're driving me crazy because now I have to rewrite my report."

I realized I had made a blunder. A clergyman who was involved in preparations for the prayer meeting did not attend because he had a high fever. His wife called me shortly before the rally and appealed to me to drop her husband from the list of organizers. I promised that I would. Prior to the prayer meeting, I asked my colleagues to delete his name from the list of rally organizers. When questioned, however, someone must have mentioned his involvement.

The investigator went through my colleagues' testimony, which had been recorded in other reports, and said, "Was Pastor X at the meeting?"

I then told the investigator what had happened.

"I'm awfully sorry. I had his name removed because his wife asked me to before the meeting. It's hard to believe. Our colleagues promised to keep that a secret. Who can beat the Central Intelligence Agency? You guys are incredible."

The investigator smiled in resignation too exhausted to argue. I was quizzed again and again, sapping me of my strength, whenever there were discrepancies between my testimony and that of my colleagues. It appeared there would be no end to the investigation.

When being transported from Seodaemun Prison to the KCIA, I could see people walking about on the street, unconcerned, and I wondered whether in the past I had had such freedom.

Whenever I was moved, a pair of brutish agents always escorted me. I initially felt animosity toward them, which made me keep my distance. As time went by, however, we got to talking and came to understand one another's position. While we continued to hold our own views, it did not prevent us from becoming friends.

I was surprised to learn that even government agents could be human. Before coming into contact with the KCIA, I had thought its agents were thugs who beat suspects without giving any thought to what they were doing. Being in their company for a while, however, I found that they had a serious outlook on life and the nation. This made me reconsider my attitude toward them.

What motivated them to work so hard? Were they subservient to an individual, Park Jeong-hui, helping him preserve his political power? Were they desperate to get promoted and wield even greater power? Or were they driven purely by their patriotism?

After looking at this matter from various angles, I came to the conclusion that they worked hard, on their own, out of duty. Their first priorities were national security and economic development, while our group attached greater importance to freedom and human rights. As I saw it, it came down to two questions: 1) Whether national security should be put ahead of human rights, or vice versa, and 2) whether economic development should be put ahead of individual rights?

The investigators claimed that the country's economic foundation could be shaken if we continued to clamor for "human rights and freedom" and that we were throwing the nation into chaos. For the sake of national security and economic growth, they argued, human rights and individual freedom needed to be restricted. They said they took pride in the fact that they were working hard to ensure social stability for the nation.

I tend to hold a positive view of people I encounter and look on any situation optimistically. As a result, at times I have failed to take decisive action and have been criticized by my friends for lacking a strong sense of resistance and political awareness. That also is why I failed to develop a hostile attitude toward the KCIA agents who grilled me. They thought they were working in the national interest, just like us, although we went about our work in different ways. I further thought that both they and we were necessary for ensuring social stability.

I was seriously injured during one interrogation. The questioning focused on whether any women were involved in the rally and its planning. I made it clear that none were. Because our preparations were conducted over such a short period of time, there was no chance for a woman to get involved, but the investigator was adamant that I should "tell the truth."

Repeatedly asked to recount what had "really happened," at one point I exploded with fury, saying in desperation, "Yes. I remember that a woman was involved in the incident."

"Ah, now you're telling the truth."

The investigator had been eagerly awaiting my reply.

"First, the conductor of the city bus I took from the Cheonggyecheon shantytown to the Christian Broadcasting Station in Jongno 5-ga was a girl. Second, a woman operated the elevator that I used to reach CBS's eighth floor. Third..."

As I rambled on, he sprang from his chair in anger.

"What do you take me for? This guy's trying to make a fool out of me!"

With that, he threw a hard punch into my left side. It was such a strong blow that the pain made it all but impossible for me to breathe. That ended the session.

It was around that time that I was given a Bible. I cannot describe the joy I felt when I got it. I began to read, beginning with Genesis. I managed to read the entire Bible between Monday morning and the following Saturday afternoon.

Reflecting on my past behavior, I admitted to myself that in the past I had gone for an entire year, carrying on my work and conducting sermons, without once reading the Bible. I said that from then on, I would devote myself to reading the Bible. A person can read the Bible in different ways. One way is to skim through it, like water flowing. Another way is to read it paragraph by paragraph, taking time to savor its meaning. On this occasion, I went through it quickly.

Something happened as I was reading it for the sixth time. When I was leafing my way through Jeremiah, the Bible suddenly changed. The printed word came alive and could breathe and talk to me. The Bible was transformed into a living organism.

I cried with joy as I read. To keep my tears from falling on the book, I held it away from me and read on. Rather than say I read it, perhaps I should say I devoured it. It seemed that every paragraph was making its way into my body, creating a force within me. I knelt on the cold floor and prayed, giving thanks to God.

"Lord! I'm grateful that despite my many shortcomings, I have had an opportunity to be imprisoned and to gain access to the Word. While incarcerated, I will pray that you transform me into a new man who will be more faithful to you, and a servant who will breathe new life into the church."

Goethe once said, "Any person, who has not had tearful bread, is not qualified to talk about life." I would change this expression to the following: "Any person, who has not shed tears while reading the Bible, is not qualified to talk about Christianity."

ONCE THE KCIA'S PROBE INTO MY ACTIVITIES WOUND UP, I was put on trial by the emergency court martial. My colleagues and I, bound together by a rope, were dragged into the court set up behind army headquarters near Samgakji.

Something unusual happened on the second day of the trial. The hearing was abruptly halted. We did not know why or what was going on and were kept waiting several hours in the army headquarters chamber. The room was very cold. After the hearing resumed, we learned that members of Hwalbin Church had held a rally in front of the building, which led to a suspension of the proceedings.

At the rally, people had rushed forward, shouting, "Set our leader, Pastor Kim Jin-hong, free!"

Army officers were put on alert. Carrying loaded rifles, the MPs shouted to the crowd, "Leave immediately. Otherwise, we'll shoot," but their threat went unheeded. Women holding babies to their chests lunged toward the MPs, shouting, "Shoot if you wish, you bastards! This is a dogs' world. We won't take it any longer."

The MPs had to retreat. Someone later said that this was probably the first incident since the military had come to power in which the MPs had withdrawn from the front gate of the army headquarters because of protesters.

News of the protest, timed with the start of our trial, proved an immense encouragement to us, cut off, as we were, from the outside world. It was evidence that people were concerned about our welfare. One of our fellow prisoners, hearing news of the demonstration, told me, "I really envy you. You've done a great job. It's amazing that they demonstrated in front of army headquarters, defying the mighty MPs."

For my part, however, I was worried that the protesters might be injured. I prayed that no one was seriously hurt during the demonstration.

Later, I approached a KCIA agent and asked, "I heard that residents of Cheonggye-cheon demonstrated when our trial began. I'm concerned whether any of them were hurt."

"What do you mean, was anyone hurt? Is it that simple? I've never seen such a demonstration. Holding up their babies, they ran at the MPs, just asking to be shot. It might have been more serious, if someone had gotten hurt." Sarcastically, he added, "No, we treated them to a bowl of hot beef soup and gave them movie tickets, before escorting them home safely."

People who are downtrodden tend to be more sympathetic to the plight of others. I was grateful that people who lived from hand-to-mouth were brave enough to mount a protest in front of the MPs.

Meanwhile, the trial went on. In the end, five of my colleagues and I were sentenced to 15 years in prison and had our civil rights suspended. This did not depress us. Rather, we took pride in the belief that our actions would contribute to laying a foundation for democracy and advancing the expansion of evangelistic activities in Korea. We appealed the sentence to the emergency high court martial, which had reopened an investigation into our activities. We were once again grilled as to whether someone else was behind our activities.

"There must be other people pulling the strings behind you, some political figures or impure elements. You'd better confess, because the truth is bound to come out," one investigator warned.

The questioning went on for several days. Finally, I answered, "Yes, it is true that there was someone behind us. It was not a human being, but God Himself!"

During one of my interrogations, a KCIA higher-up made a senseless remark to me that deserved a rebuke. "Kim Jin-hong, you are the main culprit here, aren't you?" he said.

"Yes. I am."

"Why do churches perpetrate such hostilities against the government? You know, if churches continue to be hostile toward the government, we'll just get rid of them."

Outraged by his insolence, I protested. "What are you talking about? Do you want to be quoted on that? It is not government as government that the churches oppose, but a specific regime. Who is mapping out this policy for abolishing churches? Whose big idea is that? Is that President Park's policy, or something the KCIA cooked up?"

"Why are you latched onto this like a *Jindo* dog*?"

"I don't mind being compared to a *Jindo* dog. You're talking nonsense. Let's see who'll be the first to go, the churches or this government? Let's take a poll to see who the public would rather be rid of?"

---

* *Jindo* dog is a breed native to Korea, known for its tenacity and named for the region it is from.

19

A Community of Seven

IN FEBRUARY 1974, I WAS MOVED TO A NEW CELL. I had been confined to one that was only 25 square feet. The new cell was two and half times the size of the old one, but it already held six inmates. With a toilet and our belongings, it was crowded and uncomfortable during the day, but the lack of space was particularly unpleasant at night. It was impossible for seven people to sleep in such a small area. We had to sleep with one shoulder on the wooden floor. One night it was the right shoulder, the next it was the left. We called this sleeping in the "knife" position, because we kept one shoulder in the air like the blade of a knife. If you moved and lost your shoulder space, it was gone for the night. In that case, the only thing you could do was sit beside the toilet and try to sleep upright. Under these circumstances, at night, if you had to urinate, you just held on, for fear you would lose your spot.

Two of the inmates were in for fraud, one for *arirang* robbery, one for rape, one for armed robbery, and one for larceny.

One of the swindlers had sold a 200-*won* bag of sugar for 3 million *won*, claiming it was opium, fresh from Hong Kong. It was hard to believe that anyone would be so stupid as to fall for a trick like that, but evidently the man was good at his work, or so others told me.

The swindler explained the sugar scam in detail. He said he would teach me how it was done, so I could try it for myself.

He was one of a three-man team operating in Incheon. The most clean-cut of the three dressed up in a white medical gown, put on a name tag indicating that he was a doctor, and lay in wait in the vicinity of the Incheon Christian Hospital. Of the other two, one assumed the role of a street opium seller and the other pretended to be an anxious buyer. He told me that to properly pull it off, you had to be able to instantly spot the right victim, someone who looked greedy.

Most people who get caught up in swindles are people who are greedy and see themselves as crafty, not the good and the innocent, as is commonly believed. Even when faced with an opportunity to make big money, the innocent type tells himself that he does not have the money to swing the deal and that, in any case, the deal is not honest. He lets the opportunity go by. The crafty type, however, who has a high opinion of himself, hears about a chance to make some easy money, thinks of the money as already in the bank, and does not hesitate to jump at it.

The two street men would stand on a secluded corner and wait for the right victim to come along, at which time they would launch into their act.

"Wait a minute. You mean to say you want me to give you this stuff for just 2 million *won*? No way. There are plenty of people who in an instant would give me 5 million *won* for it."

They speak just loudly enough for their intended victim to hear. Then the buyer says he will raise the price. He pleads his case, says he does not have a lot of money and offers 2.5 million *won*. The seller holds out and says no.

The victim, passing by, thinks he has come upon a windfall and jumps into the conversation. If things go this way, at this point the game is all but over. The passerby asks what they are haggling over. The seller tells him it is opium brought in from Hong Kong by sailors and if he gets caught with it he is in big trouble. He says he cannot find the right buyer, but that someone could easily make 20 million *won* on it.

The victim is suspicious and asks how he can be sure that the goods are the genuine article. The seller tells him that they can go to the nearest hospital and check. If he's really interested in buying it, then they should go to the hospital straightaway.

The victim is tempted and accepts. They get into a taxi and head for Incheon Christian Hospital. The fake buyer goes on ahead and tells the fellow playing the doctor that the others are on their way. The doctor goes into the toilet at the hospital and waits.

The others arrive at the hospital and look around for someone to test the goods for them. Then the doctor comes out of the toilet and passes them in the hallway, looking appropriately dignified. The seller draws up beside the doctor, bows his head, and asks him to do the testing.

The doctor takes the goods and goes into a room. After a while he comes out and speaks carefully.

"This is 99 percent pure. Will you sell it to the hospital? We need it. We can give you 5 million *won* for it, cash. It's dangerous to walk around with this stuff. We'll take it off your hands," he says.

At this point, the victim finds it hard to contain himself. He blocks the sale to the hospital and takes the seller outside. He quickly gets the money together and buys the goods for himself. The seller, pretending to be doing him a big favor, agrees to let him have it for 3 million *won*, and the three swindlers each walk off with 1 million *won*.

When I asked how they had been caught, the swindler said that it was because he had taken a bus instead of a taxi. It turned out that the victim had gone back to the hospital to sell the goods. He asked for Dr. so-and-so and was told that there was no doctor by that name.

The victim became suspicious and put some of the sugar that he had mistaken for opium into a bag and took it to a pharmacy to be tested. The pharmacist asked him why he wanted to test plain sugar. In alarm, the victim ripped open the bag and stuck his finger in the white powder. He tasted it. There was no doubt about it—it was sugar. He had paid 3 million *won* for a bag of sugar! Outraged, he tore through the city, looking for the gang of swindlers. He found our man on a bus.

The swindler was distracted, looking around at people on the bus, wondering whether there could be another victim among them, when suddenly someone came up from behind and grabbed him by the belt. "I gotcha, you crook! Wait 'til I'm through with you!" The swindler turned around and there stood the victim.

That was how he wound up in jail, which he constantly lamented. "I should have taken a taxi. Taking a bus was my big mistake," he would say. We gave him a nickname, calling him "Mr. Taxi."

He had a gift for coming up with money and even while in prison he had made more than 2 million *won* on the black market. Using his talent the way he did, he was always in and out of jail. He was the perfect example of how a person's fate can take him in the wrong direction, because of his attitude toward life.

The other swindler in our cell had been caught trying to fob off pieces of burnt coal briquettes as film. He had disguised the briquettes by packing them in a convincing way and had placed real film on top of a large box, ostensibly full of other boxes of film, to show prospective customers.

He had been caught making a sale. In pulling off the scam, he had taken a package of real film off the top and opened it for the customer. The buyer himself picked up and inspected a couple of other rolls. Seeing that it was good film, he made an offer. It was as the swindler was weighing the offer that a police officer came along.

"What's this?" the officer asked, pulling one of the packages out from deeper in the box. The swindler ran off, but in the crowded market he was easily caught.

The *arirang* robber in our cell had employed the same modus operandi a total of forty-seven times. This man was a serious criminal. Five of his victims had suffered a broken jaw, and one had died on the spot. In an *arirang* robbery, which is a violent mugging, the victim, a pedestrian, is slugged on the jaw and robbed when he falls to the ground. The name *arirang* comes from a folk song of that name, in which a person makes his way over a hill. It is said that the image of the victim staggering and falling to the ground is similar to the image of the person going over the hill in the song.

The rapist was a youth who had attacked his victim, a teenage girl, at a cemetery in Icheon, where she had gone to pay her respects. His trial documents said that he had threatened the girl with a knife and had inflicted wounds that took two weeks to heal.

Our armed robber had climbed over the wall of a house and threatened a couple at knifepoint. He tied them up and gathered up whatever loot he could. He was caught while waiting in the house for the curfew to end in the morning. He had become bored while waiting. Ransacking the house, he found a bottle of cognac, which he gulped down like *makgeoli*, eventually passing out. When he awoke, he found himself at the police station.

Debates often broke out in the cell. One question was whether the robber had just drunk the cognac or had raped the wife as well. The robber swore that he was a gentleman and would not have laid a hand on the woman, but no one believed him. They said that apart from his breath, everything else that came out of his mouth was a lie.

The most unfortunate among us was a youth who was in for larceny. He went by the nickname "Broken Knife" and was mildly retarded. He was from a small island off the southwest coast and had come to Seoul to look for work. Finding none, he was going hungry and decided to break into a house. He climbed over the wall and got as far as the kitchen, but his courage failed him and he could go no farther. People were sleeping in the front room. He was wondering how he could get in without being seen, when he came up with a plan.

He changed the coal briquette in the heater and opened the door to the front room. He took a fan out of a cabinet and fanned the noxious fumes in the direction of the room. He figured the people sleeping in the room would pass out from gas poisoning and then he could go in and take whatever he found.

Things, however, did not go the way he had planned. He was hungry and cold. Sitting by the coal briquette, he began to feel drowsy. He nodded off and fell into a deep sleep. When the woman of the house came out to change the briquette, she was startled to find the youth, with the fan still in his hand, fast asleep beside the heater. She woke her husband and they called the police. The police tied him up as they found him, sound asleep, and took him off to the police station.

From there he was sent to Seodaemun Prison. He was charged with attempted murder, as well as larceny, because it appeared that he was trying to kill off the whole family with gas poisoning. Smart people can come up with good plans, but when dumb people try to be clever, they are bound to fail.

To MY DISMAY, a gap between the rich and the poor was just as apparent inside the prison as in society. The use of money was not permitted so trade was in the form of barter. Things such as soap and toothpaste were the going currency. Even in our tiny cell, the rich had a stock of toothpaste while the poor cleaned their teeth using their fingers. One prisoner had two boxes of soap while others had none and had to wash their clothes without any.

Those who had money had meat sent in for their meals, while the poor could only sit and take in the aroma. Naturally, this caused

314

friction, and fights were inevitable. Arguments that started out as only verbal skirmishes very quickly became physical.

The poor prisoner would sit with his nose twitching at the smell of meat being enjoyed by his rich cellmate and would pick a fight.

"Sure does stink around here. Ginseng for some and radish for others.* Some die from overeating, while others die from hunger," he would say.

"Is something bugging you? You like the smell? Why don't you order some, too? No one's stopping you," the rich man would say, taunting him.

"Are you trying to rub it in, you son-of-a-bitch?"

"I'm not trying to do anything. You started it. I was minding my own business, sitting here eating this meat, and you pick a fight, ruining it for me. Can't you see that?"

"Shut your yap or I'll make it so you have no teeth to eat meat with."

In such a small area, when fists began to fly there was no getting out of the way. I always took a few blows, trying to intervene. I saw the cell as the Korean society in miniature. I was frustrated to see that even in prison, there was friction between the haves and the have-nots. I had a thought, which one day I brought up.

"Hey, everyone. Let's try some politics. The kind you won't get from the president or from military brass," I said.

"Politics? What do you mean?"

"Let's call it community politics. The gap between the rich and the poor is a serious problem in Korea. Let's forget about what's mine and what's yours. Let's pool our belongings and try to create a community. Whether it's money, toothpaste, soap, or whatever, let's have common ownership over these things and put them to common use."

They all stared at me blankly. No one took me up on my suggestion. A few days later, the richest inmate, Mr. Taxi, began to ask me questions. "Hey, Number 2012. Are you by any chance from the North? Are you in here for spying? The way you talk is very suspicious."

"No," I answered. "I'm not from the North and I'm not a spy. I'm a Christian and the pastor of Hwalbin Church, so you don't have to

---

* Ginseng, a rare and expensive medicinal root, symbolizes something special, while radish symbolizes something ordinary.

worry about my ideology."

"You may be a pastor, but you still sound suspicious. Commies don't write 'I'm a commie' on their forehead. Never talk that way again in this cell. If you do, I'll report you as a spy. You know how much the reward is for turning in a spy, don't you?"

It seems he felt threatened by the idea of sharing his wealth. I realized that my idea was not going to be accepted out of hand.

"I think you misunderstood me," I said to everyone. "Think simply, for a minute. Imagine that we're all brothers and sisters. Like one family, when there's food, we eat together, and if we have nothing, we go hungry together. We now fight over a tube of toothpaste, but if we pool our belongings, everyone gets rich."

"Rich! Ha! Typical preacher. You're good at mouthing off. If that's what you want, hand over your things first. You Jesus people are all alike. All talk."

"Of course I'll be handing over my things, but if I give my things to someone who has nothing, that's charity. If we all hand over our things, and pool the resources, that's forming a community. Charity and community are two entirely different things. By handing out charity, it's easy for the rich to feel self-satisfied, but in a community, everyone takes part, the rich and the poor together."

I tried to convince everyone, but I wasn't getting anywhere. I realized that for my suggestion to be accepted, I would have to gain their confidence and create an atmosphere where we could open our hearts and really talk to one another. I tried again.

"It seems you still don't understand. You have to completely understand something before you can willingly take part in it, so let's wait and see. I'll pray that in this cell we can form a community."

A FEW DAYS LATER, AN OPPORTUNITY AROSE involving the lad from the remote island. He was alone in the world. The cold came early that year. The families of other inmates sent them thick underwear and blankets, but the island youth had nothing to keep him warm. He shivered in his prison clothes and his feet became frostbitten. With frostbite, the itching is severe. Because of his retardation, he was not good at controlling his body movements. He scratched his feet until he developed an open sore. Then the sore got infected. The toes on his right foot started going black and his heel began to swell. It was not looking good.

I was worried and told him to go to the infirmary to have it checked out. He did as I suggested and returned very dejected.

"My foot is infected and rotting away. I may lose it." He laid his head against the wall and started to cry. He was a pitiful sight. Even with two sound legs, he had not been able to look after himself and had landed in prison. How would he survive without a foot? I decided to do what I could to help him.

I gave him my thick winter clothes, my warm underwear, and my socks. I massaged his foot three times a day to stimulate circulation and, of course, I prayed. I asked for some warm water and bathed his wound, praying all the while. "Dear Lord. Please help this boy. Please heal his foot so it does not have to be amputated."

After eight days, the color around the wound began to change. The part that had been black started to regain its normal color. "Look, the color's beginning to change," I told him. "The cells are coming back to life. Go back to the doctor and have it checked again. You may not lose your foot after all."

I almost pushed him out of the cell. Two hours later, he came back. He said nothing, but knelt before me. He put his hands on the floor and wept.

"What's wrong?" we asked him, worried.

"What did the doctor say?"

He kept crying. After a long time, he stammered and started to speak. "Thank you, sir. You saved my foot. I won't have to lose it. Thank you." As he spoke, the others broke into cheers.

"Hey! Good going, Jesus Teacher! The foot is saved! When you came in, we thought you were a dog, but it turns out you're a tiger."

In prison, weak prisoners are called dogs and strong ones tigers. Those who are weaker than the weak are called mice and those stronger than the strong were called dragons. I had saved the youth's foot and my cellmates now recognized me as a tiger.

AFTER THIS INCIDENT, the atmosphere in the cell changed. Fighting diminished and my cellmates began to show genuine concern for one another.

When the bedtime bugle played that night, we went to lie down as usual, in the knife position. Mr. Taxi, who was next to me, seemed to have something on his mind.

"Hey, Jesus Teacher, you asleep?" he asked.

"No, not yet."

"Looks like we have a lot to learn from you."

"Do you think so?" I asked. "I'm learning a lot from all of you, too."

"Do you remember what you said when you first came in here?"

"What was that?"

"You remember. You said we shouldn't worry about what's yours and what's mine, but share everything."

"Yes, I remember. I still pray that it'll happen that way."

"Well, I've thought about it and I think we should try it. We got nothing to lose. I'll help you, if you like."

At that I sat straight up and said, "Good. Let's take the bull by the horns, as they say, and start right away."

It seemed as if everyone else had already agreed to the idea. Only Mr. Taxi, the richest of the lot, had been opposed to it, but after the foot incident, he had reconsidered.

With Mr. Taxi on my side, I decided that we should not lose time. Actually, I was worried that he would change his mind overnight, taking back his words, saying he had been talking in his sleep. I woke everyone up.

"Wake up everyone. There's something we have to do before we go to sleep." Everyone got up, wondering what it was all about.

"What's up, Jesus Teacher? Anything wrong?"

"No. Just the opposite. We're going to pool our belongings, money, toothpaste, whatever, and share like brothers."

I went first and handed over everything I had. Everyone else followed, and from the next day, everything in the cell changed.

When the concept of ownership changes, relations between people change also. With common ownership, people became unified, and fights and resentment declined accordingly. I was impressed by how quickly I saw results.

We lived peacefully, like seven brothers, with the oldest playing big brother and the youngest being the baby of the family, everyone taking care of one another.

A FEW DAYS HAD PASSED when the island lad came up to me and said, "Jesus Teacher, you read the Bible day and night. Why don't you read it aloud, so we can all learn, instead of keeping it to yourself?"

This was a welcome request. I looked around and asked, "What about the rest of you? Do you want me to read aloud as well? If you all want me to, I'd be happy to do it."

Everyone agreed, and my prison Bible lessons began. I started with simple, interesting stories from the Old Testament, Samson and Delilah, David and Goliath, Gideon's army, and Daniel in the lion's den. I managed to hold their interest and they sat close and listened intently.

"This Bible's something. It beats the pants even off *Huckleberry Finn* and *Tom Sawyer.*"

"You said it. Seems our teacher here has a different Bible from everyone else. It was never this much fun when I went to church. Is your Bible different, Teacher?"

As their interest grew, I began a few lessons. I read from the Ten Commandments. "The Fifth Commandment is 'Honor your father and your mother.' The Sixth Commandment is 'You shall not murder.'"

I explained the Commandments, one by one. When I got to the last one, 'You shall not covet your neighbor's house,' the island lad protested.

"Teacher, that one's hard to swallow. Let's leave it out and just go with the nine. If we follow the Tenth Commandment, we'll all be out of a job."

The others agreed. "That's right. Ours is a real profession. We're in the supply business as they say. At night, we steal from the rich and during the day, we give to the poor. We're helping the economy by redistributing the wealth."

Our Bible lessons were full of such talks and on Sunday I held a service. A prison chapel had been started, so to speak. We sat in a circle, so close that our foreheads almost touched, and I started preaching. I read from 2 Corinthians 5, and tried to explain it with an easy example:

In an American port there was a fishing boat by the name of The Accident. *It was so called because every time it went out an accident occurred.* The Accident *went out to fish one day and was returning to port when it tooted its horn.*

*The villagers came out shouting. "*The Accident*'s returning.*

Let's go and watch. I wonder what happened this time?" The vil-
lagers gathered at the wharf. The Accident *let down its anchor*
and one of the boatmen came up to the land.

"What happened? Has there been another accident?" the
people asked as they crowded around him.

"No, this time there was no accident," the boatman said.

The crowd was surprised.

"How is it that The Accident *hasn't had an accident. It's hard*
to believe," they said, as they headed back to their homes, shak-
ing their heads.

"We have a new skipper," the boatmen said, stopping them
in their tracks. "The old skipper was the cause of all the acci-
dents. Whenever we went to sea, he drank and became violent,
so it was no wonder we always had an accident. The new skip-
per is a good man who has the respect of the whole crew. We've
been able to catch a whole load of fish and return safely."

"Really. Imagine that. Change the skipper and The Accident
becomes The No Accident. *What do you think of that?" the peo-*
ple said, as the crowd dispersed.

There is a lesson to be learned from this story, I explained. It's
about changing skippers. We can compare ourselves to The Accident. *As the skipper of our own lives, we cause accidents wherev-*
er we go. That's why we're all here in jail.

To believe in Jesus is to change skippers. When we let Jesus
take charge of our lives, The Accident *becomes* The No Accident,
and that's what it is to live as a Christian.

It is written, "Therefore, if anyone is in Christ, he is a new cre-
ation; the old has gone, the new has come!" (2 Corinthians 5:17)

After the sermon, we sang a hymn and took up the collection. Our
"collection" consisted simply of one-tenth of any food or money that
happened to come our way. We used it to help out a poor inmate in the
cell next door. We concluded the service by reciting the Lord's Prayer.
The reaction to the sermon was positive.

"Teacher, why don't we turn this cell into a chapel? You can be the
preacher and you can make me an elder," one of my cellmates said.
Everyone burst into laughter. A guard approached and looked in on us

with suspicion. He squinted as he looked at us, but he went away.

When he had gone, Mr. Taxi said, "Did you see the look in his eyes? Something's going to happen."

"What do you mean?" the others said in protest. "What's wrong with listening to a sermon and laughing? Nothing's going to happen."

My cellmates said they had learned a lot from the sermon and asked that I hold services often. They liked the allegory and asked for more of the same.

My first prison sermon was destined to be my last, however. The next day I was moved to a solitary cell. The guard had been watching me talking with my cellmates and had become suspicious. He sent a report to the KCIA. The intelligence agency decided that I was dangerous, that I was putting ideas in other prisoners' heads, and that it would be best if I returned to solitary.

My cellmates were sad to see me go. We had been together for only a short time, but we had grown to like each other and parted with tears in our eyes.

"Teacher, you're going to do just fine," one of them said, as he squeezed my hand. "Don't be a pastor. Go into politics. Be a politician who can deal with the problems of underdogs like us."

I did not get a chance to ask him more about why he thought I should go into politics, but he said it with such sincerity that I did not forget it.

20

Baptism by Fire: Prison 1974

I T WAS BITTERLY COLD IN SOLITARY confinement. The cell I left had not been as cold because body heat from the inmates kept it warm. Here the cold was bone chilling, even worse than it had been when I was taking off my padded clothing and underwear to give to Mr. Frostbite. As time went by, the cold became unbearable. It was as if hundreds of needles were piercing my bones.

I prayed, "My Lord, I can't stand this cold. Please help me overcome this and survive my agony."

Although I continued to pray, the cold only became worse. To warm myself, I thought about a very hot summer I had spent in our makeshift house in Cheonggye-cheon. Most of the houses there were covered with sheet metal. When the hot summer sun bore down on the roofs, the rooms became sweltering bathhouses. I recalled the days when because of the summer heat, my son would not stop crying. I remembered also when I had been an employee in an ironworks, working next to a hot furnace, but even these thoughts failed to comfort me.

I picked up the Bible to read stories about fire. This helped me overcome the cold. The first story about fire was from Exodus 2:3. Moses once could have succeeded the pharaoh, but was forced to flee Egypt after he was inadvertently involved in a murder. He went to live at the home of his wife at the foot of Mount Sinai.

One day, when he was tending a flock of goats on the mountain, he came upon a bush that was on fire and would not stop burning. Thinking this was strange, he moved closer. He then heard the voice of the Lord coming from the burning bush. "Moses. Moses. Do not come any closer. Take off your sandals, because you are standing on holy ground."

Here, Moses met the Lord and was given the mission of rescuing the Israelites from slavery.

In Judges, Gideon and his 300 men used torches to defeat a large army of Midianities. In 1 Kings, fire sent by the Lord helped the Prophet Elijah defeat 450 prophets of Baal at Mount Carmel. In Isaiah, the youthful Isaiah, at the altar, had his lips touched by a burning coal and saw his guilt disappear. In Daniel, friends of Daniel were thrown into a blazing furnace to prove their faith. Finishing the Old Testament, I went on to the New Testament.

The word "fire" first appears in Matthew 3, as John the Baptist introduces Jesus. "I baptize you with water.... But after me will come one who...will baptize you with the Holy Spirit and with fire."

I prayed. "Lord, my Lord who came to baptize me with the Holy Spirit and with fire, I am so cold that I can't even think. Please baptize me with fire again, to overcome this freezing cold."

Next, I read about fire in Luke 12:49. "I have come to bring fire on the earth, and how I wish it were already kindled!"

Having gone to church ever since I was small, I had read Luke many times, but I did not remember having seen this phrase before. "Jesus Christ came to set the earth on fire." This expression came to me as very much a surprise. Jesus said He would be pleased if the fire were already kindled.

After carefully reading this phrase, I knelt and prayed again.

"Jesus Christ, who came to set the earth on fire, please set me on fire today. When you were being crucified, you said, 'It is finished.' I understand that the fire that the Lord cast onto the earth is already kindled. Please cast fire upon me." I prayed with all my heart.

I read Acts 2:1. "When the day of Pentecost came, they were all together in one place. Suddenly a sound like the blowing of a violent wind came from heaven and filled the whole house where they were sitting. They saw what seemed to be tongues of fire that separated and came to rest on each of them."

While reading these phrases, I sensed something unusual in my body. I began to warm up, as the coldness that had gripped me melted away. At first, I could not believe it and touched several parts of my body. While my body and mind felt normal, warmth had spread through the cell and had warmed me up.

I touched the floor with my hands. It was somehow warm, as if heated. I touched the walls. They also seemed to be heated. I was at a total loss to understand what was happening. I thought to myself that I must have become mesmerized while praying for fire.

While majoring in philosophy in college, I became keenly interested in psychology and read many books on the subject. There is a branch of psychology that is called abnormal psychology. Because of my older brother's mental illness, which greatly distressed me, I studied abnormal psychology extensively. The concept of mesmerism, a form of hypnosis, in abnormal psychology was vivid in my memory. Part of the theory is that when one is completely engrossed in something, he can become mesmerized, or hypnotized by it.

I wondered if my sudden warmth was the result of being mesmerized. Only after I was overcome with elation did I realize that my sudden warmth was the result of my prayer and not an abnormal psychological state. I was unable to contain my joy, which cascaded through my body like a rapidly flowing stream.

In jubilation, I bowed in every direction because I sensed that Jesus was with me somewhere in my cell. I felt as if He had come to me in person. I prayed with tears flowing, crying more than praying.

"Jesus, I am grateful to you for blessing such an unworthy person. I send you my most grateful thanks. I cherish your grace and will faithfully serve you all my life. I will dedicate my life to honoring your will."

My excitement lasted for several hours. The small cell became a true paradise. I experienced the grace of the Lord again, after I went to sleep to the sound of a bugle playing taps.

Just after I was put in prison, I was taken every night to the KCIA headquarters for interrogation. It was particularly cold at that time and I neglected to take proper care to avoid frostbite. I survived the ordeal, but ever after that, as soon as I went to sleep, my feet and legs would itch and I would feel like scratching. My feet were often swollen, which made it difficult to walk.

Strangely enough, after I was baptized with the holy fire and my cell warmed up, my feet no longer itched. It was hard to believe, so I put my feet under the light to inspect them. As if by a miracle, my feet had healed. I kept rubbing them, realizing that the Lord had somehow relieved me of my affliction.

In college I had loved to debate and was interested in logic. I would acquiesce to nothing that was not reasonable or logical. I believed that, like everything else, faith must be reasonable and conform to common sense. I believe that when in my cell I was baptized with fire, the Lord, who knows well how I think, cured my itch as irrefutable evidence of His existence.

I was too excited about the power of the Lord to remain calm. There was a rhythm to my excitement. It would rush in like a rising tide and then, like receding water, out it would drain. To calm my excitement, I began to sing:

> Amazing grace! how sweet the sound!
> That saved a wretch like me!
> I once was lost, but now am found;
> Was blind, but now I see.

As I sang, a prison guard came running to my cell and looked in. He said, "Number 2012, pipe down. You know better than that."

In prison, inmates are not allowed to sing, even during the day, but I sang hymns well into the night, to the dismay of prison officials. When the guard shouted for me to quiet down, I replied, "Guard, I'm very sorry, but you have to understand. The Holy Spirit has descended upon me, and I can't help but sing. If I don't sing, my heart will surely burst." I struggled to calm myself down.

Stunned, the guard looked at me and made a gesture of a circle with his finger near his temple, questioning whether I was playing with a full deck.

"What's wrong with you, Number 2012? Have you lost your mind?"

I replied, "You're right, Guard. I'm out of my mind. It's probably because of the Holy Spirit. Why don't you join me and we'll go crazy together?"

The guard left, as I moved to approach him. "Number 2012 has gone completely bonkers," he muttered.

That night, while crying and clapping, I continued my singing. I got little sleep, but I was not tired. Rather, I was full of energy, which was difficult to explain.

At breakfast I was given cooked rice and soup, but I dumped them in the toilet so I could fast. I then opened the Bible to Hebrews 12:29. I read, "Our God is a consuming fire."

I prayed through the first day of my fast. "The Lord is a consuming fire. I pray that you will wipe the tears of people on earth just as you took away my chill and my frostbite. I pray that you take away the sins of those in prison. I pray that with your fire you rid the earth of all the injustice, fighting, and ill-will."

At lunch I again dumped my meal into the toilet. I then read from 2 Corinthians 5:17. "Therefore, if anyone is in Christ, he is a new creation; the old has gone, the new has come!"

I prayed, "I am grateful to you for allowing me to become a new person with the Lord. I ask that you forgive me for my misguided thoughts and actions. From now on, I am determined to renew my body, my mind, and my vision."

All afternoon, I read silently from the Bible. I flushed my dinner, my third meal, down the toilet. I prayed after reading Galatians 2:20. "I have been crucified with Christ and I no longer live, but Christ lives in me. The life I live in the body, I live by faith in the Son of God, who loved me and gave himself for me."

I then prayed, "I have now died for my Lord. My ambitions and my dreams, as well as my future, have also died. For the rest of my life, I will live for Jesus Christ by having faith in Him. Please accept me wholeheartedly."

After having fasted for three meals and prayed silently, I promised myself that I would get off to a new beginning. Since that fateful day in prison, every year, on February 23, I renew this pledge by fasting. I am reminded of God's grace whenever I read the Lord's words that I read that day. It was by the grace of God and an incredible blessing to me that in my lifetime I was able to experience such a glorious day.

As March set in, the government's investigation of me was nearing an end. The cold weather was waning, making prison life less miserable. I had no woes other than the pain in my side, so I concentrated on studying the Bible.

IN MARCH, I WAS TRANSFERRED TO A CELL on the second floor of a building next to Building 9. At 25 square feet, my new cell was too cramped to do even simple calisthenics. On one wall were three German words, written in blood:

> *Wahrheit* (Truth)!
> *Freiheit* (Freedom)!
> *Gerechtigkeit* (Justice)!

They must have been written by a political prisoner who was held in the same cell. Although there was no way of knowing who it might have been, I prayed silently that whoever it was would be able to achieve what he was pursuing, "Truth," "Freedom," and "Justice."

On another wall was a poem. The words of the poem had long since become blurred, but I could discern that it was "Prologue" by Yun Dong-ju, a poet who was born in Manchuria and who, at the age of 29, died in a prison in Fukuoka, Japan. Reading the poem word by word, I could feel his dispair, in the land of Korea's colonial aggressors.

PROLOGUE

> For a life to be led until death
> without a patch of shame;
> under the eye of heaven
> I felt painfully hurt
> by a single breath of wind
> that stirs the leaves of grass.
> I must love all things mortal
> with a spirit to sing the stars;
> I must follow the path
> destined to me.

The poem's final line, which reads "Again tonight, wind rustles against the stars," was missing. I thought that the inmate who had transcribed the poem could not remember it. I wanted to fill it in, but had nothing to write with. Inmates were not allowed to have pencils or other writing tools. Particularly, political prisoners were strictly denied access to writing materials. Still, I wanted to record the last line.

After much thought, I decided to make some ink. I scraped my aluminum dinner dish against the wall and collected the powder in a container. I then added some urine. The aluminum residue became dark ink. I now had the ink, but what could I use for a pen? I sharpened the handle of my toothbrush by scraping it on the wall. I had my pen. With it, I added the final line of the poem:

> Again tonight,
> wind rustles against the stars.

THE NEXT DAY, AN INMATE PEEKED INTO MY CELL through the window and asked, "Are you a churchman?" I nodded and, before scurrying away, he threw in a folded piece of paper. He had done this at great risk because inmates were prohibited from any contact with political prisoners.

Political inmates wore a yellow tag on their prison shirt. Yellow tags were initially worn only by prisoners who were mentally disturbed. The effect was that political prisoners were treated the same as the insane.

I picked up the scrap of paper. The paper contained a brief sketch of five men who were in prison for burglary, manslaughter, battery, and armed robbery. The five, who had grown close in prison, had read the Bible together and decided to accept Jesus as their savior. They said, however, that they had no idea where to begin and asked for guidance.

I used my homemade pen and ink to write a reply. I encouraged them in their effort and added some basic tenets for a religious life. I was unable to deliver the message for several days, but one morning, while washing up, I decided to act.

In the morning, cells were opened briefly for inmates to go outside to quickly wash their face and hands. We had only until the count of ten to finish, which required us to work quickly, before having to return to our cells. Any delay in washing would elicit a loud reprimand from the guards. Hence, on reaching the washbasin, everyone was in a rush. Taking advantage of the chaos this system created, I managed to convey my message to the men.

Engaging in secret correspondence between inmates is known as "flying a pigeon." I flew pigeons to the group a number of times, helping them adapt to their new religious life. As time went by, I noticed that their faces became brighter, suggesting that their belief in God was growing stronger.

PRISON LIFE IS OFTEN CALLED "EATING BEANS," as a beans and barley mixture is standard prison fare. My poor health, aggravated by the pain in my side, made it difficult for me to digest this concoction. I felt bad about throwing so much food away and looked for ways to utilize the surplus.

I always read the Bible until I got tired and then I would look out the window. One day I saw pigeons in a tree near my window. That gave me an idea. I would feed the beans to the pigeons.

When the next meal came, I separated the beans from the barley and placed them on the window ledge for the pigeons. For the first two days, they showed no interest, but on the third day they began to come around. I hid myself away from the window, lest they be scared away.

The next day, when they came, I inched toward the window to see whether they would be frightened off. My efforts appeared to be paying off. The pigeons did not fly away, even though I stood right by the window. They seemed to have determined that I would cause them no harm. After that I called out "coo, coo" whenever I had beans for them, and they would come over to eat.

I became particularly close to this pigeon couple. They would eat the beans fearlessly, even though I stood right next to them. While they were eating, I spoke to them, "Pigeons, would you please visit the homes of our church members in the Cheonggye-cheon slum area? As you can see, I'm not free right now to do it myself."

As if they grasped what I had said, they responded "coo, coo."

The next day, I asked them whether they had delivered on their promise.

"Pigeon couple, did you visit Cheonggye-cheon? Did you find out whether the church members and other residents were safe and happy?"

The duo answered "coo, coo," as if they had returned after flying over to Cheonggye-cheon. I decided to give them names. I called the male pigeon Min-hyeok, meaning "to reform people," and the female

Min-ae, meaning "to love people." I gave them my surname Kim.

Min-hyeok and Min-ae became the main focus of my meditation. "What must Korean churches as a whole do for the sake of our nation and its people?" I asked myself. They should love people, *min-ae* and reform people, *min-hyeok*. How, then, could they do that?

The answer, I believed, was to teach them how to have confidence in themselves and manage their own affairs, and lead them to right thinking. This, I thought, was the most crucial issue for Korean churches.

I decided that after being released from prison, if I had a son, I would name him Min-hyeok. If I had a daughter, I would name her Min-ae. If possible, I wanted to have a son and a daughter.

A year later, I became a free man. The years passed, and in 1981 my second wife and I had a son. We named him Min-hyeok. Two years later, my wife gave birth to another son. We would not be able to use the name Min-ae, because it is a girl's name. We reversed the syllables, to Ae-min, which works as a boy's name and which in Korean carries the same meaning. The children grew up quickly. Watching them grow, I often pondered the significance of their names.

21

To Be Refined as Pure Gold

I APPEALED MY 15-YEAR SENTENCE TO the emergency high court martial, but my appeal was rejected. I made a final appeal to the Supreme Court. While my case was pending, I was transferred to Anyang Prison, where my number was changed to 73.

One day, one of the guards came to my cell and asked whether I was a Christian. When I said I was, he told me to read Psalms 138:7-8, and went away. I wondered what was in those verses that made the guard seek me out and tell me to read them. I looked it up and read:

> Though I walk in the midst of trouble,
>   you preserve my life;
> you stretch out your hand against the anger of my foes,
>   with your right hand you save me.
> The LORD will fulfill his purpose for me;
>   your love, O LORD, endures forever —
>   do not abandon the works of your hands.

These words did a lot to encourage me. They inspired me to write a letter to a friend:

My day starts with the morning call. I get up, clean my cell, and go to roll call. After that, I read the Bible. As days go by, I see greater results. I consider this period in prison a trial, put before me by God, for me to endure to become a vessel worthy of His service. I devote my time to preparing myself in mind and body. My fellow inmates talk about suffering during their time in prison and anxiously look forward to the day of their release, but I am not anxious about my release. If God is using this period as a time of training for me, the date of my release will not be decided by humans, but by God.

Here I will quote from Isaiah 48:10 as my confession of faith, "See, I have refined you, though not as silver; I have tested you in the furnace of affliction."

I considered my time in prison "a furnace of affliction" and that made it easy for me to adjust. There remained, however, one problem. The pain in my side, inflicted by the KCIA during interrogation, was getting worse. I found it difficult to digest my food. My weight fell to 88 pounds and I was becoming dangerously unhealthy. My body hurt terribly.

My fellow inmates worried that I would be "going out the back door," which was another way of saying I would die in prison. My vision was dimming and I had difficulty reading. I reasoned it was because of malnutrition, since our food consisted mainly of salty soup and barley with beans.

I called the guard and said, "My eyesight is bad and getting worse. I think it's because of a lack of vitamins in our food. Could you arrange for us to have some fresh vegetables?"

"You can eat fresh vegetables when you get out," he barked. "What do you think this is, a hotel? Do you think that you can order whatever you want? Besides, if we treat you people any better, you'll keep coming back."

There was nothing I could say in response. Eyes aside, my greatest problem was the worsening pain in my side.

My ribs hurt whenever I inhaled. When I exhaled, it was as if my joints were being jabbed with pins. It hurt when I lay down or when I sat. The only way I could get any relief from the pain was to press my hand to my side and lean with my forehead against the wall.

As I leaned against the wall, I recited Bible verses to myself. I started to read from the Book of Job. Job was appropriate, I thought, because it concerns the sufferings that people often go through.

I came to a passage that, when I applied it to my own situation, made me feel greatly blessed.

> But if I go to the east, he is not there; if I go to the west, I
> do not find him. When he is at work in the north, I do not
> see him; when he turns to the south, I catch no glimpse of
> him. But he knows the way that I take; when he has tested
> me, I will come forth as gold. (Job 23:8-10)

When the pain was at its worst, I would cry out, "Oh Lord," but the Lord didn't come to my aid. I felt alone with my pain. I had been cast aside by both man and God, as if forgotten by all.

Nobody knew my situation, neither my family, nor the people of my church. God alone knew, but why He did nothing, I could not say. I could understand his silence, if He did not know, but knowing how I was suffering, why did He not help me?

Job 23:10 gave me the answer—it was to test me, in the strictest sense of the word. God had a plan for me and was testing me for His purpose.

If this was the case, for what was I being tested? It was to turn me into a person of pure gold. In the Bible, gold symbolizes faith, but there are different kinds of faith. Faith that is come by easily is just faith, but faith that is arrived at through pain and suffering, failure and adversity, is a faith of gold.

I pondered this idea and thought, God, my Lord and master, is testing me and refining me into gold, so I can work for my church and my people. This is why he is allowing me to suffer as I am now.

Having reached this conclusion, it became easier for me to withstand the pain and my mind was at peace. When the pain returned, I convinced myself that I could endure it. I consoled myself by thinking that the pain was a sign for me to pray, so I should kneel and pray.

Until then, I had refused to go outside during exercise period. Political prisoners were allowed thirty minutes of outdoor exercise daily. The guard would come around, call out my number, and open the door, yelling "exercise time." The pain was worse when I moved, so I always declined this opportunity to go outside. After reading Job, however, I asked to be allowed outside again.

Once outside, I concentrated on jogging. I would grab my painful side with one hand and recited as I went, "But he knows the way that I take; when he has tested me, I will come forth as gold." I repeated this as I jogged. After my sessions, my legs would ache and my eyes would grow even dimmer.

I was jogging one day when I saw some greenery growing under the fence. I went over to it to see whether it was edible, when I realized it was clover. If rabbits ate it, I concluded, it could not be harmful to humans. I ate handfuls of it while I ran and, after a few days, my breathing came easier. But I did not have an endless supply and, after a week, it was all gone. I would have to wait until it grew back.

SOME NEW POLITICAL PRISONERS CAME TO THE PRISON. The policy was to keep the serious offenders handcuffed and in solitary cells, but with the number of political prisoners rising, they had to double up.

One of the new prisoners was assigned to my cell. His name was Kim Yong-sang and he was in his late twenties. When he greeted me, he looked into my face and said, "What's wrong with you? You don't look at all well."

"I was hurt during interrogation and it's not healing," I said.

"I see," he replied. "Well, don't worry about it. Leave it to me and I'll cure it. Just do as I say and in one month you'll be as good as new."

"Are you a doctor?"

"No. I'm something better than a doctor."

"Better than a doctor? Are you a vet?"

"A vet? Don't make me laugh. No, I'm a yoga instructor. I was teaching college students yoga and there were some activists among them. When they were arrested, so was I. I'll teach you and help you get better. Just do as I say and don't worry."

Kim was from Jeonju and had graduated from Jeonju High School. He had not gone to university, but had studied yoga for the past ten years. Yoga was very difficult and, as it turned out, he was exactly what I needed.

As a remedy, yoga was fast and effective. After 20 days, the pain in my side had diminished and my digestion improved. In a month's time I was able to eat my prison rations. Before my yoga sessions, I had not been able to eat even half a meal. I quickly regained my strength and continued to run every day. I soon became healthy again.

At Anyang Prison inmates were required to attend services. A different religious leader came every week: a Catholic priest came once a month, a Buddhist priest once a month, and a minister twice a month.

One day, the political prisoners were sent to services with the ordinary prisoners. Minister Lee Cheon-seok had come that day. Minister Lee had had a colorful past. He was a disabled veteran and before becoming a Christian had been a famous gangster. He was a "four star" ex-con, meaning he had been in and out of prison four times.

As soon as he began to speak, we knew he was different from other ministers. "I have four stars," he began. At this, the prisoners suddenly went silent. They could not help it. They had to show respect for an ex-con.

"One day I was happily walking around in Myeong-dong* with a broad hanging on my arm, when the fuzz spotted me...," he continued.

Being an ex-con, his language was not what you would expect from a minister. He used words that are heard only in prison and his listeners were very quiet. Not only was his language different, but his sermon was also unusual. He had lived by his fists before coming to know God. He had repented and become a new person. His life had been dramatic, but it also had been filled with God's grace.

After finishing his sermon, he looked out over the 4,300 prisoners in the auditorium and said in a serious voice, "Any of you who would like to repent and become a preacher like me, stand up!"

At this, 600 or 700 prisoners shot up from their seats. My heart fell when I saw this and began to pray.

"Dear Lord, I pray that you allow those people to become useful people in the church, but not ministers. If these swindlers, robbers, and rapists repent and become ministers, the Korean church will be in for big trouble. Please make sure that they remain believers who keep the faith, but do not let them lead others as ministers."

I prayed not out of any disrespect for the prisoners, but rather because they were dear to me. Though a person may repent and be born again, it is difficult for for him to change his nature completely. At the moment of conversion, it seems possible to become an angel. As time

*A fashion district in downtown Seoul.

passes, however, the strong sense of determination that accompanies conversion begins to wear away. As that determination weakens, a person's true nature resurfaces. That is why I prayed that they receive God's blessing, change their ways and be saved, but that they only become strongholds of the church rather than spiritual leaders.

AT TIMES, WE POLITICAL PRISONERS WOULD BE SENT to spend a few days in a cell with ordinary prisoners. This happened to me, also. One night my sleep was disturbed by a strange noise. I awoke to find the two men next to me naked and huddled together in a state of great excitement. I realized I had come upon two homosexuals in the act, something I had only heard about. I could not avoid seeing them, because they were right next to me and I had a clear view.

For me, the thought of two men in an act of sex was repugnant. Obviously, the protagonists did not think so. They were enjoying themselves thoroughly.

Then suddenly I was eye to eye with the inmate taking the role of the male. He looked at me awkwardly and said, "Hey, Mr. Kim, what are you staring at? Look the other way. You're taking the fun out of it."

I turned away and after a while they finished and went back to sleep. The next day the "male" apologized to me.

"Sorry about last night," he said. "We woke you up, didn't we, but you understand, don't you?"

"Well, I'm not sure I do. Is it fun to have sex with another man?" I asked.

"What, you mean you've never done it with a man?"

"No, I haven't."

He went to some length to explain homosexuality, although it was not something in which I had a lot of interest. Having been introduced to that aspect of prison life, I began to notice that in prison, a male-only society, many of the problems revolved around love and affection.

For example, once there was a murder involving a love triangle. Three inmates in the same cell had become involved with one another. The "female" inmate was a flirt, going first with one man and then the other. With the first man watching over them jealously, the new couple was not able to make love in peace, so they lobbied for a transfer. They were moved and in their new cell lived like husband and wife.

The man left behind was resentful for having been rejected and decided to take revenge. Having been sent outside to work, he found a big nail along the roadside. Secretly, he sharpened the point of the nail and turned it into a weapon. He waited for his chance and, one day, when they were in the exercise yard, he stabbed his former lover in the back. The nail punctured a lung, and although they stitched up the victim, he died anyway.

On another occasion, there was a suicide. An inmate left a note saying that in the next life, he would find the love that could not be realized in this one. He hanged himself with a plastic bag, the kind that bread comes in. If you twist such a bag around many times, it becomes very strong. The inmate and his lover had apparently made love loudly every night and the neighbors, having had their patience tried, asked that the couple be moved elsewhere. They were separated and moved to different cells, which gave rise to the suicide.

These events were the result of people being starved for love. Just as with a person who suffers malnutrition, a person starved for love suffers from a deficiency. When normal love is not available to them, sufferers will look outside of ordinary relationships for abnormal love. Before judging such people by our standards and condemning them, we need to try to understand them and work to cure them of their disease.

IN PRISON, IT WAS COMMON for people to injure themselves purposely. In one case, a prisoner sewed his own eyes shut with a needle and thread. He said he no longer wanted to see this rotten world. Prison officials had a terrible time removing the stitches.

On another occasion, long-term inmate in the cell next to mine drove nails into his feet. I heard him shouting out in pain and turned in time to see him putting nails in his feet, driving them through by banging his feet on the floor. The nails had gone in deep and had been caught between the boards on the floor. He could not move his feet or pull the nails out, which was why he was screaming.

Prison officials worked to release him from his agony. When the inmate screamed and shouted that it hurt, the guard hit him on the head and said, "You stupid bastard, didn't you know it'd hurt?"

The prisoners abused themselves because they had no way to relieve their feelings. If they expressed their feelings overtly, they would be punished. With the intensity of their emotions demanding expression, they resorted to abusing their own bodies.

People who have lost sight of their true selves through sin and pain create a hell within themselves. They shut themselves inside that hell, suffering in a prison of their own making.

The most somber part of my day in prison was at lights out. I found it odd that at every prison I was in, for lights out, on a bugle they played only hymns. At Anyang they played, "Come, Thou Almighty King."

> Come, Thou Almighty King
> Help us Thy Name to sing,
> Help us to praise:
> Father, all glorious, O'er all victorious,
> Come, and reign over us, Ancient of Days.

Upon hearing the hymn, the prisoners became silent. Every night, when the hymn finished, you could hear inmates here and there calling out, "Mother." It was always a moment of serious reflection. To all the prisoners, mother was a symbol of home and the lost innocence of childhood. Mother was also the symbol of love, affection, and warmth. No matter how twisted a person may be, in prison he becomes introspective when he thinks of his mother.

There was a young man who at the age of twenty-three was in prison, condemned to death. Every night, when the bedtime bugle played, he would go to the window and call out, "Mother! Mother!" The voice of this one man crying out to his mother was so heartrending that everyone who heard him felt a tightening in their chest.

Listening to him, I often thought to myself, "That poor boy, to hear him call out to his mother, it's clear that he regrets his crime. They should let him live."

The day came when we no longer heard him call out. I asked the guard, "Has anything happened to the young man next door? I haven't heard a sound out of him lately."

"Didn't you know? They put a necktie on him a few days ago."

I became convinced that if mothers ruled the world, it would be a very different place. There would be no prisons, no torture, and no bombs. Goethe said, "Femininity will save the world." I think it would be truer to say "Motherhood will save the world."

To relieve the boredom of prison, there were frequent swearing competitions. People in cells facing one another would take turns yelling out the foulest language they knew, in an escalating litany of obscenities. The person who ran out of words first was the loser. I heard all sorts of strange words and expressions, some gut-wrenchingly funny and some so cruel as to be horrifying.

At times, the side that felt it was losing would come out with something related to mother, such as, "Your mother's...." When this happened, the men listening in would complain. "Hey, can it, you guys. Say what you like, but leave the guy's mother out of it."

Those competing would have to take back what they had said and come up with something else. To these prisoners, mother was the only sacred thing they had left. They were not about to lose it.

I began to think that it was important for the church to play the role of mother to distressed souls, those who were lost and weary of life. As with love a mother embraces even a prodigal son, it is important for the church to embrace the lost. The power mothers possess is the power of love, and what can be the purpose of the power of love if not to save mankind from destruction?

IN PRISON, JUST AS THE WINTER COLD WAS HARD TO BEAR, the summer heat proved to be no less maddening. The second floor of the two-story Anyang Prison had a concrete slab roof that in summer became unbearably hot. Sitting in my cell in the afternoon, my head would ache and the whole room would spin. We joked that if we threw a raw egg on the roof, it would fry.

It was during the heat of summer that the political prisoners at the prison proposed to go on a hunger strike. The strike would be held for the abolition of the *Yusin* political system, freedom of speech, and the restoration of democracy.

Prisoners were divided on the issue. Those in favor of the hunger strike said they had landed in prison fighting for democracy, so they should continue the battle. Those against said that being in prison was itself a form of protest. The best thing they could do while there was maintain their health. They thought that a protest should be carried out in a productive manner and that going on a hunger strike under such difficult conditions would hurt their health and would therefore be unproductive. It was the hard-liners, who thought that everything had to be a battle, against the moderates.

I was always a moderate. I believed that anything worth achieving came only gradually and tried to reason with the hard-liners.

"The foundation of democracy is strength. Who will fight for democracy if we starve ourselves, grow sick, and die?" I argued. "We'll be able to fight only if we look after ourselves and build up our strength. How can we achieve democracy in the space of one or two years? It'll take a long time. Political change is like a tree. You cannot force it to bear fruit. We have to persevere for a decade or two. Let's eat. Why should we starve?"

My plea was not particularly effective. The moderates were greater in number, but they were silent, while the loud voices of the hard-liners moved to the front. It is nature's way for the position of the intransigent to prevail. The more this is so, the less mature the society.

It was decided that the political prisoners of Anyang Prison would go on a hunger strike. After arriving at this decision, the next question was how long it should continue. The hard-liners were all for continuing the strike indefinitely, until our demands were met.

I argued that we should strike for just three days. Anyone who found three days too difficult should take part for at least one day and after that use their discretion. I wanted to avoid any do-or-die resolutions.

"Jin-hong, why are you always so compromising," one scolded me.

"I don't care what you think of me," I said. "My point is that we should be reasonable. I'm not saying we have to do things my way. I think we should all express our opinions and discuss them and then decide with a vote."

After arguing back and forth this way, we came up with a compromise that accommodated the position of both sides. We would all go on a hunger strike for three days, after which those who wished to would continue.

With that, the hunger strike began. After the agreed three-day period, some continued. Lee Hae-hak, a pastor in my cell, was among them. I tried to persuade him to stop, but he was determined.

340

"How long do you think you can keep this up?" I asked.

"There is no set time. We keep going until President Park listens to our demands," he said.

"And what exactly are our demands?"

"Democracy, of course."

"Then one precious life will be wasted. Park Jeong-hui is a hard man. Do you think he will bat an eyelash at the news of a handful of prisoners dying because of a hunger strike."

"It doesn't matter what Park does. The important thing is that we do what we have to do."

"I don't agree. If we want to defeat Park, we have to outlive him. The only person who'll thank you for ruining your health and buying the farm is Park. You have to live before you can help create a democratic society."

Lee, however, was unshakable. After ten days, I grew worried. It was unreasonable to continue a hunger strike for more than ten days in prison, where keeping up your health is difficult enough. Lee was carted off to the infirmary and, after a few days, came back and was eating again.

"Lee, if you knew it was going to end this way, why didn't you go to the infirmary earlier," I asked in jest. "If you were going to eat so soon after leaving the infirmary, why were you so stubborn?"

"You don't understand," he said. "I had no thought at all of eating, but they forced me to."

"How can they force you to eat? After all, you're not a child."

"Well, they made me sit in a chair like a barber's chair."

"And then?"

"They attached a machine that resembled an ox yoke to my head. Then they pressed a button and there was a whirring sound and the machine pressed on both of my temples. My mouth just opened. They put in some juice and pushed in a spoonful of rice. When I took a breath of air, the rice just went down my throat. I never imagined there could be such a machine."

"I can't believe it! Well, it's a sign that machine design in Korea is rapidly developing. Perhaps we could export this machine and earn some foreign exchange," I said in amazement.

I was sure that there was no other country on earth that had invented and put to use a machine that could force a person to eat.

Though we were cut off from news from the outside, on the afternoon of August 15, Liberation Day, 1974, a rumor filtered down to us. It seemed that something had happened to the President. By the next morning the story had emerged. There was an assassination attempt during the Liberation Day ceremony and, according to the rumor, the President survived it, but the first lady, Yook Yeong-su, had been hit by a stray bullet and died.

Some of the political prisoners greeted this news with cheers and applause, but I did not agree. The president's wife was dead and as a citizen of Korea, that was news for grief, not for cheering. We may have all been in prison for our opposition to how the nation was being governed, but in no event should we lose our reverence for human life. Hate only engenders hate.

The first lady's death created discussion among political prisoners. The question was whether it was a cause for mourning or celebration.

Those who welcomed the news said that as Yook was not an ordinary person, but a public figure, her death was a warning from heaven and therefore a cause for celebration.

Those who mourned her death said that the first lady was neither a politician, nor a dictator, but a housewife and mother and therefore it was not right to feel joy over her death.

They continued to argue that it was uncertain whether the death of the President himself would be a cause for celebration or grief. As such, it was wrong to be happy that his wife had been killed. To take pleasure in the death of another person is to display a loss of humanity and lower ourselves to the same base level as those who imprisoned us.

The debate went on and, by nature, was not one that could come to a conclusion. It showed us that there were differences of opinion even among people working for the same goal.

I DIGRESS. GETTING BACK TO MY APPEAL to the emergency high court martial, the judge presiding over my case was General Lee Se-ho. The other prisoners and I stood in court dressed in our blue prison clothes, handcuffed, and roped together. It was not a public hearing, so there were no outsiders in the courtroom. I looked at the chief judge's chair. Sitting there, bristling with authority, was a five-star general. The other judges were likewise generals, with more than ten stars among them.

Lee Hae-hak said sarcastically, "Look at these guys. Who do they think they are, pinning shiny medals on their chests like children?"

"They're emotionally immature and like to play with toys," said another pastor, Park Yun-su, in the row in front of us.

We all burst out laughing.

Our laughter seemed to alarm the judges. Authority is relative and exists only if another party recognizes it. When the other party does not, authority loses power and becomes a mockery. These generals, coming face to face with prisoners who did not recognize their authority, appeared to be uncomfortable.

The military police were flustered and shouted for us to be quiet, but we had no respect for them, either. Fearless, Lee said to them, "You don't even have any stars. What right do you have to yell?"

Another prisoner picked up on the line and said, "Who knows, maybe if they keep yelling, someone will pin a star on them."

The prison guard who had escorted us looked uneasy.

"Don't do this," he said. "You put us in a very difficult position. Please have mercy. We'll be reprimanded."

It is characteristic of churchmen to become meek before the meek. We pitied the guard and quieted down. Considered the worst offender, I was the first to be tried. General Lee questioned me.

"Kim Jin-hong, what is your occupation?"

"I am the pastor of Hwalbin Church."

"Why is a man of the church departing from his duties and getting involved in political activities?"

"The military have departed from their duties and therefore we, people of the church, have also temporarily left our calling."

"What do you mean by that?"

"The military has abandoned its duty of defending the national territory. To stop it in what it is doing, in oppressing the civilian population, we have been forced to abandon our duties. When the military returns to the Demilitarized Zone (DMZ), then we will return to our churches. You needn't worry about that."

This kind of questioning went on for several hours. We were all exhausted at the end of the day.

Our appeal was turned down and we made a final appeal to the

Supreme Court. I received a letter asking me to submit a document explaining the reason for requesting a Supreme Court appeal.

In summary, the letter said:

> *I have been accused of violating the emergency measures laid down by the president and I believe that my sentence of 15 years is unjust. My reasons are:*
>
> *First, the emergency measures go too far in suppressing freedom of speech. Freedom of speech is a God-given right. To suppress it is to go against God's will. History shows that past governments and administrations that have committed the crime of suppressing freedom of speech have been judged by God. I feel it is unjust to be sentenced to 15 years for organizing a prayer meeting for the purpose of spreading awareness of such issues.*
>
> *Second, the emergency measures forbid actions to amend the constitution. This is a measure that goes against the principles of democracy. Since May 16, the President himself has amended the constitution three times. It makes no sense for him to outlaw such actions on the part of the people.*
>
> *Third, the emergency measures set up a court martial that hands down excessive sentences. At a time when the situation in Korea and the world is rapidly changing and the country faces threats from North Korea, the army has abandoned its duty of guarding the border and is now aiming their guns at their own citizens. All I wanted to do was make the people aware of this and I see no reason why I should be punished.*
>
> *I ask that the judges of the Supreme Court use their wisdom to examine this case thoroughly and make the right decision.*

On August 20, 1974, my appeal to the Supreme Court was rejected and my sentence of 15 years was confirmed. They shaved my head, to punctuate my status.

22

Out of the Frying Pan, Into the Fire

AFTER MY SENTENCE WAS CONFIRMED, nine of the political prisoners at Anyang Prison were transferred to Suwon Prison. I was among them and was assigned to a cell for serious offenders. Of the eighteen men in the cell, six were murderers.

Suwon was a model prison, where both national and foreign inmates were housed. It had a well-stocked library. The library, however, was off-limits to political prisoners. We had always sought to gain access to it and it was in this regard that I came up with a plan.

"Let's tell the administration that we're going on a hunger strike. They'll try to keep us from doing it and we can negotiate access to the library in exchange for stopping. What do you think?"

The political prisoners welcomed my suggestion and we all began a hunger strike. Worried, the guards tried to dissuade us. Finally, the warden himself came to see us and appealed to us to stop.

"Our job is to take care of you. We are responsible for your health and we'll be blamed for this. I'm asking you to stop now."

I told him that if he gave us permission to use the library, we would give up our hunger strike. He promised he would do everything he could. Being assured we would have access to the library after passing up only one meal, we agreed. This was the first time since my college days that I was able to spend time reading great books and I considered myself lucky.

One night I overheard a conversation among prisoners. They were talking about Korea's political and social situation. One said, "Korea's future looks really bad."

The other prisoner responded, "I agree. Who can we trust? The way trials are conducted shows what horrible condition the country is in. How can we have confidence in judges and prosecutors? How can we trust lawyers? The courts run on money. The poor are always guilty, while the rich go free. People with money and connections never go to jail, while guys like us wind up behind bars, wasting taxpayers' money. It's hopeless. Do you think we can depend on the U.S. or the politicians? No, there's nobody we can count on."

Hearing these remarks, a fellow who was in for robbery, spoke up.

"Why do you guys worry about all that stuff? All we have to do is climb fences."

"No, not true. Look at it this way. Only when the country is doing well will there be anything worth stealing."

"You're right there. We may be thieves, but we still want what is best for the country. If the country's in good shape, we'll be able to live out our dreams. We won't always be crooks. Someday we may become decent citizens and lead a better life, but I'm not sure that day will ever come. Anyway, the world outside is in such a mess that even a decent man like Pastor Kim here is sent to prison."

With all the inmates nodding, the atmosphere in the cell turned solemn. I was shocked. If even criminals have no confidence in the nation's future, imagine what the general public must feel.

To survive and prosper, a country has to build mutual trust among its people. Distrust was on the rise in all sectors of society, which made me think that the nation's foundation was very shaky. I prayed and pledged the following:

> *The church is vitally important. The Korean church has to become the institution that people seek out as their last resort. The church has to be on a firm footing, so people can find refuge there when they have nowhere else to turn. Let me dedicate my life to building a church that people can truly rely on. Let me build a church that clergy and believers, as well as the masses, can count on. Let me build a church that everyone, from laborers to farmers, thieves to policemen, can always depend upon. To build*

this kind of a church, church leaders need to purge them-
selves and take the lead to rejuvenate the nation, after they
confirm and declare their own faith.

After making this pledge, I felt more empathy for my fellow inmates and tried to become friends with them.

ONE MAN, WHO AT THE AGE OF NINETEEN had committed a contract
killing, had been in prison for eighteen years. Being in the same cell
with him, I wondered how human beings could become obsessed with
the thought of doing evil. His dreams were not ordinary. While sleeping, he would grit his teeth and shout, "Stab'em! Stab'em!" It was horrifying to sleep near him. He also often stood by the cell window, after a
meal, repeatedly opening and closing one hand, with two fingers bent.

I once asked, "What's that exercise? Why do you do that?"

He replied, "Ah, this. I do this so I'll be able to gouge out the warden's eyes when my fingers become strong enough and I get the
chance." Then he demonstrated for me how he was going to do it.

"Why would you consider such a thing?" I asked.

His face took on an evil look and he shouted, "You're new here.
You talk too much." At that, he extended his bent fingers toward me
and went on, "You know what I've always planned to do? When I get
out of prison, I'm going to get a hand grenade, go to Myeong-dong, get
together a dozen pretty girls and blow 'em all to hell, putting a glorious
end to my life."

"Why do you want such a finale?"

"It's impossible for me to go to heaven. I've committed too many
crimes, so I'm doomed to go to hell. Because the Gatekeeper of Hell is
said to like girls, I want to give him a dozen as a present, so as to get better treatment from him."

He thought hard about how to get a hand grenade and where in
Myeong-dong girls preferred to gather.

With his threatening eye-gouging gesture, he had brought the inmates in the cell under his control. Everyone detested and feared him
because he had threatened to gouge the eyes out of anyone who crossed
him. One of the cellmates was a black belt in *taekgondo*. He had virtually no rival in fighting, but even he was helpless in this fellow's presence,

347

because of his unpredictability.

"If you brag about your *taegwondo*," he would say, "and don't show me proper respect, I'll gouge out your eyes when you're asleep."

I tried to make peace with the man, attempting to appeal to his humanity. I felt pity toward him for leading such a life. I assumed that, like everyone, when he was young his mother had held him close, and I wondered how he had grown to become the person he was. Anxious to transform him into a decent human being, I prayed for him, wrote letters for him, and shared with him some items I had bought.

While fasting for three days, I prayed that the Holy Spirit would help him change his character. Not thinking that I would be fasting and praying for him, he tried to comfort me. "Mr. Kim, are you sick? In prison, people can die, if they don't eat right."

I decided to teach him about the Gospel, but I mulled over the timing. One autumn day, I sat next to him and said politely, "Mr. Lee, how about you and me having a talk today?"

"What kind of a talk? What do you mean?"

"I'll get right to the point. Let's change our masters."

"What are you saying, change our masters?"

"Why are we, you and I, wasting our lives here in prison? It's because we failed to honor the right master. When we take ourselves as our master, chances are we'll get into trouble. If we honor Jesus Christ as our master, however, He'll make new men of us, with a new character."

I went on to read John 1:12 to him, where it says, "Yet to all who received him, to those who believed in his name, he gave the right to become children of God." The word, "receive" means "serve." People who receive Jesus Christ as their master, that is, who believe in Jesus Christ, become God's children.

"Mr. Lee, you have lived a difficult life until now because you had yourself as your master. You can get off to a fresh start by serving Jesus Christ. I'm sure that Jesus Christ, the Holy Spirit, will stay with you and help you. Let Him help you lead a new life."

After listening attentively to what I was saying, he asked, "Can even rotten people like me believe in Jesus Christ?"

I was delighted to hear that. It was a miracle that he had come up with such a thought. Encouraged by this, I told him as convincingly as I

348

could, "Of course, you can. Jesus isn't here just for upright people. He came to earth to make friends with misfits and troubled people as well. Even a troublemaker or a scoundrel can be transformed into a righteous person, when he believes in Jesus Christ."

"In that case, Mr. Kim, make me into a believer in Jesus Christ. Guide me, please. Show me the way, and I'll do whatever you say."

Thereafter, he underwent a transformation that was as different as night is from day. He no longer intimidated other inmates with his threats. Nor did he repeat his Myeong-dong mad bomber fantasy. He became a believer. I taught him hymns and told him stories from the Bible, all the while praying for him.

Later, on the day I was to be released, he knelt before me and, with tears in his eyes, said, "Mr. Kim, congratulations on your freedom. I know that you will be successful in life, but before leaving, please listen to me. I'm grateful for your help in turning me into a human being. Before meeting you, I had blamed others for putting me in prison, rather than myself. Since believing in Jesus, those thoughts have disappeared. I have faith that from now on I'm going to lead a decent life. When I'm free someday, I intend to do something good for society, even if it means that I pick up litter in a park. I appreciate your help. I hope that you make a great contribution to our society."

Once again, I was amazed by the power of faith, which had helped him begin a new life. For the crime he committed, society punished him with eighteen years in prison, but what he got from Jesus was very different. He now had the courage to make a new start. I thought that Jesus, who had brought hope to this convicted murderer, could also be the hope for our nation.

WITH THE ARRIVAL OF CHRISTMAS, 1974, my fellow inmates proposed that we hold a Christmas service. I read Matthew 2:16-18, before delivering the following Christmas message:

> *Because of the birth of Jesus on Christmas Day, many baby boys were murdered. They were killed on the grounds that they were born in the same area as Jesus and on the same date. How could there be a reasonable explanation for this? The Son of God came to save mankind, but*

what caused so many innocent babies to perish as soon as He arrived? We can take a cue from this. That is, we have to pay a price to acquire anything of value and if we are to lead rewarding lives.

As the coming of Jesus led to bloodshed, we must make every effort to lead a decent life. Only those people who manage to survive after overcoming pain are assured a worthwhile life. If a person tries to lead an easy life, without effort, he may lag behind others and be labeled unfit. The coming of Jesus was intended to help us to gain victory after going through pain and bloodshed.

Following the sermon, I called the names of each of my cellmates and prayed for each one individually. Some cried while bowing their heads. They said it was the first time they had ever had a prayer addressed solely for them and it was difficult for them to hold back their emotion.

On Christmas afternoon, all the inmates of Suwon Prison were brought together for worship. A young priest from Suwon Cathedral delivered what he considered a sermon, but his message was far off the mark.

He spoke at length about theologians and philosophers in the presence of criminals. During his hour-long lecture, he mentioned 28 Western theologians and philosophers, including Thomas Aquinas, Gabriel Marcel, Ernst Cassirer, Jacques Maritain, Martin Heidegger, Soren Kierkegaard, and Teihard de Chardin, none of which made any sense to the men.

The inmates became increasingly restless, sitting with their feet getting colder by the minute. They spewed all imaginable obscenities at the priest, which he simply ignored, while going through his long list of Western scholars. Most inmates, like residents of slum areas, tend to be impatient and even emotionally unstable, but the priest rambled on.

Returning to our cell after the lecture, one man said, "I'll be damned if I'll ever send my kids to church."

JANUARY 1, 1975 WAS A FESTIVE DAY FOR THE INMATES. Everyone was served beef soup and rice in celebration of New Year's Day. On January

6, five members of Hwalbin Church paid me a special visit and said, "Pastor Kim, we have decided that tomorrow morning we will begin a 40-day all-night prayer for your release."

Astonished, I replied, "What are you talking about? Nights are for sleeping. Why are you going to pray all night? It'd be better to pray at dawn, after a good night's sleep."

"Pastor, according to Acts, the prison door was flung open for Peter when the apostles prayed all night for him. We believe the same can happen today."

"That was a long time ago. The characters have changed. That was Peter. I'm Kim Jin-hong. There is a saying that deep sleep can be good medicine in winter, even when there is not enough food. Lacking food, a person needs sleep. Don't pray for me without going to sleep."

"Pastor, prison seems to have diluted some of your religious fervor. You would never have spoken to us this way in the past."

"That may be, but by the time I get out I will have rebuilt my faith. Anyway, forget about your all-night prayers."

"Pastor, this is something we have to decide for ourselves."

They then departed. I later learned that the following day they initiated forty days of all-night prayers. Although the church had no heater, the church members prayed on the chilly plywood floors. I heard there were some women who prayed through the night, without a break.

On February 14, they concluded their prayers. The next day, the exhausted church members were at work or at home when they heard on the radio a special announcement by President Park Jeong-hui. Certain political offenders were to be granted amnesty and would soon be released. My name was at the top of the list.

Upon hearing the news, members of Hwalbin Church and slum residents burst into tears, overcome with joy. They spread the word to as many people as possible and everyone gathered at the church amid a festive atmosphere. As for me, I sat in my cell, ignorant of the president's announcement.

On the morning of February 15, a guard walked up to our cell and said there would be good news that day for political offenders. We had no idea what he meant and therefore did not get excited about what the "good news" might be.

Shortly after noon, the same day, a guard informed me of my impending release. On the morning of February 16, a guard told me that I would be set free in an hour's time and that I should prepare to leave. Thirteen months had passed since I had gone to prison and forty days since Hwalbin Church members had started their all-night prayers.

It was so simple to get out of prison, especially compared to when I arrived. When I walked out of Suwon Prison, after the last iron gate was flung open, our five-year-old son, Dong-hyeok, rushed toward me calling "Daddy." My wife was carrying a baby. She had stayed at her parents' home while I was in prison, during which our daughter was born.

Upon seeing my children, my head began to spin and I became dizzy. A large crowd of church members and slum residents were on hand to greet me as I came out. They held a banner with red lettering that read, "Hallelujah! Our Good Shepherd has returned."

All of a sudden, I felt as if the earth was shaking. I knelt and, kissing the ground, I prayed for God's grace: "God, I would like to express my sincere gratitude to you. Thank you for this moment. I am determined to spend my life working on behalf of these good people and go to heaven with them. Should ever an easy road be paved for me, I swear I will not desert them and will remain dedicated to your mission."

Being welcomed by church members upon my release.

UPON MY RETURN TO CHEONGGYE-CHEON, the residents gave me a hero's welcome. Hwalbin Church members were even more enthusiastic.

I was deeply moved. I would feel no remorse, even if I sacrificed the rest of my life for these wonderful people. I swore again that I would devote myself to improving their lives.

The next day I underwent an extensive physical at Severance Hospital. My friends in Japan had sent money to pay for the checkup. I was found to be in good shape. While the health of many of my prison colleagues had deteriorated during their incarceration, my health had improved. I got to work immediately, believing that God had blessed me with good health so I could work for the people.

The Cheonggye-cheon slum neighborhoods were still being battered by a variety of problems. I delved into them and searched for ways to deal with each one.

The first problem was that missionary workers, who had come in to help during my absence, now dominated every aspect of the church's operation. Although they worked hard and with good intentions, the results were not good. In spite of what they had tried to do, they created confusion in the church and in the neighborhood.

My assessment of the situation was that the confusion had come about because they lacked an underlying philosophy for missionary activity among the needy. It is difficult to carry out missionary work for the poor, when armed only with enthusiasm. Missionaries have to have a clear understanding of issues facing slum areas and the mindset of the residents. The focus should be on helping the residents develop the capacity to manage their own problems.

Because of this confusion, the true spirit of Hwalbin had gotten lost, and the cooperation between the church and the community, which Hwalbin Church had so carefully nurtured, was coming apart.

ONE EXAMPLE OF THIS WAS THE "LUXURY TOILET." After arriving at the Cheonggye-cheon slum from Suwon Prison, I went directly to the church. There, in one corner, I noticed a "luxury toilet." Its door, however, was locked, with a sign saying that it was "for guests only."

Latrines in slum areas were not flush toilets. Rather, they were built along the edge of the creek and were "flushed" only by the rising waters when it rained. The waste flowed down the Cheonggye-cheon

The Cheonggye-cheon Creek running alongside the slum.

Creek into the Han River. When the water level in the stream dropped, piles of odoriferous human waste could be seen and around it flies swarmed.

Ashamed of having such latrines in the church, church members built a luxury toilet for guests. If they did not like the existing church toilets, I thought they should have built new ones. It was wrong to erect a toilet exclusively for guests.

I told the members of the church, "Waste is just waste. There is no difference between guest waste and that of residents. At a glance, the problem of this toilet may be considered trivial, but it poses a serious problem in light of the guiding principle of our missionary activity. This attitude creates a gap between the church and the people. The effect is that it leads people to distance themselves from the church."

I then suggested that the new toilet be removed. The church members reacted coolly to my suggestion. Rather, they suggested that we remove the sign and the lock and allow anyone to use it. I thought that was a good solution.

ANOTHER BONE OF CONTENTION CONCERNED A PIANO. A generous benefactor wanted to donate a piano to Hwalbin Church. Without much consideration, the church had accepted it. The piano was supposed to be delivered within a few days. The price of the piano was more than four times that of a house in the slum area. Moreover, the church building leaked such that it would often flood, even when there was only a light drizzle. It appeared unlikely, therefore, that the church could properly accommodate such an expensive piano. Considering that the church remained open for a variety of events all day long, the piano would soon be worn out.

I called a meeting to discuss the piano issue. At the meeting, I said, "The piano itself is no problem, but it doesn't belong in a makeshift structure such as ours. Doesn't it make better sense that, in view of our circumstances, we use a miniature organ or a guitar in our services? Why don't we accept the piano's value in cash instead, and use the money to help the sick?"

Whereas the slum residents responded positively to my suggestion, people from outside Cheonggye-cheon were opposed to it.

"How can we turn it down, since it is offered to God? It will be for the glory of God if we listen to beautiful music from a good piano, even in this makeshift church. The needy should also learn about good music, to develop their character and for the education of their children. Let's take the piano," urged a person, who represented the opinion of people in favor of accepting the piano.

Someone rebutted, however, "Do you really believe that we can bring glory to God when we play music only on expensive instruments? You mention development of the residents' character and the education of their children, but character will not necessarily be built by the sound of a piano. When we have services using the instruments bought with our contributions, our character will change for the better. The spirit of self-reliance will also contribute to our children's education."

Those wanting the piano responded, "We said nothing when Pastor Kim objected to the toilet that we worked so hard to build, but with regard to the piano, there will be no concession."

The outsiders were taking a resolute stand on the piano. I realized that the atmosphere of Hwalbin Church was not what it had once been. In the past, discussion of any matter was conducted among church members in a free and a friendly manner. Now, the lines were drawn and the atmosphere was tense.

I studied everyone participating in the discussion. Those opposed to accepting the piano were the church members residing within the slum, while those from non-slum areas favored the donation. The Christians from the non-slum areas had become used to the typical Korean church culture, since they had attended services in mainstream churches.

In particular, I was concerned that if this gap remained unchecked, the congregation would suffer from factional strife. Consequently, I adjourned the meeting and met privately with the person who had offered to donate the piano, to persuade him to change his mind.

After listening to what I had to say, he remarked, "Pastor, I appreciate your explanation. We church members are always ready to follow the suggestions of a pastor, if he helps us understand the issue. I will donate money instead of the piano, so you can have it available for medical emergencies."

While Korean churches are willing to spend on buildings and furnishings, as a rule they are very stingy in providing assistance to the poor, to projects for community development, and to educating promising low-income students. This pattern of behavior dies hard.

STILL ANOTHER MAJOR PROBLEM I ENCOUNTERED, after my release from prison, had to do with community relations. Several days after I arrived in Cheonggye-cheon, a group of resident representatives came to talk to me.

"We've been looking forward to your release, for several reasons. We would appreciate it if you could put an end to some inconveniences that are bothering people," one of them said.

I was not happy to hear that. What "inconveniences" could they be experiencing because of the church? I did not know what to say, but asked them to be specific. Someone continued, "First, there's the racket of the bell ringing every day at dawn. The church used to ring the bell only a couple of times, which was fine. It was good for residents to know what time it was. During your absence, however, they began to ring the bell longer and louder, so that everyone in the neighborhood, including children, was forced to wake up."

"Well. I would have imagined that that sort of a problem could easily have been solved, had you taken it up with the church."

"In fact, we did take it up with the church, but they accused us of being indifferent to God. They added that the bell's ringing would become music to our ears, if only we repented our sins. After that, they took to ringing it even longer. We decided not to argue with them, expecting that the problem could be taken care of when you came back."

Listening to them, I responded, "I understand your concern. I think the church is wrong. The bell ringing will stop beginning tomorrow."

"No, you misunderstand us. We want the church to ring the bell a few times, enough to tell the time. We do not mean that you should stop it altogether."

"OK. I'll deal with it. What else is bothering you?"

"It's a similar problem. We have no objection to the church holding prayers in the middle of the night, but could people make less noise and try to keep it inside the church building?"

"It's customary to conduct prayers inside the church building. Who offers prayers anywhere else in the neighborhood?"

"No, Pastor. They do pray inside the church, but they make a lot of noise, carrying on and wailing, so families living near the church can hardly get any sleep. Once, when it was late, I ran out of my house wearing only my underwear, thinking someone was shouting 'fire.' As it turned out, it was only people praying. I mistook the shrill prayers as an alarm. We would like to ask that they lower their voices when they pray."

I asked a church member sitting beside me. "Why on earth would you bring residents out of their houses, thinking there was a fire?"

"Well, Pastor Kim, that was during a revival service, when everyone cried out in unison, 'The Lord! The Lord!' This led residents to believe that a fire had broken out."

It sounded ridiculous and I was sorry that the church had disturbed the neighborhood. I told the residents, "I understand how you feel. People must have been praying fervently for my release from prison. Now that I'm out, I will manage these problems so as not to inconvenience you."

"We're glad to hear that. We've put up with it until now, hoping that everything would eventually get back to normal."

I took care of these problems during services the following week.

"It's important to pray, but we have to avoid annoying the

neighbors. The founding philosophy of Hwalbin Church is that it exists for the people. The people don't exist for the church. I hope all of you will keep this in mind, ring the bell just twice, softly, at daybreak and when it's late, pray quietly. If you want to pray in a loud voice, then I suggest you go to a mountain or use a prayer house and do whatever you please."

After the service, a stranger stepped forward and announced, "Please, will *bangjja* gather in the prayer room." I asked Deacon Kim Jong-gil as to what *bangjja* meant.

"Well, Pastor Kim, *bangjja* refers to people who have been given the ability to speak in tongues."

"It is all right to speak in tongues, but why should they separate themselves from everyone else? I see no need for that."

"Because you criticized them during the service this afternoon, I suppose they want to get together to come up with a response."

"What do you mean? When did I criticize anyone? The ability to speak in tongues is something that the church should encourage, not criticize. I wonder whether they're getting together for that purpose or for something else."

During the time I was in prison, the focus of the church members' faith had shifted. In particular, they had experienced a variety of mysterious charismata while single-mindedly praying for my release. It was all right for them to experience charismata, but the equilibrium of their faith was being thrown off because they were focusing too narrowly on mysticism, while at the same time they lacked the religious discipline to back up their charismatic experiences.

At this critical time, leaders of the church should have guided the church members in the right direction with the Word of God. On the contrary, they took advantage of this phenomenon and created an undesirable atmosphere by strongly encouraging mysticism. As a result, a belief spread among worshippers that anyone who had received the gift of speaking in tongues was somehow guided by the Holy Spirit, while anyone who did not was irredeemable.

Slum residents are prone to emotional instability. In teaching them about faith, it is important to help them develop a balanced character. If people become obsessed with mysticism, their experience will likely undermine their faith. For them, mysticism can be a narcotic.

BY WAY OF EXAMPLE, THERE WAS THE CASE of Mr. Choi, who had once been in the rubbish picking unit of the Self-Support Association. He had contracted TB previously, while working as a coal miner in Gangwon province. Initially, his condition was not serious. In fact, he was recovering from TB, having received medical treatment during the six months before I went to prison.

While I was away, however, he experienced mysticism during prayer and was blessed with the grace of God while attending a revival service. Thereafter, he stopped taking his medicine, concentrating only on prayer. Subsequently, his TB worsened, and he was again bedridden.

After I was released, I visited his home, but he and his wife would not invite me in. They told me that I was only a "person of flesh" who did not speak in tongues. They declared that they would talk only with people who were baptized with the Holy Spirit, choosing to keep their distance from worldly people.

"Pastor Kim, you have always been good to us, but since you have not experienced charismata and are unable to speak in tongues, we cannot speak with you." They then closed the door on me. I stood there, embarrassed, saying good-bye through the closed door. I never expected this sort of thing to happen.

Concerned about Choi's health, I returned to his house later with some medicine. When I asked if I could enter, they asked why. I replied that I had brought some medicine, to which Choi retorted that he would cure his disease not with medicine, but with prayers and the blessing of God.

I pleaded with him to take the medicine. "Deacon Choi, I understand that you want to cure your disease through the grace of God. But it's wrong to seek God's blessing without taking your medicine. You must know that God also created medicine. May I remind you that in the past you nearly recovered because you had taken your medicine? Now, you've stopped taking it and your condition has deteriorated. Please take this medicine. Then we'll pray together that your disease heals completely."

Deacon Choi spoke to me through the door. "People who have experienced the Holy Spirit do not need medicine. Pastor Cho Yong-gi cured his TB by experiencing the Holy Spirit and without resorting to medicine. I appreciate your kindness, but I can't take your advice. My disease gets worse when I'm with worldly people."

His mention of Pastor Cho came as a surprise. Pastor Cho, the principal pastor of one of the world's biggest churches, had contracted TB during his youth. Believing that his disease could not be cured by medical treatment, he concentrated on praying for God's blessing. Prayer helped him cure his disease. Having heard of Pastor Cho's experience, Deacon Choi sought to follow his example.

Finally, I spoke, "Deacon Choi, out of respect for our long friendship, please listen carefully to what I have to say. God's blessing comes in many shapes and forms. I know that Pastor Cho cured his TB through God and without the aid of medicine, but it doesn't work that way for everyone. You are not Pastor Cho. You are Deacon Choi. Be open-minded. Take this medicine and then let's pray together. You must think of your wife and children. You may never recover, if you continue this way."

I pushed a packet of medicine under the door. I appealed to him to accept it, even though he refused to see me. The door instantly flew open, and the package came hurling past me and into the yard. I heard a sharp-tongued voice, "Shhhh! Down with the Satan!"

I stood there for a moment, picked up the medicine, and returned to the church. On my way back, I threw the medicine packet in the trash and repeated to myself, "Down with the Satan. Down with the Satan."

Something had gone seriously wrong. People seemed to have gone insane, suffering from mass hysteria. What they were claiming was not a blessing. Mumbling to myself, I walked along the embankment of the Cheonggye-cheon Creek.

Several days later, Mr. Choi died and I was finally allowed into his room. After his cremation, I thought to myself, worse than not believing in Jesus at all is to believe in Him in a false way.

ONE DAY, I WAS SUMMONED by some self-styled "leading members" of the church. I walked up to them in disbelief, asking myself, who are these leaders of Hwalbin Church? On what grounds do they call themselves leaders of the church?

I knew most of the people in the group.

"You wanted to see me?" I asked.

360

Pastor Min, who served as the leader of the group, spoke first. He had come from my hometown, and had been my senior at the seminary. During my imprisonment, he served as senior pastor of Hwalbin Church.

He spoke as if accusing me. "We cared for Hwalbin Church during your absence, Pastor Kim. To tell the truth, we are all disappointed in your behavior since your return. That is why we, the leaders of Hwalbin Church, have gathered here to discuss you. Our consensus is that you should quit Hwalbin Church or respect the opinions of those who have struggled to keep the church going."

That made me chuckle. I was curious to see how they perceived me. The way they talked to me indicated that I was perceived as a weak person.

I asked, "Well, is that so? Let's discuss the matter of my resignation later. First, let me hear your opinions. What are the opinions that I should respect?"

Pastor Min replied, "There are many, but I will touch on a few. First, stop criticizing charismata; second, you've fired many of the people who struggled to support the church. Stop running the church in your own style; third, don't exploit the needy for your political ambitions; fourth, stop wasting church money; and fifth, stop wrangling with the KNCC. Those are our demands."

I could not find words to respond to their allegations. When I said I had no idea what to say, Pastor Min pressed me for an answer.

"Saying that you have no idea what to say sounds like you don't respect us."

I was offended by his overbearing attitude, so I asked, "What would happen, were I not to accept your suggestions?"

"It would mean that we will tell the church members about this and you would have to quit the church. Your reaction indicates that you are going to quit. We will announce your resignation at the next service."

"You may be right, but I think this affair is not something that should be settled here. We should call a meeting and listen to the views of other church members. Since I went to prison because of my conviction in democracy, I think this question should be taken up in a democratic way."

I then walked out of the gathering. I asked the church members about their opinions during Sunday service.

"You are the owners of Hwalbin Church. You will have to decide on this matter, after listening to what I have to say. While I was away, you all worked hard to put the church into good shape. As a result, the church has developed into the institution that it is today. I appreciate your dedication, but there are certain church members who believe that I should no longer be welcome here. I want to ask for your frank opinion. If you really want me to leave, I will go gracefully. I will then look for a church in some other slum area to carry out my work. Please speak freely and from your hearts."

No sooner had I wound up my speech than church members reacted. The most immediate responses were from those who had worked on rubbish-picking detail with me.

One shouted, "What on earth are you talking about? What wretches would say such a thing about our pastor? Some losers have been going around talking trash and I cannot remain silent. Who's making trouble? Speak up and stop whispering to each other behind people's backs. I'll knock you in the head."

Fazed by this outburst, the self-styled church representatives began to leave silently. By the next day, this episode had spread to neighborhood residents as well. Some angry residents gathered at the church and commented as a group. "We heard there are some strange people at the church. We'll break their kneecaps if they lay one hand on our pastor."

Pastor Min packed his belongings and left the church. Other "leaders" fell silent.

Several days later, one of the members who spoke in tongues, came to me, "Pastor. We have decided to offer prayers separately. Please accept our demands."

"No. Please don't do that. Remember the adage that time heals all wounds. All of our misunderstandings and hard feelings will fade away in time. Look back on the good old days, please. Why should we part company?"

They remained steadfast in their position, urging me to accommodate their request.

"Yes. What do you want?" I asked.

"Well, please give us the church building in Dapsimni, the organ, and the megaphone, and other church items that we need."

Listening to them, I had to smile. Their demands revealed their simplicity. I responded, "All right. I can give you all of that, and anything else you need, except for one thing. Also, please don't leave here fighting. You can return only if you leave here smiling."

"OK, but Pastor, what is the one thing that we should not take?"

"The name of Hwalbin Church. You can take anything, but the church's name."

"Ha! Hwalbin! Hwalbin! We don't need it, and why would we try to take the name, anyway? We wouldn't take it, even if you gave it to us."

That part of the congregation devoted to mysticism and those members who spoke in tongues left the church. Hwalbin Church once again returned to normal.

23

Against All Odds

THE MOST SERIOUS PROBLEM I confronted after being released from prison concerned my family. Two weeks after I
arrived home, my wife took me to a quiet place to talk. I welcomed this, thinking that she might have some ideas about our future
together.

Her proposal, however, was very different from what I had hoped
or expected. She wanted a divorce. She confessed that she had been waiting for my release to mention it to me, after having made up her mind
several months before. She explained that she was unable to continue
supporting the path and the vision that I was pursuing. Having grown
up in a well-to-do family, she wanted to live like a normal housewife,
without taking part in crusades for the poor and for democracy.

Without understanding how bad the situation was, I tried to persuade her to change her mind. "I think I understand you. You must
have suffered terribly, to be willing to take such a step. While in prison,
I always regretted having caused you and the children such pain. Let me
have a chance to make up to it," I said.

She would not be moved. "No, it's too late," she replied. "No matter how hard you work, the slum is the slum. Nothing you can do will
make a difference. If you change your mind, and want to save our marriage, we can all emigrate to the U.S. You could get a doctorate there.
After that, you could return to Korea and resume your work. It is impossible to improve our situation under these circumstances. You
need to choose between your family and the shantytown."

"My dear, how could I dare go off to the U.S.? The Hwalbin missionary activities have just gotten off the ground. People like me, who live with a mission, are obliged to put their work ahead of their family. It's impossible for us to remain faithful to our families, if it requires us to abandon our mission."

"If that's what you want, it's best you continue your work, but let me and the children go. I'll take them to America and raise them to be decent people. You do what you want."

Her parents were then living in the U.S. and she would go live with them. She would not change her mind, demanding that we all go together or that we separate.

I thought about it for several days. Should I go to the U.S. with my family and leave Cheonggye-cheon behind? That would not be possible. How could I turn my back on what everyone there had done while I was in prison? They had held all-night prayers for my freedom. Forming groups, church members had taken 3-day shifts, praying and fasting. In light of all their efforts, it would be unthinkable for me to leave so soon after being released. At the same time, I did not want to be separated from my family.

I tried once again to persuade my wife, but without success. After several months of arguing, she and the children left for the U.S.

After that, we did not communicate for a long time. I did not know where she had moved to or what she was doing. Four years passed before I finally received a postcard from her. It had no return address. It read, in part, "I have remarried and am leading a happy life. The children are adapting well to their new father, so live your life as you please."

That's life, I thought.

I dispatched the postcard to the wind and climbed a mountain. I prayed for my children, while trying to drive my wife out of my mind. Because I was still considered a political prisoner, I was not able to travel abroad. Even if I had been able to go, in such a vast country, I would not be able to find my children. All I could do was pray for them, hoping that they would grow up happy and healthy.

Having by then launched the Doorae Community project, I responded quickly, whenever I heard about orphaned or abandoned children. I always brought them to the church, where I would hold their hands firmly and pray for them, saying, "Dear Jesus, while I take care of these children in the Doorae Community, please protect Dong-hyeok and Eun-song in the U.S. They are now far away, where I cannot talk to them."

Nobody knew that I was praying for my own children, asking Jesus to watch over them, and that I longed so much to see them. Believing that I should do something in return for His protection of my children, I started a project at the Doorae Community to look after abandoned children.

Later, a nationwide clemency was granted, enabling me to travel. When I was on a plane to the U.S., I prayed. "Jesus, please allow me to meet my children during this trip."

I looked for them in New York City, having heard a rumor that they were living there. I was unable to find them, however, and returned to Korea dispirited. Where are they now? Do they live in a ghetto? Are they sick? What kind of person is their stepfather? Are they abused? Sitting on the runway, waiting to take off on the return flight to Korea, these thoughts gave me a severe headache and a great pain in my heart.

THEN ONE DAY, AFTER A FOURTEEN-YEAR SEPARATION, I received a lengthy telegram from the United States. It arrived just three days before Christ-mas. It said that my daughter, Eun-song, was hospitalized for some undiagnosed illness. Saying that Eun-song wanted to see me, her mother asked me to travel to Orlando, where they were living.

As soon as I finished the Christmas services, I rushed to Gimpo Airport and took the earliest possible flight. Upon arriving in Orlando, I took a taxi directly to the hospital. I met Eun-song's mother in the hallway. She was surprised to see me.

"Thanks for coming. Before you meet the children, listen to what I have to say."

"What's wrong with her? Why is she here?"

"Well, she was initially diagnosed as having a serious form of stress, having fainted at school. I brought her to the emergency room. She was talking deliriously, suffering from a high fever. She kept crying out, 'Seoul Daddy, Seoul Daddy.'"

"I realized then that I had committed a terrible sin. She ordinarily would never have mentioned her 'Seoul Daddy,' but when she was ill she called out for you. I realized then that she missed you very much and that I had been erecting a wall between the children and you. For that, I apologize. I did it because I was outraged by your lack of interest in them. I sent you the telegram, thinking that I should arrange for them to meet you. I appreciate your coming, even though you must be busy with year-end activities."

"Well, I'm to blame too. Let me see Eun-song."

As I entered the room, my son was seated next to the bed, while my daughter slept. I went over to her and spoke her name. "Eun-song, your father has come from Seoul."

My voice woke her up. With sparkling eyes, she said, "Oh, Daddy, you're here. You're here for me, aren't you? You came here for me, not because you had work to do in the U.S."

"Of course. How could I take time out to visit the U.S., in light of my tight schedule at Christmas? Learning that you were sick, I put everything aside and came."

"Daddy, I'm so happy."

"Well, I'm happy to hear that. Please get well soon. Let's have a good time, traveling together."

"Yes, Daddy. I'll get better. Do you remember when you took Dong-hyeok and me to Changgyongwon Zoo? You twirled me around and you bought us ice cream. Do you remember that?"

"No. When was that? I can't remember it. How can you remember that, you were very little when we separated?"

"It's not because of my memory. Whenever our stepfather hurt us, Brother would take me into another room and say, 'Our Seoul Daddy was different from stepfather. He was kind and gentle. A long time ago, he took us to the zoo, where he twirled you around and bought us ice cream.' That's how I can remember."

Hearing that broke my heart. Tears streamed down my face, and I was unable to see clearly.

"You've suffered a lot. Let's have better times from now on. When you recover, we can go anywhere, not only to Changgyongwon Zoo. Let's go to Disneyland and the Grand Canyon and eat as much ice cream as we want."

I turned to Dong-hyeok. "Dong-hyeok, I'm so happy to see you. Have you been wanting to see me, too? I missed you both and always prayed to Jesus, asking Him to help me find you."

367

"Daddy, of course, I have. Looking up at the sky over the Pacific Ocean, Eun-song and I prayed, wishing that we could meet our father in Seoul and live together, even if for only a few days."

"It's heartbreaking to hear that. Jesus must have answered our prayers."

"I'm the president of the student council at our church."

"That's great."

"Some time ago, a student asked me. 'Do you know Reverend Kim Jin-hong? He's a great man.'"

"What did you say?"

"Can't you guess? I bowed my head and pretended not to hear."

"I guess you've gone through a lot. From now on, I want to help you. What can I do for you?"

Thinking about it for a second, my son shook his head.

"Nothing, really. I only want to be able to tell my friends, 'Reverend Kim Jin-hong is my father.' Please make it so we can tell them."

I was so touched, I found it difficult to speak.

"OK, let's do things right from now on."

Afterward, I went to my hotel. Covering myself with the bed sheets, I cried for a long time. I felt that the ground I had walked on for the past two decades had suddenly collapsed.

What had I accomplished? I had stayed in the slums to help the needy, built the Doorae Community on reclaimed land after the shantytown was torn down, and did a few other things, but none of it held any importance for me. What had I done, while my children were ill and hurting in the U.S.? It all seemed so meaningless.

I told myself that I would quit my work in Korea and go live with them. I would stop work on the Doorae Community project, give up my position in the church, and start a business, such as a laundry or a grocery store, to fulfill my role as their father.

Thinking it over, I stayed up the entire night. At dawn, I opened the Bible. I came to a revelation, after reading the story of Elijah in 1 Kings 19.

The prophet Elijah exercised absolute power throughout Israel. One day, as he prayed for rain, rain came, ending a three-year drought. He killed 450 prophets of Baal, who had worshiped graven idols. Elijah's spiritual authority was at its peak, but in the next chapter he ran for his life into the wilderness.

The reason was that he received a message from King Ahab's wife, Jezzebel, saying, "May the gods deal with me, be it ever so severely, if by this time tomorrow I do not make your life like that of one of them," referring to prophets that Elijah had killed.

Elijah was afraid and fled. He walked the whole day in the wilderness. He stopped and sat down in the shade of a tree and wished to die.

"I have had enough, Lord," he prayed. "Take my life; I am no better than my ancestors." He lay down and fell asleep under the tree.

Suddenly an angel came to him, saying, "Get up and eat." He looked around and there by his head was bread baking on hot coals and a jar of water. He ate and drank and then slept some more. The Lord's messenger appeared again and said, "Get up and eat, for the journey is too much for you." So he got up and ate and drank. That meal gave him strength to travel forty days and forty nights until he reached Mount Sinai.

I regained my strength while contemplating Elijah. The meal that Elijah was given that night was now in front of me. I believed that "the bread baking on hot coals" and "a jar of water" were prepared for me to demonstrate the power of the Bible and the comfort of the Holy Spirit.

Bread in the Bible is symbolic of the words of the Lord, while water symbolizes the Holy Spirit. Now that I had been comforted and had gained courage, I decided to approach my tasks with greater enthusiasm, rather than plunge into despair.

EARLY THE NEXT MORNING, I BOARDED a flight for Korea. Dong-hyeok came to see me off at the airport. I told him, "I'll come back soon, after attending to some things in Korea, and we can spend some time together."

Four months later, I returned to the U.S. and called my children to Los Angeles. After staying together at a hotel for three days, I asked them how they felt, getting together after being separated for fourteen years.

Dong-hyeok hesitated for a while. He then said, "Canaan seems in sight, after years of roaming in the wilderness."

I was touched by his remark and said, "Spoken like a true son of a pastor."

An American publishing house was publishing an English

translation of my book, *I Will Awaken the Dawn*, and had asked me to write a prologue for it. At the time, I had not heard from my children, so I ended the prologue with a dedication:

> *I dedicate this story*
> *to my son and daughter,*
> *Joshua and Grace,* *
> *who live in the United States.*
> *I hope*
> *they can understand*
> *how I struggled in the search for truth*
> *and how their father met Jesus Christ.*

After writing the prologue, I had taken the envelope containing it to the post office and sent it to the publisher by registered mail, kissing the envelope and praying before posting it. "Jesus, I pray that I can meet my children, after this book is published."

As soon as the book was printed, the publisher sent me two copies by courier service. By that time, I had learned my children's address. I sent the two copies of the book to them by express mail.

After staying with them in Los Angeles, I asked them whether they had read the book. They nodded.

"What was your impression?"

My daughter replied, "I'm proud of you!"

I was very much moved by her response. It was as if a dam that had held for fourteen years had suddenly burst. I felt a refreshing breeze sweep over my entire body. How much I had worried about them and missed them.

I had lived in agony, beset by concern for them. Having met them again, I was happy to see that my daughter had recovered and to know that she was proud of me.

I rented an apartment in Portland, Oregon and asked them to live there. In doing so, I could be something of a father to them. I visited them and stayed with them whenever I traveled to the U.S.

When I arrived in Portland on one of my trips, they were at the

---

* Dong-hyeok and Eun-song's English names

airport to greet me. They gave me an envelope.

"Daddy, we have a present for you."

"Oh, really? What kind of a present? Let's have a look," I said, opening the envelope.

It was their school report cards. They had both earned straight A's.

In awe, I asked them about it. "You both got straight A's? How did you manage it?"

"It was possible because we were so grateful after meeting you."

"We were both determined to study harder to please you. We did well and that's why we're giving you our report cards, as a gift."

"I'm truly grateful and I thank you. You've become healthier and have done better in school than ever before."

I HAD STARTED A NEW FAMILY four and a half years after my first wife left. Back in Korea, I told my two sons what had happened in the U.S.

In Catholicism and Buddhism, a clergyman's celibacy is institutionalized, so marriage is not an issue. It would have been impossible, however, for me, a Protestant, to remain unmarried. It would have been particularly difficult when visiting a church member's home or when I was sick.

At the time, my two sons from my second marriage were young. My first son was a fifth grader and my second a third grader. When I told them about my meeting with their older half-brother and -sister in the U.S., they looked at me in surprise. Recalling stories about early Korea from their history lessons, where a king would have a wife and a number of concubines, one of them asked, "Then, Daddy, are we children of a concubine?"

I was shocked by this unexpected question and wondered what they could possibly be thinking. I spoke about it to my wife. "Dear, you should have explained to them about my trip to the U.S. Why should I hear such things from our children?"

My wife did not mince words. She replied, "Why do you blame me for what you've done? Why don't you tell them? I wouldn't know how to begin to explain such a thing."

"How uncooperative you are," I told her.

I was embarrassed by my son's abrupt question. I was relieved after meeting my children in America, having agonized over them for so

371

long, but I didn't know that my two sons in Korea would pose a problem for me.

Meanwhile, I received a lengthy fax from Brazil. It said that a one-month speaking tour of four South American countries that I had been planning was being canceled. The tour had been arranged after a year of preparations in which a number of faxes were sent back and forth between Korea and church figures in South America. The reason for the abrupt cancellation was my family situation. People in South America pointed out that despite my being a pastor, I had been divorced and that I had even neglected my duty of taking care of my children.

The final lines of the latest fax read, "We hereby cancel our invitation. It would be impossible for us to accept you as a preacher at our gatherings because of your unethical behavior. We suggest that you not go abroad, but stay home, remain silent, and reflect upon yourself."

I stuffed the message into the drawer. My wife saw me, however, and asked what I was doing.

"What was that about? Why did you close the drawer so quickly?"

"You don't have to concern yourself."

"No, tell me about it."

My wife opened the drawer, read the fax, and said, "So now I'm living with an unethical person?"

"Let's get some rest, now that we can take a month off work," I suggested.

"Yes, let's do that, and spend more time with the children."

Several days later, I received a letter from Europe requesting me to preside over services in some European cities. I accepted and told the organizers that I would appreciate it if I could take along my family.

Their reply was, "Of course, Pastor Kim. That will be no problem. Please feel free to do so. At night, you will conduct services, while during the day you and your family can go on tours. Don't worry about a thing. We will make all the arrangements." Thus, I agreed to tour Europe.

On that tour, when we visited St. Peter's Basilica in Rome, I felt cornered. In the cathedral was a statue of St. Peter, with a long line of people in front of it. There is a legend that anyone who kisses the feet of the statue will see their dream come true.

Our family was among the crowd. My oldest son kissed the statue's feet and prayed loudly, "Jesus, I pray that I will not get married twice, the way my father did."

Hearing his prayer, I could hardly express my feelings. When I entered the seminary, after abandoning my original plan to become a professor, I harbored great ambitions. I aspired to become a prominent, not a little-known, pastor, but life never works out according to plan. I wasn't even an ordinary pastor, let alone a distinguished one. What could I say? What had I made of my life?

WHENEVER I WAS IN A PREDICAMENT, the expression "In spite of…" always came to mind.

Since moving to the slums at the age of 30, I have tried hard to be a good pastor. At times, I have been criticized for my mistakes, but I cannot let criticism affect my work. I have to continue, "In spite of…."

Despite my unwitting blunders, Jesus has supported and encouraged me. What more could I want? Since I made up my mind to become a servant of Jesus, I want nothing more than for Him to approve of me. I have often had to think, "In spite of…."

After leaving prison, I had to overcome a spate of problems. At the same time, I was working to rebuild the community organizations, which had fallen into disarray. My first task was to reestablish the Cheonggye-cheon Shantytown Residents Society and streamline its activities.

I was told later that after I was sent to prison, four KCIA agents stayed in the shantytown for several months to spy on the community and the activities of Hwalbin Church. They were reportedly investigating whether I was a communist who had infiltrated the slum, disguised as a Christian social worker.

I had to laugh at their analysis. Kim Jin-hong, they said, was "a home-grown communist," having become a communist on my own, without intervention from North Korea. Upon hearing this, I said that, if anything, I should be considered a biblical communist. Should they call me just a communist, I would not be differentiated from secular communists.

What would be the difference between a secular communist and a biblical communist? Secular communists would contend that the driving force of history is "materialism," whereas for biblical communists the driving force would be God.

While we were busy reinforcing the Residents Society, one day we received a notice from the Seoul city government that the entire Cheonggye-cheon slum would be demolished to construct a subway train garage.

The central government announced that the demolition of shantytowns in Seoul was in the interest of national security. I asked a high-ranking government official to clarify the rationale behind such a move. He provided the following explanation:

"When South Vietnam fell to the communists, Saigon collapsed more quickly than anticipated. The reason was that Cholon, a slum area, was located in the heart of the city. Cholon resembled Seoul's Cheonggye-cheon. A massive number of enemy had infiltrated the shantytown, where they stockpiled arms. At the signal, armed guerrillas poured out of the slum area, quickly plunging the city into turmoil. This accounted for Saigon's quick collapse.

"The Korean government cannot afford to allow Seoul to follow suit. Seoul, also, could plunge into confusion in the event of an emergency, because of the thousands of slum residents in the center of the city. To prevent such an eventuality, the Cheonggye-cheon slum must be cleared. Should the North start firing rockets at Seoul, which side do you think slum residents would support? We can never count on their loyalty. That's why we consider the demolition of the Cheonggye-cheon slum a matter of national security."

Upon hearing this, I was reminded of the remarks made by one resident when Inter-Korean Red Cross talks were announced. It was reported then that the KCIA director had recently visited North Korea.

"Pastor Kim Jin-hong, a better world seems to be in sight," the fellow had said.

"Why do you say that? A better world?"

"Don't you read the newspaper or listen to the radio? South Korea will establish relations with the North."

"Of course, I heard that, but on what grounds do you say that establishing relations with the North would usher in a better world?"

"Let's face it. In the North, the government provides the people houses and food. Nobody has to worry about their house being demolished or having no rice."

"Perhaps that's true, but they have no freedom!"

He stared at me silently, as if he thought I was strange.

"Pastor, you don't understand anything. Why on earth would a hungry person need freedom? Do you enjoy freedom now? The only freedom I have is the freedom to go hungry."

Startled, I told him, "While you say you have freedom only to go hungry, here we enjoy genuine freedom. In North Korea, people are coerced into labor, but here in the South, people are free to choose their jobs and can lead a better life through their own effort. Don't you agree?"

"Pastor, if there is any such work available, let me have it. As for me, I see no job."

Having become disenchanted by his ten years in the slum, he was depressed. Watching his house being razed, he cursed the demolition crew. "You bastards. Now I have no home. Send me to North Korea any day of the week. I'll go gladly!"

He paid for his remarks. First, they reduced his house to rubble. Then they took him away and subjected him to severe beating. Five days later, he returned, a changed and sullen man.

REPRESENTATIVES OF THE NEIGHBORHOOD met several times at Hwalbin Church to discuss the public notice issued by the municipal government, but nothing came of it. The residents were faced with only two options. One was to comply with the city's decree. The other was to use force to obstruct the removal of the houses.

The city promised that it would provide each family facing relocation with 150,000 *won* or the right to buy a small apartment. Only a limited number of the small units were available, however, and anyone taking the apartment would have to put up 10 million *won*. People's only real choice was to accept the 150,000 *won* in cash compensation and move on. Still, there was nowhere in Seoul where they could rent a house for that amount.

We searched for ways out of the predicament, but saw no practical solution. After days of discussions, we decided to comply with the government's order. In this regard, two propositions were on the table.

The first was to purchase land in Seoul jointly and build apartments on it. Che Jeong-gu, who had been working with us in the slum after being expelled from the university for organizing anti-government protests, would be responsible for this project dubbed the "Let's-have-our-own-home Campaign."

The second suggestion was a farm project, which would be for people who had been farmers before moving to Seoul. I was put in charge of this project, which was called the "Hwalbin Farmers Homecoming Program."

Two hundred forty households took part in the "Let's-have-our-own-home Campaign" and banded together to purchase a large tract of land in Bangi-dong, near Jamsil, in southeastern Seoul. Each family was offered a 350-square-foot site.

This group faced a serious obstacle, however. Seoul refused to grant permission for construction of the proposed apartments. City officials were worried that the previous Cheonggye-cheon slumdwellers might stir up trouble in their new location. The 240 families set up tents on their tract, where they lived through the winter in a bid to obtain construction permits from municipal authorities, but in the end their effort was unsuccessful.

Che then had the families move to another shantytown in southern Seoul, in Sillim-dong, where they forged strong solidarity. Later, they were successfully relocated en masse to Siheung, in Gyeonggi province. In 1986, Che received the Magsaysay Award for his contribution in settling displaced slumdwellers. In 1992, he was elected to the National Assembly, representing Siheung. In February 1999, he died of lung cancer. His death was a great loss to the nation, as well as to his family.

Meanwhile, the collective farm project, for which I was responsible, went ahead, despite a number of hurdles.

At one of the meetings of residents whose dwellings faced demolition, one man spoke up, "I came from an island off the south coast. I moved to Seoul because I was fed up with living the life of a poor farmer. The only work I do here is that of a porter, but I often go hungry because porters aren't in demand. "Now, the government wants to tear down even my shack. I'm tired of living in Seoul. I want to go back to the countryside, to return to the earth, to sweat and pay taxes, while raising my children. I want to live like a human being, but I can't go back to my hometown because I sold off my field before I left. If we could get hold of some farmland somewhere, anywhere, I'd go in a second. What do the rest of you think?"

Unexpectedly, his remarks were well received. Many people reacted positively, with comments such as "That'd be great," "Good idea," and "Me, too." I then realized that these people were longing for the rural life they had abandoned.

Another person stood up and remarked, "I couldn't agree more with your suggestion. I'm from Hapcheon, South Gyeongsang province. I worked a number of farm plots and was well-off, but I lost it all to gambling. I had no choice but to come to Seoul and settle in this slum. I don't like to think about how miserable I've been since coming here. I'd like to get my hands on some farmland again, too. I'd work it until I die, and then I'd be buried there, but where could we get land in this God-forsaken country?"

Then I spoke. "Everyone, listen, please. I'm surprised to be hearing a lot of things that I never would've expected. I now realize that many of you are still attached to the countryside and that you'd like to go back. It may not be as impossible as it sounds for us to find land to farm. Although Korea is small and crowded, there could be tracts of land in different parts of the country that are unused.

"If we talk with the authorities and get plots that we can work collectively, it would be a boon to the country in terms of increased food production. Let's talk about how we can get some land. There is a saying that when three people work together, there is nothing they can't accomplish. I'm sure that if we put our heads together, we'll come up with a solution."

"You're right. Let's try to get some land and go back to farming, and raise our children to become good citizens," urged one resident.

That is how the Hwalbin Farmers Homecoming Program came into being. Hundreds of families on the verge of losing their homes submitted applications, of which 100 households were selected as initial members of the program.

The following is the program resolution, adopted at its inauguration:

RESOLUTION

Years after we moved to Seoul in pursuit of a better life, we have degenerated to the status of squatters and have joined the ranks

*of the needy. Poverty, illness, and despair are all we now own.
We have sought an exit from a struggle to survive that tolerates
no escape. If one person stumbles, many should join hands and
help him up. God helps those who help themselves.*

*We have studied, discussed, and prayed, and have decided
to return to the land that we turned our backs on long ago, demonstrating our renewed will to live. Herewith, 520 people from 100
families inaugurate the Hwalbin Farmers Homecoming Corps
and declare our resolve.*

*Let's now join hands and labor with hoes and shovels, in-
stead of indulging ourselves in alcohol and gambling.*

August 1975
Members of the Hwalbin Farmers Homecoming Program

THREE TEAMS, EACH CONSISTING OF TWO PEOPLE, were formed to
explore potential sites for our farm. One team was told to survey abandoned land near the DMZ, north of Seoul, while another team was to
inspect mountain areas in Gangwon province, to the east. The third
team was to look into reclaimed land on Namyang Bay, in Hwaseong-
gun,* Gyeonggi province, to the west.

Members of the program met at the church, after the groups
returned from trips to the countryside. They came to a consensus that
abandoned land near the DMZ would be the best site. From having
served in military camps along the DMZ, many of the men knew of
tracts that were not being farmed.

The group drafted a petition to submit to the authorities. It read:

*We are looking for a way to comply with the Seoul city's reloca-
tion policy, while facing demolition of our homes. We have no way
to pay the 10 million won required to purchase small apartments,
although such a purchase would be a privilege. We cannot lease
a dwelling with the 150,000 won relocation allowance that the
municipality offers as compensation for the loss of our houses.*

---

*A *gun* (pronounced *goon*) is an administrative district, roughly equivalent to a
county in the U.S.

378

Therefore, we have decided to return to the countryside and engage in farming.

We can no longer afford to live in the farming communities where we used to live. We petition you to provide us land that we will till as pioneer farmers. In particular, we request access to plots that are sitting idle near the DMZ, to which no one claims ownership. Although these plots were fertile farmland before the outbreak of the Korean War, they have remained uncultivated since the war and their owners are nowhere to be found.

This petition was presented to the mayor of Seoul. Three days after we submitted the petition, three black jeeps roared into the shanty-town, looking for me. The men in the vehicles were hostile and intimidating. When I approached them, one of them told me, "I'm sorry, but you have to come with us."

"Go with you? Where?"

"You'll see when you get there."

"Gentlemen! What are you saying? I have to at least know where I'm going."

"You should know well enough. It's obvious."

"So, I should know? What should I know? I have no idea. If you know anything about this, please tell me."

"We're to take you to Mount Nam." I knew he was referring to the headquarters of the KCIA.

"Oh, I see. I can imagine that the ruling camp is busy trying to shore up its power base these days. I don't know why you people continue to bother us. We're small potatoes. Why don't you just leave us alone and let us get on with our work?"

"We don't know anything about that. We're just here on an errand to pick you up, so come along quietly."

Smiling at a growing crowd of anxious residents, I said, "I'll return soon. There won't be any problem." Then I got into one of the jeeps.

We arrived at the KCIA through a familiar back alley. Once inside, an investigator with hawkish eyes peppered me with questions, while holding the petition we had sent to the mayor of Seoul. Scanning the petition, he began to question me. "Kim Jin-hong, what's the real intention behind this petition?"

"The real intention? The petition speaks for itself."

"Well, it may and it may not. Admit it, isn't there some hidden agenda to your proposal to move to the DMZ, along with your destitute mob?"

"What do you mean 'hidden agenda'? I assure you, there is no 'hidden agenda,' as you call it. As we state in our petition, we only want to work land that has been abandoned."

"We have no problem with what you say your purpose is, but we don't think that's the whole story."

"What else could there be? What agenda are you referring to? Can you be more specific?"

"We think that with you living near the DMZ, your people can cross the DMZ into North Korea when the time is ripe. From there, it'd be easy for you to make contact with the North."

I was aghast. How could he have come up with such a fairy tale?

"What are you going on about? Are you saying that we might cross the DMZ? Why on earth would we want to go anywhere, leaving behind our land and our country?"

"Kim Jin-hong, just come clean. I heard that residents in the slum prefer the North because they think the government hands out houses and grain, and education is free. Here in the South, they think that houses are razed unfairly and that they aren't respected."

"Goodness! Stop making such a fuss. I've lived with these people for years. They are entirely sincere and I know them to have a deep affection for their country. Don't distort their intentions of turning wilderness into farmland and wanting to lead a decent life."

"Regardless, the DMZ is out of the question. It's too close to the North. You may have good intentions, but if even a few of your people were to defect to the North, you'd be held responsible."

"If that's the case, find us some other place, far from the DMZ. Jeju Island or Busan or Yeosu, we're ready to go anywhere, as long as we can get land to farm. We don't insist upon land near the DMZ. We only figured we could resettle there because there's a lot of idle land."

"That's outside my responsibility. Anyway, the DMZ is off-limits."

Then they sent me home. I called members of the program to a meeting. After hours of discussion, we decided on reclaimed land in Hwaseong-gun, Gyeonggi province, on the west coast, as our second choice. That is how, ultimately, we came to relocate to Namyang Bay.

We submitted our petition to the city authorities, the Ministry of Agriculture, Fisheries, and Forestry and the Blue House. At first, the authorities turned us down, but our persistent efforts eventually paid off, enabling us to initially secure 125 acres of farmland.

24

Starting a New Life

I N LATE 1975, OUR TASK FORCE ARRIVED at the site on Namyang Bay and began to lay the groundwork for our farm project.
The government had built a dike across the mouth of the bay,
pumped out the water, and created an area of 7,800 acres, where the
land would have to be developed to become fertile.

When our task force got there, the coastal area was but a barren
mass of weeds. Our plan called for converting the salty soil into farmland and leveling off a nearby hill for homes, but we were at a loss as to
how to even begin with our project.

We first assembled at Ihwa-ri,* where the dike had been built, and
rented a storage shed as our meeting room and office.

On a cold winter day, the entire membership of the Hwalbin
Farmers Homecoming Program left Seoul behind and headed for Namyang Bay. Dozens of rented trucks were loaded with an assortment of
belongings, including kitchenware, blankets, and lumber salvaged from
houses before the Cheonggye-cheon shantytown was razed.

Passing Suwon, we drove across the countryside, along endless unpaved roads. The closer we got to Namyang Bay, the worse the roads became and the more people had to struggle to stay aboard the bouncing
trucks. As their leader, I wondered whether I had committed a major
blunder, moving people out there. I had had no experience farming and
we had little money. I pretended to be confident, however, because I

---

*A *ri* is a subdivision of a *gun*, or a county.

could not reveal my true feelings and many misgivings.

With the trucks rocking violently on the unpaved road approaching the bay, a pregnant woman cried out from behind, "I'm afraid I'll miscarry at any minute." I stopped the truck and asked the woman get in beside the driver. I then told the driver to go more slowly, even though it would take us longer to reach our destination.

First days of Namyang Bay.

At long last, the vast reclaimed land of Namyang Bay came into sight. Everyone was very excited. "It's so big," people commented. For the moment, we were flush with expectations. The land was icy with frozen rainwater. Trucks became stuck in the mud and were unable to continue. We had to stop. The women and children remained on the vehicles while the men all got down, took shovels, and cleared the track.

Eventually, 7,800 acres of farmland were reclaimed and divided among 1,200 households that took up the challenge of developing it. Among the 460 households from Seoul, 100 families were from Cheonggye-cheon, half of whom were Hwalbin Church members.

HWALBIN CHURCH MEMBERS had wanted to build a single community, with collective ownership of land, on the order of Israel's *kibbutzim*. The authorities turned that plan down, however, commenting that the

383

proposed communal system too closely resembled the collective farm of a communist state. Moreover, they did not want us to live together in a single village, thinking it would make their work of dealing with members of the "notorious" Hwalbin Church, that much more difficult.

Having no option, we went along with the directive of the authorities and settled in 15 separate villages throughout the Namyang Bay area. We initially expressed strong opposition to this plan, but on reconsideration decided we could live with it. It would give us an opportunity to spread the Hwalbin Spirit throughout the bay area.

As expected, residents of the entire area were eventually influenced by our activities. We managed to combine all the 15 villages and 1,200 families into a unit and established seven churches. Around this time, I was ordained as a pastor, which gave me a renewed sense of responsibility and new hope. We set up tents for living quarters, having first erected outhouses. We were indeed living the life of pioneers.

To survive, we would have to transform the salty soil into farmland as quickly as possible, although we lacked everything necessary to accomplish the task—money, equipment, and experience. Shovels and hoes were our only tools.

That winter we dedicated ourselves to building waterways to draw water from the lake behind the dike and then to desalinating the soil. The winter winds coming off the Yellow Sea were strong and biting cold. Confronting the frigid weather, our hands bled as we worked. Our fingernails became deformed because of the cold and the salt, but despite the conditions, we persevered.

Getting proper nutrition was our greatest problem. Living out of tents, we had neither cooking nor dining facilities. Sometimes we put barley into a large pot with water and fresh fish, and boiled it. We ate food that was normally eaten by animals, including acacia leaves, plantain, and sagebrush, accepting that it was fit for human consumption.

Meanwhile, seven churches that we built throughout the Namyang Bay area served as centers for our charity work and community development efforts. During the day, they were used as daycare centers, in which 27 teachers took care of more than 600 children.

TO ENCOURAGE VILLAGERS TO SAVE MONEY, I took the initiative to open a community bank, the Namyang Bay Credit Union. I made the rounds of homes, accompanied by teachers from the daycare centers, to persuade residents to deposit their money in the bank.

I told them, "Please save some money, even if it's only 10 or 20 *won*. If money is not pooled, it is of little value. Only when it is pooled does it become useful."

My argument drew a cool response from residents. One said, "Dear Pastor, you really are out of your mind, aren't you? Think about what you're saying."

"What do you mean?"

"You know we are barely scraping by. We don't know where tomorrow's meal is coming from and you're asking us to save. You're not old enough to have become senile, but you wouldn't know it to listen to you."

"You don't know what you're saying. The rich don't need to save. Only the poor need to. Rich people lead their lives, blessed with everything they need, but why are we living on this barren coast if not to improve our situation? We have to collect even a small bit of money from everyone to get enough money for some productive activity. We will have a bright future only when we save and invest wisely, even though for now we will go hungry."

Oddly, members of Hwalbin Church were more adamant in their opposition to my campaign than non-members.

"Pastor, stop this nonsense, please."

"Why?"

"You know how tough our lives are. If we have to save money, we'll have nothing left to donate to the church?"

"That's not logical. To eat pork, we have to raise pigs. In this context, church members need to build their economic power, so they can later donate to the church. How much money can you contribute now? If you were better off, I think you would be inclined to donate more money to the church."

Despite an outpouring of rebukes and cynicism from villagers, I continued my campaign to save money. The criticism that irritated me most was that any money we saved would end up in the hands of the wrong people.

"Pastor, I think you're wasting your time," someone said.

"What do you mean?"

"Even though you make the rounds of villages and make your pitch, you'll only wind up padding the pockets of thieves."

"What are you talking about?"

"Take my word for it. Ask yourself, who can you trust? If you push this and people go along with it, you will be blamed when someone runs off with the money."

"Well, we'll never accomplish anything worthwhile, if we don't trust people. I'll guarantee the money, should something happen to it. If you have so little faith in other people, at least have faith in me. I will see to it that no one steals the money."

Despite this initial negative reaction, today the credit union's assets have mushroomed to 16 billion *won*, enabling the organization to extend substantial financial assistance to area residents. The credit union's success demonstrates that if the poor unite, they can achieve great things.

SPRING FINALLY ARRIVED. We were about to prepare seedbeds for rice seedlings, when we received a letter from the Ministry of Agriculture, Fisheries, and Forestry. It informed us that we should not plant rice seedlings on the reclaimed land because the soil still contained too much salt. The letter went on to say that if we had a bad harvest, the government would accept no responsibility.

I called a meeting of representatives from the 15 villages. Thirty people, two from each village, assembled to discuss the matter.

"I've asked you to come here to discuss a letter we received from the Ministry. They advise us not to plant this year because the soil is still too salty. As representatives of the farmers, what's your opinion?"

"Well, Pastor, I say it's ridiculous! There are 1,200 families living here, not one or two hundred. What'll we do if we don't farm? If we give it up, overnight we'll turn into a community of beggars. Do you want to become the King of the Panhandlers?"

"That's what we're here to discuss. I want everyone to voice his opinion."

"Pastor, as far as I'm concerned, this isn't worth discussing. It's cut and dried. We have to count on God to provide, not the Ministry. I say we should always do the opposite of what the government tells us to do, and this applies to whether we plant this year. Since the government has warned us against planting, if we move ahead and do it anyway, we are bound to have a good harvest. What do you think? Am I wrong?"

People spoke up. "No, You're right! We're talking survival here. What does the Ministry know about farming? Let's go ahead with it, as we planned."

"All right! Let's do it!"

Everyone attending the session expressed a strong commitment. For my part, I was worried about the profound distrust of the government that I saw within the group. In Korea, it was the generally accepted view that anyone who acted contrary to the directives of the government would be successful. Such a high level of distrust did not bode well for the future of our overcrowded land, which had little in the way of either resources or capital.

At the close of the meeting, we had a small party with *makgeoli* and roasted pig knuckles.

THE VILLAGE LEADERS RETURNED to their neighborhoods and visited every home to explain how to prepare seedbeds. Because rice seedlings could easily wither in the salty soil, residents were told to sow more seed than would ordinarily be necessary.

I came up with the following suggestion for the seedbeds. "As you know, each household in our village has approximately five acres of arable land. If each one were to create its own seedbed, it would be an enormous drain on labor, money, and time. I suggest that we set up one large seedbed for ten households to provide seedlings for fifty acres, and that the households take turns taking care of it. That way, they could all engage in other activities and still get seedlings. In the end, I think this would allow us to save money, time, and labor."

Ten households agreed with my plan and moved to create a joint seedbed. Each household would take turns watering and weeding. Reality, however, does not always conform to vision. There were early signs that the joint seedbed project was doomed to fail. The seedbed often was too dry and overgrown with weeds. This was a big disappointment to everyone, particularly because our seedbed stood in marked contrast to individually managed seedbeds in nearby neighborhoods.

We became impatient because seedbeds are crucial for rice farming and we were losing valuable time. I went to the ten households responsible for the seedbed and inquired about the poor management of the joint seedling nursery. Everyone blamed others for the sorry situation.

"When I took care of the seedbed, it was brimming with water, but things went haywire after Mr. Lee took over."

"Aw, c'mon! What are you talking about? You let it go dry. I'm the one who filled it. You should be honest about your failure and hold your tongue."

"Golly! Mr. Lee, are you trying to lay the blame on me? You should own up to your deficiencies."

This sort of wrangling went on, with no improvement in the state of the seedbed. We had to change our approach. We divided the seedbed into ten sections and put one family in charge of each section. The new arrangement yielded good results and everything improved. The weeds were kept down and the beds were always filled with water. After many twists and turns, the time arrived for us to transplant the seedlings into the paddies.

Carrying rice seedlings to be planted.

After they were planted, however, because of the salt in the soil, the seedlings turned red and died. We were disappointed, but we had anticipated the loss. We cheered up and replanted with new seedlings. I took part in the replanting, praying with every sprout that I put in the ground.

"Jesus, please protect these seedlings to ensure they grow to become healthy plants. Indeed, while in this world, you brought Lazarus back to life. Likewise, you are able to revive these rice seedlings. Please resuscitate these plants and reward these pioneering farmers for their efforts."

As the farmers lined up for planting, I busied myself with prayers, at times hindering their efforts. They often waited behind in a line, while I offered prayers.

One church member asked, "Pastor, what're you going to do, plant rice or pray? Hurry up. If you're going to take so long, you'd better just stand aside."

"Well, I'm praying for our rice."

"That's fine, but why not do it over there, out of our way?"

Despite our best efforts to keep them alive, the seedlings we planted the second time also withered and died. The farmers' disappointment was beyond imagination. They were worried that because of their crop failures, they might eventually become beggars, with neither money nor jobs.

We planted a third time. In villages, planting is usually a festive event, but there was no sign of an upbeat mood this time. The thought that we might all end up with nothing weighed heavily on us.

At dawn, the day after the third planting, I rushed to the fields to see if the seedlings had survived. Once again, our hopes were dashed. The plants were turning red. No one could smile, in the face of this tragedy. With the adults all somber, the children were also quiet. Even the dogs were subdued. Some residents wanted to sell their land off cheaply and move elsewhere.

Knowing that in difficult times, the actions of a leader are crucial to the community, I went about encouraging residents.

"This is not the time to despair. Cheer up! Let's give it another try."

"Pastor, it's no use. It's too late in the season, and besides, we have no more seedlings."

"I don't know if it's too late, but let's see if we can't find some more seedlings and plant anyway."

"Good heavens. How could we get rice seedlings, when there are none? Do you think we can go out and buy seedlings like we buy things from a shop down the street?"

"Well, don't be so pessimistic. This is not the time to give up. Let's go at the problem from a new angle."

At dawn, we loaded people on trucks and sent them out in search of seedlings. I told them to go around to farms and bring whatever they could get from seedbeds.

"If you can't find the owners of seedbeds, bring the seedlings anyway. Planting season has passed and anything left in seedbeds will go unused. If you do that, however, leave our address in the field, in case they come back. Otherwise, we can be accused of stealing."

As THE DAY PROGRESSED, PEOPLE RETURNED with their vehicles full of seedlings. Still, we failed to secure enough seedlings and held a meeting to discuss how to make up for the shortfall. Exhausted, I left the discussion and went home to go to sleep. As I was about to fall asleep, three people came to talk to me. They were men who had worked with me in Seoul as rubbish pickers.

"Pastor, we want you to pretend that you are not aware of what's going to happen tonight, since you went to sleep early."

"What are you talking about? What's going to happen that I'm not supposed to know about?"

"We're still short of seedlings. We talked it over and decided that we should filch seedlings from fields that have already been planted. If we're exposed, we won't let on that you knew anything about it. We'll take full responsibility for it."

Startled, I spoke firmly, "You must be out of your mind. You would dare to commit such a horrible deed? How on earth could you even think of uprooting other farmers' seedlings? You can't do that."

"Who's to find out? Right now, all we can think about is rice. How can we leave our paddies unplanted?"

"Do you think that God will protect us, after doing such a thing? God helps us only when we do the right thing, in spite of our hardship. Don't even dream of doing what you suggest."

"Oh, well. I thought that you'd react this way. We shouldn't have told you about it."

I told them repeatedly not to take other farmers' seedlings. Oddly enough, rumors that Hwalbin Church people might try to steal their seedlings had already reached the neighborhoods, and people were keeping an eye on their fields.

Finally we gathered enough seedlings and set them out in the fields. The mood in our village worsened after we finished our fourth planting. Our fate would be drastically changed, if our rice did not survive.

Without being called out, residents began to assemble on the ridges around our rice fields to pray. These people were not members of our church. Many, in fact, had never set foot in a church, but they apparently believed that in times of crisis prayer helps. They told the dispirited church members, "Hey, you guys, why don't you pray? Pray hard for God to help us out of this."

Our prayer was simple. We prayed for rain. Rain was thought to be the only solution to help rice survive in the salty paddies. If the paddies dried up, salt residue would attack and kill the young plants. Successful rice farming depends on the rice taking root in the paddies while the salt is washed away by rain. In the past, rain had not come and our paddies had been exposed to an assault of cruel sunshine.

Members of Hwalbin Church began to pray along, children as well as adults. Third and fourth graders assembled separately. The adults were deeply moved by how the children prayed, with their hands clasped tightly, looking up at the sky.

"Lord Jesus, please give us rain. Keep our rice alive. Send rain so the seedlings that our parents worked so hard to plant won't die."

I could not suppress my tears at the sight of these children praying. I went to the shore and prayed, crying.

"My Lord, while you may not respond to the prayers of the adults, I implore that you answer the prayers of the children. If the children's prayers are not answered and no rain falls, we will watch our rice wither and die. If this happens, how can I deliver sermons about the goodness of God? Please answer their prayers and send us the rain we so desperately need."

Into the night, most of the villagers returned to their homes, but some church members remained in the fields and continued to pray.

As DAY BROKE, A MIRACLE WAS IN THE WORKS. Rain began to fall. For a while, there were only a few drops, but in no time, it was pouring down. The villagers were ecstatic.

"Is this rain I see?"

"Are we getting rain at last?"

"Yes, it's raining. Look at those clouds over there. We're in for a real downpour."

"Oh, it's really raining! What can I say?"

Drenched by the driving rain, I prayed. "Dear Lord, I want to thank you. I am grateful that you have answered our prayers, in spite of our many shortcomings."

The rain was now falling in torrents and continued for a week. After it stopped, I went out to the fields and found the seedlings looking fresh and healthy. I kissed the rice and said in earnest, "Dear Lord, I am grateful to you. Even if these seedlings do not survive to harvest, I will thank you all my life for helping us this far."

My pent-up fatigue instantly vanished and I walked along the paddies, loudly singing hymns. "This is my Father's world, And to my list'ning ears…"

THE RICE THRIVED AND AT THE END OF THE SUMMER we had a bountiful harvest. Looking over the golden fields, I pledged to myself, "I will live out my life as sincerely as I can, since the Lord has helped us like this. I will remain devoted to this work, instead of pursuing worldly goals."

One day, while thinking that we would be able to harvest soon, one resident called out to me and said proudly, "Pastor, our rice is ripe and we're ready to harvest it."

"Oh! Congratulations! Yours has come in ahead of everyone else's."

"Yes. We think it's great."

"When are you going to cut it? I hope I can help."

"Indeed, we'd planned to talk to you about that."

"Is there something you need to talk to me about?"

"Yes, frankly, there is. We started harvesting today, but stopped because we thought we should first consult with you."

"What about?"

"Well, as I began to cut the rice, it occurred to me that had it not been for the rain after our fourth planting, this harvest would have been impossible. Don't you think?"

"Yes, that's right. Heaven really helped us out."

"So, I think it'd be good if we were to hold a harvest ritual or something like that to express our gratitude. What do you think?"

"That's a great idea. I'd never thought of that. Christians call it the

Thanksgiving Prayer. We usually give thanks on the third Sunday of November, but there's no reason we can't advance it a bit."

As a result, Hwalbin Church offered its 1976 Thanksgiving Prayer in October. It was a festive day. A big party followed the service. The party featured *songpyeon* (rice cakes) made from newly harvested rice, *hobakjeon* (zucchini fried in batter), and *maeuntang* (spicy fish stew). The villagers all relished the food tremendously. Everyone was very happy.

One woman said, "This rice is great! Let's have a feast. We'll lick the platter clean, even though we burst from overeating. They say that even the ghost of a person who dies from overeating is good-looking."

Another woman responded, "A ghost that didn't taste this rice should regret it. Cooks, please put on more rice. This is wonderful! Let's eat until the sun goes down."

Amid this merrymaking, some people wept, overcome with joy. Afterward, we had a good time, playing traditional music in the church yard. Our party continued well into the night. I was pleased that the Thanksgiving Prayer turned into a festival for all the villagers and thought about my mission.

I felt as though on that day I understood the true meaning of missionary work. To serve the church by respecting the will of Jesus is to serve people the same way that Jesus loved people, without reservation, which cost him his life. To serve people means to laugh and cry with them, to be with them in joy and in sorrow.

At the news that we had a good rice crop in our first year, two officials from the Ministry of Agriculture visited us one day.

One of them said, "Pastor Kim, we're here to find out how this reclaimed land could have yielded such a successful harvest in the first year. It usually takes five or six years for crops to reach normal levels on reclaimed lands, but everyone's talking about your big crop. Could you tell us what method you employed? We think that perhaps your technique can be introduced in other reclaimed areas."

"I'm sorry, but I'm not in a position to answer your question. I wasn't directly involved in the planting, but I'll call in two members of our church who were and you can address your inquiry to them."

I called in deacons Kim and Lee. "Deacons, these gentlemen are from the Ministry. They heard about our good crop and want firsthand information about our method. Please give them details about our technique."

No sooner had I completed my remarks than, with great pride, Deacon Kim said, "What method did we employ? We call it the prayer method."

"Please, stop joking. We'd really like to hear about it."

The officials were holding notebooks and pens ready to take notes about our method. They obviously thought that we were not serious.

"Joking? Who's joking, and why should we joke? In the spring, the Ministry sent us a letter saying we shouldn't plant and that the government would assume no responsibility should our crop fail. When we planted our seedlings, we always followed up with a prayer. We were successful because God sent us rain. What other name could we give it? We've always hoped that the government would stop issuing directives to farmers on rice cultivation, because whatever the government says only harms. Instead, why don't you spread our method to other farmers? I'm sure our country would be a lot more prosperous."

We had good harvests three years in succession. Naturally, we were all greatly encouraged.

PART THREE

Darkness Unto Light

25

Disaster Upon Disaster

T HE SEVEN CHURCHES BUILT THROUGHOUT the Nam-
yang Bay area became center stage for community activities for
the 1,200 households in the fifteen villages that had sprouted up
on the bay's 7,800 acres of reclaimed land.

In the beginning, Hwalbin Church, located in Ihwa-ri, served as
something of a mother church for other churches. More than 400 people attended services, which gave everyone a sense of collective power
and interdependence.

After two years, as the six other churches grew to become independent, putting down roots in their communities, the Hwalbin Church congregation disbursed to the local churches.

To serve the community, the villages all established residents soci-
eties, which joined together to form the Namyang Bay Residents
Society. This organization, combined with Hwalbin Church, created
the Namyang Bay Community Development Association.

As the representative from Hwalbin Church, I was made the head
of the Association, while the chairman of the Namyang Bay Residents
Society became deputy head. We also appointed a secretary-general to
manage overall activities of the Association.

Within the Association, committees were formed to develop activities in five categories: resident education, community health, cooperatives, agricultural development, and cultural activities. The committees
were expected to define their roles and identify and solve community
problems in their respective categories.

For instance, there were five areas of activity in the resident-education category: community schools, sitting-room classes, guest-room classes, senior classes, and leadership training.

There were five stages of education in the community schools:

The first stage was pre- and postnatal education for women, which continued until their children reached the age of three.

The second stage was a daycare center for children, from the age of four until they began school.

Visiting a daycare center in one of the Namyang Bay communities.

The third was education for elementary-school children. The program provided remedial classes to help meet the needs of children in rural settings, who generally trailed their urban counterparts in cultural resources and academic achievement.

The fourth was classes for students attending middle and high school.

Finally, the fifth was for the young adults who were unemployed after graduating from middle school or high school.

Of the five stages, the second stage was the most dynamic. Seven daycare centers were set up in the Namyang Bay area, minding children from eight o'clock in the morning until five in the afternoon.

Twice a year, meetings for parents were held at the head office of the Association. The district head and the police chief were invited to answer questions concerning community administration and policy. The officials were surprised that hundreds of residents would gather to ask about and work to correct community problems.

The programs offered by the Association were organized such that all of the residents of the communities were involved in one way or another.

Whenever a plenary session of the Namyang Bay Residents Society was held, with representatives of fifteen villages, a sense of unity and enthusiasm for working together became evident. One result of this was that the post of chairman of the Society became a coveted position.

The post was regarded as having considerable influence because whenever a new district head or police chief was named, they would soon pay a courtesy call on the office of the chairman, in recognition of the growing importance of the Society, and on special occasions would send cards and gifts. Unfortunately, what might have been a source of strength and community pride became a source of strife.

Tragedy struck during the second generation of leadership of the Society. A Mr. Yoon was then chairman and a Mr. Park deputy chairman. Both had worked as core members of Hwalbin Church in Seoul. I had baptised them and they worked hard on behalf of the church.

ONE DAY THE SECRETARY-GENERAL CAME to inform me that Yoon and Park were not on good terms.

"I'm sorry to have to tell you this, Pastor," he said, "but could you please do something to get them back together?"

"What are you saying?" I asked. "Is there some problem between them?"

"It's not easy to talk about," he replied.

"That's OK. Feel free to tell me," I said.

"All right. You understand, this is not unusual when two people work together. These guys have developed something of a dog and cat relationship," he began.

"Why is that?" I asked. "I'd have thought they'd have developed a strong friendship, after all they've been through since we were all in

Seoul. Do you think something happened to cause a problem between them? It'd be easier to help them mend their fences, if I knew what was causing the rift."

"Well, I don't know how to say this. The plenary meeting of the Society is coming up."

"Yes, and what does that have to do with their argument?" I asked, still trying to get to the bottom of the problem.

"Well, Deputy Chairman Park wants to stand for chairman in the upcoming election," was his reply.

"That's not unreasonable. He probably has a pretty good chance of being elected, having served as deputy chairman. What's wrong with that?" I asked.

"Nothing, I suppose, except that Chairman Yoon isn't yet ready to step down."

"I see. He seems to have commitment as well as leadership. I assume this means that Mr. Yoon and Mr. Park are going to compete for the chairmanship."

"That's right."

"What's wrong with that?" I asked again, "The one who wins becomes chairman."

"Yes, but it's not that simple."

"I see no reason to think it's complicated."

"You're taking the matter too lightly," he continued. "The competition has soured their relationship and now they don't even talk to each other."

"That's not right. If they've had a falling out over something as ridiculous as this, they're behaving like children. I don't think it'll cause any serious trouble. I'll call them in and talk to them. By the way, which one do you think the other representatives favor?"

"The conflict arose because opinion has swung in favor of Mr. Park."

"Well, he's a good man, which I'm sure has won him support."

After this conversation with the secretary-general, I was tied up with the daily routine and could not give proper attention to the Yoon-Park relationship. This was later to cause me regret that I have had to live with ever since. Soon afterward, Chairman Yoon brought up the issue of Deputy Chairman Park at a meeting of the Society.

"Why hasn't Deputy Chairman Park been around lately?" he asked.

"I don't know. He was here the day before yesterday. He's absent today, but he rarely misses a meeting."

"Is there any chance that rumors about him are true?" Yoon went on.

"What rumors are those?"

"Deputy Chairman Park is said to have been having an affair."

"No way, Chairman Yoon. Do you know what you're saying? It's impossible that a man of Deputy Chairman Park's integrity would have an affair."

"Don't be a fool. You can't tell a person's nature by looking at him."

"You should never speak ill of such a decent person."

"I'm only repeating the rumors. I was afraid that he might have run off with the woman."

DEPUTY CHAIRMAN PARK DID NOT SHOW UP for some days after this conversation and was nowhere to be found. In the meantime, Chairman Yoon asked around as to Deputy Chairman Park's whereabouts.

A while after, a dog was seen sniffing at a mound behind the village. Out of curiosity, a passerby approached the dog and spotted a piece of clothing sticking out from the mound. Concerned by it, he dug around it, only to find a dead body. It was the missing deputy chairman.

A police investigation established that Chairman Yoon had murdered Park. It was a heartbreaking day when Chairman Yoon was taken away in handcuffs. Everything was falling apart and I lost completely my ability to concentrate.

How on earth could this have happened? I had introduced both of these men to Christianity and had baptized them. I had groomed them to become leaders in the church and to play a lead role in the Namyang Bay Residents Society. Now, one of the two was dead while the other was dragged off to prison. It was unimaginable. What was happening?

I was completely at a loss as to how to deal with the situation. The murder did not end with consequences only for Yoon. His whole family was cast into misery, as if they were trapped animals. Shortly after Yoon's arrest and his story was broadcast on television, his daughter was thrown out by her in-laws. She had been married only two months.

She burst into tears, on entering the front yard of her family's house. "My father's to blame for this." she cried out. "If you had to do this, why didn't you wait until after I had had a son and settled down with my new family? I had just gotten married. How can I live now? I blame you for all this, Father."

The sobbing daughter was embraced by her mother, who was also in tears. The sight of the daughter and the mother holding each other and crying was so touching that the neighbors wept in sympathy. The depth of grief suffered by the daughter was understandable, considering she had been sent back to her family after only two months of marriage, for no reason except she was the daughter of a murderer.

The agony of Chairman Yoon's family was small compared to the hardship suffered by Deputy Chairman Park's family. Deputy Chairman Park's wife went insane after seeing her husband dead. She went about picking up flowers on the day of her husband's funeral and strolled around in back alleys, flashing a seductive smile at people, exposing her breasts. It was his children, however, who most broke peoples' hearts. At the funeral, Park's weeping daughters would not leave his coffin.

"Father, how can we go on living? How can we get on with our lives, with Mom insane?" they cried.

People were unable to hold back their tears, witnessing this heart-rending scene. Sitting in a corner, I also was unable to control my tears during the funeral services. I could hear people say, "What good does a service do, after members of the church kill each other? He should be buried without a service."

"That's right. Hwalbin Church has had too much of a good thing. It got carried away and ran out of steam."

For the first time, I regretted having become a pastor. I am in this situation because I was not meant to be a pastor, I thought. How can I continue to preside over services after all this tragedy in my own church. After the funeral, I am going to hang up my collar and return to the life of a layman. I'll start my life all over again, whether as a cosmetics salesman or a farmer, raising cows and pigs.

TORMENTED BY THIS CONFLICT, immediately after the funeral I went off to a mountain with only a blanket.

402

I spread the blanket out on a flat rock among the pines on the deserted mountain. I meditated and prayed. I would walk down to the valley only when I was thirsty. Otherwise, I remained seated, dozing off when I was sleepy. A week passed.

Through meditation and prayer I sought an answer to the question of giving up the ministry. How should I disengage myself from the projects I had started? What criteria should be used to decide which projects should be allowed to continue? Who could take over the unfinished projects?

Whenever night passed and dawn was approaching, I had to hold onto a stump to dispel the notion that an evil spirit had descended upon me. "Please help me, God. Please help me." I cried out repeatedly.

On the sixth day of my retreat, I felt a revival of spirit from within. I opened the Bible and read from the book of John, "In the beginning was the Word, and the Word was with God, and the Word was God." (John 1:1)

In this verse I looked for the root of my failure. Leaning against the stump, I reflected on John 1:1 in relation to my mission with the farmers. What did the message mean for my work? What was the message? After much thought, I realized that what I had done was wrong.

The foundation of my missionary campaign in the rural community was based not on "the Word," but on increasing farmers' income. I centered my pastoral effort on the formation of resident organizations. It should have been built on "the Word," but I had worked day and night only to boost farmers' income.

The final objective of working that hard, my ultimate concern, was not about man and God, but the construction of a materially well-off rural community. No part of my missionary activity had been founded on "the Word" as the foundation of life, truth, and love. I had relied on the frail means and methods of human beings.

I came to the conclusion that instead of leaving Namyang Bay because of the Yoon incident, I should remain and chart for myself a new course. I resolved that instead of leaving the mission, I would be reborn as a pastor true to God's purpose.

I returned to Ihwa-ri to a warm welcome from church members.

"Where have you been, Pastor? We couldn't eat or sleep out of concern for your well-being."

"I have been praying on the mountain," I replied.

"You should tell us where you're going, even when you're going out for prayer. We were so worried. Why do you look so haggard?"

"Don't worry," I said. "I'll be OK soon."

"Do you want something to eat?"

"No, thanks. Well, on second thought, I would appreciate a bowl of soup and a place to sleep."

After eating, I quickly fell asleep. My energy returned after a two-day rest.

I was about to get up when I was told that I had visitors. The visitors were people who had been fishermen and farmers on the coast before the Namyang Bay was reclaimed for development. They had survived previously by catching fish offshore and picking up crabs in the tidal flats, while at the same time growing what crops they could.

They had been economically hurt, having lost their fishing spots, when the bay was reclaimed. We thought they were at odds with our newly relocated residents, although, as we discovered later, that was not the case.

"I'm glad you have come," I welcomed them.

"Thank you for welcoming us, despite all the trouble we caused you."

"Not at all. It's an honor to receive you. Tell me, what brings you here?"

"We've come to cheer you up because we were afraid the recent incident might have discouraged you."

"Oh, the matter involving the church people. You've heard about that."

"Of course. How could we not have? It's been on television and the entire country knows about it."

"Yes," I said. "I'm very embarrassed."

"No, why should you be embarrassed?"

"I'm to blame because it happened in my church."

"Don't think like that. We know of what you've done, even though we aren't close. We were all moved by your efforts to help the farmers and their communities."

"Thank you for your encouraging comments."

"We wanted to come see you earlier, but were afraid."

"Why were you afraid?" I asked.

"It may sound silly, but we'd heard that you were a spy."

"A spy?" I asked, puzzled.

"Didn't you know?"

"No, this is the first I've heard of it."

"Before you came, the police spent some time here and told people that we'd better watch out because a communist spy-pastor would soon be coming. They told us not to have any contact with you, but if you showed up, we should report anything you had to say."

"Are they still coming around?"

"No, not recently. They came by for six months, but after that they haven't been back."

"They should have arrested me, if they thought I was a spy, instead of telling people to avoid me."

"That's what we thought."

"I didn't know about this. I sensed a cold reception when I went to the villages, but I thought it was because people had lost the bay to us," I said.

"No, not at all. That was no problem for us because we were compensated for the loss, even if the compensation wasn't much. Also, it was the government that made the decision. It had nothing to do with you. We were afraid because they kept referring to you as a spy."

"What do you think of me now?" I asked. "Are there people who are still suspicious of me?"

"No, that's all history. How could we dare to come see you if we still had suspicions?"

"I'm glad to hear that."

"People's attitude started to change about six months after you and your people moved in. They realized that you had the courage to speak out against the government's wrongdoings and it was absurd to think of you as a spy."

"I appreciate your support. Let's try to get along and work together," I said

"We'd like that. We would also like to help you with your work."

This meeting with representatives of the fishermen bore fruit in the form of increased cooperation between the newcomers and the original residents, and their participation in rural development projects.

ALTHOUGH I BEGAN TO PLACE MORE EMPHASIS on spirituality, I could not avoid the reality that even successful rice farming afforded only limited opportunity. To make up for this limitation, I encouraged farmers in the community to set up a swine park to raise pigs.

To secure a good breed of pigs, I had asked Reverend Brown from an Australian church to bring in ninety-two good pigs. Reverend Brown had been my mentor when I studied at the seminary. The pigs he sent were of the best stock, costing us 420,000 won each, when on the Korean market the going price of one pig was about 60,000 won.

The residents were excited when the pigs arrived. They were happy because pork was selling at a good price. One year after we brought in the pigs, however, pork prices plummeted. The plunge was caused by a surplus of pigs. Just to break even, the price of pork would have had to have been at least 700 won per *geun*.* Instead, pork was fetching only 200 won per *geun*. The residents suffered a double setback because as pork prices fell, feed prices rose. To add to their problems, there was no market for piglets. They started to blame the church.

"We're going to be left with nothing, because we trusted the pastor." No one hesitated to voice their complaint, whenever I visited their village.

A woman commented, "Pastor Kim has ruined us by encouraging us to raise pigs. He even looks like a pig. He should have stuck to his preaching."

"Ma'am, that's not fair. I may not be good-looking, but don't you think I look a little better than a pig?" I shot back, embarrassed.

"Don't take it personally, Pastor," she replied sarcastically. "I spoke in haste. You're right. You do look a little bit better than a pig."

I did not have the nerve to go into the villages, in the face of accusations from the villagers that the church was the cause of their misery.

The situation grew worse, to such a point that one day some women dumped their piglets in the tidal flat because they could neither feed them nor sell them at market.

ONE DAY, AS THE TIDE ROSE, piglets that had been left on the tidal flat floated to higher ground and wandered into the village. Two hundred

---

*A *geun* is a unit of measurement equal to 600 grams, around 1.3 pounds pigs, covered with mud, were rooting about in people's yards.

Enraged, village women picked up the pigs and put them in a cart. "Let's take these damn pigs over to pig-loving Pastor Kim."

They stormed to the church. I heard people calling me and ran out. I thought perhaps that had brought some news.

"Pastor Kim," they called out. "You like pigs, don't you? Here, you have them, one for each meal." They threw the pigs out of their cart and onto the ground. The pigs ran into the church and made a mess of it, turning the kitchen upside down.

I called youths from the church. We dug a big pit and herded the pigs into it. I had intended to cover them over, but I could not bring myself to do it. It would have been cruel to bury the animals alive. At the same time, however, I could not leave them in the pit, because they would not stop their squealing.

I was stuck. It was then that I saw a newspaper article that said the government was selling imported pork. I called the youths again.

"Guys. Go get a truck."

"What are you going to do with a truck, Pastor?" they asked, "Are you going to haul the pigs off and dump them?"

"No. Read this article." I explained, "The government is importing pork to sell in Seoul, while pig farmers are being ruined. We can't let them get away with this. We'll take the pigs to Seoul and release them in front of the National Assembly. We'll tell them to have our pigs for dinner."

Their faces lit up at this suggestion. "Great, let's do it, but don't you go chickening out on us," they told me.

They came back with a two-and-a-half ton truck, which we loaded with pigs and headed for Seoul.

In those days, Korea was still ruled by a military dictatorship. Someone saw us on the road and reported us to the provincial government and the police. Long before we reached Seoul, the head of a county government blocked our way with his jeep.

"Reverend, I was anxious to see you," he pleaded. "You don't really want to do this. If you go any farther, I'll lose my job. Please turn your truck around. Do it voluntarily, so we don't have to force you."

A police car was deployed further along and still other police seemed to be standing by, ready to move in. Confronted with this show of force, continuing on was not an alternative. I handed the whole lot of pigs over to the head of the county government.

"Sir, I give you this whole truckload of pigs," I said. "You and the police chief can eat pork for a month."

26

A Telegram to Heaven

B ECAUSE THE FEUD BETWEEN the chairman and the deputy chairman of the Namyang Bay Residents Society had resulted in the deputy chairman's death, I tried to concentrate my missionary activity on people's spirituality. I wanted all of our programs to reflect the teachings of the Bible. That wish, however, was difficult to translate into action, which caused me concern.

In the meantime, democratic movement activists, Hwang In-seong and Suh Gyeong-seok, joined the Namyang Bay missionary team, bringing strong leadership to the group. As it turned out, their naive ambition and enthusiasm suffered from lack of experience, which would later become a source of problems.

One day at dawn, two black jeeps drove into the church compound. Police alighted and snatched up three members of our team to take them away.

"What's going on?" I asked.

"We're investigating these men because we've received a report on an espionage suspect," one of the police replied rudely. The three were released the same day, because the report turned out to be groundless, but the incident was not to be laughed off.

On the first day of their education program, the two activists had lectured residents that the government was a dictatorship and should be overturned. They were preoccupied with their objective of enlightening the population and failed to consider the effect that such outright anti-government statements would have on a politically naive rural community. After the lecture, some of the people filed a report with the police that a suspected spy had given an anti-government lecture. The police who raided the church were acting on that report.

After the incident, I convened our team members and spoke to them. "You cannot go about vilifying the government without going through a process of getting to know people. You have to take your time, if you expect your movement to have any success. The process of enlightening farmers is very much like farming itself. You have to select good seed, plant it, fertilize it, tend the plants all summer long, and harvest in the autumn.

"To enlighten farmers," I continued, "you have to educate them. Educating them requires that you work with them and gain their trust. You have to talk to them, identify their problems, and work to solve them. Jumping into anti-government lectures, calling it education, indicates that you are not prepared to educate anyone," I scolded. "It tells me that you're a bunch of amateurs. To achieve your purpose, you have to take a professional approach."

After that, nobody discussed sensitive issues, such as politics, with residents of the community. Instead, we concentrated on matters that were important to their immediate existence.

AS ONE SOLUTION TO INCREASE FARMERS' INCOME, we came up with two projects, a clothing factory and a livestock co-op. The factory was to produce belts for kimonos to export to Japan. It employed about 100 local women, but it shut down shortly after going into production because Japanese buyers insisted upon cutting the prices in half.

Farmers blamed the church for this failure, but this was not the only example of a situation where the church started something in good faith, only to be blamed when things went wrong.

Late in 1977, the agricultural development committee of the Association initiated the livestock co-op. They decided to first establish a farm for beef cattle. The committee would manage the entire business collectively, from purchase and raising of cattle to butchering and selling the meat. They then went about purchasing calves.

It was not an easy task to buy hundreds of calves at one time. They went as far away as Jeju Island to buy animals, but without success. After a series of brainstorming sessions, we decided to import calves

410

from abroad. The plan was to decide how many calves each individual household needed and then to contract directly with ranches overseas. This approach allowed us to buy at a lower cost by importing in quantity and without commissions that otherwise would have been paid to middlemen.

A contract was signed with a farmer in New Zealand for 500 calves at a cost of 397,000 *won* each. This totaled just short of 200 million *won*. I assumed that for everyone to pay would take at least three months, but in only 18 days they had come up with the money.

We were all excited about the new business. The enthusiastic response from the residents meant a lot to me because it was sort of a midterm test to assess our missionary activity. Leaders of the residents society in each community and members of the Hwalbin Church missionary team were encouraged by the trust the residents were putting in them. We were elated to witness the history-making sight of low-income farmers importing breed stock with their own money.

At the end of August 1978, a total of 493 head of Angus cattle arrived at the port of Incheon. At his own expense, Reverend Nomura from Japan, had taken the trouble of going all the way to New Zealand to inspect the cattle.

Delivery of the cattle to individual households was carried out by the residents society in each community. After balancing the books, each household was refunded 17,000 *won*. The per head price amounted to 380,000 *won*. This was a bargain when compared to the corresponding cost of 900,000 *won* on the domestic market at the time.

Coincidentally, a government organization had brought beef cattle in from New Zealand on the same ship. The cattle brought in by the government sold at 600,000 *won* per head. We thought it strange that the same cattle, brought on the same ship at the same time, under government auspices, sold for 220,000 *won* more per head and wondered who was pocketing the difference.

A problem arose after the allocation of cows to each household. Cattle prices in the domestic market crashed while feed prices soared. Worse yet, people from slums in Seoul and small farmers lacked experience and training in raising imported animals. A series of failures followed. Cattle that had been grazing on New Zealand's lush, expansive grasslands failed to adjust to Korea's confined sheds, feeding on straw.

An animal represented a considerable part of a farm's assets. For this reason, any news that even a few head of cattle had died was enough to scare farmers into selling at knockdown prices. This was more likely to happen for beef cattle than for milk cows. An investment in beef cattle could be recouped only in the long run, because they calved only once a year and the calf would be their only contribution to revenues.

An alternative livestock that provided better cash flow had to be found. We decided that milk cows would provide a quicker return on our investment because they produced milk on a daily basis.

I ASKED REVEREND BROWN to introduce a company that could provide a good breed of milk cow. He recommended Dalgety Australia Limited. The Namyang Bay Residents Society decided to buy 600 milk cows from Dalgety at a price of 640,000 *won* per head, which was about half the price for milk cows in Korea.

I organized a meeting of farmers wanting to buy milk cows to select representatives to travel to Australia to inspect the cows before we bought them. The selection was arrived at by a vote, after a competition that was hotly contested because it provided a rare opportunity for farmers to travel abroad. Two men were chosen to go to Australia.

On June 24, 1979, a ship bringing the cows arrived at the port of Incheon. In the quarantine process at loading, many of the cows had failed to pass, and only 356 were shipped. Dalgety promised to send the remainder of the cows in a follow-up shipment.

But things took an unexpected turn in the process of customs clearance. Upon arrival, the cows were supposed to be sent to a quarantine station for 15 days of observation. For them to clear customs, however, we had to produce a certificate of origin.

The certificate was supposed to have been airmailed immediately after the cows were loaded in Australia. Although it should have arrived before the ship, it had not arrived, even after the 15-day observation period had passed.

We had to pay expenses incurred from the cows overstaying at the quarantine station. By every possible means—telegrams, telex, and telephone calls—we urged the Australian company to send the certificate, but they replied that they had already sent it.

The money we had collected for the cows that were not delivered was used to care for other cows in the quarantine station at a rate of 800,000 *won* per day. It later turned out that the Australian bank involved in the deal had not typed the complete address on the envelope when sending out the document, and it was undeliverable. To compound the problem, the bank had sent the document by regular mail, not by special or registered delivery.

The original certificate never arrived. Figuring out what had happened, we contacted the Australian company again and urged it to resend the certificate on an emergency basis.

To make matters worse, Australian postal workers went out on strike just as Dalgety was about to reissue the document, bringing the postal system to a halt. We were frustrated, but there was nothing we could do. It was early October before the certificate arrived, more than three months after the cattle had arrived at Incheon.

In the meantime, disputes arose among the Hwalbin missionary team and the Namyang Bay Residents Society. No one had managerial skills up to the task of dealing with a contingency of such complexity. Some funds had been embezzled or misappropriated and the financial management system suffered greatly because they had to borrow to pay for the cattle's stay at the quarantine station. In the end, everyone held one another responsible for the failure.

I was at a loss to find a way to untangle the mess. After overcoming all of the hurdles, I managed to distribute the cows to the farmers and demanded that Dalgety pay us 70,000 US dollars in compensation. Dalgety insisted that the bank was responsible because the delay had been caused by the bank's error. The issue went to court for a ruling between Dalgety and the bank.

The trial dragged on, unresolved. Residents who had paid money but had not received cows protested at the church.

ON OCTOBER 3, 1979, on the 8th anniversary of the founding of Hwalbin Church, our balance statement showed that we had a deficit of 140 million *won*. There were two options—either give cows to farmers who had paid for them or refund the money. Unfortunately, we could do neither and I was held personally responsible for the loss.

At Sunday service, the creditors sat in a group at the back of the room. When the service began, they raised their voices and shouted, "Hey, Pastor Kim. Those are fancy words you're spouting, but where's our money? You pocketed it, that's where it is." Later, they would disrupt the service saying, "Why don't you send a telegram to heaven? Ask them to send you some money."

When I raised my hand for the benediction, they would say, "Hello, who are you trying to distract by raising your hand? He may try to sneak out the back door. Send someone back there to keep him from getting away."

Sometimes they would stand over the collection box after the service and say, "How much did you collect today? You have no objection if we take that, do you?"

"Look," I scolded them, "I understand what you're going through, but do you have to do this at the service? Please come some other time and talk sensibly."

"Sensibly?" they asked sarcastically. "You like sensible talk. Think about it. We can't find you when we come on weekdays. We came today because we knew you'd be here. Sunday is like market day at church. Give us our money and we'll never set foot in this place again."

The creditors thronged the church on Sundays and trashed the service. Church membership, which had once reached more than 200, had rapidly shrunk to only thirteen. Senior members prayed, crying, "Dear God, give our pastor power to endure this hardship and to emerge victorious."

Realizing that their pestering would get them nowhere, the creditors took the matter to court. I was charged with fraud and stood trial twenty-one times during 1979 and 1980. I was always acquitted, but times for me were extremely difficult, nevertheless.

IT WAS THANKS TO A PROSECUTOR that one day all of the lawsuits came to an abrupt end. I received a notice from the prosecution that I should appear at the district court. By that time, court appearances for me had become routine. I went to the prosecutor's room at the appointed time to find most of the creditor-farmers already assembled.

When I entered the room, the prosecutor looked around at the creditors and said, "Here is Pastor Kim, against whom you have made so many accusations. I will be out of the office for a while, so you can have a good chat. I hope that by talking with him you can put an end to the charges against him." The prosecutor then left the room.

After he left, one creditor said, "We're sorry to hound you, Pastor Kim. We know that you didn't take our money, but we have no choice. We have to do this to get it back."

"Yes, I understand what you're saying," I said to them, "but you have to keep me alive, if you ever want to get your money. Coming after me as you have been will get you nowhere. Who will pay you back, if I'm not around? I'm not irresponsible. You have to understand what I'm going through and stop pestering me."

"We know that you're innocent and that you're a man of integrity," they responded, "but please understand our position. We paid for our cows with borrowed money, on which we are paying interest. Now we have no cows and we're left with huge debts. In such a situation, we cannot while away our time sitting on our hands. We think that if we pester you, you'll find a way to get the money."

In the middle of this conversation, the prosecutor came back into the room and scolded the creditors.

"I heard everything from outside. I set this up to find out the real story, because you guys have been filing all these charges against Pastor Kim. I taped this entire conversation. From now on, anyone who brings a lawsuit against him over this matter will be subject to charges of false accusation. You cannot charge him while you know that he is innocent. Please go home now and don't come back."

My district court appearances came to an abrupt halt, thanks to the prosecutor.

IN AUTUMN 1979, THERE WAS A CHURCH BOARD MEETING following a week of my usual district court appearances. Halfway through the meeting, a member addressed me with hostility.

"After putting the church in such disarray, if you have so much as a shred of conscience, you will resign your post and leave. You have a lot of nerve, staying in office! We suggest that you take responsibility, and leave your post. Otherwise, this mess will never go away."

Strangely enough, I felt relieved by this accusation and looked around at the people. "Do you agree with his suggestion that I take responsibility and leave the church?" I said. "I'm ready to resign any time you want me to. I have stayed at my post under the impression that I needed to sort this out and help the church get back on track."

I glanced around at people, but no one said anything. They remained silent. I asked again, "I take your silence as a sign that I must resign. If that's the case, I'll leave here this week. But even after leaving, I will continue with my other work and do my best to pay off the debt. I would like to ask a favor, which is that you keep Hwalbin Church going, however difficult that may be. Hwalbin Church has yet to see its best days."

Making this farewell statement, I became emotional and my eyes filled with tears. The following day, the church's bookkeeper gave me 100,000 *won*, saying that he was sorry he could not give me more.

"We have 700,000 *won* to 800,000 *won* in the budget set aside for a situation like this, but it has to be held for a pastor who will come to fill your post," he added.

At the age of thirty-nine, with 100,000 *won* in my pocket, I left the church I had started in a slum, eight years before.

I had not expected to be leaving, so I had no plan for my future. A friend suggested that I start a new church in Jocheon, an area at the foot of Mount Halla on Jeju Island, off the south coast. I sent my mother, who had been living with me, to my sister's and shipped my belongings to Jeju Island. After paying for shipping and buying a plane ticket to the island, I had only 5,000 *won* left. I went straight to Jeju, where I started a new church.

HARDLY TWO MONTHS HAD PASSED when one day members of Hwalbin Church came to Jeju to invite me back. They said that a consensus had been reached among church members that it was wrong to have let me leave the church.

I became sarcastic and asked, "I came here because I had nowhere to go. Now that I have settled in and made a new start, why have you come to get me?"

One of them, a deacon said, "Pastor Kim, that's not true. We didn't tell you to leave. It's true that we strongly urged you to take responsibility to work out your problems, but we didn't mean for you to leave. You simply took our criticism as a statement that we wanted you to leave and gave us no time to respond. Did we tell you to leave?"

"I left the church because a lack of response in such a situation was a tacit agreement with the suggestion that I leave, although you didn't say specifically that you wanted me to leave," I quipped. "If I had stayed, refusing to leave under those circumstances, I would have been making an idiot of myself. In the worst case, it would have resulted in a division in the church."

"Everything happened before we could figure out what was going on," they pleaded. "Forgive us and return with us. Please come back, sort out the problem, and revive the church."

I felt a responsibility for what had happened to the church and decided to return to Namyang Bay. My return, however, changed nothing. I continued to be hounded by my creditors and depended on church members for my meals.

27

Against the Wall

ON DECEMBER 30, 1979, JUST ONE DAY before the end of the year, I went on a retreat to the Daihan Christian Prayer Hill in Cheorwon, Gangwon province. My plan was to meditate, but also I wanted some time alone, away from my creditors. I had decided to stay at the retreat through the New Year, to pray and to fast, asking God's help in overcoming my difficulties.

The head of the Prayer Hill suggested that I have a body massage prayer. This massage prayer is different from a laying-on-the-hands prayer, which simply requires the laying of hands on the head or infirm parts of a supplicant's body. The massage prayer requires supplicants to have their bodies pounded upon or rubbed while praying. I turned down his suggestion because I do not subscribe to that kind of prayer.

"I'd like to pray quietly, making the most of the rare occasion I have to visit such a serene place as this," I responded, "but thank you for your thought."

"I'm not suggesting that prayer for just any reason," he said. "I recommend it because I sense spirituality in you. This rarely happens."

"Thank you for your consideration, but I'd rather not. I prefer to pray in my own quiet way," I explained.

He did not let up, saying "Understand, Pastor, your persistence can be interpreted as arrogance. Please be humble and give it a try."

He was so persistent that his suggestion seemed to be more on the order of a demand. I finally accepted his offer because I agreed with him when he said that my refusal could be taken for arrogance.

A while later, two sisters and a brother came and told me to lie down. They started to pray, while hitting my entire body, with the palms of their hands, in short strokes. The pain from the blows was so acute that I felt it to my bones. I could have thought that these people had come from the KCIA to interrogate me, but I endured the pain without complaint.

Amid all the pounding, they foretold my fate. The brother told me that I would have power to manage a large fortune. I made light of his prediction, becoming sarcastic, saying that, if anything, my power would be to manage a large debt.

Considering my situation, what he said did not make sense to me. I had come to this mountain to fast and pray, after my effort to help people had ended in failure, leaving me owing 140 million *won*.

A while later, one of the sisters told me that I was meant to go to America. I smirked to myself. I had been blacklisted as a political offender and banned from traveling abroad. I did not believe in such predictions, thinking that they were nothing more than random guesswork.

After the prayer session, the head of the retreat house came to speak to me, "You withstood surprisingly well, Pastor. I was told you didn't flinch during the session, which even young men find difficult to endure."

"I have a talent for absorbing beatings," I joked.

"You're so funny," he said. "By the way, what did you think of the prophecies?"

"I'm not sure," I replied.

"What do you mean, you're not sure? It sounds as if you didn't like what you heard," he said.

"I don't know."

"Please, tell me what you really think," he urged.

"I don't want to offend you."

"You needn't feel that way. Just tell me what you think."

I decided to level with him and told him exactly what I thought. "If you insist," I started. "They told me that I'll have power over a big fortune. I don't believe it because I came here to get away from my creditors."

"You may have a lot of debts right now, but that doesn't mean that you'll always be in the same situation. We can't guarantee that you'll be given power over a big fortune, of course. We have merely relayed the words we heard from the Holy Spirit."

"OK, that's fine. They also told me that I was destined to go to America. As a political offender, I'm banned from travel. Although I may be able to go to America one day, it cannot be said that the prediction proved right because going to America has become so common that there's nothing special about it that could raise it to the level of a prophecy."

"You're not an easy person," he said. "You'll be allowed to go to America, if God intends it to happen. You say that it is no longer a special thing to go to America, but your purpose in going to America will be special or at least different from that of other people. Don't try to make sense of the predictions, please. Just accept them with your heart."

I had no desire to contradict him and ended the conversation, responding with a smile. I carried the bruises from the prayer session for some days. With the bruises gone, the predictions also eluded my mind.

TWO YEARS LATER, I RECEIVED AN INVITATION from the White House to go to America. It was from President Reagan, inviting me to speak at a special prayer breakfast, ushering in the New Year. I applied to the Korean government for a permit to make an overseas trip. It was issued without a hitch.

The breakfast, hosted by the president, was much like a revival service. The event actually lasted two nights and three days, was attended by 1,600 leaders in various fields, and consisted of lectures, prayers, and seminars. I felt awkward and out of place because it was the first time for me to attend such an event.

The day after I arrived, I had lunch at a table with five other men. I said hello to a man sitting next to me, as other people introduced themselves to one another. My greeting must have sounded odd because my English was not fluent and I had never carried on an extended conversation with an English speaker.

"I'm Kim Jin-hong. I come from Korea. I'm a pastor in a Presbyterian church," I said to him.

It took considerable effort to get through my greeting and for me to reach out to shake his hand. To my embarrassment, he gave me a quick glance and turned away, pretending not to notice me. His impudence upset me.

After a moment, my unease turned to anger. It was rude of him to ignore my greeting, although I might have lacked refinement in how I had gone about it. My dismay was all the greater because I was among Christians. I was not about to let it pass.

I confronted him, pulling his wrist, "What's the matter? Don't you like yellow people? Well, I'm just like you. I don't like white people. I guess we should get along just fine."

I said this out of bitterness because I had assumed that his rudeness was race-motivated.

Watching what was unfolding, other members at the same table burst into laughter and clapped in approval. The man whose wrist I had been holding turned red, whether with anger or shame I do not know. He must have been upset because he looked down at me with an unpleasant stare.

I ignored his stares and faked a smile in reply. I thought to myself, if you want to come to blows over this, I'm ready for it.

At the next session, I made a twenty-minute speech. People seemed to have been moved by my story because afterward they applauded enthusiastically. I stepped down from the podium after the speech to see the man I had confronted earlier approach me and offer an apology.

"I apologize for behaving in a way so unbecoming a Christian. I hope that you accept my apology," he said. I shook his hand willingly because I was also uncomfortable with my brashness and for having shamed him before other people.

Having watched the whole incident, the man responsible for arranging the program invited me to a prayer with some senators. I had a good time at the senators' gathering and became friends with some of them.

FOLLOWING THE PRAYER BREAKFAST, I went to a Korean church for a Sunday service. After a delay of twenty minutes, it had not yet begun, while the congregation was kept singing hymns. Then a member of the church came forward to ask, "Is there anyone who can conduct the service? We've just heard that our pastor has been in an automobile accident and was taken to the hospital. He's all right, but will not be able to join us today. Please, anyone who can give a sermon, come forward and do so."

I looked around, but saw no sign of anyone volunteering. I was born with a penchant for standing up in front of others. Taking my Bible and hymnal in hand, I stepped forward.

"May I officiate the service, if there is no one else?" I asked.

The church member looked me up and down skeptically.

"Will you tell me about yourself?" he asked.

"Yes, I'm Pastor Kim Jin-hong from Korea," I replied.

"May I ask where you practice your ministry?"

"I belong to Hwalbin Church. I'm sure you've never heard of us because ours is a small church in a rural area."

Taking into consideration that there were so many self-styled ministers in Korean churches, it was understandable that he asked a number of questions to establish my credentials. I went into detail about my background and education, to dispel his doubt.

"I went to Presbyterian College and Theological Seminary in Seoul and belong to the Presbyterian Church of Korea," I explained.

The man's face lit up, as his doubt receded. "I see," he said, leading me to the pulpit. "Please proceed with the service."

I was not properly prepared for a sermon, so I told people stories based on my experiences practicing ministry in a rural church and associated them with verses from the Bible. It was something of a "storytelling" sermon.

The man who had asked me to improvise a sermon came up to me during the social session after the service and said, "I was very impressed with your sermon. The congregation would like to hear more. Could I ask you to preside over a special congregation for one hour in the afternoon?"

"Let me think about it," I hesitated. "I have no experience in this sort of thing and I didn't come prepared for it."

"You don't need to prepare. Just tell people your stories, like you did this morning."

"If that's all there is to it, then there's no problem," I said, accepting the request.

In the afternoon, I conducted the sermon more casually,

interspersing it with occasional jokes, because the time limit on the afternoon session was not as strict as in the morning. After the sermon, three church members got together and addressed me. "Pastor," they said, "we're having a revival over the next three days and would like to hear more of your sermons. Could you join us?"

"I'm sorry. Practicing ministry in a small church in a rural area, I have no experience presiding over revival services."

"There are no special rules for revivals. You just carry on as you did today. It's fine, as long as people feel blessed. Please don't turn us down. Your presiding over the congregation will serve as great inspiration for our spiritual life."

They were so sincere that I accepted. Their compliments on my performance in the previous service also gave me confidence.

I led services for three evenings. To my surprise, these sermons were marked an "unprecedented hit," if I may use a dramatic expression to describe it. The taped sermons were circulated around the U.S. and were sent to Korea. Afterward, in Korea, I was flooded with invitations asking me to conduct services.

That was the start of my career as a speaker at revival services. Since then, I have enjoyed a reputation as a speaker who can attract a large audience. My life had taken a new direction.

The prophecies about me had been fulfilled. Their predictions about me going to the U.S. and having power to control a fortune turned out to be correct.

I do not have cash holdings or real estate of my own. The fortune mentioned in the prophecy referred to funds I use to help people in God's name. Those funds have grown year after year. Testament to this is the Doore Community. I started the communal settlement in Namyang Bay, but its influence has expanded to other places, across the nation and to the U.S., China, and North Korea.

AFTER MY RETREAT IN THE DAIHAN Christian Prayer Hill, I returned to Namyang Bay only to be greeted once again by my creditors. They were becoming exasperated because New Year had come and gone, and they still had not been paid. My unannounced disappearance to a retreat house had only fueled their rage.

The day after I returned from the retreat, seven or eight creditors barged into my house and forcibly took me out to the center of the village. I was intimidated by their menacing behavior. "Why are you doing this to me?" I asked, while they shoved me around.

"You're a cheat. We're going to teach you a lesson," they shouted, making a big scene. They forced me to stand in the center of the village, while they spoke to the residents.

"Hey, folks, gather round. We're going to teach this fraud a lesson."

They shouted this several times, until a crowd gathered to see what was going on. One creditor pitched his voice high, as if he were a peddler.

"Folks, this Kim Jin-hong is a fake. Taking advantage of his position as a pastor, he has cheated innocent farmers out of what is rightfully theirs. We're going to teach him a lesson."

Two bulky men held me up by the arms while others began to remove my clothes. First they took off my shirt.

In a mock auction, they spoke to anyone who would listen, "This is Kim Jin-hong's shirt. How much are we asking for it? Ten thousand *won*? Are we going to sell it at the full price? No, we are not. We are going to cut the price in half. No, on second thought, we're going to give it away."

They walked around, among the villagers, waving my clothes, shouting. Next they took off my undershirt.

"This is Kim Jin-hong's undershirt. How much are we asking for it? One thousand *won*? The full price? No, half is fine."

They proceeded the same way with my trousers and then my socks. I grew more humiliated, as the auction progressed to my underwear, my last remaining garment. I closed my eyes and prayed.

"Oh, Lord. Please let them stop here. They do not know what they are doing. Please, please let them stop here and not strip me naked."

The leader of the creditors' group made a motion as if to take off my underwear. Then one of the others stepped forward and suggested they stop.

"Boss, let's stop here. We've gone far enough."

"What do you mean? Look at what we've gone through, because of this scoundrel."

"Let's stop here. It serves no purpose to go any farther. Enough is enough."

While they squabbled, I continued to pray. The leader finally spoke up. "OK, enough is enough. I wanted to leave you buck naked, but you're lucky. I'll stop here."

They left the site, leaving my clothes strewn about. I was unable to look at the villagers who had gathered. I collected my clothes, put them on, and left. I went straight to the dike. On one side were fields created by blocking off the sea. On the other side was the sea itself. Walking closer to the sea, I took off my shoes and then I put them on again. I did this five or six times. When I took off my shoes, I was contemplating suicide. I wanted to jump into the sea, but something held me back and I would put them on again.

How could I stand before God after having committed suicide? That thought held me back. By the time I got back to the dike, however, I had set aside that argument. I was tired of creditors who were certain to attack and heckle me, beginning again at dawn the next day. I had had all I could take.

I can't go on like this. Let's end it here, I thought. Reaching this conclusion, I would turn around and walk back toward the sea. Finally, I put on my shoes and returned to the prayer room at the church. I decided to pray, thinking that only in heaven would I find a way out of

Looking out to the Yellow Sea over reclaimed land. The lake on the right was created by a dike across the bay.

my situation, because here on earth I had failed in everything.

I will confront God in the prayer room. If God does not show me a way out of this, I will die on the spot. I would rather die praying than jumping into the sea. I cannot go on like this.

Before starting to pray, I summoned a deacon. "I want no one to interrupt me while I attempt to speak to God. Don't let anyone come near me until I come out. Even if the place burns down, leave me alone. I will throw myself entirely into the mission of confronting God. I will come out only after I'm successful. If I'm not, I'll die here. Please don't bring me any food, drink, or anything whatsoever."

The deacon became solemn, "Yes, Pastor. We will join you, in a prayer fast outside the room. I'm sure that Jesus will answer your prayer because he knows you are sincere."

I went into the prayer room, locking the door behind me. I covered the windows, making the room as dark as night. I got down on my knees, facing the wall, and began to pray with all my heart.

"Lord, it's unfair. Although I cannot say that I have done well, I have done my best. Have I not? Have I taken so much as a single penny or bought a single patch of land for myself? You know that I have not misappropriated even so much as a pair of shoes and have always done my best. For all my effort and hard work, how could you let me endure this suffering? I am your servant. How could you sit back, watching me suffer so at the hands of others? Please show yourself to me. If not, I will die right here."

Some while after I started praying, I found tears streaming down my face. I could not suppress the sorrow in my heart. I cried out, my palms pressing against the wall in front of me. I calmed down after a good cry.

It was then that I thought of the story about Hezekiah appearing in 2 Kings. King Hezekiah had been sick and faced death. He sat down, facing a wall, and prayed. Moved by his tears, God answered his prayer and extended his life by fifteen years:

> In those days Hezekiah became ill and was at the point of death. The prophet Isaiah, son of Amoz, went to him and said, "This is what the LORD says: Put your house in order, because you are going to die; you will not recover."

> Hezekiah turned his face to the wall and prayed to the LORD, "Remember, O LORD, how I have walked before you faithfully and with wholehearted devotion and have done what is good in your eyes." And Hezekiah wept bitterly....
>
> "Go back and tell Hezekiah, the leader of my people, 'This is what the LORD, the God of your father David, says: I have heard your prayer and have seen your tears; I will heal you.... I will add fifteen years to your life....'" (2 Kings 20:1-6)

I thought about this passage and continued praying, thinking that the wall in front of me was the same wall that faced Hezekiah when he sat down to pray.

"My Lord, I am not praying that you add fifteen years to my life. My only wish is to be able to make up for the financial loss to the farmers and keep this church, to which I have devoted eight years of my life, going. Lord, this church is not mine. It's yours. Please keep this church from falling apart. You can take my life, but please keep the church alive and find a way for the farmers to recover from their loss."

I prayed, wiping away my tears with the back of my hands. Whenever I was sleepy, I dozed off, but would return to praying as soon as I awoke. This routine went on and on. I drank no water and became so involved in my prayer that I did not know whether it was night or day.

THEN, AT ONE POINT, I HEARD A KNOCK AT THE DOOR. I remained seated, ignoring it. Having no response from inside, someone outside called me, "Someone has come to see you, Pastor."

"Didn't I tell you to leave me alone?" I responded.

"I know, but she is very eager to see you."

I was in no mood to see anyone. "Send her away, please. Don't interrupt me. I'm in no condition to see anyone."

There was some murmuring outside and the knock came again.

"She says that just a few words will do, Pastor. Please step out briefly."

"I'm not ready to see anyone. I know that this is not courteous, but please send her away."

"Pastor, the lady has come all the way from Seoul, just to have a few words with you." The man outside was also persistent.

I was annoyed and told him.

"If she insists, ask her to speak to me from outside. I will stay here to hear what she has to say."

There was another quiet exchange and then the woman spoke.

"I will speak to you through the door, Pastor. You have problems, don't you? I just want to suggest that you read Romans 8:12-13."

I was bewildered and upset at the same time. A woman is visiting me at this critical moment and she is telling a pastor to read the Bible. I was insulted, but it would not be courteous to reject her suggestion outright.

I got to my feet and turned on the lamp to find my Bible. I had difficulty focusing my eyes, because I had been in the dark for so long. I finally managed to find the passage and, rubbing my eyes, attempted to read.

> Therefore, brothers, we are debtors—but not to a sinful nature, to live according to it. For if you live according to a sinful nature, you will die; but if by the Spirit you put to death the misdeeds of the body, you will live. (Romans 8:12-13)

Of these verses, a word that first registered with me was "debtors." I am sure that in my lifetime I had read Romans scores of times, but never had I taken note of the word "debtors." I am sure I noticed the word because I owed so much money. "Therefore, brothers, we are debtors...."

These words seemed to mean, "Therefore, Pastor Kim, you are a debtor owing 140 million *won*." Reading the next words, I felt a realization: "But not to a sinful nature, to live according to it."

I came to understand that I had not lived up to the life of a pastor, which is to live spiritually. Instead, I had lived a life of a sinful nature. Once again, I had been too worldly. The Lord has put me in this situation to make me realize this.

I had neglected my Christian mission as a pastor in the name of helping farmers. My life was on a fast track with regard to such worldly projects as importing cattle, creating a livestock co-op, and strengthening residents organizations. My preoccupation with these matters, however, left me little time to prepare a proper sermon, not to mention time for prayer.

It was not unusual for me to ask people attending the early morning service to pray silently to themselves. I would also ask people to pray and study the Bible by themselves at Wednesday service, offering the excuse that I was too busy to preside over the service. Sometimes I found myself looking for phrases from the Bible for the day's sermon only after I was standing at the pulpit, after asking people to sing hymns. It was not surprising that church members had fallen into spiritual confusion.

One day, not long before, a church member had scolded me, saying, "You have to come to your senses, Pastor."

"What do you mean?" I asked.

"Why is it so difficult for church members to see you. It's easier to see the president than it is to see you."

"I'm sorry," I replied. "Please be patient a little longer. I'll come back to my job, once this cow thing is resolved."

"I'm sorry, too, Pastor. I don't want to hear any more of this cow stuff. It's not right for a pastor to talk only about cows, neglecting his work, which is to preach the Gospel. God will not let you get away with this."

"It sounds like you're threatening me."

"No, I'm not threatening," he said bluntly, "but I'm sure that God will not forgive you for this. Please set aside all those matters and come back to your real job. Otherwise, you are sure to regret it later."

Now I realized what I was doing wrong and came to accept that, as Romans said, I had been sinful.

This, then, was the source of my problem. All the trouble I had experienced because of the cows was a wake-up call from God. The failing was spiritual, not financial. The solution, therefore, should also be spiritual, and not financial or social.

I found a thread that led to the solution to my problem when I moved to the next verse: "For if you live according to a sinful nature, you will die; but if by the Spirit you put to death the misdeeds of the body, you will live."

Here was the solution to my problem. These words brought home to me that the spiritual solution is to discard the "misdeeds of the body" and return to a life that subjected the body to the spirit.

I felt a release deep within and realized that God had created this anguish to make me understand what was happening. This realization relieved me of a heavy burden. I knelt and prayed. This time my prayer was of gratitude.

"Lord Jesus, thank you for freeing me from my worldly ways. I realize that you sent me these difficulties to awaken me. It was not an easy lesson to learn, but I am grateful to you for it. I know that you resorted to strong medicine to break me free of the mold because you knew that I was preoccupied with a worldly life. Lord, I will go back to a life of spiritual pursuit. I will live off your spirit and as pastor lead a life that is true to the Bible. Please hold me and guide me."

I got up and left the prayer room.

Having come to understand God's purpose, the service at Hwalbin Church the following week was full of emotion. I spoke to the congregation, "Hwalbin family members! You have suffered from my inadequacy as a pastor. I repent before you because your sufferings are all my fault. During prayer last week, I read Romans 8:12-13 and in those words saw my reflection. There was nothing pastor-like about me. I did not understand God's effort to awaken me through hardship."

I had tears in my eyes as I spoke.

The congregation was also crying. One of them spoke, "You have committed no sin, Pastor. You have gone through all of these hard times for us. We are to blame."

I replied, "Let's begin again. Leave behind the life of the flesh that we have led so far. The life of the flesh caused us to fail with both our spiritual and our temporal pursuits. Let's take our lives beyond the flesh, not allowing worldly ways to obstruct our spiritual path. Let's revive our church and live a life becoming of God's creatures. Let's embrace a life in pursuit of the spirit that does not fear death, in this land of salt, granted by God. Our bodies, will fertilize the land after us. As pioneers, we will work till death overtakes us. Let's apply ourselves to this task so that, when their time comes, our grandchildren can say that our sweat and sacrifice made possible the development of this prosperous farmland and the establishment of our blessed church."

Standing at the pulpit, I lost track of what I was saying. Everyone was crying, so we began to sing a hymn.

Father, I stretch my hands to Thee; No other help I know;
If Thou withdraw Thyself from me, Ah! wither shall I go?
I do believe, I now believe, That Jesus died for me,
And that He shed His precious blood, From sin to set me free.

What did Thine only Son endure, Before I drew my breath!
What pain, what labor, to secure My soul from endless death!
I do believe, I now believe, That Jesus died for me,
And that He shed His precious blood, From sin to set me free.

O Jesus, could I this believe I now should feel Thy power,
And all my wants Thou wouldst relieve, In this accepted hour.
I do believe, I now believe, That Jesus died for me,
And that He shed His precious blood, From sin to set me free.

We sang several hymns. The day's service was brought to an end with everyone crying. As the congregation and I renewed our faith, Hwalbin Church was reborn. We prayed with one heart, praised God's blessings, and sought to build a more spiritual church. The weight of the debt was no longer the burden it had been.

Before this, we all felt as if we were under a dark cloud and that there was no way out. Now the farmers, who had been depressed, recovered their spirit. At long last, the clouds were dispelled and there was dazzling light.

This reawakening on our part brought about a change in the creditors' attitude. They continued to come by, to squeeze me for money, but would leave without making a fuss, after seeing me in a joyful mood.

One day they addressed me, as if they were talking to one another. "Pastor Kim, you're looking better. You must have had some good news. If it proves good for you, it'll prove good for us as well. We know you mean well and believe that you will keep your promise. We're sorry for having bothered you so much. We see no reason to come all the way down here any longer. We'll wait at home. Please let us know when things change for the better."

Saying this, they went away. When they arrived in their village, a neighbor, who also had not received his cows after paying for them, asked them, "You've seen Pastor Kim, haven't you? Is there anything new?"

"Yes, he looked much better. We went too far with him. He won't forget us, if he comes into money. We've decided not to bother him any more."

"Then I probably shouldn't bother him either."

The creditors came less frequently. Encouraged by this, I banded with church members and embarked on the mission of reviving the church and rebuilding its foundation.

The woman, who was worried about me and who visited me to suggest that I read from Romans, later became my wife. When she first came to me, I thought she was unusual. She was telling a pastor to read his Bible! I became grateful to her because after accepting her advice, I learned a valuable lesson from the Word of God.

28

Refuge in a Storm

HAVING GONE THROUGH SUCH ADVERSITY, it occurred to me that, if I had a family, it would provide me refuge and stability. When my first wife left me and went to the U.S., taking our children, I resolved to dedicate myself to my work. Indeed, I had done so, but the work I had thrown myself into had ended in failure. I felt utterly abandoned. A man without a family is like a tree without roots or a bird without a nest.

I set a date for a wedding, thinking that it would be good to get married when I had no other pressing matters. On my calendar, I penciled in January 17, the date on which I had been arrested in 1974. I then started looking for someone to marry.

There was, in fact, a woman who had expressed interest in marrying me. She worked as a nurse and had been married to a pastor who was killed in an auto accident. She was raising a son and a daughter by herself, and I thought she might agree to marry me.

With that in mind, I went to Seoul to propose to her. I told her that I had set a date for our wedding. Her response was not what I expected.

She replied, "You are not the kind of person who is content to settle down with a family. You are destined to live alone. I have no interest in marrying you. If you want to marry, you'll have to find someone else."

I was not expecting a rejection and certainly not such an adamant one. "Pardon me? Why, then, did you once say you were interested in marrying me?"

"Perhaps I did say that, but that was before I got to know you. When was the last time I mentioned that to you? It was some months ago. Since then I've changed my mind. As a person, you are attractive, but you are not a person to marry."

It was as if my spirit had left my body. Even though I felt dejected, I told her, "What you say makes sense. You must have learned a lot over those months."

I turned around and walked off, only to hear her coming after me. "Oh, and by the way, Pastor. I would appreciate it if you could pay me back the 150,000 *won* you owe me."

"Yes, I know, I owe you, but I haven't been able to pay my debts. Could I pay you back later?"

"I'm afraid not. I need the money for my children."

She was right to ask, but I didn't have so much as a penny in my pocket. I was in no mood to suffer ridicule because of my poverty.

I collected myself and told her, "I understand. You need money to support your children. I'd always planned to repay you, but right now I don't have the money. I'll get it, even if it means selling the clothes off my back."

On the way home, I experienced an inexplicable mix of emotions. One reason I had asked her to marry me was because I wanted to give her children a good home. I suppose now that I was thinking, in part, that I could make up for the loss of my children. I was embarrassed that she had turned me down.

Fortunately, some days later, I earned 140,000 *won* and thought I would repay her. I took a bus to Seoul early one morning because I was afraid I might change my mind.

"I've come to return your 150,000 *won*," I told her, "but I'm 10,000 *won* short. Please regard the 10,000 *won* as a contribution to the church. I hope you understand the effort I've made in taking an early bus to come here, to keep my word."

She thanked me and gave me back 5,000 *won*, saying that she would like to make a further contribution.

On my way back to Namyang Bay, I remembered that I had set January 17 as the date for my wedding. Instead of returning home, I continued south to Gwangju, in South Jeolla province, to ask about someone else.

I recalled that there was a devout couple in Gwangju who had a daughter. Her husband had been killed in a car accident before her very eyes, only a few days after their wedding. The shock of the accident was such that she became mentally imbalanced.

I had had first-hand experience of caring for a mental patient, because of my brother's breakdown after being discharged from the military. I knew what she was going through. I felt a lot of sympathy for both her and her family. I thought God would be happy with me for marrying a mentally disturbed woman, if I were to marry anyone at all.

I went to their house, thinking to myself that it was a good idea. Her mother answered the door and invited me in. I told her that I had traveled all the way to Gwangju to ask to marry their daughter. The mother looked at me in blank amazement, saying that she would discuss it with her husband. She then served me a big meal.

Two days later I received the answer. They said that although they appreciated my intention, I should abandon the idea. The reason they gave was that their daughter was not good enough for me.

I WAS FRUSTRATED because although I had already set the wedding date, my efforts to find a wife had met with no success. A Miss J came to mind as another possible candidate. I had gotten to know her when I was working in a slum in Seoul.

She was Catholic, but I thought that she could convert to Protestantism, were she to marry me. I proposed to her.

"I like you, too, Pastor, but...." Her voice trailed off.

"So? What more can there be?" I asked impatiently.

She replied, "I have a condition that I'm not sure you can meet."

"A condition? Tell me what it is. A man should make every effort to satisfy a woman's desires, if he wants to marry her."

"My family is Catholic. If we were to marry, you would have to convert."

I gazed at her in silence. "Do you know what you're saying? You're saying that I should convert to Catholicism? Do you think I'm that anxious to get married? You'd have better luck asking Cardinal Kim Soo-hwan to become a Presbyterian."

I was speechless. She put her head down and said through her tears. "I thought you would agree, if your love for me was sincere."

By that time, I had decided that the conversation was going nowhere. I rose to my feet. "Love may count first for women," I explained. "For men, however, work, honor, and belief in their way of life precede love. I cannot change how I live my life, just to get married."

She was intelligent and good-natured, but her demand was not acceptable. I recalled one time having tried to hold her hand during a date and her unexpected reaction. I apparently startled her and she stiffened. Shuddering, she exclaimed, "Oh, Mary, Mother of God." I released her hand saying, "How can you call out to Mary at a moment like this?"

It was her innocence that had prompted me to propose to her. I had the impression that I would be able to remain true to my soul, if I were married to her, but converting to Catholicism would have been too high a price to pay.

THIS EXPERIENCE IMPRESSED UPON ME that my attitude toward marriage was overly sentimental and I needed to take a more practical approach.

Sitting in the prayer room at Hwalbin Church, I pondered marriage. The realization came to me that my future spouse should be sent by God in response to my prayer. Any rush on my part to find a wife would end in failure.

I set aside a few days to think about marriage. In my solitude, I read the Bible and prayed quietly. Out of this experience emerged the memory of the woman who had come to me while I was on a fast, praying, because of the cow business. It was she who suggested that I read the Bible.

She worked at the Korean Association of Presbyterian Women, where I went to see her. On my way there, I developed a toothache. The pain became worse as time passed, to the point that by the time I started talking to her in a coffee shop I had taken her to, I could hardly bear it.

Seeing me grimace, she asked, "Are you OK, Pastor?"

"No, I'm not. I'm sorry, I have a terrible toothache."

"You should see a dentist. You don't have to put up with pain."

"I know where I should go, but it started only after I left the house this morning and I didn't bring any money."

"If that's all it is, I'll lend you enough to go to the dentist. You can pay me back later."

"Thank you. I promise, I'll pay you back."

This is how our relationship began, with me borrowing money from her. Even now, after more than two decades of marriage, she makes a joke of it, because I have yet to pay her back.

I proposed to her after we met three times. I said, "Miss Kang, I would like to ask you to marry me and have set January 17 as our wedding date. You will accept, won't you?"

She hesitated, "I don't know if I will, but I'm not happy about your already having set a date. Couldn't you at least have waited until I decide whether I want to marry you?"

"I can understand that. How long do I have to wait?"

"I have to pray. I will let you know as soon as I have an answer."

What can a pastor say to having to wait until a response comes from prayer? There was no point in arguing. Two days later she responded. She said that she wanted us to go to the Daihan Christian Prayer Hill to pray together. I agreed and we set a time and date for visiting the retreat house.

Three days before we were to visit the retreat house, I was arrested. Some farmers in Anseong had charged me with fraud in connection with the cow business.

Without so much as an explanation, police from Anseong came to the Korea Christian Building in Seoul, where I had gone for a visit, and took me away in handcuffs. Right in front of the church people, I was put into the police car and taken away.

I had gotten by so far, but now I was afraid I had encountered an insurmountable barrier. After two days in jail, however, I was released. The prosecutor had dropped the charges against me because they determined there was insufficient cause to hold me.

Upon being released, I went straight to the bus terminal in Majang-dong, where I was supposed to meet Miss Kang to go to the retreat house. I arrived only five minutes before the bus was to leave.

My wife tells the following version of the story. She had been praying because she could not decide whether to marry me. She decided that she would marry me if we could go together on a prayer fast at the Daihan Christian Prayer Hill. She would give up on the marriage, however, if something happened to prevent us from going. With this in mind, she was waiting for me at the bus terminal. Because at five minutes before the bus was to depart I had still not shown up, she was thinking that it was not God's will for us to marry. When I arrived, short of breath, she says she was relieved.

We went straight to the retreat house. There we offered prayers and went on a three-day fast, after which we agreed to marry. She also agreed to the January 17 wedding date, but money remained a problem. I still had none. For the wedding, I managed only to buy her a pair of shoes, at a cost of 20,000 *won*. I felt sorry for myself. Speaking to her in front of her mother, I said, "Your husband-to-be has a great personality and good health to make up for the lack of wedding presents for you and your family."

Her mother took this remark as a joke and was disappointed when it turned out to be true. There was nothing I could do about it. I had no money, no job, and no prospects. I could not even get around, because I could not afford bus fare.

JANUARY 17, 1980, WAS A BITTERLY COLD DAY. Seosomun Church, where the wedding was taking place, was full of well-wishers in the main hall and creditors on the lower level. The air on the lower level was filled with smoke because of the many chain smokers. They did not care that the building was a place of worship.

At one point, there was a telephone call. The caller asked, "Is this where that so-called pastor, Kim Jin-hong, is getting married?"

My future mother-in-law had answered the phone, only to hear a barrage of invective. "How could that fraud dare have a wedding ceremony in a holy place? We won't let it happen. We're on our way over."

It was fortunate that it was she who had answered the phone. Had it been anyone else, they might have panicked. My mother-in-law turned pale, but soon calmed her pounding heart. She told my wife-to-be, who then came to find me, worried about the situation. "I'd like to know what kind of people are going to show up," she said.

"Please don't worry. Nothing's going to happen. I've done nothing to provoke anyone to interfere with our wedding," I said, trying to put her mind at ease.

She was relieved to see that I was taking it so calmly. The real nuisance, however, was not the phone call, but the creditors on the lower level, who thought I was marrying into money. They threatened to disrupt the wedding, if they were not going to be paid. This made me uncomfortable, but I decided to be brave and hold my chin up.

As it turned out, they did not interrupt the ceremony, although they did take all the money that guests had brought as gifts, which left us with no money for our honeymoon.

For our first night, I had reserved a room at a hotel in Seoul, over-looking the Han River. Upon arriving and looking around the big hotel room, my wife asked, "Why did you reserve such a big room?"

"I thought we'd need a big room because I've invited some people to join us later," I answered.

That night, a group of a dozen or so creditors came by. They sat around the room. One of them asked my wife, "Why would you want to marry a penniless bum like Pastor Kim here? It's not too late to put your shoes back on and leave."

My wife was not one to tolerate this kind of insult. She shot back.

"It's none of your business whether I put my shoes on or not. I do with my shoes as I choose."

"You're really something. You two make a good pair," he jeered. Other creditors joined him.

Our wedding day.

"I can read in her face that their fortunes will turn for the better after she turns forty," one said cynically.

"Then we don't need to worry about our money."

Indulging in this banter, they ordered from room service expensive dishes and drinks, signed my name to the tab, downed everything, and left.

The next morning my wife called one of her friends and asked to borrow enough money to pay the hotel bill.

LATER, MY WIFE CAME TO NAMYANG BAY. She brought a wardrobe, a kitchen cabinet, a television set, and some other furniture aboard a 2.5-ton truck. I had hired someone to renovate our quarters, but they had not yet finished. There was no light, no door, and no bathroom. My mother-in-law did not like the idea of her daughter living under those conditions. After looking around, she left without comment.

Darkness set in while we were moving in and arranging the furniture. We hung a blanket over the doorway and lit a candle. I was getting ready to sleep when the wife asked, "Where's the bathroom?"

I was too ashamed to tell her that there was none, so I took a flashlight and told her, "I'll take you to it."

She followed me, unaware of what was about to happen. We went out and I walked her to a big chestnut tree on the edge of the yard.

"Do your stuff, while I watch out," I said.

"Do my stuff?" she asked, exasperated.

"Yes. You told me that you would like to go to the bathroom. For now, this is the bathroom."

"Here?"

"The bathroom isn't quite ready yet."

"Oh, my goodness! In this open place?"

"Why not? Just imagine that this is a bathroom in an open place." She hesitated, but soon realized she had no alternative. We went back to the house. Later, she went to sleep without having said a word all evening.

Married life proved difficult for her at first. The church was in a shambles because of the fiasco over the cattle and we had no money. Sometimes I earned a little, doing one thing or another, but it was of no help because it all went to pay debts.

Failing to come up with anything else, my wife lectured part time at a college and we survived on her small income. She worked hard and without complaint. I felt sorry for her and was grateful for her effort and forbearance.

Some months later, she became pregnant. At term, when she went into labor, I had her admitted to the Min Obstetrics and Gynecology

Clinic in Seoul. We chose the Min because we had a doctor acquaintance there.

My wife experienced so much pain from the complications of labor that she had to have a caesarian section. She gave birth to a baby boy. They both came through it in good condition.

Since our wedding, we had saved 10,000 *won* every month to pay maternity expenses. By the time the baby was born, we had accumulated 150,000 *won*. That was nowhere near enough to cover the clinic bill, which came to 1.15 million *won*.

Visiting the head of the clinic, I put on a brave face and begged him. "Sir, I thank you for helping us to have a healthy son. I'm ashamed to say this, but I have no choice. I'm a practicing minister in a small rural church. I do not have enough money to pay the bill. We've saved for months for this, but have saved only 150,000 *won*. My wife had a caesarian delivery and the bill comes to 1.15 million *won*. I'm sorry to have to ask, but I would very much appreciate it if the hospital could discount the bill."

Watching me stammer in shame, the clinic head thought for a moment and replied that he could reduce the bill by 400,000 *won*, leaving a balance of 750,000. I realized that the 400,000 *won* was a big concession on his part, but I could not appreciate it because the difference between what they required and what I had remained so great. Leaving his office, I told him, "Thank you. I'll come back and get my wife, as soon as I can get the money together."

I went back to the ward to see my wife.

"Dear, you'll be able to leave the hospital today, but first I have to go out and make some arrangements. In the meantime, please prepare to check out."

"Make arrangements?" she asked. She knew what I meant by making arrangements. "Will you come back soon?" she asked, looking down.

I was not sure, but I did not want to let her down. I said, "Yes, of course. I'll be back straightaway. Pack your things and be ready."

I left the clinic, but there was no one in all of Seoul from whom I could borrow that kind of money. Walking around downtown, I tried to think of people I might ask. In my head, I made a list of possible sources, prioritizing who to visit and in what order. I made the rounds, one by one, visiting people and asking for a loan of 600,000 *won*, but to no avail.

I was not good at borrowing money. I managed to get people to meet me at a coffee shop, but when it came time for me to ask for a loan, I found myself beating around the bush, unable to get up the courage. In some cases, I even wound up paying for the coffee.

On the few occasions when I mustered the courage and brought up the subject of money, I was turned down flat.

I did not regret having become a pastor, but after meeting seven people, with no success, I pitied myself. Here I was, at the age of forty, having a child, and wandering about the city trying to borrow enough money to get my wife out of the clinic.

I had only a few friends in Seoul who I could ask for money, so I had to turn to classmates I did not know well. I felt awful about going to them. The terrible feeling was compounded when I saw the expression on their faces. They were saying, "Kim Jin-hong, you were once the campus rising star, but now you've proven to be just like everyone else, coming around asking for money."

I had no choice but to endure the humiliation, thinking of my wife back at the clinic holding our son in her arms. She was waiting for me to return, having packed her belongings to leave. It was when I was on my way to visit the eighth person that from deep within my heart I felt a surge of emotion, telling me not to give up.

OK, I'll see how many more visits I have to make to come up with what I need, I thought. God must want me to learn something from this experience. He must have something in mind, making me wander around the city like this to borrow 600,000 *won*.

I thought positively. How lucky I was to have places to go for help. Think about other pastors, living in remote locations, who have no one to go to. How would they handle this situation? How sad and alienated they would feel. I became convinced that God had sent me this trial to make me understand that, in the future, I should help them.

These thoughts made me realize that my situation could be worse. My spirit was renewed and the self-pity left me. After thirteen visits, I had come up with 650,000 *won*.

It was after six o'clock when I finally returned to the clinic. My wife, who had packed her things early and had waited all day, welcomed me warmly.

"I was worried that you might have had an accident."

"No, not at all. There were some places I had to go."

"You don't need to explain. I know."

I paid the clinic its 750,000 *won* and we took a cab to Namyang Bay. We named our son Min-hyeok.

That was an experience I would never forget. Nine years later, I put my resolution into action, when I started helping pastors from rural churches.

ONE MORNING IN NOVEMBER 1989 I came across a notice in a church community newspaper announcing a seminar for full-time Christian workers. The qualifications for attendees caught my attention. Attendance was reserved for ministers of churches whose membership was greater than 1,000. The venue was a posh hotel in Gangnam, an upscale section in Seoul, and a well-known American pastor was the featured speaker. Participants were supposed to go on a group tour of holy places across the world. The registration fee was the equivalent of one year's pay for a pastor working in a rural community.

"They exclude participation of pastors working in churches of fewer than 1,000 members. They scorn people from small churches," I grumbled to myself.

Then I had an idea. I would hold an event for full-time Christian workers serving in small churches in rural areas and on islands, whose membership totaled fewer than fifty. Instead of a tour of holy places across the world, we would take a tour of the Doorae Community in Namyang Bay.

I became excited about the idea and got to work on it right away. While planning the event, deciding the theme, explaining its purpose, and preparing leaflets, my thinking evolved and I came up with another idea. It concerned the wives of Christian workers.

Pastors gain respect because of their service to the church, but their wives' hard work is barely acknowledged. They are excluded, toiling under the combined disadvantage of a hard life and a lack of recognition.

Families of Christian workers in small churches must be more mindful of their behavior than families of Christian workers in large, anonymous settings, because their behavior comes under closer scrutiny and they are, therefore, rightly or wrongly, held to a higher standard by church members.

Korean churchgoers are no different from anyone else. When they get together, they like to talk about other people. The problem is that they usually talk about other people's negative traits rather than their positive ones. The less sophisticated the population, the more socially conservative they are.

In the rural environment, family members of Christian workers often come in for criticism. The effect of this pressure is evident in the life expectancy of pastors' wives. While, on average, in Korea, women live longer than men, in families of Christian workers it is the opposite, the chances of pastors' wives dying before their husbands being higher than for their counterparts in other households. I suspect that pressure from church members contributes to their early death.

MY WIFE LIKEWISE SUFFERED from this community pressure. She is full of vigor and outspoken, but by no means overbearing. Once some women church members came to tell me, "This is difficult to say, Pastor, but your wife is out of line. Her behavior is often unbecoming of a pastor's wife. We are telling you this to let you know that it would be wise of you to restrain her."

I felt uncomfortable relaying this message to my wife. I told her, "Dear, I have been told that you have overstepped the boundary of proper decorum."

"Excuse me? I have overstepped my boundary, have I? And who says so?"

"That's not important. The fact that people have said it can only harm both you and the church."

"This is how I am. How can I change?"

"As the wife of a pastor, you have to try to restrain yourself. If you insist upon doing things your way, it'll hurt the church."

She sulked at my cautioning her, but after that she kept silent at church meetings. This behavior, however, gave rise to still another complaint.

"The pastor's wife has become arrogant these days. She said nothing to us the other day when we were with her, as if she's ignoring us. She acts as if she's too good for us."

My wife liked dressing up by wearing makeup and earrings. I liked her caring about her appearance, so I would buy cosmetics and accessories for her occasionally when I traveled.

Church members faulted her for her appearance and expressed disapproval. They thought it was not appropriate for a pastor's wife. I heard this from people on several occasions and told her about it.

"Dear, people say that you like expensive items. Perhaps you should wear more modest clothes. It does no good for you to make yourself the object of that kind of talk."

"I don't understand. I have no expensive clothes. The ones I have just look good on me. I bought these clothes at a discount at Dongdaemun Market. How could they think they are expensive?"

I could tell that she thought the comments about her appearance were unfair. Still, she could not ignore the criticism and attended services for a number of weeks wearing more modest clothes. Then people started to complain that she looked like a servant.

One person commented, "It doesn't look good that our pastor's wife dresses like a servant. The other day a visitor to our church sat right next to her, but he didn't know she was the pastor's wife."

I realized belatedly that if I kept listening to criticism from the congregation, and that if she tried to please everyone, she would become a mental case. I decided that I needed to give her a hand.

I told her, "I see now that you are often the subject of gossip. Please pay no attention to what anyone says. I've learned that they don't make sense. One day they say that your clothes are too expensive. The next day they say you dress like a servant. One day they say you are overstepping your boundary and the next they say that you are arrogant and aloof. Do as you like and ignore everything they say about you."

"Do you think that'd be OK? That's great, but I can't do it without your support."

"Of course, I'll support you. I promise."

After this conversation, my wife became herself again and regained her enthusiasm for her work. It was no surprise to me, then, when a church member approached me one day saying, "You need to talk to your wife, Pastor. People are complaining."

I had been waiting for just this opportunity and rebuked him.

"I don't want to hear any more complaints about my wife. It's enough to turn a normal person into a complete idiot. I know from my experience of living with her that she is a sensible woman. She is none of your concern."

He was caught off guard by my strong reply.

"What's wrong with you? You don't sound like yourself."

"I don't care whether I sound like myself or not, " I continued. "If I listen to what you and others have to say, it'll drive her insane. Please, leave her alone, as long as she does nothing outrageous."

My siding with my wife had an immediate effect. After that, no one complained about her again.

A PASTOR'S WIFE IS NOT THE ONLY ONE who suffers from community pressure. The same applies to children. My second son, Ae-min, is a laid-back, good-tempered boy. It's rare that he gets into fights, but one day he came home crying. He was in the third grade. I scolded him because I did not like to see him being overly emotional.

"Why are you carrying on like a baby? You're a man. If you get in a fight, you should fight to the end, win or lose. It's not manly to weep."

"I'm not crying because I lost."

"Then why are you crying?"

Hearing what had happened, my heart went out to him. On his way home from school, he got into a fight with one of his classmates. A member of Hwalbin Church recognized my son and said, "Why are you fighting? You're the pastor's son, aren't you? A pastor's son should be better behaved."

My son was distracted by her scolding, which caused him to lose. He was crying not because he had been beaten, but because he was frustrated, since as the pastor's son, he was told he couldn't fight back.

Feeling sorry for him, I told him, "She was wrong. Pay no attention to that kind of talk. If you run into someone who tells you that when you're in a fight, tell them, 'My father is the pastor, not me. Do you think I chose to be a pastor's son?' Now, go back and find the guy who beat you up and knock him down. Never let anyone talk to you like that. Do you understand?"

He seemed consoled by my words and stopped crying.

"I'm OK, but I don't think I'm going to go knock him down. He's one of my best friends," he replied.

HAVING IN MIND THE DIFFICULTIES that pastors' families experience, I changed my plan from holding a get-together for church workers to holding a get-together for pastors' wives.

I announced the program, limiting participation to wives of pastors whose churches were located in rural and fishing communities and had fewer than fifty members. The maximum number of participants I thought I could accommodate was 150. I received 800 applications. Of the 800 applicants, I invited the 200 poorest applicants.

At around 7 a.m. early, the morning of the event, I received a phone call from a pastor's wife in a distant rural community.

"Pastor Kim, I have packed my things to participate in your program."

"Wonderful? Where are you calling from?"

"We are at a church in a rural area at the foot of Mount Jiri in South Jeolla province."

"You'd better leave quickly. You're already late, even if you leave right away."

"I know I have to leave now, but I haven't been able to because I don't have money for the fare."

"Please, don't worry about the fare. We cover fares for participants by selling eggs and cabbage. If you don't have fare to get you here, borrow it from somewhere."

"It's not easy to borrow money from people in a backwater like this."

"Ask anyone in your area. Tell them you'll pay them back in a few days. I can't imagine that you can find no one anywhere to lend you money."

"Do you really think it's that easy, Pastor? That may be how it is where you live, but not here."

"I'm sorry. What do you mean? I don't understand."

"I suppose it's difficult to understand people like us who are working at the bottom. Last week eight people came to our service and we collected 110 *won* in contributions. Who is going to lend money to a pastor's wife whose church has only eight members and collects only 110 *won*. You shouldn't take this so lightly."

I was at a loss for words, listening to her. I took on a kinder tone and told her.

"I was wrong. What is your address and where is the nearest post office? I'll send the money to your post office. You can pick it up there. I won't let you down."

I sent the money to the address she gave me. She managed to arrive, but not until we were nearly finished.

THE PROPGRAM WAS HELD IN THE SECOND WEEK of January 1990. I delivered an opening speech.

"Welcome, Ladies, to the Doorae Community. You are spouses of pastors serving in churches located in the most remote villages and on the most distant and inhospitable islands in Korea. I will go straight to the point. During the program, please don't worry too much about religion. Relax and consider this an opportunity to take a break.

"As far as blessing is concerned, you have been blessed enough. Who else could devote their lives to working in remote locations, as you have, unless they had experienced sufferings and made their confessions? You have all had your own spiritual experiences. During this get-together, you deserve to have a good rest. To help you rest, we are not going to hold an early morning service. You can sleep in. In the mornings, get together and chat about whatever you like. You can complain about your husbands or disparage the leaders of your congregations who get on your nerves. By doing this you will be released from your grudges and the animosity that has built up in your hearts over the years."

My speech prompted a burst of applause from participants, and they chanted, "Amen-amen-amen." Their morale rose immediately and their faces lit up.

The program proved a success beyond anyone's expectation, although there were times I could not continue, so overwhelmed was I by their emotion. One woman sitting in the front row, especially, cried harder than the others.

On the last day, during recess, I asked her, "Is crying your gift from God?"

"I'm sorry, Pastor," she replied.

"You don't need to be sorry, but you cry so hard. Is it usual for you to cry so hard?"

"No, it's not. Strangely enough, since coming to the Doorae

Community, I have not been able to hold back my tears. I can't help myself."

"Where do you live and what do you and your husband do?"

"Nine years ago my husband quit his job as a government employee to become a pastor. He swore to God that he would live a life as His servant, wherever his service was needed, and we settled down on the island where we now work. The island is in the far southwest, a two-hour journey from Mokpo by ferry. This is the first time in nine years that I've been off the island. When I reached the mainland, I put on the shoes that I had worn nine years before on my way to the island and that since then had sat in the closet. Your story about your hard times was amazingly similar to our experience. That made it hard for me to stop crying. I kept telling myself not to cry, but, simply by looking at you, I begin to cry. Sometimes I close my eyes, so as not to see your face, but then your voice makes me cry."

The woman's face was stained with tears, even while she spoke.

"Wonderful. Our Lord will be glad to find both of you committed to His work. You believe that Jesus is happy with both of you, do you not?"

"I do, indeed. That's why my husband and I work so hard. We are determined to live, work, and die on the island, and have already picked out a site there for our burial."

What she said brought home to me that these people's hard work was the foundation of the Korean church. It is not grand churches towering here and there in the center of Seoul that serve as beacons to guide lost souls to Jesus. It is these unknown people, serving in distant churches on remote islands, who are the foundation of the church. It was God's blessing that Doorae was given an opportunity to hold this event for them.

THE FIRST PROGRAM FOR WIVES OF PASTORS in rural and fishing communities ended with a big feast. The feast, however, which was supposed to cheer up the participants, turned into another weeping session. It started with a few people who became emotional, talking about their religious experiences. Their emotion was contagious, and a woman who had come from a remote area in the mountainous Gangwon province became the detonator.

She came forward to the front row, removed a gold necklace she was wearing, and hung it around my wife's neck.

"I want you to have this," she said. "I had thought that my husband was strange. He set up a church in one area and then moved to another, handing over the helm of the church to another pastor when it became established. When the new church overcame all of its difficulties and became established, he moved to still another area. He repeated this many times, while our family suffered from every move.

"I managed to make a life for us, but often gave serious thought to divorce. Listening to the experiences of other people here, however, I realize that I'm not the only one who has suffered like this. I see that many of you have survived far more difficult times than I have had to put up with, and you never allowed yourselves to succumb to your hardship. It dawned on me that Pastor Kim owes his wife a lot, for what he has done.

"This necklace is the last of my wedding presents, all of which we have sold off, one after another, when we needed money. I give it to Pastor Kim's wife, as a token of my gratitude for the blessings I have received during the program. I swear that when I go back, I will serve our church without complaining."

She fought back her tears while putting the necklace around my wife's neck. It was then that the whole room burst into tears.

We have held this event every year since, and always with great success.

29

The Doorae Community

IN 1974, WHEN I WAS IN PRISON, I thought about establishing a communal settlement. At the time, six other inmates and I were living in a cell that measured only 60 square feet. With time, a communal spirit developed in the cell and people who had been antagonistic toward one another became more considerate. This attitude of cooperation and sacrifice enabled us to make the most of limited space, benefiting everyone.

With the new spirit of cooperation, men who previously had talked only about crime started to exchange concerns about their families and their future, talking about their intent to reform their lives upon release and live like proper citizens. Their personalities changed, and eventually they were able to pray and study the Bible together. A spirit of community took root.

My experiment in communal living in prison was based on a fellowship of believers described in the Book of Acts, where it states:

> They devoted themselves to the apostles' teaching and to the fellowship, to the breaking of bread and to prayer.... All the believers were together and had everything in common. Selling their possessions and goods, they gave to anyone as he had need. (Acts 2:42-45)

From this, I determined that I would someday build a community embodying this principle. I gave the community the name "Doorae,"

451

which has a historical background in Korea and means "sharing in a communal-living environment."

As one example, in the old days in Korea, there was a well in every village that belonged to no single person and that everyone shared. At each well was a gourd that people used to draw water. It was known as a "doorae" gourd. I adopted the name and, thus, as an outcome of my prison experience, the Doorae Community was born.

Upon being released from prison, I returned to the Cheonggyecheon slum. A few months later, the government issued an order to raze all of the makeshift houses and close it down. After exhausting all efforts to prevent it, we resigned ourselves to the reality that we were going to lose our homes and would have to reestablish ourselves elsewhere.

People from the slum area and I made an exodus to the reclaimed land of Namyang Bay. In moving to the bay area, I envisioned building the communal settlement that I had pondered during my time in prison.

I applied to the government for land, expressing my intention, but they were strongly opposed to the idea, claiming that it was inspired by communist ideology. They reasoned that my plan could be labeled communist because the concept was akin to North Korea's collective farms. Consequently in the early stages of moving to the bay, I had to put my plan on hold.

It took three years to develop a viable village, after transforming the mud belt of the sea into rice paddies. Once the farm project had taken hold, I turned my efforts to building the community.

ON OCTOBER 3, 1978, HWALBIN CHURCH adopted a draft for founding the Doorae Community. It proposed to establish a community with twenty households on a 50-acre parcel. In April 1979, the first Doorae Community started with eight households.

There were five problems that at the time defined the structure of Korean farming and farm living conditions. Those five were responsible for stagnating Korea's agricultural sector and for making the life of a farmer difficult.

First, the land held by one farm was too little. An average Korean farm had only two acres of land. A village could not prosper with holdings of that size, no matter how hard farmers worked. Additionally, of course, a certain percentage of the land on a farm was not arable. The future of Korean agricultural industry and farmers boiled down to how to overcome the limitations of both farm size and fragmentation.

Second, farmers suffered from a chronic shortage of capital. The accumulated debts of Korean farmers had grown with time and changes of governments. The government once discussed the possibility of writing off farmers' debts, but that was not a solution, as long as structural problems remained.

Third, Korean farming still focused on rice cultivation. That resulted in a waste of labor during the slack season and limited sources of income. It allowed farmers to work only four or five months out of the year, forcing them into idleness for the rest of year.

Fourth, a series of government policies emphasizing national industrialization had left farmers alienated with no effective policy to help them. One of the most damaging policies for farmers was that there was no price guarantee for agricultural products. Farmers often found themselves stuck with their goods because they could not sell them at high enough prices, and often could not sell them at any price.

Fifth, the lack of culture in rural society posed a serious problem. Culture is a mental element that enriches people's lives and makes them worthwhile. That there was no culture in rural society had made farmers feel as though they were leading meaningless and empty lives. That prompted youth in rural areas to abandon the countryside and head for urban centers.

Hwalbin Church started the Doorae Community in an effort to find alternatives to these problems. I wanted to form a communal settlement, where land, finances, labor, and skills were centrally managed. This approach would correct weaknesses in the Korean agricultural sector and help farmers overcome their difficulties. Furthermore, it would provide farmers with a culture model and give them hope.

We announced our plan to build the Doorae Community and asked for applications from people who wanted to take part in the project. We put out a prospectus with a detailed plan, based on words from 1 Peter:

> ...in your hearts set apart Christ as Lord. Always be prepared to give an answer to everyone who asks you to give

the reason for the hope that you have. But do this with
gentleness and respect. (1 Peter 3:15)

This verse served as the foundation for the project. We set up three
guiding principles for the community:

First, Jesus Christ is the head of the Doorae Community.
Second, there is only one law in the Doorae Community,
    the law of love.
Third, work within one's ability and spend as necessary.

The first principle is testament that the Doorae Community is a
communal society based on Christianity. Christians become Christians
by accepting Jesus as their savior and by confessing it. Those who do
not accept and acknowledge it are not Christians. How a person's life is
shaped depends on who he considers his Lord and how he lives, based
on that belief.

The Doorae Community is a settlement of people who serve Jesus.
Thus, it is a community of Jesus Christ. It is a community of truth because members rely on Jesus' teachings for direction in their lives. It is a
missionary community because the people spread Jesus' teachings to
the world. The Doorae future depends on how sincerely members believe in Jesus, how faithfully they practice His teachings, and how far
afield they carry His Word.

The second principle implies that the more laws there are to keep,
the greater the hostility in a society. In the Garden of Eden, there was
only one law. In the desert, where Moses led the Israelites, there were
only the Ten Commandments. In our society, however, there is a multi-
tude of laws. We live in a state of legal pollution. In Doorae, members
are expected to live up to only the law of love, decreed by God.

The Doorae Community was founded on the spirit of owning nothing, so there could be no dispute as to whom an asset belonged. Nor could
there be any dispute to decide who was the leader because Jesus was
the head of the community. There could be no disparity because the community was established on the principle of helping the weak. There could
be no cheating because the community was set up by people who had
resolved to be honest. Even when someone pocketed someone else's

money, he or she was not to be condemned for thievery. The money was only moved from one place to another, and it did not matter where the money was because it belonged to all.

Whoever becomes a member of the Doorae Community should discard his or her claim of ownership, break free from desire for fame, and become selfless by throwing off selfish attitudes.

People today are exhausted both physically and mentally. Jesus' way of life should be taught so people learn gentleness and humility. In this, they can find serenity. The vision of the Doorae Community was to build a society reflecting these values. We read the following in Matthew:

> Come to me, all you who are weary and burdened, and I will give you rest. Take my yoke upon you and learn from me, for I am gentle and humble in heart, and you will find rest for your souls. For my yoke is easy and my burden is light. (Matthew 11:28-30)

Anyone joining the Doorae Community should read these words to say:

> Come to the Doorae Community, all who labor and carry a heavy burden, and Jesus, who is the owner of the community, will give you rest. Take Jesus' yoke upon you and learn from Jesus, for He is gentle and humble in heart, and you will find rest for your soul. For Jesus' yoke is easy and His burden is light.

The third principle is rooted in teachings in Acts about assets, labor, fellowship, and brotherly love. On Pentecost, the Holy Spirit descended upon the people who had gathered. On that day, the church as a community of the Holy Spirit, was born. With the beginning of the church, communal living followed:

> First, members in the community were in fellowship with one another, based on the apostles' teachings.
> Second, the community endeavored to pursue religious

lives and confessions by having communion services and
praying together.

Third, assets were shared and used for one another's needs.

Fourth, members gathered with hearts united, lived, and
prayed together. Their daily lives were intertwined.

Fifth, the community sought to add to its number daily
newly saved souls.

Times have changed and so have society's values. It is unrealistic
and undesirable to try to mold a community after the way things were in
the early days of the church. What should be kept, however, are the spirit and principles of living that the early church community espoused. The
church, which began in the form of holy settlements two thousand years
ago, has lost much of its original communal spirit and its ability to
serve as a model for people's lives. The Doorae Community started with
an objective to revive the spirit of such a way of life and to recover the
church's original integrity and passion.

In the Doorae Community, all assets, labor, ability, and talents
were supposed to be shared by everyone, and everyone was to be devoted to Jesus. There was to be no discrimination between the able and the
less able, the educated and the less educated, the powerful and the less
powerful, and the healthy and the less healthy. All were expected to live
as devout members of the community, sharing Jesus' love. Those who
were able to work were to do as much as their ability allowed them.
Those who were in need were to have whatever they required.

ON APRIL 1, 1979, WHEN THE FIRST DOORAE COMMUNITY was initiated,
along with abovementioned guiding principles, it aspired to four
qualities:

The Doorae Community is a community of joy.
The Doorae Community is a community of faith.
The Doorae Community is a community of service.
The Doorae Community is a community of cooperation.

The Doorae Community is a community established by Christ's
disciples. Who are the disciples of Christ? They are people who follow

in the footsteps of Jesus. What, then, was the path that Jesus trod? A path that leads to truth and happiness.

The way of life represented by Jesus urges us to lead a humane existence. Because His is the most humane way, it leads to genuine happiness. A happy life is one believing in Jesus.

It should be easy and joyous to believe in Jesus. If believing in Jesus makes a person feel unhappy, he or she does not truly believe. No matter how difficult their environment and life are, people who are imbued with the Holy Spirit find happiness by following Jesus.

Some religious people say that although they do not have a happy life in this world, they will find happiness in the next. They are mistaken, because the happiness that they cannot find on earth is not to be found in heaven, either. Our goal is to bring those people together and to undertake endeavors to create a community of joy.

Happiness comes from believing. Believing is the catalyst that makes a joyous life possible. Believing in Jesus and His Word and believing in men, for whom His love was so great that He died for them, is the foundation for happiness. We often think that we do not need to believe in man, as long as we believe in Jesus, but that is not the Bible's message. The person who believes in Jesus should reach out to man. Happiness is to be found by believing in both Jesus and man.

What, then, is believing? Believing is serving. People misunderstand what serving and believing truly mean. They think that those who are served should be happy. On the contrary, Jesus' teaching is that it is those who serve who are blessed.

It is difficult for a single person, working alone, to serve both Jesus and man. It requires fellowship. A life of service is achieved through collaboration, through which faith grows. In faith, we can achieve a life of happiness.

THE DOORAE COMMUNITY WAS ON THE ROAD to achieving this goal, but the way was not without its obstacles. Although members of the founding families were all Christians and were enthusiastic about the new way of life, that did not guarantee success. As it turned out, when they got together, every imaginable conflict arose.

In one incident, fish garnished with radish was served at lunch. Doorae families sat down at the table and began to eat. A mother from

Jeolla province moved the serving plate closer to her son, saying that he liked it very much.

A woman from Gyeongsang province furiously disapproved of this and moved the dish closer to her son. "What are you doing? My son also likes fish," she protested, rolling up her sleeves.

The woman from Jeolla fought back. "Come on. Your son always gets more. Today it's my son's turn."

"What? You sneaky woman. Is there some rule that I don't know about that decides who gets ginseng and who gets cabbage?"

This tug-of-war over the fish caused the bowl to overturn, strewing the table with pieces of radish and fish. Looking on while this was happening, the men observed, "Women are making a mess of things. They should be left out altogether. It was a mistake for God to have created woman in the first place."

Saying this, the men expressed their concern about the future of the community. Some months later, however, a fight over finances broke out among the men. The women's squabble paled by comparison. The men's fight was of a magnitude to pull at the very roots of the community.

Throughout all this, Doorae families worked as best they could to achieve their goals. They broke ground to build houses, dug wells, and raised chickens in coops they had set up. They grew vegetables and raised pigs. They worked hard, day and night, determined to build a happy and prosperous community.

We hit a snag in that we had difficulty finding markets for our products. Products without markets became a source of concern, leaving professional middlemen as the only alternative. Not surprisingly, they always put their interest ahead of ours.

At the time, prices of agricultural products were unpredictable and subject to sharp volatility. The more produce we grew and the more chickens and pigs we raised, the greater our deficit was bound to become. Our situation contrasted with that of the middlemen, whose profits grew apace with our losses. It was unfair that we, raising chickens, suffered losses, while the middlemen selling our chickens, bought land and houses with fortunes made at our expense.

The economic foundation of the community became shaky and families began to lose confidence in it. They blamed one another and arguments broke out all the time. The suggestion was raised at one of the community meetings that the Doorae Community be disbanded.

I was strongly opposed to it. "Folks, we cannot allow that to happen. The road to success is riddled with potholes. Success can be achieved only after navigating past them. The community movement is the only way to breathe life into Korea's agricultural sector. Nobody is willing to take it on because it requires a lot of hard work. The community movement will be successful only when pioneers are ready to make the sacrifices. It was our blessing and good fortune that we set out to achieve something that no one had tried before. Now you want to drop out, less than a year into the project. It's not right. Come on. We'll make it."

I tried hard to persuade them, but they had already lost their enthusiasm. What was worse, however, from my point of view, was that they held a grudge against me and did not trust me.

"Pastor Kim, you lured us into this mess, but you refuse to hold yourself accountable for it."

"Are you saying that I'm responsible?"

"Who do you think I'm referring to?"

"It's not fair."

"Isn't it? We're stuck here, thanks to who? It was you who talked us into coming all the way out here. Except for you, we wouldn't be here. You should feel sorry for us. Don't tell us to do our best to the end. How far away is this end you talk about?"

"I'm not saying that I've done well, but you must have faith and see it through. If you trusted me enough to follow me in the first place, the day will come when you will thank me, once we overcome the difficulties."

My efforts to persuade them got nowhere because they were beyond persuasion. Losing control of himself, one day one of them slapped me across the face. Rubbing my chin, I told him, "Please, continue hitting me, if it makes you feel better, but this is going too far."

"Too far, you say? I feel like tearing you to pieces, but I won't because I still have respect for pastors."

He was shaking with rage. I looked at each person, one by one, standing around me, only to sense that they all harbored hostility toward me. I left without saying anything and walked down to the bay.

Why has this happened? I can say without a moment's hesitation that I have worked hard for them, not for myself. Why do I always end up complicating things?

The next day we held a meeting and decided to disband the community, on the condition that each person should decide for himself whether he would stay or leave. That was in December 1979. The Doorae Community, which was launched only nine months before, ended in failure.

ON THE DAY DOORAE WAS CLOSED, I made entries in my diary with a view to record the reasons for which the community had failed. There were four:

> First, preparations to establish the community had been inadequate. Any project that has a hasty beginning, without proper research, discussion, preparation, and commitment, is destined to fail.
>
> Second, the dive in livestock prices became an important factor. The Doorae Community relied on livestock for its income. A downturn in prices of beef, poultry, and pork all occured at once, leaving the members to suffer losses.
>
> Third, Hwalbin Church, which was supposed to aid the Doorae Community, could not assume its supportive role because it also was riddled with debt, resulting from the failure of the imported cow business, and was struggling to survive. It, too, had been stripped of its will to sustain itself.
>
> Fourth, there was a lack of harmony among the people. The cardinal ideal that the Doorae Community had sought to achieve was a harmonious relationship among people. Nevertheless, personality conflicts prevented the membership from reaching agreement.

These four factors, taken together, constituted a recipe for failure. I made other notes that I could refer to, in the event I ever decided to launch a second Doorae Community:

First, being religious in the church does not necessarily lead to having a communal spirit. Thus, the religiously faithful are not always fit for communal life.

In Korea, the religiously faithful may exhibit any or all of the following characteristics: listening to church workers; observing Sunday services and early morning prayers; tithing; abstaining from smoking and drinking. Anyone who exhibits these attributes is considered religiously devout and an exemplary church member.

When these exemplary church members become involved in community movements, however, they often obstruct progress. When a person is devout, it only means that they serve the church well, follow the order of the church and do what the pastor says.

In establishing the first Doorae Community, I did not take into consideration these behavioral characteristics of churchgoers and brought together people who had a reputation for being devout Christians. The result of my misjudgment was a breakup of the community before the end of its first year.

Second, I learned that people had a natural need and desire for material goods, personal property, and privacy. This lesson brought home to me that whenever I set up another community, privacy for the individual and his family, and the family's own living space, should be guaranteed as much as possible within the principle of maintaining a community spirit. Subsequently, there was a need to prepare a guideline for governing people's public and private lives.

Third, good intentions or principles can end up hurting people unless they are properly managed and directed. An ideal not backed by appropriate management skills runs the risk of doing harm to all.

Fourth, no effort can succeed when it depends upon support from outside. Work should be planned and carried out autonomously, throughout the entire process. Projects that are undertaken with the expectation of support from outside hold the potential for failure when promises are not kept. Any work should begin in the sprit of independence and proceed on a foundation of prayer and hard work. It means that any work a community takes on should not be beyond its capability.

Fifth, when I established a second Doorae Community, I would begin with a few core members who have common interests and develop it step by step.

These were the lessons of the first Doorae Community. Seven

years passed before I would start a second Doorae Community, which I did on April 1, 1986. During the intervening years, I carried out a series of preparations to lay a proper foundation for the second launch.

BEFORE STARTING A SECOND COMMUNITY, I needed to secure land. I prayed to God to help me find it. While praying, I went about looking for land in the Namyang Bay area. I found a place that I thought had potential. It was Mount Bonghwa and overlooked the sea from one of the best locations on the bay.

The place was named after a signal fire (*bonghwa*) station that had been there during the Silla Dynasty. The Silla used signal fires to send warnings to the capital when pirates or enemies, such as Japan or China, invaded. A single fire indicated the appearance of enemy, two its coming ashore, and three its approach. During the day, smoke was used as a signal while at night flame was used. Once raised, the signal was relayed to the capital efficiently and rapidly by a series of stations.

I liked the location of the hill and its historical significance. I prayed that one day I could purchase it, although I had no idea who owned it.

"Lord, please give this land to Hwalbin Church. On this mountain I would like to raise a beacon for Korea's farmers, a beacon of Holy Spirit and hope for impoverished people living in this, our motherland. Please let us become stewards for this mountain."

I prayed for seven years. During that time, the land changed hands several times, but that was of no interest or importance to me. I kept praying. Between prayers, I would go to the mountain and look around, imagining what we could do with it, if it belonged to Hwalbin Church. I pictured in my mind which area would be used for training and which area would house Doorae families.

One day, after years of praying and planning, the owner spotted me walking about on the mountain. Miffed, he asked me, "Why are you sneaking around on my land? Why don't you just say what you want?"

I replied, "I'm just looking at the area for personal reasons. I mean no harm."

"Whatever your reason is, I don't like you on my property."

After that I would go to the mountain only very early in the morning, right after dawn prayers, or late in the evening.

LATER, THE THEN OWNER OF THE MOUNTAIN CAME to see me and said, "Pastor, I would like to sell you the mountain and have you look after it."

"I'm sorry, I don't understand. What do you mean, you would like me to look after it?"

"I need money urgently and have decided to sell the mountain. I have put it up for sale through real-estate agencies, but the only people who are interested in it are speculators from Seoul."

"I appreciate your going to the trouble to come to me, but I wonder why you have."

"Around here, Mount Bongwha is a very special place. I don't want to sell it off to speculators for no reason other than that I need the money. I've come to you to ask whether you would like to purchase it. I figure that were you to take it, you would put the mountain to good use. I can give it to you for a good price. Please consider it."

"Thank you for being so thoughtful. I have been looking at the area for a long time because I like it. Could I ask what price you have in mind?"

"My offer is that you give me now the amount of money I urgently need and pay the rest, over time, at a low interest rate."

It hit me that the man's offer must have been a response to my years of prayer. We agreed on a price of 40 million *won.*

I gathered church workers and campaigned for donations. I managed to collect four million *won,* a tenth of the settlement price, from the campaign. With that, I made a down payment and promised that the rest would be paid the following month.

Thereafter everyone in the church prayed together. Wherever we gathered, we prayed that God would let us come up with the money to pay for the mountain.

In the meantime, I went to every potential source to get a loan. My efforts, however, bore no fruit. The due date for final payment was only three days away, when a deacon came to me after dawn prayer.

"Pastor, we have no hope, do we? It's water under the bridge."

"What are you saying? What water? What bridge?"

"I'm referring to our deposit on the mountain. We have only three days left and no hope of getting the rest of the money. We could have used the deposit for something worthwhile. We put the money in the owner's pocket for nothing."

"Now I see what you're getting at, but we still have three days."

"Yes, only three days. Then it's all over."

"Let's not worry about things ahead of time. Anything can happen. If we start to worry three days from now, we won't be late."

"You seem so unconcerned, you must have something up your sleeve."

"No, I don't have anything up my sleeve. I'm only saying that we started this to do God's work, not as a business. Whether this works or not is in God's hands. You needn't worry about it before anything actually happens."

THAT AFTERNOON, WE HAD A VISITOR. A tall man in his late thirties came round to the church and asked to see me. I received him in my reading room. He introduced himself as a deacon from a church in Philadelphia. He said his name was Park, but refused to tell me more, preferring to remain anonymous. I became curious and asked him, "What has brought you all the way from America?"

"I read your book, *I Will Awaken the Dawn*, and was so impressed by it that I've come to make a donation, hoping to be of help to you in your work," he replied.

Upon hearing his reason for coming, I expressed my thanks to him. Thereupon he proffered a sealed envelope.

"May I open it? I would be embarrassed to find out later that it was empty," I said jokingly.

"You may open it. It's not empty," he assured me, with a smile.

I opened the envelope and took out a check. Seeing the amount of the check, I could not believe my eyes and had to look a second time. The amount was exactly 36 million *won*, the amount that we had been praying hard for two months to come up with.

"This check is for 36 million *won*. How did you know that we have been praying for two months for this exact amount?" I asked.

"Being in the U.S., how could I possibly have known? I came straight to you because that is the amount that I had that I could donate to God."

I was amazed. God had responded to our prayers. I did not know how to express my gratitude.

"Mr. Park, this is unbelievable. Our prayers have been answered

464

through you. I am truly grateful."

Mr. Park, too, was surprised and said, "You needed exactly that amount? It is amazing. I feel blessed, as well."

"You need to join us in a prayer of gratitude. If you don't mind, please come to Hwalbin Church this Sunday and let us pray together at the service, before you return to America."

"Thank you for your invitation, but my schedule requires me to leave tomorrow."

"Ah, but there is something here that you do not understand. You see, I'm in charge of this community. You may come at your will, yes, but you cannot leave without my permission. Therefore, you must set aside your schedule and come to our church to pray with us this Sunday, please."

It was Friday and Mr. Park accepted my invitation. I informed church members that Mr. Park would be coming to the Sunday service. At the service, I asked Mr. Park to stand up and introduce himself to the congregation.

"Folks, our guest today is Deacon Park from Philadelphia, Pennsylvania in the U.S. He has made a donation for our church. Can you imagine how much it is? Exactly 36 million *won*. Our prayers have been answered and now we will be able to complete the transaction for our land.

A deacon in the congregation, who had a reputation for his sense of humor, spoke out. "I wish we had prayed for twice that amount. After we buy the land, we still need to register the deed and dig wells. I wish that God was not so accurate in his accounting and had sent us a little extra." Everyone burst into laughter.

At last, Hwalbin Church could buy Mount Bonghwa and build the second Doorae Community.

COMPLETING THE TRANSACTION FOR THE MOUNTAIN, the first thing we set out to do was remove all the small pine and acacia trees and build lodges for Doorae families. After that, we set up chicken coops, with capacity for 2,000 chickens each, and built facilities for communal living.

Halfway up the mountain was a flat area. It was the site where for seven years I had sat and prayed to get the mountain. Kneeling in the same place, I launched another round of prayer to ask God to help us establish a facility there to educate farmers.

It was not until three years later that we could construct the Education Center for Doorae Community farmers. The building cost us around 700 million *won*, but it was worth it. We have educated farmers and youths in the building ever since. Today it is used as part of the Doorae Nature High School.

After deciding on the location for the Doorae Community at the foot of Mount Bonghwa, we set about to lay the community's foundation. I checked all of the details, one by one, not to repeat the mistakes that I had made with the first one.

For the second Doorae Community, I emphasized, in addition to the principles applied to the first, that the community should help people in difficulty. They would have an obligation to reach out to others who suffered, physically or mentally, or were deprived and alienated from society.

The Doorae Community. On the left is the Education Center. The large building in the center is Hwalbin Church. Above right, a sign in the community carries the reminder, "Always remember that from dust you came and to dust you will return."

The second Doorae Community was founded with the following charter:

CHARTER

"Whatever you did for one of the least of these brothers of mine, you did for me." (Matthew 25:40)

One hundred years have passed since Protestantism was introduced to Korea. A nation suffering and in despair gained hope from stories of people having been saved through Jesus Christ. The Korean church has been called a miracle in the history of Christianity. There is one thing, however, that the Korean church should be ashamed of—lack of love for the unfortunate and its failure to look after the poor, the sick, and the emotionally scarred.

In our society there are many broken souls, deprived of human comfort. Among them are brothers released from prison, sisters eager to break free of wretched and painful lives, the disabled left abandoned, the homeless perishing in the street, and the mentally ill. These souls are mired in wretchedness and are without support.

Jesus Christ, who saved us by His crucifixion, sent these people to us. They are our responsibility. We are all of the same blood and as Christians share a mission. Yet, we have neglected them.

Marking the 15th anniversary of its founding, Hwalbin Church has embarked on the establishment of a community to help these people. It is called the Doorae Community. The word Doorae derives from a Korean tradition of collaboration and sharing in a communal environment. Drawing on both the collaborative religious settlement from the Book of Acts and our nation's ancient spirit of "sharing," our Church has established this community, where the infirm and the abandoned may live in peace.

This job cannot be achieved by one person or a single church. It must be the mission of all Christians. Our Lord has called upon us to do this and will watch over us as we undertake this task.

April 1, 1986

Once organized and productive, the next task the Doorae Community set about to accomplish was the distribution of agricultural products. One of the causes of the failure of the first Doorae Community was the absence of distribution outlets for agricultural products and livestock, which was why it was given priority for the second Doorae Community. My wife and I became responsible for selling the community's products.

Clad in workers' overalls, we would go to Seoul with our products loaded on a one-ton truck. We moved about to sell them in such posh areas as Apgujeong-dong and Daechi-dong. Some churchgoers recognized me and talked among themselves, questioning. "That fellow looks just like Pastor Kim Jin-hong."

"Do you really think so? A lot of people look alike."

"No. His voice is also the same as Pastor Kim's. By any chance, is Pastor Kim your brother?" They would ask.

I answered, "No. I'm the only son through three generations of my family."

Our most strenuous chore was rice delivery. It was hard work delivering a big bag of rice to residents in apartments without an elevator. One time I had to deliver a 175-pound bag of rice to a fifth-floor walk-up. Reaching the third floor, I could go no farther. My vision became blurred under the load and my legs were shaking. In the end, I put the bag down on a landing, filled smaller bags, and carried the rice up one bag at a time.

We were proud of our merchandise, but we had difficulty persuading consumers to buy it because the Doorae Community was not well known. When we said to housewives that we did not use pesticides, they were often skeptical and questioned whether they could trust us.

"You can, indeed," I would reply. "We guarantee our products. If we weren't truthful, it would jeopardize our reputation."

One time, looking me up and down sarcastically, a housewife replied, "You talk about losing your reputation. You don't look like you have much of a reputation to lose."

30

Bless This Calf

I LIKE LIVING AND PRACTICING my ministry among farmers, one reason for which is that they are not tainted by big city ways. One day a farmer and his wife came to see me at one o'clock in the morning. Alarmed, I asked what had brought them around at such a late hour.

"Is something wrong? Are your children OK?"

"We're sorry to bother you so late, Pastor," said the husband. "The kids are fine, but our calf is sick."

"Really? Well, don't you think you should probably be calling on the vet?"

"We were, in fact, going to go see the vet, but changed our minds and came here instead. We trust you more than we trust him."

"I'm flattered that you have so much confidence in me, but I don't know what I can do for you."

"Could you come to our house and lay your hands on our calf to heal it."

"You want me to pray for a sick animal?"

"Yes. We would appreciate it very much."

I did not know how to respond.

"You know, I'm not sure I could cure a person with laying on of hands, much less a calf."

"Please, Pastor. This is no ordinary calf. If it dies, it'll be devastating for us. We came to ask you for help, although we knew you might say it was nonsense."

They were justified in saying that the calf was not ordinary. It was a product of ten years of work and prayers on the part of the couple. It would have broken their hearts, had anything happened to it.

THE HUSBAND HAD TENDED DAIRY CATTLE when he was single. His wife was a kind and down-to-earth woman. Right after their wedding, they agreed to work hard to save money to buy milk calves and start a herd. Raising milk cows was then very profitable, a single cow bringing in about 100,000 *won* per month. It took about two years to raise a calf to maturity.

This couple had nurtured a dream to raise one calf, increase the number to ten, and eventually have a herd. After ten years, they were still working on getting started. Instead of owning a herd of cows, however, they found themselves the parents of four children.

When they were married, a calf cost 450,000 *won*. By the time they had accumulated the 450,000 *won*, the price had risen to 700,000 *won*. They resolved to save the 700,000 *won*, which was a more difficult goal because they now had more mouths to feed. By the time they saved the 700,000 *won*, the price of a calf had risen to 1.2 million *won*.

They then set a new goal of 1.2 million *won*, but were afraid that the price of a calf would go up again.

I had heard the story two months earlier. It moved me so much that I guaranteed a loan of 500,000 *won* for them at the credit union, enabling them to buy a calf.

The couple were so excited that their dream was finally coming true that they prepared rice cakes and treated church members at a Sunday service.

Now their calf was sick and they wanted me to lay my hands on it to heal it. I was at a loss. How could they ask such a thing? Although I was uncomfortable with their request, it was so sincere and was borne of such naive faith that I could not refuse.

I gave up trying to say no and asked myself what choice I had. I should be ready to embrace this kind of thing as part of my missionary work among farmers. I'll go along with what people want, even if it concerns animals.

I told the couple to lead the way. It was nearly 4 miles to their place. The calf was in the barn, covered with a blanket.

The couple signaled me to go ahead with the prayer. I began to pray in a loud voice, closing my eyes and laying my hands on the calf's head.

"Lord Jesus. Please bless this calf. The calf is coughing so hard, it's very sick. If this calf gets pneumonia, the ten years of effort of these good poeple will turn into nothing. God, I, too, guaranteed their payment of a loan to buy the calf. I pray in your name, believing that you are going to restore its health." I finished the prayer saying "amen," which the couple repeated.

Two days later, the wife came to my house with smile as wide as her face. "The calf has recovered, Pastor. It's fine now. Thank you very much. I'll have you back again, the next time something goes wrong."

"Please don't. Are you asking me to become a vet?"

In gratitude, she brought me a bottle of after-shave lotion. A cold is supposed to go away in time, in both man and beast, but this couple was sure that the calf had recovered because of my prayer. They made a donation at the Sunday service the following week, writing on the envelope, "Thank you for helping our calf recover."

I told church members during recess, "Mr. and Mrs. So-and-so fetched me one night last week to lay hands on their sick calf to heal it. Today they conveyed their gratitude for the calf's recovery."

In response to the announcement, there were chants of "amen" from among the people standing around.

After the service, men approached the husband to offer their congratulations. Women held the wife's hands and said, "That's wonderful. We hear that your calf has recovered, thanks to the pastor's prayer. We know how hard you worked for the calf. Nothing should happen to it."

This story of the calf brought happiness to everyone in the church.

IN ADDITION TO THE NATURAL NAIVETE OF RURAL PEOPLE, there are several other reasons for which I like rural life.

First, rural life makes it possible to live honestly and modestly. Land has no pretensions. People's deceptions do not affect it. It produces only what has been sown. I encourage anyone who wants to live an honest life to move to the countryside.

Second is that rural living assures a healthy lifestyle. Physical labor makes people healthy physically and mentally. You can get up early and go to sleep early in the fresh air and have clean water. Your life can be free from want. I tell my sons confidently, "It's better to be a healthy farmer than a professor suffering from a nervous breakdown."

A third reason for liking rural living is that you learn. Rural life is not regimented and presents constant opportunity for learning. The soil, insects, wild flowers, and grass and the whole process of growing crops, from sowing to harvest, you can learn from all these things, if only you pay attention to what is going on around you.

A French elementary-school teacher, Fabre, became a renowned entomologist by recording his observations of insects in his surroundings. The contribution of his work to mankind's store of knowledge was far greater than that of a professor giving lectures at some university.

God has endowed us with intellectual curiosity and has provided us the capacity to think, prompting us to pursue learning throughout our lives. It enables us to find happiness from learning by paying close attention to nature.

The fourth reason is that rural life enables me to produce uncontaminated food and make it available to urban consumers. For the past 40 years, Korean farmers have used too much pesticide and chemical fertilizers. This overuse has harmed farmers and consumers alike.

Natural farming has become a must for survival. This realization motivated the Doorae Community, from the beginning, to grow crops organically. We use only compost and manure for fertilizer. This has required us to work harder at every stage of cultivation, including weed control, making compost, and attending to the soil. Our approach, however, has enabled us to grow quality produce, free of contamination.

Times have now changed and environmentally friendly farming has emerged as an important technology and one to be universally encouraged. The Doorae Community pioneered natural-farming techniques in Korea and we are proud of our accomplishment.

My fifth reason for liking to work in a rural area is that it lets me practice my love for the nation by attending to its soil and the environment. The globe is suffering from the massive destruction of nature, requiring each nation to protect its environment.

The role of farmers in this effort is crucial, although the entire nation should take part. Farmers suffer from the burden of heavy debts, however, and grand issues such as the protection of the environment are often too remote for individual households to deal with. This is where the importance of a communal settlement like the Doorae Community becomes apparent. Collective settlements are positioned to make the best of resources, labor, and technology because everything is in one place.

I have traveled in many countries and have had an opportunity to compare other lands with ours. I have found that Korea is no less beautiful than any other. Nature on the peninsula is so well arranged that it looks like a meticulously tended garden.

Working in the Doorae fields.

A person can never become bored with our landscape. The more a person looks around, the more welcome he feels. The waves of mountain ridges, villages clustered in mountain valleys, brooks streaming down to rivers below—all these reach out to the visitor. As such, pollution of the environment is an affront to God's work.

In recent years, I have visited North Korea several times. Looking at the depleted land and its people, it is difficult for me to suppress my grief. The country is so beautiful and the people are so good, but everything there is breaking down. This is one of the greatest catastrophes ever to hit our land.

The mountains in the North have been stripped of all vegetation. The absence of trees causes flooding during the rainy season, inundating the fields, leaching them, and rendering them unproductive. People have no motivation to control the damage because they are fighting their own battle against hunger. This creates a cycle of starvation. Whenever I return from trips to North Korea, I am reminded that in the South we must protect our environment.

IN 1996 A DOORAE COMMUNITY WAS ESTABLISHED on a 1,200-acre tract of land in Yenbian Korea Autonomous Region, China, near the border with North Korea. It consists of fifty households, ten brought in from other Doorae communities and forty from among Koreans living in the area. Excess grain produced here goes to North Korea.

The Doorae Community in Yenbian served as sort of a beachhead, paving the way for the establishment in 1998 of another community in the twin-city area of Najin-Seonbong, North Korea. Three farmers from South Korea worked on that farm with North Korean farmers. Their primary crop was potatoes.

I originally planned to establish a model farm there, where farmers from South and North Korea would work together on an 80-acre parcel. I wanted to expand the experiment with a division of responsibilities in which Doorae communities in the South would provide seed, fertilizer, and equipment for North Korean farmers working an area of 8,000 acres. Theoretically, the harvest would be assigned in proportion to everyone taking part, although it was expected that North Korean farmers would receive it all, because the purpose of the project was to help the North.

I visited Najin-Seonbong on a day when farmers were harvesting a crop of a new variety of potato that had been developed by South Korean scientists. Doorae had sent them 400,000 potatoes for seed.

People were busy working their way along the rows in the field. I was helping with the harvest, although behind me stood a "security guard" whose job was to keep an eye on me. Working beside me was a woman with a towel around her head to protect her from the sun. She appeared to be in her thirties.

A while later, I looked back at the security guard and saw that he had wandered off. I guessed that he had probably gone off for a cigarette. I took the opportunity to talk to the woman. "How do you do?" I asked. "The harvest has turned out to be better than anyone expected."

"Yes, it has. The plants did well, considering all the bad weather," she replied.

After this short exchange, we said nothing for quite a while. I was thinking as to how to continue the conversation, when she broke the silence.

"I've heard that there are many poor people in South Korea. Is that true?" She was addressing me, although her face was turned away. I supposed that she did not want to be seen talking to me.

"No, that's not true. On the contrary, there are many wealthy people," I replied, without looking at her, in consideration of the situation.

"I've heard that South Korean people live off American imperialists."

"No, that's not true, either. In fact, we buy things from the Americans. We buy food from them with money we earn from selling them cars, television sets, and textiles."

"I see. Then it's different from what I've heard. I hope that we reunify quickly."

"Indeed. I would say we are already on the way to reunification, now that a South Korean, me, has come to North Korea to harvest potatoes alongside your people. Don't you think?"

"Yes, I'd say so. Come here as often as you can."

That was in late July 1998. The three South Korean farmers who returned home after the harvest were kept from returning by a change in policy in the North.

THE DOORAE COMMUNITY INCORPORATES five principal projects. The first project is farming. The Doorae Community began as a communal farming settlement and developed through farming. Doorae farms have increased their value and productivity by engaging in a wide range of farm activities, from production to processing to distribution.

The second project is an educational facility for young people. Of the Doorae education activities, the best known is the work-study program. Youths work during the day and get an education at night. This program helps young people improve their mental and physical health and nurture their youthful spirit. The youth curriculum became more diversified with the opening of an alternative school in March 1999. The alternative school, called Doorae Nature High School, pursues "open education," the objective of which is to educate youths to become moral and hardworking contributors to society.

The third project is the Doorae Rehabilitation Center. At the Center, a doctor, a pastor, a cook specializing in nutrition, a physical therapist, and an administrator work as a team to treat and rehabilitate people who are afflicted in one way or another. They receive full-time support from five non-professional staff. The doctor serves as the team leader, while the administrator is responsible for the overall operation.

The fourth project is the Bible Education Center. Life in the Doorae Community is based on four living principles: the Bible, labor, service, and learning. A proper understanding of the Bible is the bedrock of communal living. As such, the Doorae Community holds seminars for Bible study, distributes taped sermons, and publishes related books. The Bible requires Doorae families to conduct their lives according to biblical teachings.

The second living principle, work, refers to Doorae families' resolve to work hard. This principle requires not only healthy people, but also the disabled, to do their share. The contribution of the disabled is often limited in terms of net accomplishment, because they are able to do only a small part of what might be expected of an able-bodied person. What is important, however, is that they have a mindset that values honest work.

The spirit of hard labor has lost acceptability in our society. Our economy is still at a stage in which it requires us to work hard, instead of indulging in extravagant and wasteful behavior. This dislike for work was partly responsible for the ignominy of Korea having to turn to the International Monetary Fund for aid in 1997. The Doorae Community thinks highly of manual labor and its role in a person's life. Even more than that, manual labor is regarded as inspiring and as a part of practicing our religion.

On the wall of the kitchen in the Doorae Community is a motto: "Prayer is work and work is prayer." This line emphasizes that working as best one can is the same as praying one's hardest.

The third principle, service, refers to a life serving others who are less fortunate. The thought that only the healthy and the affluent can help others is wrong. Even the disadvantaged can help others.

Some years ago a 23-year-old man suffering from depression came to the Doorae Community. According to his mother, he had become depressed, confining himself to his room, after his teacher slapped his face when he was in the third grade. Listening to her story, I was touched by her devotion as a mother. She cried as she spoke.

"That terrible teacher ruined my boy's life. I have looked all over and have used every medication imaginable to treat him. I've even had shamans perform exorcisms and have gone to temples and retreat houses. I've been anywhere I heard there might be the slightest chance of helping him recover. My heart breaks whenever I see him close himself in his room. The only thing he does now is breathe.

"I'm getting old. I can take care of him while I'm alive, but who will look after him after I'm gone? I've come here to ask you to take us in. If you allow us to stay, I will do housework for the community until my last breath. I will do anything, regardless of how hard it might be, if only you promise to care for him after I die."

Listening to her, I guessed that her son was suffering from what we call *han*, a combination of grief and a grudge, accumulated over time. Her plea moved me to accept her son at the community, but I decided to send her home.

I comforted her and told her, "Don't worry about your son. We will care for him as if he were our brother. Go on with your life and visit him here whenever you like. He will be better off here than at home."

She went home, after thanking me many times over.

Then I sent for a Mr. Keum, a man who was generally considered the most sympathetic person in the community.

"Mr. Keum, where are you working?"

"On the farm."

"I'll tell you what. Leave your job and come and take care of this fellow. He is 23. I was told that he has stayed in his room since his teacher slapped his face when he was in the third grade. It's a shame. From now on, stay with him and look after him as if he were your brother. Who are you sharing your room with these days?"

"A Mr. Kim."

"Is he suffering from any condition?

"No. He's plenty healthy."

"OK. Move Mr. Kim to another room and put this fellow in with you. Taking care of him will be more than enough to keep you busy."

"I'll do my best."

"Yes, I'm sure you will. Thank you for taking on this job so willingly. You must never become angry with him, or browbeat him because he acts dumb. Treat him kindly and respect him as a person. You must never call him an idiot. A clever person can laugh off being called an idiot, because he can take it as a joke, but if you call someone who is mentally unstable an idiot, it's like hammering a nail into his heart, so never do it."

"I understand."

One week later, Mr. Keum came to see me. "I've done it, Pastor."

"You've done what?"

"That fellow you told me to take care of, he's started talking."

"That's good news. What does he say?"

"When he came here, he knew only his name. Now he remembers three more names."

"What names are those?"

"Yours, mine, and the name of our leader."

"Our leader? Who are you referring to?"

"Come now. You've always said that our leader is Jesus Christ."

"That IS progress. It means that he has potential for recovering. Keep it up. Don't give up on him."

Another week passed, and Mr. Keum came to me again.

"Now he knows seven names. What's more, yesterday he smiled. This is great progress, don't you think?"

The man slowly improved. At that year's Christmas party, he sang a popular children's song, "Calf, Calf, Spotted Calf." People applauded him, not because he was a particularly good singer, but because he had gotten the song right. One of the community members smiled and said, "Wonderful, this fellow has made us all happy."

Someone added, "Yes, he has. Life is worth living."

After that, he made considerable progress. His mother saw him improving and emerging from his depression, slowly getting back to being his old self. Wiping her tears, she would tell him, "I now have nothing to wish for. I'm grateful to the Doorae people for bringing you back, my son. Now I can die with no regret."

Once I happened to pass by his room late at night. I heard someone's voice rumbling from inside. I could tell the voice was his and knocked on the door, thinking that he was talking to himself and perhaps was having a problem. It is common for people suffering from depression to talk to themselves.

"Why are you up so late?" I asked him, opening the door.

What was going on in the room took me by surprise. He was teaching another handicapped boy to read the letters of the Korean alphabet.

One man serving another is doing God's work. God sent Jesus to serve the human race. Jesus said, "For even the Son of Man came not to be served, but to serve, and to give his life as a ransom for many." (Mark 10:45) Christians live serving Jesus Christ. The advantaged serve the disadvantaged, the educated the uneducated, and the healthy the ill. Thus, the Doorae Community is a community of service.

The fourth principle of the Doorae Community, learning, does not refer to formal education, certificates, diplomas, or degrees, but rather, to a life that takes pleasure in learning. People should find happiness in learning. Learning, however, should be put to the service of the entire community, and not just serve a purpose for the learners themselves. It refers to an attitude of enjoying learning to serve in the name of Jesus. In the Doorae Community, therefore, study is recognized as labor and must be productive and creative.

In medieval Europe, the monastic movement made it possible to maintain the spiritual heritage. Monks pursued a modest life with hard work and study. Their way of life was the candle that lit the way for civilization during centuries of darkness.

This belief led the Doorae Community to establish its fifth and final project, the Doorae Research Center, as both theoretical and practical support for the community's work. This Center concentrates on four areas: organic farming, alternative education, reunification, and *Mokmin* Theology.

THE FOUNDATION FOR ALL THESE PROJECTS is the church. In establishing the Doorae Community, I wanted to restore the communal spirit of the early church .

One of the roles of the church is to exercise the power of healing. In Exodus 15:26 God is referred to as "the Lord, who heals you." In Malachi we read, "But unto you who revere my name, the sun of righteousness will rise with healing in its wings. And you will go out and leap like calves released from the stall." (Malachi 4:2)

Jesus himself declared that he had come to heal broken hearts. This healing power is inherent in the nature of any church.

There are approximately 40,000 Protestant churches in Korea. The reality, however, is that they're losing their ability to heal. They have failed to address the ills of our society and have turned their backs on their role as healers. The movement toward communal settlements will help them recover this lost ability.

Through communal living under Jesus Christ, greater healing took place than I had expected. Over the years, the community came to realize that people living among them were becoming healed for no reason other than that they lived together.

From this experience, I can say to a certainty that the Holy Spirit brings healing through communal living and that, as in the past, the Doorae Community will continue to heal people in the years to come.

A YOUNG MAN, WHO I WILL CALL D, lives in our community. When he came to us, he was addicted to drugs. His father, a pastor, pleaded with me to take his son in. He blamed himself for his son's addiction. Although his son had been admitted to a rehabilitation center on three occasions, and twice had gone to prison for possession of drugs, he had made no progress toward recovery. I sympathized with the father, but could not dare to accept his son.

I told him, "Heavy drug users like your son should go to a specialized treatment clinic. The Doorae Community cannot take on such a responsibility. We have neither doctors nor professional counselors. Our community is a gathering of ordinary people, working and living together." I pleaded with him, "Please send your son to a treatment center."

"No, Pastor Kim, they can't help him. Do you think I haven't taken him to clinics? I've taken him three times, but with no success. You are my only hope. Please, just give him a place here with you. It would help me immensely."

"I see. Well, if you think so, send him to us. We'll do what we can."

"Thank you very much. How grateful I would be if you could bring him back to normal."

Ten days after this conversation, D came to the Doorae Community. He looked awful. He seemed to have been good-looking at one time, but drugs had taken their toll on him.

I pitied him and wanted to help him. I took him out to a field and showed him how to weed red pepper plants. I explained how to pluck the weeds, rake soil in around the plant, and cover the base of the plant. I taught him how to use a hoe to loosen the dirt, to let air and moisture permeate the roots. Explaining all this, I got to talking to him.

"You're a fine kid and your father is a pastor. I heard that when you were young, you were a good student. I don't understand why you turned to drugs instead of the Bible. Did you not find the help there that your father found? I'll give you a word of advice. Get off drugs. They will destroy your body. I can't stop you from taking them. That's your business. You can do whatever you want with your body, but I suggest you get off drugs and onto the Bible."

I continued to talk to him. He said nothing, using the hoe to poke at the soil. A close look at what he was doing revealed that it was the plants themselves that he was hoeing, not the soil around the plants, and he was damaging them.

By his careless approach to the task, he was demonstrating his chagrin at having to work in the field on a hot summer day. I could sense his hostility, but I did not react negatively. I spoke in a quiet voice. "We'll end up with nothing to harvest, if you damage the plants. Why don't you rake the soil to cover the base of the plants? I know you're not happy with this situation, but don't take it out on the pepper plants. They're innocent."

Finally, in a grumpy voice, he spoke up, "Pastor Kim."

"Yes," I responded.

That was it. He said nothing more and went on with his hoeing.

"C'mon," I said. "I'm waiting for you to say something. Feel free to say anything you like. A man is expected to be decisive. It's not becoming to be shy and hesitant."

"How can you force me to work like this? How much are you going to pay me for this work?"

I could not suppress my laughter at his demand for payment. In response, I lectured him.

"What are you saying? Did you ask about your pay? Do you know what most people would say in this situation? Wake up!"

"What do you mean?"

"Yes, you should wake up. Think about it. How much do you think your labor is worth? Do you know how much hard work Doorae families are doing to take care of you? You ask about your wages. It is I, not you, who should get paid for this. You have to come to your senses. I'll tell you why we're having you work.

"It's called 'work therapy.' You know that music therapy uses music to heal physical or mental illnesses, and art therapy uses artistic expression, such as making pots or drawing pictures, for the same purpose. When work is used to treat patients, it's called work therapy. The drugs will wash out of your body when you perspire, and then you can get back to being yourself. Don't let other things distract you. Concentrate on your work. That's the only way you're ever going to recover. Do you understand?"

I was tough with him, but he remained hostile and pretended not to hear me. After that, for a long time, his attitude showed no change.

Drug addiction is so damaging. He would scream when he became desperate for drugs. His cry sounded like it was coming from a wild animal, rather than from a human being. At one point, he broke his arm, banging on the wall with his fist, because he could not overcome his dependency. I felt sympathy, even pity, toward him, as I tried to grasp the magnitude of the outrage he was dealing with. I consoled him whenever he lost control. I would hold his hands and pray for him.

"You need strength. You will never get back on your feet if you fail to overcome this. You'll be able to go back to a normal life only when you get through this critical stage."

Several months passed. I was returning home one evening, after eleven o'clock, when passing a row of pines at the back of the community I heard someone crying at the top of his lungs.

When I got home, I asked Doorae people, "Who's that in the woods crying?"

"It's Mr. Drugs."

"What's his problem? Did he get in a fight?"

"No, he wasn't in a fight. The spirit of repentance has finally touched him. He's been crying for three days, without eating or sleeping."

Hearing this, it occurred to me that D had finally regained his mind and would now be able to lead a normal life. We say that the spirit of repentance has worked when the Holy Spirit enters our mind and makes us repent our wrongdoings and rectify them.

Having been unable to get off drugs, D had not been able to live a normal life. Now the Holy Spirit had descended upon him. He was born again and could embark on a new life. Nobody had been able to provide direction for his broken soul. His father and I were within reach, but neither of us could help him. The Holy Spirit entered his mind and altered it so he could begin again.

I went out to the woods to be with him. After three days in the woods, his clothes were muddied, his voice was hoarse, and his eyes were swollen. He was clutching the stumps of trees. He was exhausted, but he was praying, although his prayer was more akin to a cry.

"Lord Jesus, forgive this miserable sinner. Please forgive me for my stupidity. Please accept me, although I deserve to die for the sins I have committed."

He shouted. I was proud of him and consoled him. "Everything is fine now," I said. My consolation came from deep within, as he repented his past with tears in his eyes.

"Thank you. It's a blessing to repent. Repent thoroughly and get off to a new start." I continued to comfort him.

I held his hands to pray. "God, I'm grateful to you for blessing this young man. I'm grateful to you for giving him an opportunity to repent. Please guide him, to undergo a thorough repentance and be born again as a new person."

He prayed for repentance for one week and came out of it a changed man. First, his appearance changed. His eyes were more gentle and his expression took on a softer look. He became sensible and enjoyed his work. We reassigned him to the poultry farm, where he went about his chores happily and with enthusiasm.

ONE DAY, ONE OF HIS FELLOW WORKERS CAME TO SEE ME. "Pastor, you need to scold Mr. Drugs."

"Stop calling him Mr. Drugs. He wasn't born with a habit of drugs and has now abandoned them. Give him back his name."

"OK, if you say so."

"Anyway, what's wrong with him? Is he causing trouble?"

"No, it's not that."

"Then what?"

"He's been dating a girl."

"Has he? That's good news. There's nothing wrong with that, is there?"

"No, I can't say there is."

"Why, then? It's natural for single men and women to date."

"But the girl is too good for him."

"What are you talking about, 'the girl is too good for him'?"

"Yes. It's not right for such an innocent girl to go around with a drug addict."

"I still don't get it. You're saying that an innocent girl is getting mixed up with a drug addict. Who's the girl?"

"She's Miss Park, from South Gyeongsang province."

"Oh, that pretty girl!"

"Yes, that pretty girl. It's not right to let such a pretty girl get mixed up with a good-for-nothing like him."

"I can tell. You're jealous, aren't you?"

"Me? Jealous?"

"You're jealous because you like her and you're upset to see her dating somebody else."

"Come on. That's nonsense."

"It makes sense to me. Otherwise, I see no reason why you should concern yourself with who she dates. You don't need to go to any effort to help them, but don't try to break them up. He went astray once, but now he's been born again. He's working hard to start a new life. You should help him. Don't look down on him. People can change."

"I knew you were going to say that. You only see the positive. It was foolish of me to try to talk to you about this. I have to go."

"I understand what you're trying to say. Anyway, it's good of you to pay attention to him, but I'll tell you again. Don't try to change what's going on between them."

That afternoon, I called in Miss Park. She had been cleaning eggs on the poultry farm. She came to my reading room with her apron still on.

"Did you want to see me, Pastor?"

"Yes. There's something I wanted to talk to you about, just between you and me."

"You make me nervous. What is it?"

"I've heard that you're seeing someone these days."

"I'm seeing someone?"

"Yes. I heard that you've been dating D. Everyone is aware of it. I was the only one who was in the dark."

"It's not exactly dating. We work in the same place and have gotten friendly."

Seeing her face turning red, I could tell that their relationship had already passed the friendship stage. I spoke to her cautiously, so she would not feel embarrassed.

"It's not unusual for two people to develop a friendship and become close. That doesn't bother me, but I would like you to do me one favor. It's not actually a favor. It's more a piece of advice."

"Yes, Pastor. What is it?"

"When dating, you have to maintain your decency. You should not go together to the mountain or the barley field for no purpose."

"I should not go to the mountain or the barley field?"

"Yes. I'm telling you this because you are mature enough to understand what I mean. Men have little patience, so you have to exercise discretion. Everything in nature has its time. Don't get ahead of yourself. Do you understand?"

"Yes, Pastor, but you don't have to worry about me. I'm not a child and I know what I'm doing."

"You may well trust yourself, but men are not always honorable, so I'm cautioning you."

"I'm fully aware of it, Pastor."

"OK. He might have had a rough life, but he's a nice guy. Please help him."

D and the girl continued to date and eventually got married. Weddings in the Doorae Community are generous and festive events. There is always a lot of food, including barbecued pig and Korean pancakes. A band played in the wedding hall and the community became happy and vibrant with the joy of the event.

I presided at the ceremony. "This wedding means a lot, not only to the bride and the groom, but to everyone at the Doorae Community. The groom should be particularly happy. His soul was suffering when he came here, but through God he regained his health. He has now found his lifelong companion. As members of the Doorae family, we are happy to have such people among us. I hope that, being one, the bride and the groom work together on the farm and increase our productivity. I also hope that they produce children, to ensure the prosperity of the Doorae Community."

Guests at the wedding came out with a loud "amen" to my address.

"What's with you?" I asked. "It is the bride and the groom, not you, who are supposed to say 'amen.'"

Guests burst into laughter and chanted "amen" again.

TODAY THE GROOM IS A RELIABLE MEMBER of the Doorae Community. One day I recalled what he had been like and asked him, "You are now trustworthy. Why were you such a troublemaker in the past,?"

"I was stupid then," was his reply. "I blame myself for my stupidity, but I also bear my father some ill will."

"How can you bear your father ill will? He's a pastor."

"Yes, I know."

"Why would a pastor's son bear his father ill will?"

"I have no idea what his reputation as a pastor is, or how hard he works for his church, but he was not a good father. I don't remember ever in my life having had a good conversation with him."

"Listening to you, I'm ashamed of myself," I said. "You have to understand, being a pastor is very stressful. It takes a lot of time and there is little time left for us to take care of our children. I'm not talking only about your father. It's the same for all of us."

"I realize that, but I don't accept it. My father never said I did anything right. Ever since I started school, I wanted him to compliment me for something. Whenever I thought I had done well and went to him with it, he'd reply, 'What do you know? You always get in the way of my church work, you good-for-nothing troublemaker.'

"I'd become depressed at the very thought of his frowning face, even when I was playing with my friends. He was unbearable. Do you know how painful it is for a son never to get any recognition from his father? No, I don't suppose you do."

As he talked, his face became dour. It brought home to me that no matter how hard a pastor works for his church, he is bound to have problems, if he neglects his children.

That evening, I called my sons into my study.

"Did you want to see us, Dad?"

"Yes."

"What is it?"

"I thought the three of us should have a father-son conversation."

"Yes, but we have to study, Dad."

"I know you have to study, but some things are more important than studying. You know D? His father's a pastor. Like me, his father was always very busy, which was one of the things that caused D to resort to drugs. I'm worried that you may follow in his footsteps because we don't talk very often. That wouldn't be good, so tonight we're going to have a conversation."

"OK, Dad, but please make it quick."

"Excuse me? How is it possible to speed up a father-son conversation? It can't be called a conversation if we have to hurry through it. A conversation is a relaxed exchange of thoughts."

I asked my wife to bring us tea and tried to create an environment for a friendly chat. We were not used to it, so it did not go smoothly. I did not know where to begin. The three of us stared at our tea. I broke the silence, asking whether they had had dinner. They replied they had.

Then we were silent again. I was uncomfortable and asked, "Is there anything you'd like to tell me?"

"No, not really," they said.

Unable to find anything to say, I told them to go and do their homework. That was the end of our conversation.

31

Bridge Over Troubled Waters

A COMMUNITY CAN DEVELOP IN THE right direction only if members communicate among themselves. I encourage people to take every opportunity to talk to one another. I emphasize particularly that to have a healthy family life, parents should provide an environment where family members get together and talk. I have to admit that I have not always lived up to my words and I greatly regret it.

A community in which members do not talk to one another will fail in its mission. These days, however, people find little time to talk, whether in church or with their family. This lack of communication is bound to result in problems.

Juvenile delinquents often come to the Doorae Community, young people who either have run away from home or have been expelled from or voluntarily dropped out of school. I ask them, "Why have you run away, wandering the streets alone? You could have a comfortable life at home, being cared for by your parents. What drove you to become a delinquent?"

The reply is always more or less the same.

"You say the same things that my teachers and my parents say. You ask why I ran away. I'm not a puppy or a rabbit to be raised at home. I'm a human being, an individual. What I need is not three meals a day or money. I need people who can talk to me. I need parents and teachers who treat me with dignity."

One day in 1997, a couple brought their high-school-age daughter to the community. Hearing their story, I became very sympathetic to her situation. For some reason, the girl had run away from home. Her parents had looked for her and, after a year of searching, managed to find her. By then, she was seven months pregnant. The parents were shocked to find their daughter pregnant. They had heard about the Doorae Community and brought her to us because they were at a loss as to what to do.

I took them into my study. The parents blamed each other for their daughter's predicament.

Her mother spoke first. "She has ruined herself because, like her father, she always wants to have a good time. She's only a child. It's shameful that she's going to have a baby."

Looking at her husband, she said, "She's just like you. She left home with no fear of the consequences. Now she's gotten herself pregnant and doesn't even know who the father is. Our family has been ruined." The husband only grunted.

I felt sorry for them. "Your daughter seems to resemble both of you," I said. "There's no point arguing who she resembles most. We need to come up with a solution. Blaming your daughter gets no one anywhere. First, you two have to understand your daughter and look at things from her point of view. Can you fathom the severity of what she went through before she decided to run away?"

I turned my glance to the girl, sitting with her head down. I saw tears welling in her eyes. The tears gave me hope for her future. In most cases, tears portend potential for correcting past wrongs and starting a new life. By comparison, people who show no emotion under such circumstances give little hope for their future.

Watching her eyes, I saw that she would be able to reform, once given direction. I told her parents to leave her with us at the Doorae Community and go home. I summoned a manager responsible for rehabilitation and told him to assign her a room.

The next day I had to leave on a three-day trip. I returned to the community to receive a visit from the girl who was sharing a room with her.

"Pastor, I'm sharing a room with Hyang."

"Yes. Who is Hyang?"

"Don't you remember? The high-school girl who came here with her parents a few days ago."

"Oh, now I'm with you. How is she? She's undergoing a very critical period and needs your help."

"Yes, she's fine, but she's weird."

"She may be, but you have to be understanding. How can you expect her to behave normally, after what she's been through?"

"No, you don't get my point."

"I'm sorry. How is she weird?"

"She has your picture stuck to the wall. She says good night to your picture every night and the first thing she does after getting up in the morning is go to the picture and say good morning."

"That does sound 'weird,' as you say. What do you think is going on?"

"That's why I'm telling you that I think her behavior is weird."

"Yes, it surely is. I'll call her in this afternoon and talk to her."

In the afternoon, I called her in.

"Did you want to see me, Pastor?" she asked.

"Yes, I did. I have something to discuss with you. Your name is Hyang, isn't it? I hear that you are very courteous."

"I don't think I understand what you're saying."

"I heard that you greet my picture every morning and every night."

"Yes, I do. I'm sorry, Pastor," she said, her face flushing.

"You don't need to be sorry, but I need to know why you do it."

"The other day I went to your study because I wanted your advice. You were away. I saw your picture on your desk and took it. I'm sorry, Pastor."

"OK. You might well take my picture, but why do you greet it?"

"Do you remember what you told my parents, when we came to see you? You may not remember. I was deeply moved after hearing what you told my parents."

"Did you? What was it I told your parents?"

"After hearing my parents condemn me for running away and shaming my family, you rebuked them for blaming me. You asked them whether they could understand the difficult times I had been through."

"That was true, wasn't it? It must have been very hard for you at home, for you to have run away, even though life would have been more comfortable under your parents' care."

"What you said made me cry. I'd wanted to hear that, but no one has said it until now. I was so desperate for someone to talk to that I would have talked to a dog. Do you know the real reason I ran away from home?"

"No, I don't think I do. What was the real reason?"

"I left home because I didn't want to go crazy. I'm not saying what I did was right, but I'd have gone crazy if I hadn't left."

"Why was that?"

"Mom kept telling me to study. She was obsessed with my grades. She kept saying, "Study, study, study," whenever she saw me. Just to look at her gave me a headache. Dad would come home drunk late at night and yell at everyone. I was forced to sit at my desk from eight in the morning until late at night, even though I didn't want to go to college. I had no friends. I thought I was going mad. I ran away from home because I wanted to keep my sanity."

"What did you do after you left?"

"I worked at a coffee shop. I thought my job there was doing chores, but it wasn't. Men my dad's age called me 'young chick' and paid my employer so they could sleep with me. If I refused, they beat me. One day I found myself pregnant, but I had no idea who the father was."

"Men are pigs. How could they sleep with a young girl like you?"

"I went to a hospital to get an abortion, but they said I was too far along. I don't know what to do now. I deserve to die. There is no other way."

My heart went out to her; not only to her, but to so many young people in our country. Adults seem to all gang up on the kids to ruin them. It is a church's mission to take in these broken souls, to nurture and heal them.

I REALIZE HOW CRUEL THE WORLD IS whenever I see a young person undergoing hardship. I ask, "How can I heal this sick society? What can I do to transform this rotten society into a healthy one? Is it possible for a society in which people so disparage one another to become a society where people help one another?"

It dawned on me that the Doorae Community's raison d'être is to reach out to help confused youth as if they were our own sons and daughters and brothers and sisters. In fact, the Doorae Community has seen many youths, who have gone astray, set out on a new life after staying at the community.

Another girl came to the community from Seoul. She was an honor student in a high school from a district that had the best schools. All of a sudden, when she was a junior, she lost interest in her studies. She was fed up with everything—her school, her family, and the idea of going to college. She wanted to go to a quiet place and live the life of a hermit. That desire led her to the Doorae Community.

We accepted her as a member of our family. I encouraged her to dedicate her life to the service of others, rubbing the backs of senior citizens and doing their laundry in the evening, and collecting eggs on the poultry farm during the day.

When she came to the community, I worried because she was physically weak and rarely smiled. She transformed herself by working hard. A smile came back to her face and her eyes sparkled. She came to me one day, ten months after coming to stay with us.

"Please allow me to study again, Pastor," she said. "I'd like to study."

"Why do you want to go back to that? You found it such a headache before. You wanted to do physical work and live quietly for the rest of your life."

"Yes, that was what I wanted when I came here, but I've changed my mind."

"May I ask why? I'm curious."

"There's no particular reason. Working here and helping others, I realize that there's a limit to what I can do for them simply by working. I think that to really help people I need training, so I'd like to study."

"That's a good idea, and you're right. To help people, you need training. You've learned a good lesson."

Then she asked me, "What should I study?"

"Let's think about that for a while, but social welfare, psychology, medicine, and nursing come to mind. Whatever you do, your work will be appreciated because you're smart and kind."

"Do you really think so? You're not just saying that to encourage me, are you?"

"No, you really are a good person. Now that you understand

492

yourself better, I'm sure you'll be able to do much better than you could've before."

"Your confidence in me means a lot. I'm going home to my parents tomorrow and tell them what I want to do."

"That's a good idea. By the way, I'm not sure that your school is going to take you back."

The next day I went to her school to plead to have her readmitted, but her place had been taken long before. Because the system provided no acceptable alternative, her parents wanted to send her abroad. They could not afford to, however, so the Doorae Community decided to support her. We sent her to England, where her academic performance exceeded our expectations. She did well because she had waged an internal battle and had won. That gave her strong motivation to succeed. She is now studying for a doctorate in social welfare.

THERE ARE A GREAT MANY OTHER STORIES that attest to our success at rehabilitation. The case of Mr. Park and his daughter is another such story.

On a cold day in 1989, a Mr. Park and his daughter arrived at the Doorae Community. It was in the afternoon, when the mountain behind the community was already casting its shadow on the buildings, that a taxi drove into the courtyard to drop off a girl and her semiparalyzed father.

The girl got out first, then her father, holding their belongings. Perhaps I should say her father rolled out, because he could not get out in the normal way. After the taxi sped off, they remained stationary, the girl standing and the father sitting on the ground.

A member of the community approached them and asked why they had come. Without answering, the father produced an envelope containing a letter. The man read the letter and hurried to show it to me. The envelope read, "To Pastor Kim Jin-hong." I opened the letter and read it:

Dear Pastor Kim, who to me is like Jesus Christ,

This father and daughter stayed at our retreat house for some months. His wife abandoned him after he suffered a stroke. I am sending them to you because he has not shown any improvement. I believe that you will take good care of them. Hallelujah.

I showed the letter to the Doorae people standing around. Some people became furious upon reading it. One of the young members in the community fumed, "Who is this man to call you 'his Jesus Christ.' Why doesn't he call himself Jesus Christ? Let's send them back. The retreat house has always claimed they have miracle cures and now they send us a paralytic, asking us to cure him. There's nothing here to discuss. They have to go back."

"Sir, please don't send us back. We have nowhere to go. Last night we slept in the street. Please take us in." The girl begged the young man, clutching at his clothes. She then burst into tears. The father sat on the ground, with his head down.

Doorae families have a soft spot in their heart for people in tears pleading with them. After some discussion, someone said in a low voice. "Let's take them." Other people agreed. "Yes, we should accept them. How can we expect to be blessed, if we send people away who have nowhere to go."

I stepped forward and spoke to the girl, "We'd like to hear how you ended up coming here, but first let's go inside where it's warm and get you some food."

The man's story was a sad one. He had been fairly well-off, but at the age of forty, suffered a stroke. He survived, but he was partially paralyzed. Then his wife ran off, leaving him and their daughter, who at that time was in the fifth grade. He exhausted his savings and had no means of support. He went to a retreat house in hopes of curing his illness.

He had gone there after hearing its reputation as a place that had cured even cancer patients, but he experienced no miracle. There seemed to be some patients who were cured at the retreat house, but a greater number died there. The truth was that the patients exaggerated their experiences when speaking to others, while the stories of the dead were never told outside the retreat. Mr. Park and his daughter had been there for one year before they were sent to us.

The first response of the Doorae people to Mr. Park's story was,

"Women today are faithless. They stay with their husband as long as he's healthy, but at the first sign of trouble, they run off. We need to look after ourselves so we do not suffer the same fate."

We gave them a warm room with comfortable beds. Mr. Park became emotional and thanked us profusely.

The Doorae Community lacked facilities for paralytics like Mr. Park. When he wanted to go to the bathroom, he needed his young daughter's help, frail though she was.

One day I was returning from a week-long stay in Japan. Entering the community, I saw Mr. Park walking around the grounds. He was ambulatory, although he moved with a pronounced limp.

"What happened, Mr. Park? How did you manage to make yourself walk?"

"Jesus helped me to stand up and walk like this, Pastor. I'm so grateful."

He wiped tears from his eyes as he spoke. I was amazed and asked him to tell me how it happened.

"I thought that I was going to die on the street, Pastor, but Doorae took me in and provided me with a warm room and hot meals. I was so grateful to the community that I prayed to Jesus. All of a sudden, in the middle of a prayer, I felt my strength returning. I tried to pull myself up and here I am."

"That's wonderful. How did you pray?"

"I merely gave thanks for living here and my wish for Doorae to prosper. I also prayed that my wife would meet a good man and have a good life. I had never before prayed for my wife. I'd always wished her ill. Since coming here, I've learned how to forgive. I cried while I was praying for her. After a good cry, joy sprang into my heart and my strength returned. Then I stood up."

"Congratulations, Mr. Park. You keep praying like that. Jesus must have heard you praying for others, rather than only for yourself."

"That's how I figure it. What else can I pray for now? I guess I'll keep praying for Doorae and for the poor people around me."

My joy was such I could not express it.

At a gathering that evening, someone said, "Doorae made it happen, Pastor. A paralyzed man was cured here."

"Yes, it's a great day, but don't let out the secret. We'll be in trouble, if word gets around. The number of paralytics across the nation is not just in the hundreds. There are thousands of them. Mr. Park cured himself through prayer, but stories often become distorted when they are told. If word spreads that the Doorae Community can cure people, paralytics from everywhere will swamp us and occupy every room we have. We'll have to sleep outside, giving up our rooms for them."

Someone spoke up. "None of us will mention it, but just make sure you don't go around talking about it." At this, everyone laughed.

Time passed and Mr. Park's daughter grew up, attended college, and is now working in a company. Mr. Park's case demonstrates one of the virtues of the Doorae Community. He would not have a place in other households or workplaces, but with Doorae he has a role to play, although because of his limp, he is not able to work as much as a healthy person.

There are many events at the Doorae Community that are attended by outsiders. When the events take place, it is a big job to greet people. Located in a remote area on the west side of the peninsula, the Doorae Community is not a place that outsiders can find easily. Visitors are encouraged to use public transportation from Seoul, getting off at a bus stop near the community. From there, they have to find their way to the community. Mr. Park's job is to give directions to visitors.

He stands at the bus stop with a band across his chest. Written on the band is, "Visitors to the Doorae Community, please come this way." Seeing the band, visitors gather round him. When ten people have gathered, a van from the community comes by to pick them up. If not for Mr. Park, we would have to send someone else, perhaps even a healthy person. Although he lacks capacity for physical work, Mr. Park does his part for the community.

In the Doorae Community, everyone is assigned work duties. Older women take care of babies whose young mothers go out to the fields. Others work in the kitchen, the laundry, or elsewhere.

THERE ARE THREE QUESTIONS THAT ANYONE WHO JOINS the Doorae Community is not supposed to ask, and three questions that they have to answer.

They should not ask about a person's academic background. Members of the community have a range of education, from Ph.D.

degrees from overseas universities to no formal education at all. Everyone, regardless of their education, is assigned work. After joining the community, people are no longer cognizant of their academic qualifications.

They should not ask about a person's assets. One of the guiding principles of the community is that people have no claim on possessions. It does not mean that Doorae families do not like having assets or that they want to be poor. They work to increase their holdings, but what they have, they hold in trust for Jesus.

Some people join the community with assets and some with debts. Those with assets turn them over to the community and have them returned when they leave. More likely, however, is that people joining the community will come with debts.

And finally, they are not supposed to ask about a person's past. Among the residents of the community are people with criminal backgrounds. One person arrived with a record of seventeen convictions. It is likely that he lived a greater part of his life behind bars than walking free, but he has reformed himself. He had a revelation from Jesus and today has a new life. Whenever I see a person like him, it brings home to me the great influence that religion can have on a person. What else could transform a criminal with seventeen convictions? It is possible only when he decides to serve Jesus as the Lord.

Also, there are three questions that everyone must answer. One question they must answer is whether they are willing to live a life of hard work. One of the teachings of the Bible is, "If a man will not work, he shall not eat." (2 Thessalonians 3:10)

Another question they must answer is whether they are willing to get along with other people in a communal setting.

The last question to answer is whether they are ready to help the poor and the weak.

The ideal form of life pursued by the Doorae Community is of people getting along together, working hard, and helping others.

Wanting to live up to an ideal is one thing, but practicing it is another. As with many things, there is a gulf between the ideal and reality. The Doorae Community has an ideal of living up to the spirit of communal living, but while giving lip service to cooperation, people in the community sometimes show themselves to be selfish.

ONE DAY, A WOMAN VISITED THE COMMUNITY. She said that she had come because she could no longer stand her husband's beatings. "I could stand his slapping and kicking, but when he hit me with a baseball bat, that was too much," she said weeping. "I tolerated the beatings for five years, persuading myself that it was a cross I had to bear, but I finally gave up."

The woman was attractive and neatly dressed. I felt sorry for her.

"How did you meet such a man?" I asked.

"It was my fault. I'm to blame."

"It's not right to blame yourself for everything."

"In this case, it is. I dated a man when I was a member of a choir at church, but the man was afraid to make a commitment, always postponing our wedding. I got impatient and in a fit of anger married another man. After we got married, whenever my husband drank, he beat me. I waited for him to change, because I thought it was my fault, but the beatings just got worse. I wanted to commit suicide by jumping out the window of my apartment, but I decided against it and came here."

"What are you going to do with your children?"

"Fortunately, I have no children. We haven't even registered our marriage."

"I'm not sure whether it's fortunate or not, but it's good because you have less to worry about. Now that you're here, rest for a few days."

"Please don't tell me to go back. I'm ready to do anything here. Please let me stay."

"Let's take some time to think it over."

The next day she started working at the poultry farm. She was a quiet and pleasant woman and got on well with other people. A while later, I heard that she had become close friends with a man working in the same place. He was from Daegu and was a good worker.

It struck me that they both had gone through difficult times and it might be a good idea if their friendship were to lead to marriage. Rumors had it that her previous husband had remarried and was already beating his new wife.

A month or so later, they came to ask me permission to get married. Without hesitation, I told them, "You're mature adults. You don't need my approval to get married."

"No, we don't, but you're our spiritual leader and we would like your blessing," the man said.

"It's a wonderful thing. I'm more than willing to give you approval. You've been through some hard times and your fiancee has also suffered the bitterness of life. Those who have experienced a broken heart can develop deeper insight and have a wider scope for understanding, once they overcome their trauma. You met each other after overcoming your trauma. Live happily." The woman's face was streaming with tears. The man became solemn, looking down.

A while after this visit, five Doorae women came to me. I welcomed them with open arms because it was rare for them to visit me together.

"What a surprise! What's going on? It's a major event when five women leaders come to see me all at the same time."

"Please excuse us for coming without an appointment, Pastor."

"No, it's not something to excuse. It's something to welcome."

"We have a question to ask you, Pastor."

"Of course. Ask anything you like."

"Are you going to allow their marriage?"

"Whose marriage are you talking about?"

"The young man's, the fellow who works on the poultry farm."

"Oh, the fellow from Daegu. Is there a problem with the marriage?"

"Yes, there is."

"What is it?"

"He's too good for her."

"How so? What do you mean?"

"He has never been married. He's too good to marry a woman with a past."

Although people are not supposed to know about other people's backgrounds, human nature demands familiarity and it is often difficult to keep one's past hidden.

"My goodness!" It had taken me a while to grasp their point. When I realized what it was, I became annoyed. What they were saying was that the young man had something to lose by marrying a woman who had run away from an abusive and uncaring husband. I was furious at their narrow-mindedness, but I kept my composure and told them in a quiet voice.

499

"She can wash her past away, if she bathes, can't she?" I said sarcastically.

"It's not that simple, Pastor. The woman was so clever that she seduced him while they were working together. Such a marriage should not be allowed in the Doorae Community."

"Ladies. I don't understand. How can you talk this way? You are branding her because of her past. What makes you think that you are any better? You should be grateful for your good fortune for having husbands and happy lives. You should not point an accusing finger at your neighbors who have suffered. Rather, you should praise them for having kept their faith and for not giving in to the temptation of going astray. I suggest that you go to her and congratulate her on her wedding."

"We're not sure about that. We'll go along with you and say nothing, but we are not about to congratulate her."

They sulked as they left. I was very uncomfortable that Doorae families had responded to others' misfortune in such a way. Living in a community is meaningless unless the members abandon such prejudice. Communal life starts with understanding others and recognizing their suffering. A community can survive and mature through human understanding. After they were gone, I knelt to pray.

"Lord Jesus, help the Doorae Community to grow so as to understand others' sufferings. Help us to be receptive to our neighbors' misfortune with minds as accommodating as yours. Help us become an oasis in the desert in an age devoid of humanity and love. Help us create a community filled with an understanding of human pain and heartfelt love for the soul."

THERE WAS ANOTHER SITUATION that particularly bothered me. My son, Min-hyeok, was subjected to bullying by other Doorae children. One day when I came home, I found my wife hugging him, crying.

"What's going on? Why are you both crying?" I asked, surprised. At first, my wife could not talk, she was so upset. Finally, she calmed down and told me what had happened.

She was worried because although it was dinner time, Min-hyeok was not around. She went into his room to find him crying. She asked him what was wrong.

"I want to die, Mom," was his reply.

His comment stunned her and she got him to open up.

"They've been bullying me."

"What? Who are they?"

"The big kids."

"I can't believe there are bullies at Doorae."

There were some 150 people at Doorae at the time, so there were bound to be a lot of children among them. There were also children who had lost their parents or who had been abandoned.

Many of children in the community lived in dysfunctional families. Men and women who have been traumatized by their experiences, whether as children or as adults, have a tendency to take their misfortune out on others. Their children sometimes suffer the brunt of their parents' misfortune. As the son of the pastor, my son was considered privileged, which made him the object of bullying.

Other children would hit him and tell him not to act like he's better than others because he's a pastor's son. They would take my son's favorite things and say, "Everything should be shared in the community. Nothing belongs only to you. Haven't you heard?"

My son is generous and understanding by nature. Previously, he would bring home other students who had fallen behind in class and help them with their studies. He would hang a blackboard on the wall of his room and give them lessons. He was that kind of a kid, but lately he had become less communicative and did not smile as much. My wife and I did not take the change seriously.

"Min-hyeok seems to be down these days," my wife had observed.

"It's just a part of growing up. It happens as kids get older."

The situation, however, had gotten worse. Listening to his story, my wife became furious. "Who did this to you? I won't let them get away with it. Tell me their names," she insisted.

"I'm not telling you because I know what you'll do," he said.

"What? What do you mean?"

"If you know who they are, you'll have them thrown out of the community, won't you?"

"Of course, I will. That kind of person does not deserve to live here. They deserve to be run out."

"Is that the right thing to do, Mom? Can you send them out of the community because they're bad? Then what would they do? They have nowhere to go."

My wife was speechless at what he was saying and fell silent. Then she spoke, "You're right, there's no choice. You're very considerate, but we cannot tolerate bullying."

"I'll put up with it. I'll tell myself that I'm helping Daddy, because he's running the community."

"But you told me that you'd like to die."

"Yes, I did. I said it because, in spite of myself, I didn't want to take it any longer."

There was nothing I could say. All I could do was sit there, helpless, swallowing the lump in my throat. "It's what children do," I said, and went to my study.

That night we discussed how to deal with the situation. We sought to find a way to create an environment free of bullying without hurting either my son or the bullies. We hit upon an idea.

Some days later we gave a party for children and invited the kids involved in the incident. When the atmosphere was right, I raised the issue of bullying and explained how important it is to understand and to talk freely with one another. I spoke in a way that left the impression that I wanted to prevent the bullying from happening again. My effort worked. The bullies apologized and asked for forgiveness.

My son was so happy that they made up by shaking hands. After that, everyone sang songs and the party ended with everyone in a festive mood.

MANY ABSURD THINGS HAPPEN IN THE COMMUNITY. Some have been so upsetting as to make me question the wisdom of my decision to remain there. One such incident was the so-called "tofu incident." I like tofu. The problem came about because one time I, alone, had been served tofu.

I was returning home from a four-day trip to visit churches in Daegu. Seeing how tired I was when she met me at the bus station in town, my wife said, "Dinner at the community is almost over. Why don't we have dinner here in town?"

"You know I don't like eating out. If I missed dinner, you can make something for me."

"OK. I'll make you a tofu stew, the way you like it."

We bought two pieces of tofu and arrived at the Doorae Community. My wife went into the kitchen, which had already been cleaned up after dinner, and prepared the stew. She put one chunk of tofu in the stew and boiled the other in hot water to put on a separate dish. The two of us then sat at a table in the kitchen and ate. Some people passed by and saw the dish of tofu, which was what caused the problem.

When matters of interest to the entire community arise, we hold a community meeting to discuss them and arrive at a solution. The meeting is part of our approach to direct democracy, as an ideal form of government. A community's maturity is reflected in how receptive members are to criticism. The community will lose its openness if criticism is not applied equally to everyone, including community leaders.

That week, as usual, we held a community meeting. Several issues were discussed and, finally, a woman brought up the tofu.

She began, "The community's principle is sharing and living together, is it not? As with everything else, that principle should also apply to food."

"Yes, of course," I agreed, not knowing where she was going with it. "Was there an occasion on which the principle was not observed?"

"Yes, there was."

"Then you should explain it, so everyone can understand."

"Very well. Two days ago, after everyone else had finished dinner, I saw you and your wife having tofu. All we had for dinner that day was *gimchi* and lettuce. It is not right for you to have tofu, only because you are the pastor. Do you think that was in keeping with the community spirit?"

Others joined her in her criticism.

"No, it was not right. It's no longer communal living if people don't eat the same things."

I realized that it was my fault and quickly apologized.

"You're right. I made a mistake. That day, I was tired after returning from Daegu and had missed dinner. It was wrong for me to have had a different menu, whether tofu or whatever."

I made a hasty apology in an effort to settle the matter, but my wife saw it differently.

She got upset and spoke out.

"What are you talking about? Enough is enough. What's wrong

with me cooking a piece of tofu for my husband when he comes home exhausted? This community stuff has gone too far."

She said this loudly enough for people to hear. The situation immediately became very awkward. People were divided. Some said, "She's right. This should not have even come up." Another group disagreed. "The manner in which it was presented may not have been right, but the principle is sound."

I pleaded with people to calm down and ended the meeting with another apology.

Arriving home, I sat down to talk to my wife, who was holding back her tears.

"How long do we have to live like this?"

"What do you mean? What are you referring to?"

"I'm talking about this community stuff that prevents us from even cooking tofu."

"Don't make a big deal out of it. They have a point. We talk about the communal spirit, but then we had a different dinner. I can understand why someone would complain."

"You may understand it, but my heart isn't that big. I'm going to confront them on it."

I was sympathetic to her, as she tried to repress her anger. At the same time, I was sorry to see her in that situation. I was concerned that this argument could contribute to the destruction of the community. The incident taught me that however well-meaning a community might be, it can easily get distracted in working out insignificant details.

The next morning, to my relief, the same women who had complained came to my wife and apologized for having overreacted. My wife accepted their apology and offered her apology for having lost her composure in public. Everyone made up and the matter was put to rest.

32

Religion, Life, and Work

ONE OF THE MOST DIFFICULT ISSUES in communal life, and one that is constantly raised, is finances. The Doorae Community was founded on the principle of no private ownership. This does not mean that the Doorae Community should not have a profit motive in its work. Rather, profits derived from community effort belong to Jesus and not to individuals and should be used for His work, helping neighbors. We put this principle into practice, defining it as "work within one's ability and spend as necessary."

The Doorae Community has another principle, the "Trinity Principle," which refers to the balanced pursuit of religion, life, and work. This principle requires Doorae members to put their lives at the disposal of their beliefs, practicing their religion in their life and work. This may sound simple, but its application to communal life often turns out to be both complicated and stressful.

When Doorae was first founded, members were allowed to take money from the community's finance department whenever a need arose. This approach, however, turned out to be flawed. Diligent workers, who contributed most to the community's economy, were too busy with their work to think about spending. Other members, who were physically ill or who by nature were less diligent, spent their time looking for ways to spend money.

This was bound to lead to conflict. Everyone was aware of the problem and endured it as long as they could, but it finally got to the point where the allowance system was put up as the topic for a community meeting. Presiding over the meeting, I explained the reason it was being held.

"We are meeting today to discuss the allowance system. The system appears to be creating difficulties in how we manage the community. We have been living on the principle of common ownership. This principle has proven to be impractical. Thus far, we have addressed the matter in terms of the individuals involved, but we recognize that the principle has created an overall negative atmosphere in the community. This has made life difficult for everyone.

"Above all, this is a matter of fairness. People who work hard have neither time nor inclination to spend and therefore take little money. A small number of other members, however, all but monopolize spending. In still other cases, there are people who, as a matter of dignity, hesitate to ask for money, although they require it. Today we want to address this situation and come up with a solution."

We discussed the matter at length, finally coming to an agreement. The new policy provided for each household to receive a certain amount of money at the beginning of each month. Any money that was left over at the end of the month would be returned to the common fund.

This seemed to be a good idea, but in practice it, too, proved to be flawed. There were households that would send one of their family members to a nearby town to spend whatever money they had left at the end of the month, to avoid having to return it. These trips took people away from their workplace, compounding the community's loss, and the matter continued to create enmity among residents.

After three months, we revised the policy again. The newly revised policy called for each household to retain any balance of their allocation at the end of the month. If, during a month, anyone experienced a shortfall, they could submit details of their shortfall to the finance department and receive a supplemental allotment.

The revised policy proved workable, although harmony was not easily come by. The worst aspect of the original system was that the laggards had an adverse effect on the diligent members of the community, sapping them of their will to work. When new workers joined the community, having initiated their communal life with enthusiasm and hard work, they were sometimes taunted.

"Hey! Why are you working so hard? What, do you want Pastor Kim to adopt you?"

Subjected to jeers, new workers lost their enthusiasm for the communal movement and wanted to leave. For my part, I was grateful to see newly recruited members working hard. I tried to encourage them to grow to become the backbone of the community. It was devastating to watch those same people lose their enthusiasm. One day one of them visited me, saying he wanted to leave.

"Why do you want to leave?" I asked. "I have high expectations of you. When you joined the community, you said your resolve was such that you would stay with us to the last day of your life. What made you change your mind?"

"I'm sorry. There's a lot I want to say, but I can't."

"Please tell me what's on your mind."

"What's the point of telling you, if I'm leaving? I might want to come back later." He went without telling me why, which left me with a feeling of isolation. After he was gone, I asked other members.

"Why do you think he left? When he came here, he was full of enthusiasm."

Some of the members avoided me, but one answered, "There are a lot of things going on that you are not aware of."

Wondering, I pressed him to explain. "What are you talking about? What's going on that's being kept from me?" Still, my inquiries went unanswered.

As time passed, and the issue was not being dealt with, it became clear to me that communal settlements were not as easy to run as I had expected. I gave a lot of thought to how to tackle the difficult issues. It also dawned on me that the process of finding solutions to problems was a necessary rite of passage for any community to mature.

WHEN I WAS THINKING about setting up a community, many people were opposed to it. The first reason they gave was that a communal spirit did not conform to the character of Koreans, who were disposed to spread out like sand. One of those opposing my plan was Deacon Kim Yong-gi, the founder of the Canaan Farmer's School, who I visited to ask his advice. He strongly opposed my plan, based on personal experience managing a communal settlement. From his youth, he had dreamt of founding a community, which he finally did and devoted himself to its success. Although the community failed, he still could not give up his dream. As a consequence, he established the Canaan Farmer's School, with only his family members.

"Don't expect much to come of your effort, although I know you are well intentioned," he cautioned me. "Communal living may be good as an ideal, but it is not realistic. It is destined to end in failure and will only hurt those who pioneer it." At first, I agreed with his advice, because he had had a lot of experience in the field.

"I won't undertake anything that is beyond my ability," I told him.

I returned home, but later, I began to question it. Are Koreans really of a character that makes it difficult for them to get along with one another in a communal setting? Are they that selfish and uncooperative? If so, wouldn't that make it impossible for us to extricate our nation from its underdeveloped status?

From the bottom of my heart, another thought emerged. Everyone says that this cannot be done, but is it not worth a challenge? Would life not be much more worthwhile, if I were to attempt what is regarded as impossible and succeed?

I began to ponder communal living, as described in the Bible. I also thought about the role of the Korean church in a reunified Korea. My thoughts led to the conclusion that the establishment of a community would be a major accomplishment.

The first Doorae Community was set up in 1979, but did not survive its first year. The second Doorae Community was launched in April 1986 and has passed the test of time. After the first seven years, I was confident that the community would succeed.

HAVING CONFIDENCE IN THE COMMUNAL MOVEMENT was one thing, but running a community is quite another. In its early years, the Doorae Community went through a series of life or death crises.

The most difficult problem we encountered was a shortage of people capable of managing the community. Many people visited the community who aspired to communal living, but most of them lacked the ability to manage. For a community to grow and develop, it needs managers. People who visited the Doorae Community were, for the most part, unfortunate souls who were unable to control and manage their own lives. After a little training, we assigned certain people to managerial positions. We needed to work quickly, so the result was bound to be far from perfect.

The Doorae Community depends primarily on farming for its livelihood. Doorae prides itself on carrying out only natural, organic farming, because this approach conforms to God's principle in his creation of the world. In the beginning, no one was technically qualified for organic farming. Although fields were managed by people who were well meaning, we experienced a great deal of trial and error, with low productivity. Weeds grew to such a degree as to make it difficult to tell whether the fields were for grain or weeds. Debts piled up in the processing plant. Sales of Doorae goods were so sluggish that they hardly covered wages of workers at its sales outlet in Seoul.

In 1996, ten years after the start of the second Doorae Community, the farm was operating at a monthly deficit of 30 to 40 million *won*. I had to work very hard to cover the losses. After several years of living this way, I found myself stretched to the limit, both physically and mentally. I realized that I would not be able to continue indefinitely and reached a point where a decision had to be made as to whether the community should continue.

In October 1996, we held a meeting to discuss the issue. I opened the meeting. "I appreciate that Doorae people have worked very hard. Any success we have had is to be attributed first to God and then to your efforts. Still, we have to be honest with ourselves. Our community is coming to the point where we must decide whether we can continue.

"Three crises now confront us. The first is one of identity. We started as a Christian community, with the objective of achieving a life on this land faithful to the Bible. Over the past ten years, however, this ideal has weakened to the point that today the Christian spirit has vanished.

"The second is a crisis of a communal spirit. One hundred fifty people came here to live communally, but the communal spirit has broken down, leaving in its place selfishness and egotism.

"The third crisis is money management. Debts are now running at more than 30 million *won* per month. With such a deficit, we cannot restart our community. Today we have to decide how we are going to deal with these crises. Please do not hesitate to express your opinion and to participate in the discussion. I hope we can work together to overcome our situation."

We discussed all of these matters openly. In the end, we devised five strategies to overcome the crises.

The first strategy was to sell part of the real estate owned by the community to pay off our debts.

The second was to shut down money-losing businesses and increase investment in profitable ones.

The third was to persuade workers who were unable to adjust to the communal movement or who lacked enthusiasm for their work and failed to pull their weight to leave the community. About twenty people left as the result of this approach, but anyone who was disabled or too old to work independently was allowed to remain.

The fourth was to cut back on expenses. This included reducing by one half the monthly allocation to each household and scaling back on the use of vehicles, telephones, and electricity.

The fifth strategy was to give each department independence for its financial management. Under the previous system, finances were managed centrally. Under the new system, any department that produced greater profit than others would receive greater benefits. Department leaders were afforded more autonomy and authority as a way to increase motivation.

At first, the community was in a state of confusion, as some people left and some departments were shut down. These changes gave rise to rumors that the community was about to go under.

Some of my acquaintances came to me to suggest that I rid myself of the headache of the community and opt for an easier life, practicing my ministry. My response would be to smile and suggest that we give it a little more time.

THE STRATEGIES TO IMPROVE THE BUSINESS of the community began to have a positive effect after about a year and by the end of 1997 deficits were reduced. Coincidentally, at the same time, Korea experienced an economic crisis of its own, and in December of that year came under an IMF bailout program.

The national economy fell apart, but the financial situation of the Doorae Community contrasted with that of the country as a whole.

Doorae continued to reduce its deficit and showed improvement each month.

One example of recovery was in the processing department, which had undergone restructuring. Before the national economic crisis, it had been a deficit operation. By the time the crisis set in, the department's management had put it on track.

When other processing plants around the country were shutting down, our plant picked up the slack and was deluged with orders. During the 1998 Thanksgiving holiday, when workers ordinarily would have taken a few days off to travel to their hometowns to celebrate with families, they were so overwhelmed with work that they could not go home. The holidays found them still at their machines.

I asked them, "What are you doing here? Why are you working when others have gone off to be with their familes?"

"This is exciting, Pastor. We have so much work, we don't dare take the time."

"It's good to hear that so many orders are coming in, but you need a break."

"We want to fill these orders. Plants elsewhere are shutting down and we have to make the most of the opportunity."

The Doorae Community was off and running. Three years after it began to restructure, Doorae had turned around and was operating at a profit.

In restructuring, we had laid off about 20 people. As economic conditions improved, we needed more workers. At a May 1999 community meeting, we discussed accepting new families. We decided to take in an additional one hundred households and raise the profile of the community. We adopted the term "second founding," which was being used in corporate and government circles, and applied it to the community. We concluded that Doorae needed a spirit of second founding and should strive single-mindedly to move forward.

It is often said that the future of Korea's farm villages is gloomy because the Uruguay Round, under the auspices of the World Trade Organization, will force Korean farmers into bankruptcy.

In my view, that is a hasty conclusion, made after only a superficial analysis of Korean farming. I am confident that, if properly managed, Korean farms can become internationally competitive, enabling Korean farmers to prosper and enjoy a high standard of living.

Work is accomplished much more efficiently when people team up and pool their resources than when they work as individuals. This is particularly true in farming. More than any other sector of the society, agriculture needs cooperation and alliance. We recognize this in the Doorae Community and it is how we have always run our farms.

Opening ceremony at the Doorae Community in Bakersfield, California.

PROPELLED BY ITS AMBITION TO PIONEER global management in agriculture, the community launched the *BeSeToVA* Project.

In the *BeSeToVA* name, *Be* refers to Beijing, representing the whole of China. *Se* refers to Seoul, or Korea. *To* means Tokyo, representing Japan. The letter *V* refers to Vladivostok and *A* is for Los Angeles. In a nutshell, the *BeSeToVA* project is a vision of the Doorae Community for the future, linking the five geographic areas to take advantage of global management.

The project envisions China, Russia, and North Korea to produce agricultural goods, South Korea to serve as a center for management, and South Korea, Japan, and the U.S. to become distribution centers.

To advance this project, we have established Doorae Communities in Russia, China, Japan, and the U.S. in addition to those in Korea.

The *BeSeToVA* project is managed out of the headquarters of the Doorae Community in Namyang Bay. Branches in Korea are in Hamyang, South Gyeongsang province, in Boseong, South Jeolla province, and in Munmak, Gangwon province, as well as elsewhere.

The goal of the Doorae Community Movement (DCM) is to establish communities wherever Koreans reside. In the future, borders and ideological differences among the nations will disappear. What will remain will be peoples and their cultures. The past was an age of conflict in which nation clashed violently with nation. That is now becoming history. A new era of coexistence is dawning, in which people will help one another because of differences rather than similarities.

33

Nurturing Leaders

THE DOORAE SCHOLARSHIP PROGRAM, established in 1989, is the most successful of the projects that the Doorae Community has undertaken. In July of that year, I had an opportunity to go on a ten-day prayer and fast retreat in Japan. I realized that I needed time to rest and recharge in a quiet place because I was feeling run down from overwork. The retreat center was located halfway up Mount Fuji, not far from Tokyo.

Twenty-eight participants took part in the program at what had previously been a Buddhist temple. Of the participants, 25 were Japanese and two were Japanese-Korean. I was the only Korean.

I learned a lot in those ten days. Japanese are different from Koreans in their attitude toward prayer. In Korea, retreat houses are visited by people who tend to pray loudly and ostentatiously, calling attention to themselves by making far too much noise, deafening others to distraction. I find it difficult to adjust to this environment because I prefer to pray in quiet setting. To make matters worse in Korea, people often recognize me and invite me to speak.

"Ah, look who's here," they say. "You're Pastor Kim Jin-hong, aren't you? We're honored to have you here. We'd appreciate it if you could deliver a sermon at our service."

Although I plead with them to allow me to rest and to concentrate on meditation, they do not take no for an answer.

In Japan, on the other hand, even though there may be as many as thirty people in a house, everyone is so quiet that the house appears to be unoccupied. The sound of their footfalls, as they walk about the house, is inaudible.

Retreat houses in Korea ceaselessly lead people in prayer and hymns. In Japan, our everyday activity was climbing the mountain. After a few days of fasting, while climbing I would become short of breath and my legs would shake. Drenched in perspiration, I protested to the leader of the retreat.

"Why are you making people exercise so hard? I am supposed to return to Korea, but I don't think I'll survive, if I go on like this."

He provided an elaborate explanation.

"Mr. Kim, hard training does good for both your body and your soul. Moving your body during a fast will stimulate life energy with which God has endowed you. Then, muscles that you do not ordinarily use are stimulated, and impurities that have accumulated in your body are expelled with the perspiration. You cleanse your body. If during a fast you do not exercise because you have no energy, you will get only half of the benefit that you could otherwise achieve. So, Mr. Kim, move as much as you can. You can observe a fast of about ten days and still have energy to move normally. Climb to the top of the mountain every day. You will be rewarded for your effort."

I felt the leader was a man to be trusted, so every day, as he suggested, I climbed the mountain. After five or six days of fasting, I found the climb exhausting, but I worked to overpower the exhaustion. After that, on each climb the feeling of exhaustion persisted for only the first 500 or 600 meters. Then I felt renewed and by the time I descended, I would feel that I had enough energy to go up again.

One thing I learned about the Japanese was their custom of reaching a consensus through discussion. A fast requires that a person bathe frequently, but the institute lacked a proper bathing facility. People had to take turns bathing. At the beginning of the retreat, they gathered to discuss how to prepare the hot water and take turns. They all respected the group's decisions in these matters and took turns without complaint.

One day, I asked the leader whether I could change my bathing time, from morning to afternoon, because something had unexpectedly come up for me in the morning.

Although he was usually very accommodating, on this occasion his response was an emphatic "no."

"It's impossible, Mr. Kim. It would be wrong to change the order, which at the outset was agreed upon by all, because of one person. If you cannot keep to the schedule, you will just have to pass up your turn. You cannot change it."

I was embarrassed by his rejection and thought, "This man has hit the nail on the head. What he says is exactly right." I was ashamed that I had asked, but it taught me an important lesson. Koreans exercise too much flexibility, often resulting in a blur between public and private affairs, and they do not respect rules.

AMONG THE RETREAT PARTICIPANTS was a reporter from the *Mainichi Daily News.* During the introductions, he said that he was participating in the program to stop smoking. He smoked two or three packs of cigarettes a day. He realized that he had reached the point where his heavy smoking could cost him his life.

Three days into the fast, he developed a rash all over his body. He was told to endure, because the rash was from the nicotine being purged from his body. It became worse, however, to such a degree as to cause others to worry for his health. After a week, the rash disappeared and the man recovered.

Another participant, a man who owned a small business, slighted me in our first meeting because I was a Korean and a pastor. When I introduced myself to him, he responded with a sneer, "Oh, you're that *Josenjin** pastor."

I was offended, but managed to respond courteously, "Yes, I am." Then I quickly excused myself and left, all the while smiling. To my surprise, at the end of the 10-day session, when it was time to say good-bye, he came to me and got down on his knees.

"Mr. Kim," he said, "please forgive me for being rude when we first met. I am ashamed for what I said."

He was seeking my forgiveness for having referred to me as *Josenjin.*

"Of course, I do. I've already forgotten it. Let's keep in touch," I said, shaking his hand. His face lit up at my conciliatory response.

"By the way, are there many pastors like you in Korea?" he asked.

---

* *Josenjin* is a derogatory term used by Japanese to refer to Koreans and originates from the period when Japan colonized Korea.

"What do you mean, like me?"

"I mean, are there many pastors who are as decent as you."

"I wouldn't know. In Korea, I'm just an ordinary pastor."

"Staying here with you has removed my prejudice against Korean people. I regret deeply behaving as I did to such a respectable pastor like you."

"I'm glad to hear it. Why don't we make an effort to help Koreans and Japanese get along better, both on an individual and a national level? Thank you."

The next day, we had a meal to end our fast. It consisted of only a bowl of soup.

"What's this?" I asked. "Do you mean to say that we're to have only this soup, which is not much more than the teardrop of a chick?"

The retreat leader responded to my protest with a smile. "Mr. Kim. This is the most critical part of fasting. How you eat right after a fast is more important than the fast itself. You benefit from a fast only when you gradually increase the amount of food you have at each meal over a period three times longer than the period of fasting.

"We have fasted for ten days. That means that you should increase the amount of each meal gradually to reach a pre-fast level only after thirty days. If you fail to do this, you will find that you derive no benefit from the fast. In the worst case, your health is at stake. You did a good job during the fast. Now continue with your effort for the post-fast period." His explanation was so convincing that I had no choice but to go along.

THE MOST IMPORTANT BENEFIT I had from the retreat was that it gave me the idea of establishing the Doorae Scholarship Program. During the fast, I focused my meditation on how to nurture leaders. By the end of the retreat, I had begun to work out the details of the program.

The first step would be to select a group of students who had proven themselves and who stood above others intellectually, spiritually, and socially. Those students would receive two years training. Following the two-year training period, scholarship recipients would be selected. They would receive support for studies through completion of their Ph.D. degree.

Five criteria would be applied to select scholarship recipients.

The first criterion was distinction. Distinction, as a quality, embraces the comprehensive person, including intelligence, personality, religious faith, and social leadership.

The second criterion was destructive power. This refers to the person's willingness and ability to stand up against injustice and, when necessary, refuse to be subjected to it or to compromise.

The third criterion was creativity. The destructive power in the second criterion is meaningless, however powerful it may be, if it is not combined with creativity and constructive power. Christian destruction should be creative destruction. This is what distinguishes religious movements from secular movements. Many movements have as their purpose merely the destruction of unjust systems or orders, with little thought as to how to fill the resulting void. Religious movements should be devoted to destroying in the name of creating.

In Genesis 1:26 we read that God created man in his own image. What is His image? God's image refers to the ability to love and the ability to create. Christians, thus, devote themselves to creating with a loving heart.

The fourth criterion was sustainability. Anyone is able to perform a good deed at a particular time. The person must be able to sustain that power over a lifetime. Sustainability is indispensable in a servant of God.

The final criterion was commitment. It is said that 99 percent is not good enough for God. Only one hundred percent will do. One's entire being should be committed and invested to serve the people and the church in the name of Jesus Christ. We read in 2 Chronicles 16:9, "…the eyes of the Lord range throughout the earth to strengthen those whose hearts are fully committed to him."

One can be called to become the Lord's person only when he or she has the will and ability to commit his or her entire self to God's mission.

During the scholarship selection process, candidates meet twice a month to study the Bible and leadership. They also go through ten days training twice a year, in summer and in winter, to discipline their minds and bodies and strengthen their fellowship. This training consists mainly of manual labor in the Doorae Community. They are assigned the hardest tasks. Among other jobs, they dig ditches, clean out pigsties, and mix cement. Those who fail to prove diligent or keep up with the work are excluded from the list of candidates for scholarships.

This screening procedure is based on my philosophy that a leader should understand the joys and sorrows of people at the bottom by experiencing their life and must be ready to put themselves in the other person's shoes.

As a consequence of having young people perform hard labor, I have learned that the more outstanding they are, the more adaptable they are to hard work. This may be because people are open-minded and self-effacing only when they have confidence in themselves.

Having planned the scholarship program, I let others know my intention of establishing it. People immediately began to donate to it. Among the first contributors were a Chun Do-seok and a Jin Gi-cheong. Mr. Chun was a businessman who donated fifty million *won*. Mr. Jin, a former school principal, donated his entire retirement money, amounting to one hundred million *won*. The money donated by these two generous men became the seed money for the Doorae Scholarship Program.

The first recipients of the scholarship were Kim Ho-yeol, Kim Hae-kwon, Lee Moon-jang, Lee Seong-rok, Chung Hyeon-gu, and Choi Dong-mook. Every two years, since the inception of the program, a new group of students is awarded scholarships. To date, 120 scholarships had been awarded. Students in the program have gone on to study at the world's most prestigious universities, including Harvard, Yale, Princeton, Chicago, Stanford, Heidelberg, Oxford, Edinburgh, and Tokyo University.

People who know the profiles of these Doorae scholarship students say that the next decade will be the Doorae Era. They are referring to the important role that these students will play in our society, after returning with their education.

I AM SURE THAT DOORAE'S APPROACH to funding its scholarship program is unique. There is no single major funding source, only a bank account in the name of the scholarship. On the 20th of each month, the money deposited in the account is sent to the scholarship students, leaving only a small balance. When the account is again accessed the following month, the balance has once again grown to more or less the amount required to sustain the scholarships. Doorae families living in Korea as well as abroad send donations to the account, each ranging from some thousands of *won* up to millions of *won* at a time. The motivator behind the scholarship program is faith.

One acquaintance, who knows how the scholarship is run, once asked , "Aren't you worried about the budget for the following month?" My reply was, "No, I'm not worried." It is because Doorae families are bonded by trust.

An incident during one selection process serves as testimony to this trust. We had originally planned to select twenty students, but the qualifications of the candidates turned out to be too good for us to reduce the pool of aspirants. The result was we selected 48 students for the scholarship.

"How can you possibly raise funds to support more than double the number of students originally in the budget?" asked one of the workers at our office, wearing a worried look.

"I know what you're thinking, but look closely at the qualifications of the candidates. Can you name one person who does not qualify for a scholarship? We have no choice but to go forward, confident that God will help us."

Having awarded scholarships to the 48 students, I went to the bank on the 20th day of following month to find, to my amazement, the amount of donations had increased sufficiently to accommodate the additional scholarships. Such experiences convince me that God recognizes and supports our work.

Doorae's commitment to identifying and nurturing future leaders is global. We have launched projects to develop leadership potential in Korean communities outside Korea, as well as inside.

The number of Korean immigrants residing outside Korea in the other four *BeSeToVA* countries are estimated to be around 5.5 million. There are 2.7 million in China, 400,000 in Russia, 800,000 in Japan, and 1.5 million in the U.S. Korean immigrants reside in 172 nations, attesting to the adaptability of the Korean people.

Abroad, just as in Korea, it is important to nurture leaders to guide Korean communities. Having established the scholarship project in Korea, the Doorae Community recently launched a project in China to develop leaders. We set up the Korea-China Scholarship Association, through which we select scholarship students from areas bordering North Korea and in Beijing. These students go through the same training and selection process as students in Korea.

Korean immigrants in these four nations—the U.S., Japan, China, and Russia—will carry out a critical role in a reunified Korea in the 21st century. One of the missions of the Doorae Community is to create a Korea in which the history of its people becomes one with the history of Korean church.

This mission has not been given attention within the church proportionate to its importance. This is because church leaders have a limited view of history. Now is the time to change. The church should take a lead role in fashioning a Korea that will serve as a world leader in the 21st century.

Communities of Korean immigrants have settled successfully in the U.S., Japan, and China, but in Russia, Korean immigrants have a bitter history. During Stalin's rule, they were forced to move from their enclaves in coastal areas, bordering North Korea, to Central Asia. After surviving their initial difficulties, they managed to settle in. With the breakup of the Soviet Union, however, they again lost their land and are now having to relocate back to the coast. A settlement movement, led by Kim Temir, is helping to relocate Koreans to seven coastal areas.

Based on its experience of moving and settling large numbers of farmers, the Doorae Community can play a role in the relocation effort. Doorae will provide settlers with agricultural equipment and advice on how to establish and run a community, including agricultural technical support and consultation on the export of agricultural products. For Doorae, the most important challenge is how to provide honest, capable, and devoted leadership to this relocation effort.

Korean communities, whether in Korea or elsewhere, are generally riddled with factiousness and dispute. Although they usually manage to elect a leader, they fail to rally around the leader's banner. Unless the nation can break this habit, it will never be able to advance. How can our people overcome this situation? As I see it, the solution lies in establishing a Christian community based on love and truth.

ALTHOUGH THE DOORAE SCHOLARSHIP PROGRAM seeks to develop a leadership elite, the guiding principle of the Doorae Community

Movement (DCM) is to serve, in the name of Jesus Christ, our neighbors who are outcast and alienated from society.

The DCM has set up a school, the Doorae Nature High School, to work directly with young people who do not fit in. The school accepts youths who have failed to perform in traditional school settings. In one year alone, more than 55,000 middle-school and high-school students are expelled from schools in Korea, with an additional 60,000 plus students voluntarily dropping out. The mission of Doorae Nature High School is to provide direction and hope for these young people.

It goes without saying that the youth of Korea are the victims of the nation's education system, which is oriented exclusively to a college-bound population. The idea of establishing this school came to me in the early 1980s. I had read about Alexander S. Neill's Summerhill School and was inspired to set up a similar school. To gain approval, I went to the Ministry of Education and explained my intention to a government official.

His reply was quick and to the point, "The school you have planned, Pastor, is against the law."

Irritated by his reply, I imitated his manner with an equally quick and to-the-point response. "If that's the case, then change the law," I said.

"Amending the law is the National Assembly's job, not ours."

"Then what do you do here?" I asked.

"How can you ask me that? I have a job to do."

"What is your job? You keep saying 'no.' Is it your job to say 'no'?"

"Have you come here to start an argument?"

I left the office with no result, having spent my entire time arguing. That was in 1983. In the fall of 1997 I visited the Ministry of Education again and made the same pitch I had made fourteen years earlier. Under our democratically elected government, however, the response could not have been more different.

"Thank you, Pastor. We very much appreciate your intention to take on work that the government is supposed to be doing. You will surely get our approval."

Securing the government's support was almost automatic. It indicated the degree to which the social environment had changed. The official continued, "Although approval for the establishment of schools is the responsibility of the Education Administration Office in each province, we will do everything we can to help. You should first get approval for the establishment of a foundation to set up a school. To get that approval, however, you should have considerable funds."

"How much are we talking about?" I asked.

"You'll need three to four billion *won*.*"

"My goodness! Why so much? I can't possibly raise that much money."

"In that case, we'll have to find a way for you to apply under a different regulation. This regulation refers to the establishment of a regular school, but yours has a special purpose."

AS A RESULT, THE AMOUNT NEEDED TO BUILD A SCHOOL was reduced to only one billion *won*. I returned to the Doorae Community and discussed it with our people.

"We need to raise one billion *won* to build the school. Do you have any thoughts about how to go about it?"

"I don't understand why so much money is needed to build a school, Pastor. I thought that teachers teach and students learn and a few rooms were all that's needed," said one person.

"I don't understand it, either," I replied, "but it costs about one billion *won* to set up a foundation fund for approval. The amount was originally much higher, but I was able to get it reduced."

"For now, we can raise half a billion, Pastor. The rest will be a problem."

"Really? I don't think half a billion should be so difficult."

"It may not be hard for others, but it is for us. It's beyond our means. Think about it. How many eggs and vegetables does it take to make half a billion *won*? I'll tell you, it takes a lot."

"I know, but as I see it, we have no choice. We just have to do it," someone said.

"Every year our education system turns away 120,000 young people who are then left to wander the streets. We cannot wait. We have to find a way," I said.

After thinking about it, I decided to fast and pray for seven days,

---

*One billion *won* at the time was approximately one million dollars.

over the New Year's holiday. My prayer concentrated on raising the half billion *won* for the establishment of the alternative school. For one week I prayed and drank only water.

"Heavenly Father, we need an additional half billion *won* to establish a school for our young people who are lost. Please open the way for us. In the name of Jesus Christ, I pray. Amen." I repeated this prayer time and again.

A week later, having finished my fast, I returned to my work, confident that God would respond.

ON A RAINY SUNDAY, ONE MONTH LATER, a woman telephoned me while I was resting at home. By her voice, I could tell that she was elderly. I assumed that, like so many others, she had nowhere to go and wanted to come live in the Doorae Community.

"If you are looking for a place in the Doorae Community, I'm sorry to say, there are already too many people who want to live here. We have a waiting list of nearly 600 applicants. We can take in people only one by one, as a vacancy arises, because we are short of space. I'm afraid that if you were to sign up now, your turn would come only after you are gone."

"Oh, no, Pastor. I'm not looking for a place to live. I have some money that I've saved. I would like it to go to a good cause. I would like to donate it for the work you are doing."

I realized my mistake immediately and hastily tried to recover. "Oh, I'm so sorry. There are so many people these days who want to come here. Please forgive me."

"Don't apologize. That's all right. I understand. Could you please come to my house, since I'm too old to find my way to yours?"

"Yes, of course." I replied. I took down the directions and went to see her. She was 86 years old. As is the case for most of our mother's generation, her appearance revealed how hard her life had been. She held my hands and said, "Pastor, I have wanted so much to see you and make this donation before I die. Thank you for coming."

At that, she handed me a bankbook made out in my name and said, "This is not a lot of money, I know, but it is what I have saved over my lifetime. I have no doubt that you will put it to good use. I've wanted it to be used to help delinquent young people, but I have no objection should you want to use it for something else. I leave that to you."

I opened the bankbook and saw that the account contained slightly more than the half billion *won* we needed. I closed my eyes and offered a prayer of thanks. I said to her, "This is amazing. I am very grateful. I fasted and prayed for one week during the New Year's holiday because I needed a half billion *won* to set up a school for dropouts. Now, through you, it will come true. Thank you very much."

Speaking to students at Doorae Nature High School.

Pleased with my gratitude, the old woman went on. She asked, "You are helping North Koreans, aren't you? I saved out one million *won* for that, too." Thereupon she handed me a check for one million *won* for use in helping North Koreans.

A church deacon, Yu Jong-yeol, donated 20 acres of land at the base of Mount Suri as a site for the school. A corporation was formed to set it up. I then petitioned the Education Administration for approval, which was granted. We named the school Doorae Nature High School.

The school was opened with a prayer on March 5, 1999, with twenty students, thirteen teachers, and 500 well-wishers looking on.

In opening the school, the most difficult part was selecting students. Everyone knew that we were preparing to open it, and we were overwhelmed with applications. Finally, we decided on the school's first twenty students.

Not bound by the restrictions that apply to other schools, Doorae's curriculum plays down academics, emphasizing instead how to work and get along in the work environment and society. Its curriculum includes classes in farming, building low-income houses, paving roads, training for community living, and exercise.

During the first mid-year vacation, the school's entire faculty and student body visited the Chinese Doorae Community, near the North Korean border, where they studied for one month. Class activities included climbing Mount Baekdu, Korea's highest peak, and visiting battlefields and other historic sites.

The goal of the Doorae school is to take at-risk young people and nurture them to become contributing members of society, with sound minds and bodies, yes, but also with dreams and expectations for their future.

34

A Bruised Reed He Will Not Break

HEALING IS ONE OF THE DOORAE COMMUNITY'S major activities. To carry it out, we established the healing center, based on healing performed by Jesus:

> Jesus went through all the towns and villages, teaching in their synagogues, preaching the good news of the kingdom and healing every disease and sickness. When he saw the crowds, he had compassion on them, because they were harassed and helpless, like sheep without a shepherd. (Matthew 9:35-36)

Jesus expressed particular concern for the poor. Sympathetic to people's predicament, Jesus sought them out, preaching the Gospel, and healing the sick. Isaiah anticipated Jesus' work:

> A bruised reed he will not break, and a smoldering wick he will not snuff out. In faithfulness he will bring forth justice. (Isaiah 42:3)

Israel had waited a long time for its Messiah. They expected him to descend, with thousands of soldiers under his command, to rule the world. Jesus came down as Messiah, but He was not what people had expected. He came as a servant, practicing love. He came to shelter weak souls who were like bruised reeds and embrace the poor who were like the smoldering wick. He came to bring justice. He himself said, "It is not the healthy who need a doctor, but the sick." (Matthew 9:12)

For all the progress in medicine and science, our age sees an increasing number of people who are sick, in both body and soul. Those who have money can afford medical treatment, but there are many who cannot afford a doctor. Ours is an age of chronic adult diseases, most of which have no cure. The church's mission is to take care of people suffering from illness.

THE DOORAE COMMUNITY HAS ESTABLISHED a healing center to look after people whose bodies are sick and hearts are bruised.

Not all patients who are admitted to the Doorae Community are cured. More patients fail to get cured than are cured, but that does not diminish the importance of the center. The healing center emphasizes the need to care for people who have been abused and abandoned by their families and by society.

One day, in 1994, an admiral in the Korean Navy brought his son to the Doorae Community. The boy had been an honor student at a prestigious high school until suddenly, in October of his senior year, he snapped from pressure to excel. It was shortly before he was to take the college entrance exam. His father had insisted that he get a high score on the entrance exam, to ensure himself a place in the College of Law at Seoul National University.

After his breakdown, the boy would sit all day in a single place, with a blank stare. His father threatened him and, with tears in her eyes, his mother pleaded with him to return to his senses, but without success. As a last resort, they brought him to us.

On the day the admiral came, he behaved as if he were an admiral not only of the Navy but also of our community. He asked that his son be admitted to the community, but his arrogance was such that his request was put in terms that indicated we were obliged to take the boy. Doorae people were upset by his attitude and complained.

"I can imagine how he treats people under him, seeing how he's ruined his son. He's making a fool of himself, behaving the way he does."

I called the admiral and his wife in and told them that in dealing with Doorae people, they should be more courteous, if they wanted the community to look after their son. Then we accepted to take him in. The admiral asked whether he could stay for a few days to watch his son's progress.

I replied, "My read on this is that you are at least partly responsible for your son's condition. I don't think that your staying will do him any good. I suggest that you go home. Leave your son with us and visit him from time to time. It would be best for everyone."

I assigned the admiral's son to the poultry farm and asked members of the team to look after him with special care. A week later, the head of the team came to me and complained, "Why did you saddle me with this useless guy? What did I do to deserve him?"

"What are you saying? I sent him to you because you're such a reliable person. What did he do?"

"What hasn't he done, Pastor? Transfer him somewhere else, if you don't want me to go crazy, too."

"Tell me what he's done."

"I asked him to collect eggs. He went out. The next thing I know he's standing dead still, clutching two eggs. I told him to put the eggs in the basket. He put his hands in the basket and stopped, frozen. He can make only one move at a time, and only when he's told. I told him to go away. He took one step. He stood there for a long time, before finally taking a second step, and then, again, he just stood there. Please assign him to some other detail, where they can deal with him."

"I put him on your team because I knew his condition. I thought that you were understanding and could help him. At one time, he was an honor student. He cracked under the pressure, just before taking the college entrance exam. We have a mission to work with people like him. You don't have to do anything. Just stay with him and do what you can for him. When you succeed, it'll be a big accomplishment."

In the beginning of his stay at the community, the admiral's son ate three or four times more than an ordinary person. Asked why he took such big helpings, he answered that it was because he was malnourished. Later, he changed and began to eat only very little. Asked why he was taking such small helpings, he answered that a person who is disciplining his body and soul should eat little. For six months he went back and forth, between overeating and undereating, before finally getting back to normal eating, working, and living.

BIZARRE CASES, SUCH AS THE ADMIRAL'S SON, are not rare in the Doorae Community. On another occasion, there was a young woman who had studied microbiology at Seoul National University. She must have been a prodigy, having gone to SNU after graduating from an obscure country high school in North Gyeongsang province. She had undergone psychiatric treatment and had come to the Doorae Community when she was close to graduation.

There have been twenty or thirty such youths at Doorae. They are referred to as the "Foreign Legion" because they are so erratic in their thought and behavior. The leader of the Foreign Legion is Dr. Ahn Guk-bin. He lives and works with them, interacting with them on a daily basis. Because his influence on the Foreign Legion is comparable to that of the chief of a political party, in the Doorae Community Dr. Ahn is referred to as "the Chief."

The Foreign Legion has developed into a special unit, working during the day and praying at night, under the leadership of Dr. Ahn. They have taken over a variety of responsibilities, such as waste disposal, grass cutting, and weeding. The Doorae Community took them in to help them. Having become an indispensable part of the community, now it is they who are helping everyone else.

Doorae people are sorry that they cannot accommodate everyone who wants to join. Almost daily, people with broken souls visit or call the community, asking whether they can come live with us. The community has only a limited number of rooms and can accept new people only as vacancies arise. In addition to a lack of space, however, we have limited capability to take care of people. When our numbers grow beyond our capacity to cope, we cannot provide proper care. For us, it is important to maintain an environment that allows people, however small the number, to help each other and become rehabilitated by living in a community.

There is a way to overcome our limitations, however. There are many influential churches in Korea. They will spend 50-60 billion *won* to build a new church or 20-30 billion *won* to build a retreat in the mountains. These same churches could establish their own communal settlement, similar to the Doorae Community. The churches could have a major effect on the social welfare of the nation, if they were to redefine their mission and take action.

AMONG THE PEOPLE WHO CAME TO THE HEALING CENTER was a woman who had been a nurse in the U.S. She was suffering from exhaustion and depression and could not adequately care for herself, let alone take care of her husband and children.

Her husband had sent her to her family in Korea for rest and to be treated. During her stay in Korea, for whatever reason, she and her husband divorced. After that, she was unable to return to the States.

She had no choice but to stay with her family. Matters became worse for her when her father's business failed and creditors seized the family house. With no home to go to, she came to the Doorae Community.

When she first came to us, she was a problem for other Doorae members. She would neither eat nor wash. Doorae people worked to help her overcome her condition. To brighten her life, they went to her room every day to sing hymns and pray. They encouraged her to come out of her shell and into a world where there were so many things to do and so many ways to enjoy life. As time passed, she showed signs of improvement. She emerged at last and recovered to the point where she was able to comfort others around her. She now applies her nursing skills to community needs, taking care of others.

BECAUSE MOST OF THE PEOPLE coming to the community come with their own sad past, the Doorae Community is bound to become involved in all kinds of unpredictable and problematic situations. Sometimes the incidents are so outrageous as to leave me speechless.

Once my wife went to visit her parents in America. I returned home after finishing my work, to find in bed a person I thought was my wife. Glad to see that she had come home ahead of schedule, I went over to the bed and, as I pulled back the cover, spoke.

"When did you come?" I asked. "I thought you were going to stay longer." Then I got a shock.

A strange woman was lying there naked. Embarrassed, I ran to my mother, who was in the next room. I did not go into detail as to what had happened, but I asked her to go to my room and deal with the situation. Perplexed by my request, she went to my room to find the woman.

"What's going on here? You are evil. Put on your clothes and get out immediately. Who are you trying to ruin? Get out! Out!" she scolded.

Despite my mother's shouting, the woman did not budge, holding tightly to the sheet. My mother wielded a broomstick and threatened her. Wrangling with my mother, she finally sat up, saying, "I'll leave, but go out while I put on my clothes."

A while later, she came out of the room, fully clothed. She was in her late thirties and not unattractive. When pressed to explain her behavior, she answered in a calm and clear voice. "You don't understand. You're not supposed to treat me like this. God told me to become a wife to Pastor Kim. I came here to do God's will. I was prepared for us to spend our first night together, which I would have done with the same sincerity as when I pray. Don't you see?"

Doorae people who had gathered looked at each other in bewilderment. "You're a lunatic," they said to the woman. Then someone looked at me and added, "It must be nice to have two wives, Pastor."

A similar incident happened to my wife. It was around three o'clock one morning and she was home alone. A man slipped into her bed and said, "Ma'am, I'd like to be breast-fed." My wife was mortified.

On another occasion, my wife and I were sound asleep. I awoke to the sound of someone scratching about. A young man, who happened to be new to the community, was looking down at us. I poked at my wife and said, "Dear, wake up. We have a visitor."

"What? Who's here?"

"Yes, we have a visitor. Look on your side of the bed."

"A visitor? Who could it be at this hour?"

She looked around to see the man standing beside the bed. She lost her composure and screamed, "Who are you? Why are you standing there?"

Hearing my wife scream, he turned around and slipped out of the room as silently as a ghost.

I have only limited capacity to help people who are disturbed. I have not been trained as a counselor, nor am I so understanding as to be able to embrace everyone with love and self-sacrifice. I wish I had Jesus' ability to cure people, simply by saying, "My daughter, your belief has saved you," or "My son, break free of your disease and be healthy." Lacking this ability, I am often frustrated.

In fact, my limitations have often driven me to question what I do and to seriously consider giving up my work. Whenever I begin to doubt, I convince myself that my only option is to work harder.

My conviction comes from my belief that God is pleased by my efforts, regardless of whether I am successful. My object is to please Jesus, not achieve success, which was all he asked of his disciples.

ONE DAY IN MAY 1997, AT AROUND MIDNIGHT, a sister came to the community from Seoul. I was not happy with the visit because it was late and I was about to go to bed. I was called out and went to my study, where I met a woman in her mid-thirties. She had a disheveled look about her.

Catching sight of me, she slumped to her knees, wrapped her arms around my legs, and burst into tears, rubbing her forehead on my knees. I was embarrassed. I stood there, awkwardly, wondering what I should do next.

The young man who had brought her in asked me curiously, "Do you know this woman, Pastor?"

"No, I've never seen her before." I could tell by the expression on his face that he suspected that I was not telling him the whole story.

I became concerned that if I did not assert myself then, I could create a misunderstanding. It was then that my wife came to see what was going on. She also asked me whether I knew the woman.

I told her the same thing I had told the young man, "No, I've never seen her before."

"Why then do the two of you look so cozy together, if you've never met?"

There I was, called out, half asleep, still not knowing what was going on, and people were jumping to conclusions. The woman stopped crying and sat back.

"I'm sorry, Pastor," she said. "When I saw you, I felt like I was reunited with my father. I apologize. I was overly emotional."

"Yes, you were, but I assume you have a story to tell me. Feel free to speak."

"I'll tell you tomorrow morning. It's too late now."

"No, I want to get this out of the way. Tomorrow you'll need to have another cry before we can talk. That'll take time that could be saved if you tell me now. I'm a busy man. This is your chance."

"You're funny, Pastor."

"It's you who are funny, crying and holding onto another woman's husband. You can't say I'm the funny one," I said jokingly. I injected some humor into the situation because I thought she needed to relax to say what was on her mind.

She regained her composure and related her story. She had been beaten by her husband during eleven years of marriage. As a result of the beatings, she lost sight in one eye and sprained her back. She had been able to endure the beatings only by praying. Whenever her husband hit her, she would say. "Jesus, I don't mind if my head splits open and my body is torn apart, if only my husband can be born as a new person."

Her patience did not pay off, however, and her husband became increasingly violent.

Then, two months earlier, her husband fell into a drunken stupor. She perceived him as an animal. It occurred to her that there was little point in continuing to live the way they were. She went to the kitchen and picked up a knife, thinking she would kill him and then commit suicide.

Only thoughts of her son and daughter held her back. She could not suppress her tears at the thought of her children. She felt compelled to see them one last time. She went to their room and turned on the light. Seeing them asleep, she realized that she could not kill their father. She sat in the living room until daybreak, crying. Her tears washed away thoughts of how sad her life was and she resolved to continue living.

Some while later, she felt something was wrong. Her body began to shake whenever she was in the kitchen and picked up a knife. A voice from within would say, "Ah, you're so hard-hearted. You say that you believe in Jesus and yet you wanted to kill your husband. You're a horrible person."

Cooking was a daily routine and she had to use a knife all the time. Finally, she could stand it no longer. Leaving her children with her parents, she came to the Doorae Community. She had heard my sermons on the radio and made a mental note of the community's location on Namyang Bay.

"I'm sorry it's so late. I left home at six this morning, but only now managed to arrive here. What should I do? I can't live and I can't die. I came here because I decided to do whatever you tell me. What should I do, Pastor?"

There was nothing I could say. I could not tell her to put up with her husband's beatings. Nor could I suggest that she leave her husband and come stay at the Doorae Community.

I thought and finally I spoke, "Your husband is a cruel man. How could he do that? I'd like to see him and give him some advice. Tell me his telephone number. I'll go see him tomorrow."

"No, that's not possible. You can't see him. He'll hurt you. He's not normal."

"Don't worry about me. I'm not your ordinary pastor."

The next day, I telephoned her husband at around seven o'clock in the morning, to be sure to catch him before he went off to work. "Who's calling?" he asked.

"It doesn't matter who I am. I hear that you're good at beating people."

"Who are you?"

"I'm Pastor Kim Jin-hong from the Doorae Community. Your wife has gone insane because of your beatings and now she's staying with us. I will come to your house this evening. When I do, you can show me how good you are at beating people."

"Are you saying that my wife is with you? Did she go of her own free will?"

"Of course she did. Why? Do you think I'd take in a person like her, someone who's been beaten until she's sick, against her will? I'll come to your house at eight this evening. See you then."

I went to his house at around eight o'clock. It was a small apartment. His attitude had changed. He spoke to me as if he wanted to pick a fight.

"Did you say that you're a pastor? Is this about a pastor kidnapping a married woman? I'll sue you."

Caught off guard, I decided to dispense with talk of reconciliation and go back to being tough with him.

"What? You sue me? Are you going to sue me, you coward? A man like you, beating his wife, brings shame on all men. You're trash. How could you beat such a fragile woman? Trash like you should be sent to North Korea or the Amazon. If you have anything to say, say it to me."

Cowed by my aggressiveness, he stammered, "Are you a thug?"

"No, I'm not a thug, but I can play the thug to trash like you. Do you know what could have happened to you two months ago? Your wife, who had put up with all your beatings, was about to kill you with a kitchen knife, but decided against it because of your children. You would have been dead. Do you think that women have no guts and will endure beatings forever?"

Then suddenly, he fell on his knees, with his hands on the ground. Tears filled his eyes. He said, "You're right. I'm trash. Hit me."

"Why should I hit you? Not every man can hit other people. Those who beat others belong to a different breed."

"I didn't hit her because I wanted to, Pastor."

"What are you talking about? Your wife told me that you have beaten her for eleven years. If you didn't want to hit her, then why did you do it?"

"My wife is a good woman. Whenever I hit her, I always said it'd be the last time, but things never worked out that way."

Wiping away his tears, he told me the story of his life. It had come apart when he was only six years old and his mother died of cancer. Two months later, a stepmother came to live with them. She hated him and treated him wretchedly. What hurt him more, however, was that his father would side with her, yelling at him and calling him stupid. After finishing primary school, he left home and lived on the street, sleeping wherever he could. After the death of his mother, no one ever treated him decently.

Finishing his story, he said, "Pastor, I love my wife and my children like my own life. I can't live without them. I don't know why I hit my wife. I always tell myself that it's not right. I know it isn't. I must be possessed by an evil spirit. Please help me escape from it."

Hearing his story, I thought how deep-seated his suffering must be. He did not come into this world by choice. Growing up, he wanted love, but found only abuse. That abuse distorted his character. He took to drink because he could not deal with who he was. He looked to alcohol to give him courage to overcome his condition, but it only made matters worse. As a result, he destroyed the only place where he could have found love and happiness.

I took pity on him and thought about how I might help him. "After hearing your story, I think I understand," I said. "I don't agree with how you've lived your life, but I can see why you do the things you do.

It could not have been what you wanted, but it was because of neither alcohol nor an evil spirit. You have a diseased mind. You suffer from a deficiency of affection. When people are deprived of love, they do not know how to love others. This may account for why you hit your wife, even though you say you love her. The question now is, how to cure you."

"I'll do whatever you tell me, Pastor. Please help me. Please have mercy on my family."

"Let's join hands. There is no other way. Only love can cure your disease, because it stems from a lack of love. I will tell your wife to come back to you. When she does, you'll continue to beat her, won't you?"

"No, never. I'll never lay another hand on her."

"Don't make promises you can't keep. You told me that you could not stop beating her, although for eleven years, whenever you hit her, you swore that it would be the last time."

"Yes, that's true."

"The Bible tells you not to swear on false promises. You may swear now that you won't hit your wife, but you have a sick mind. You were not able to keep your pledge before because you were not of sound mind. I don't think you can stop all at once. You can, however, cut back, bit by bit, on the violence and frequency of your beatings. If you do so, you will find that one day you will stop altogether. I will take time out from my schedule to visit you once a month. Regard me as your brother, and we'll get through this like family."

I returned to Doorae to see his wife. I told her about my encounter with her husband.

"Sister, I went to see your husband."

"Thank you. I'm glad you've come back safely."

"Men know how to talk to other men."

"Was he rude to you?"

"No, he wasn't rude. We had a good talk. I need something from you. You say that your husband has beaten you for eleven years. I would like you to go home and endure the beatings for one more year. They will diminish. After the death of his mother, when he was a boy, your husband became emotionally sick. It didn't happen overnight and won't go away overnight. He is sick because his stepmother treated him cruelly, when what he needed was love.

"There is only one thing that can cure your husband's disease. His twisted character has to be changed. The way to do that is by showing him the affection he has always lacked. Once he recovers, he will develop a capacity to love others. The best way to make him experience love is to let him know God's love. Your husband is now in such bad shape that he is not in a state to feel and accept God's love. A broken mirror cannot give a true reflection of the face. If he is to be rehabilitated, people around him have to reach out to him. That will prepare him to accept God's love. Go home. Put up with him for another year. If in that year he fails to come around, you and your children will be welcome to come live with us here."

She wiped her tears. "Yes, I'll do as you say. I could endure it for ten years, if I thought it would cure him."

She went back to her husband. Afterward, I would visit them. When I visited, we prayed, shared a meal, and chatted.

There was a change in their house. They became more civilized. The most noticeable change, however, was with the children, who became much more cheerful. The wife, of course, was much happier too, and the man became more stable. The following year, during the lunar New Year's holiday, the couple dressed in traditional clothes and paid me a visit, bringing a five-pound package of beef. They gave me a traditional New Year's bow, which in Korea is a sign of respect.

"Pastor, you are like my brother. Please accept our well wishes. You have saved our family."

When she stood up from the bow, I saw her teary eyes. "You are still good at crying," I told her. I said to her husband, "You call me your brother. I say this as your brother. You will never be a man, if you make your wife and children cry."

He turned to his wife and said, "You're crying again. It makes my brother think I've done something to hurt you," he chided his wife.

She responded, "My tears today are different from those in the past. I'm happy now."

As a pastor, I am happiest at moments like these, when I can help bring a family back from the brink of destruction, their sorrow turned to joy. These times recall for me the words from Matthew, "It is not the healthy who need a doctor, but the sick."

As with Jesus, who came to heal the sick, the church should reach out to cure the ill and sustain the weak. As the head of the church, Jesus is able to transform a stricken society and create a new world only when the church does its part as a healer in the community.

For this reason, the church should not limit exercising its healing power to individuals. It should expand its power to embrace entire communities, regardless of where they are, or the age in which they live.

35

A Sack of Corn

D OORAE'S ONGOING EFFORT TO help North Korea, among its other activities, stems from my belief that we should be ready to pay a high cost for work that promises to benefit the people and the church. It was in 1993 that the story of North Korea's food shortage began to emerge. At first, I thought it was no more than a one-time bad crop or natural disaster. That was not the case, however, and people were starving.

In the spring of 1995, Doorae members gathered to hold prayer meetings for North Koreans. With the passage of time, we began to discuss how we could do more to help them. In one of these discussions, someone from the Doorae youth group spoke up, "We believe that our experience can be of help."

"Such as?" I inquired.

"We moved here from the slums of Seoul, reclaimed land from the sea, and founded a community on otherwise useless property. Don't you think our experience could be of help?"

"I suppose, but it's impossible to help someone who doesn't want to be helped. They have to want to learn from our experience."

"You don't sound like yourself. Why don't we do something and find out later whether they accept us?"

"I agree, but you can't expect North Koreans to think the way you do. It's not a matter of what we want."

"There must be a way, Pastor. Let's do something."

After this exchange, we started to look for a way to approach

North Korea. In early winter of 1995, I went to the region of the Duman River, which runs northeast along the border between China and North Korea. Standing on a mountain ridge, looking across the river at the North Korean landscape, I prayed, "God, who governs history, please take pity on our North Korean brothers, suffering from hunger. Innocent people are starving. Please give them your blessing and open a path for us to help them."

Having prayed, I drove along the road, following the river. Passing through a town, a man stopped us. He came over to me, as I rolled down the window.

"Excuse me. Are you from South Korea?"

"Yes, we are."

"I'm a Korean-Chinese living here in the town."

"I'm glad to meet you. It's exciting to meet a countryman in a town like this."

"I'm daring to talk to you because I need your help. There's a girl in my house who crossed over from North Korea early this morning. I would appreciate it if you could help her."

"Of course. We're glad to hear this because we're going around looking for ways to help people such as this girl. We'll do anything. What can we do?"

"Thank you. I'll go get her. Please park your car in the woods, over there, where it won't be conspicuous. The Chinese may become suspicious."

An hour later, he showed up with the girl. The minute I saw her, I felt sorry for her. She said that she was 19 years old. Her face was puffy and her clothing was shabby.

"I hear that you've come from North Korea. We'd like to help you. To begin, however, please tell us your story."

She spoke in barely a whisper. We had to hold our breath to be quiet enough to hear her.

Her mother and father had died a month or so earlier. Her mother's last words were, "Daughter, go to China and get food for your younger brother and sisters. She buried her parents near her house. After that, she stayed home with her three siblings, starving because they had no food. She thought that they were going to die, but her mother's last words kept coming back to her. Although she was exhausted from hunger, she walked north some 50 miles to the river. She hid in a pine forest on the other side and crossed when the mist spread across the river at dawn. She went into town and met the man who had just introduced her to us. She had breakfast at his house and had slept there. The man woke her up to bring her to meet us.

My heart went out to her. I told her, "Please tell us, what can we do to help?"

She hesitated at first and then said, "Get me a sack of corn, please."

"A sack of corn? Your siblings are starving. Are you sure that a sack of corn will help? You can ask for more."

"No. That's all I can carry."

She was right. She was malnourished and ill. Her condition would not allow her to carry more than one sack. I was desperate to help her.

"My dear girl, you've managed to cross the border safely. It's sad to say, but you will not be able to save your family. Why don't you stay here? We can provide a place for you. How many days do you think you and your siblings can survive on one sack of corn? And what will you do after it's gone?"

"I can't stay. I have to go back. My brother and sisters are waiting for me."

"I understand that you have to go back for them, but you cannot carry more than one sack of corn and it is not enough to feed them. You cannot help them and you will perish in the effort. You must survive."

"No. Please get me the corn. I prefer to die beside my family."

I was touched. What a good person she was. She could have stayed in China, but she chose to return to her brother and sisters. How terrible it is to see such good people suffer, only because they were born at the wrong time, in the wrong place, and have the wrong leader.

The Korean people should break free from this condition. They have the right to cast off this sorrowful fate, to be happy, and live a decent life. Looking at her, I thought, we have to find a way to unify the country. We have to bring our people together, to achieve a reunified Korea in the 21st century.

I sent for the corn and gave it to her, along with some US dollars and what Chinese money I had in my pocket. I said, "You're right, my dear. You have to go back to your family. Take this money. Come back again and contact me when it runs out. Feel free to contact us any time.

Come either by yourself or with your brother and sisters," I said, giving her details of how to find me.

She said nothing. She walked off, with her head down. Watching her, I prayed, "God, please help them to survive."

After going about twenty paces, she turned and came back. I was hoping she had changed her mind. Standing next to the car, she asked,

"Are you really from South Korea?"

"Yes, we are. We're from Seoul. We are believers in God, so don't be afraid. People who believe in God are always ready to help their neighbors, regardless of where they are from. Crossing the border, if someone asks you where you got the money, just tell them that a Korean living in China gave it to you."

"I will. Have a good trip home. Thank you."

AFTER THIS INCIDENT, I PRAYED EVERY DAY for God to open a way for the Doorae Community to help the people of North Korea.

I returned to the Doorae Community and told people about the girl. Her story moved their hearts such that they wanted very much to find a way to help other North Koreans.

Since then we have cherished an ambition to build a Doorae farm somewhere in North Korea. Doorae people have a twenty-year history of making barren land productive, while building a self-sufficient community. We aspired to repeat our experience in North Korea.

We set out to find ways to act on our plan to build a Doorae Community in the North, as a way to help relieve the food shortage. We were told to approach North Korea by way of contacts in the U.S.

Professor Stephen Linton, of Columbia University, is enthusiastic about helping the North Korean people. To do so he has set up the Eugene Bell Foundation.* I asked Professor Linton to play a brokering role to help the Doorae Community establish a farm in North Korea. He introduced me to a North Korean government official, a Mr. Lee, who had once worked in New York. I met with Mr. Lee at a hotel in Beijing, where he was accompanied by the director of the Beijing office of the Gwang-Myeong-Seong Business Federation, whose last name was also Lee. I explained to them the Doorae plan.

---

*Eugene Bell Foundation at *www.eugenebell.org*

"I'm pleased to meet you," I told Mr. Lee. "I heard about you through Professor Linton in New York. I'm working for a South Korean farming settlement, the Doorae Community. Doorae is a communal settlement, where people have developed barren territory and land reclaimed from the sea to turn it into farmland.

"We at the Doorae Community have a plan to build a community in North Korea, using our skills and experience, modeled after our community. I am a pastor, but my interest is not in converting North Korean people to Christianity. Nor am I interested in politics or ideology. With regard to this project, I am concerned only with farming and with helping the North Korean people. Please let us help them."

"I like your honesty. We've already looked into you and your Doorae Community. You've done a lot of good work. We trust you and will work with you."

"I'm glad you've heard about our work. I believe you've received details of our plan from Professor Linton. We're very excited about it. What do you think of it?"

"We believe that Doorae's plan is well suited and, we think, necessary for North Korea. I hope you can establish a Doorae Community farm in the North, so farmers from the North and the South can work together. I'd imagine, however, that it'll take a considerable while for such a plan to be implemented. Perhaps you should begin with a less ambitious project than the establishment of a full-fledged Doorae farm. You could implement the farm project in stages. What would you think of that?"

"You're probably right. What other project do you have in mind?"

"Why not devise a project in support of children's education institutes?"

"What are these institutes?"

"That's what we call orphanages."

"I see. There's no question about it, helping such institutes would promote the Doorae spirit. I'd like to hear more about these institutes."

They replied, "There is an education institute in every province. Each institute has an average of 1,200 children."

"Twelve-hundred!" I expressed amazement.

"Yes, the scale is a bit large."

"Yes. Which education institute would you suggest we support?"

"I'd recommend an education institute in Pyeongyang, where children of revolutionaries live. What do you think?"

"My guess would be that the children of revolutionaries already receive considerable attention from the government and the institutes for them are relatively better off. Our Doorae Community has traditionally shown strength in helping people alienated and outcast from society. We'd prefer to help an institute that is not in a major city and is not otherwise in a good situation."

"Then I'd suggest the Wonsan Institute. It's located close to Mount Geumgang. The location will make it easy for you to stop by later, when you visit the mountain."

"OK. Let's work with them. What support would be appropriate and how should we go about it."

"What you do is entirely up to you. We cannot tell you what to do or how much to give."

"Well, we can discuss that later. It's getting late. Why don't we continue this over dinner?"

The next day I began planning and wrote to Mr. Lee to request other information. When I returned to Seoul, I received the following letter via fax:

> To: *Mr. Kim Jin-hong*
>   *Chairman*
>   *Doorae Community*
> *From: Director Lee*
>   *Gwang-Myeong-Seong Business Federation*
>   *Beijing*
>
> *I received your fax dated September 30. It is difficult to work out the cost required to take care of a child because each nation has its own special circumstances. If we were to work out a figure, it would be little more than a guess. I suggest that you come up with a figure and prepare a budget based on it.*
>
>   *As soon as the account is set up, you may proceed to make purchases. If you would like our help, you may transmit money to our designated Chinese trading company.*

> *The trading company will purchase goods in China to ship to the institute. In the latter case, you would receive documents related to the purchase. The Wonsan Education Institute, which we discussed earlier, is located in a mountainous area and is exposed to extremely cold weather and flooding. Please consider our suggestion and let us know what you decide.*
>
> *October 1, 1997*

Another letter arrived shortly afterward:

> *To: Mr. Kim Ho-yeol*
> *Headquarters, Doorae Community Movement*
> *From: Director Lee*
> *Gwang-Myeong-Seong Business Federation*
> *Beijing*
>
> *I apologize for failing to reply to your fax of October 3. Details of the requested information are as follow:*
>
> *Name: Wonsan Children's Education Institute*
> *Founded: October 1954*
> *Address: Bongchun-dong, Wonsan, Gangwon province*
> *Facilities: One main building and two annexes*
> *Number of Children: 1,100 (Boys 620, Girls 480)*
>
> *October 8, 1997*

We decided to send aid in the amount of 17,000 US dollars per month. The figure was arrived at based on a calculation of 10 dollars per child per month, coming to 11,000 dollars per month for the 1,100 children, plus an additional 6,000 dollars per month to cover opeaing expenses for the orphanage. We transmitted the money as soon as we raised it, having already decided that the earlier they received it the better.

We heard from them within fifteen days of remitting the first allotment, saying that they would like to meet me at a specified date and time at a Beijing hotel. At the hotel, Mr. Lee introduced me to his boss.

"I wanted to talk to you because I wanted to ask how you could send us the money so quickly," he asked.

"What do you mean?"

"Nobody, whether from South Korea or anywhere else, sends us money until they have met with us at least fifteen times. You sent the money after just one meeting. We were amazed."

"It's not a complicated matter. We concluded that once we decided to help the institute, it would be better to send the money as soon as possible."

"Wonderful! I've come all the way from Pyeongyang because I wanted to hear that from you in person. To show our appreciation, I promise that we will always be forthcoming in any matter related to the Doorae Community."

"Thank you. I'm relieved to hear that. We'll do our best to do what we can." We enjoyed each other's company so much that we talked well into the night.

At about 8 o'clock the next morning I received a message saying that they would like to see me again before they left for North Korea. In the middle of our conversation at the second meeting, Mr. Lee's boss said, "When do you think reunification will come about?"

"I don't know. Although I know nothing about reunification, I'm confident that frequent contacts and communication between the North and the South, such as ours, are certain to open the way. Talking with you over the past two days, I feel that in a certain sense we have already reunified."

"I agree. We have already reunified, haven't we?"

Since then, Doorae's effort to help North Korean children has expanded to embrace three institutes involving 3,500 children. It costs ten US dollars per month to maintain a North Korean child. Elsewhere, children are starving for want of so little money.

WHILE ENGAGED IN HELPING NORTH KOREAN CHILDREN, we have also proceeded with a project to develop a full-fledged Doorae farm in North Korea.

As an initial step to setting up the farm, we built a Doorae Community in the Chinese city of Yenji, about 60 miles from the border of North Korea. This project was made possible because of the enthusiastic support of President Kim Jin-gyeong of the Yenbian University of Science and Technology.

Twenty years ago, when no one was interested in working in China and North Korea, President Kim, a Korean living in the U.S., moved to China and established a university for ethnic Koreans living in the region.

The Doorae Community took out a 50-year lease on 1,200 acres of farmland in a valley near the city of Yenji. The valley is called Yenwhacheun, or Lotus Village. During the Japanese occupation, an army of Korean independence fighters lived nearby, hiding in the recesses of a vast gorge.

Ten households from South Korea's Doorae Community teamed up with forty households of ethnic Koreans from the area to farm barley, beans, corn, and other crops. Today, the farm is a successful operation. Its products are all sent to North Korea. Six months after we began work on the farm, a deputy minister from North Korea visited us. We fed him a hearty meal.

"Why don't you build a farm like this in North Korea?" he asked.

"As a matter of fact, we established this farm as a first step toward building one in North Korea."

"Very good. Our country needs farms like this."

"We're ready to move into North Korea any time, but I'm not sure the North Korean government will give us approval."

"What do you mean? Of course we will. I'm afraid, however, that South Korea's intelligence agency might stand in the way."

"Don't worry about them. I'm sure we can get their approval. Please find a way for the North Korean government to open its doors to us. If you could designate an area on the rail line between Pyeongyang and Sinuiju, we'd like to put a farm there. We'll bring seed, fertilizer, farm equipment, and processing facilities from South Korea."

"That's good. We've done well under our self-sufficiency farming campaign, but it'd be better if we could join forces with South Korea to bring in seed and equipment."

Two months later, we heard from North Korea. They were

reluctant about our suggestion to set up a farm between Pyeongyang and Sinuiju, saying that conditions were not yet right in that area. Instead, they suggested that we set up a farm in Najin-Seonbong, a region that was set aside for foreign investment. They added that success there would help us expand our activity later to other parts of the country. We accepted their suggestion that we proceed with the work in phases.

At the end of February 1998 we went to North Korea and signed a contract to establish a farm. This time, again, President Kim of the

Signing the agreement with North Korea in Najin-Seonbong.

Yenbian University of Science and Technology, brokered our meeting and the signing.

In the first year of the contract, Doorae Community sent three people to establish the farm. They took with them 400,000 seed potatoes of a new variety and 300 tons of fertilizer.

I visited the site in July and joined the workers in the harvest. The potatoes grown from the new seed were well received. The workers were excited to see so many potatoes on each plant.

"Wow! Twenty-four potatoes on one plant!"

"Yes, they all seem to have flourished."

"And nothing has rotted."

Hearing this, listening to their comments, I figured their old pota-to seed must have been diseased and many potatoes rotted on the plant. The seed we brought was free of disease and very prolific. People were amazed by it. The lesson of this experience was that if we were going to help North Korea, we would have to supply good seed, farming tech-nology, and equipment.

If aid organizations concern themselves with providing only food, to make up for the shortage, North Korea will never achieve self-sufficiency. Self-sufficiency can be achieved only when accompanied by motivation and ability to succeed.

THREE PROBLEMS CAUSED ME MOST CONCERN, as I looked around farm sites in North Korea.

The first was that the soil was dead. When I was looking for a site to establish the first Doorae farm in North Korea, I was taken around by an official of the Agricultural and Livestock Department in Najin-Seonbong. It was right after the harvest. Looking at a field, because the stubble of plants left after harvest was thin, I thought it had been a field of millet.

"Was this a millet field? Did you have a good crop?"

"No, that's not millet. It's corn."

"For corn, you must have had a bad crop, the stubble is so thin."

"Yes, it was a terrible crop."

"It was a bumper year in both South Korea and Manchuria. Why was it so bad here?"

"It was the will of heaven. First, there was a drought. Then there was a flood, caused by a series of storms. We had no magic to counter a succession of natural disasters."

I scooped soil up with my hand and blew it into the air. I could see that the cause of the bad harvest was not heaven, but man.

The soil lacked composition. For farming you need fertile soil, which is why farmers cultivate the soil before planting. The soil in North Korea had become infertile. It was obvious that it had not been taken care of. Certain crops, such as corn, remove nutrition from the soil. Other crops, like beans, which are nitrogen-fixing, increase its fer-tility. Corn had been planted here year after year, sapping the soil of its nutrition. With erosion that followed years of flooding, the foundation of farming was bound to break down.

The second problem that concerned me was that, as I looked around, there were no trees on the mountains, no animals on the farms, and no equipment for farmers. Crops grow in fields, but what happens on the mountains has a profound effect on them. Trees help prevent drought and flooding. Where leaves fall, an environment is created for the growth of enzymes, which are necessary for farm production. Unfortunately, however, the mountains in North Korea are bare. In addition, North Korean farmers had few livestock. For the small farmer, animals produce fertilizer. Without animals, North Korean farmers are deprived of the means to produce fertilizer. The absence of trees and grass on mountains and the lack of animals on farms are two reasons for which the North Korean agriculture sector is so impoverished.

Proper tools motivate farmers to work hard, because they see results. Any equipment that North Korean farmers had was so old and dilapidated that it was of little help. I saw that the greatest need of North Korean farmers was for simple tools, such as hoes, shovels, sickles, and manually operated thrashing machines.

Even in this grim situation, I still came upon farmers who had enthusiasm for farming. I asked them what we could provide that would help them. Their answer was unanimous.

"Please send us seed and fertilizer. We can do the rest. Some people send us used clothes. We don't need any more clothes. If we get seed and fertilizer, we can work our way out of this."

I was proud of them for being full of enthusiasm, even in such adverse circumstances. These men had been deprived of an opportunity to exercise their talents. This has left them at the bottom of the economic development ladder. South Korean leaders and people must work together to help North Korea achieve economic prosperity. That prosperity will lead to the nation's reunification.

The third problem that concerned me was the endemic inefficiency of management. One day we were unpacking, after arriving at a hotel. We received a message, inviting us to have dinner with an important person, someone on the order of a mayor. We were told to stay in our room until we received further instructions. We got dressed and waited, but at nine o'clock we still had heard nothing. We had exhausted our patience and went down to the restaurant. Dinner was on the table, but we were told to wait a while longer. We returned to our rooms. It was nearly ten o'clock before we sat down to dinner.

We heard later that the reason for the delay was that they had to wait for approval for the dinner to come from Pyeongyang. We had no way to confirm the veracity of the story, but we knew that the lower echelons of government departments are not allowed to make decisions.

People in the North do not lack a spirit of progress and creativity, but they have long suffered under a bureaucracy of unimaginative officials, while having no autonomy of action. Some people in the South are very negative about the future of the country. They say that unless the system changes, help will make no difference. Their point bears some truth. For me, however, there could be no backtracking, once I determined to work with them.

On the subject of political systems, I want to relate just one more experience. During a visit to North Korea, I went up to my hotel room after dinner one night and turned on the television. All televisions in North Korea are permanently fixed on one channel, with programs broadcast in black and white. It was only a few days after Kim Jeong-il's birthday and on the program being televised, an announcer was reading a poem for Kim's birthday:

> Buddha toiled for seven years on the Himalayas
> to save the human race, but failed.

> Jesus Christ paid with his life on the cross
> to save the human race, but was unsuccessful.

> But our Dear Leader, General Kim Jeong-il,
> has succeeded where all others have failed,
> bringing salvation to mankind.

I was overwhelmed. How could a legitimate state-run television station broadcast such a bizarre program? Deification of this sort is impossible for outsiders to understand.

IN THE CENTER OF NAJIN-SEONBONG is a billboard that reads "Long live General Kim Jeong-il, the sun that shines on the 21st century." When I arrived there, large billboards advertising IBM and Sony were being taken down. The reason for the demolition was that they stood higher than the board on which General Kim appeared. Three days before I visited, Kim Jeong-il had seen the foreign companies' billboards over-looking his and became furious, "Those capitalist rats are looking down on me? Tear them down immediately." This single word from him was enough to mobilize an army of soldiers to remove the billboards.

In North Korea there are two slogans that capture the eye of any visitor. They are, "Father Kim Il-seong lives with us forever," and "Let's pledge loyalty from generation to generation." It seems that the entire nation exists only to sing the praises of the late Kim Il-seong and his son, Kim Jeong-il.

One time, during the month of February, I was going over a mountain in North Korea's North Hamgyeong province. The roads were covered with snow and going was hazardous. We were moving along in a jeep, when we came upon a boy of twelve or thirteen, walking along the road. He was barefoot.

I said to the guide next to me, "That boy's not wearing shoes. His feet may become frostbitten. I know that giving him a lift is against the rules, but I ask you to give him a lift anyway. He looks so pathetic."

The guide turned away, pretending not to hear. I took his response as acquiescence, asked the driver to pull over, and invited the boy to get in. Seating the boy next to me, I asked him, "How old are you and where are you going?"

"I'm 12 years old. I'm on my way home after going out to meet my mother."

"Meet your mother? Where has she gone?"

"She went to get food. She left two months ago."

"Two months ago? Was she supposed to come home today?"

"No, she wasn't."

"Then why did you go to meet her, if she wasn't supposed to return today?"

"It was because my brother is dying. Mom should come before he dies, so I went out to meet her yesterday and again today."

I guessed that somewhere over the mountain was a train station. I was moved by the young boy who went over the mountain every day to meet his mother, even though there was no reason to think she would come.

"You must be suffering a great deal. What's your brother's condition?"

"There's blood in his feces."

"Why is that?"

"I don't know. After Mom left, we ran out of food. I boiled some corncobs for him. It started after that. That was some while ago."

I gathered the rugged surface of the corncobs might have hurt his insides. Whatever the reason was, the young boy kept going over the mountain to meet his mother at the train station. I gave the boy bags of biscuits and bread and asked him.

"How are you going to manage?"

"It's no problem. I'm fine, thanks to the General."

His answer made me shudder. For him, no matter how difficult his situation was, he was fine, thanks to General Kim Jeong-il.

What amount of brainwashing had it taken to make the child say such a thing when confronted with overwhelming adversity? Children must have the right to be children.

I WILL RECOUNT ONE MORE INCIDENT. It took place in Najin-Seonbong. Some years ago a limited market economy was introduced in North Korea. In Najin-Seonbong there are small mom-and-pop stores along the streets and alleys. The stores resemble kiosks seen on the streets of Seoul and bear a serial number, which I assume is a registration number.

There is also a market in the heart of the city. The market is about the size of an elementary-school playground and is usually crowded with hundreds of people. The people are thin, but they maintain their passion for life.

As I walked around the marketplace, I sensed someone following me. My shadow was a slightly built woman of around forty. She kept her distance, but when I stopped, she stopped. When I hurried, she hurried. I thought she might have something to tell me, because she did not seem to mind that I had noticed her. She did, however, mind the presence of the guides accompanying me. To find out what she wanted, I snuck away from the guides and went around to the other side of the market. Looking back, I could see them wandering around looking for me.

It was then that she shot past me, whispering one word in my ear. The impact of what she said was so strong that I felt like bursting out in tears. I was transfixed, overwhelmed by emotion. I did not see which direction she took when she left, and could not even think about trying to find her. To this day, deep in my heart, I carry the word that she whispered in my ear. It was "hallelujah."

I could not have imagined that I would hear the word "hallelujah" in the middle of a North Korean market. What inspired the woman to muster the courage to utter praise for God? Was it her belief in God, handed down from other generations? Was it faith she had adopted by reading the Bible? Hearing that single word from her was more than enough to make up for the expense and effort to which we had gone to enter North Korea. With my head down, in the middle of the market, I prayed.

"God! I believe that you are responsible for history. I believe that the history of both North and South Korea has evolved under your direction. Please let me witness history evolve in our belief. Please let us see evidence that you are leading us.

"Please show us the day when all of our countrymen, North and South, shout 'hallelujah' at the top of their lungs, standing on the banks of the Daedong River, flowing through Pyeongyang. Please let all of our countrymen sing 'hallelujah,' free of all restraint, from the summit of Mount Baekdu. I dedicate my life to bringing about such a day. Amen."

36

Raise Up the Age-Old Foundations

AS 1999 DAWNED, THE DOORAE Community Movement (DCM), beginning to take shape, which previously had not had a clear direction, was taking shape. July 6-9 of that year, twenty DCM leaders from around the world met in Scotland for the Doorae Theology Seminar. Their purpose was to define the movement and put it on a solid footing for future activities.

Attendees held a series of discussions, which led to the promulgation of a community mission statement that embraced five principles:

1. *The Doorae Community Movement (DCM) has a vision to build a Biblical Korea, a Reunified Korea, and a Missionary Korea.*

2. *The DCM has its theological and ideological root in* Mokmin *theology. The missionary activities that the DCM carries out, based on this theology, are called* Mokmin *missionary activities. The* Mokmin *theology and* Mokmin *missionary activities will be systematically theorized and published.*

3. *The DCM in the past acted outside the mainstream of the Korean church. To be able to lead the church reform movement and play a central role in serving churches and exercising influence, it has to join the mainstream Korean church movement.*

4. *The DCM will lead an effort to extend Korean Christianity as a central force, supporting the spiritual world on the Korean Peninsula for the next one thousand years.*

> 5. *The DCM will restructure and reorganize itself to be able to efficiently carry out these missions.*

What do these five principles mean? The Doorae Community Movement pursues a Biblical Korea. This means that the DCM will contribute to the building of the nation, basing its work on biblical values. Each age has its own spirit. Buddhism was the spirit of the age under the Silla and Goryeo Dynasties. The Joseon Dynasty, which lasted 500 years, had Confucianism as its governing spirit.

What, then, is the spirit of the age for a Korea liberated from colonial rule? It will be the discipline of Jesus Christ. In the era of a reunified Korea, the Bible's teachings will serve as the spiritual guiding light for the 70 million people of the Korean Peninsula. We should strive to make it happen.

This vision is enunciated in the Book of Isaiah:

> The wolf will live with the lamb, the leopard will lie down with the goat, the calf and the lion and the yearling together; and a little child will lead them. The cow will feed with the bear, their young will lie down together, and the lion will eat straw like the ox.... They will neither harm nor destroy on all my holy mountain, for the earth will be full of the knowledge of the Lord as the waters cover the sea. In that day the Root of Jesse will stand as a banner for the peoples; the nations will rally to him, and his place of rest will be glorious. (Isaiah 11: 6-10)

What a wonderful and encouraging vision! It bespeaks an age of peace on the Korean Peninsula. That the wolf shall dwell with the lamb, the leopard with the kid, and the calf with the young lion, symbolizes communism and capitalism forming one community, the North and South Korean armies joining into one.

It points to a future in which the knowledge of God will flourish on the peninsula and people will no longer cause one another pain and anguish. It points to an age in which Jesus Christ will become a banner that our countrymen look up to and in unity follow. Finally, it heralds an age when our people will achieve respect on the world stage.

The Biblical Korea movement will increase people's knowledge of God and of the Bible, and will exalt its influence. The movement will fill every corner of the peninsula with the knowledge of the Bible, educating the people concerning God. In 2 Corinthians the Bible talks about freedom that people will enjoy when they are in the full knowledge of God:

> Now the Lord is the Spirit, and where the Spirit of the Lord
> is, there is freedom. (2 Corinthians 3:17)

People who are full of the knowledge of God are guided by the Spirit of the Lord. The Spirit of the Lord is a spirit that brings about freedom. The Biblical Korea movement will build an age in which 70 million of our countrymen enjoy freedom and spread the Word of God throughout the world.

WHAT IS A REUNIFIED KOREA? As of today, Korea is the world's only divided nation. Other once-divided nations, such as Germany, Vietnam, and Yemen, have been reunified. How mortifying and deplorable this is! What evil have our people committed to deserve this fate? It is not fair.

Now is the time for us to focus our resources and energy on bringing about reunification. Christianity has made remarkable progress in Korea in the 100 years since Protestantism was introduced, but Protestants have made some mistakes. People have worked hard to bring growth to the church, but have devoted little effort to achieving reunification. As for God's response to heart-felt prayers, we read in Matthew:

> Again, I tell you that if two of you on earth agree about
> anything you ask for, it will be done for you by my Father
> in heaven. (Matthew 18:19)

Of what use are a church's grand edifices and large congregations when people are suffering in shameful conditions? The church demands that people serve the church, not the other way around. Shin Chae-ho, an independence activist under the Japanese occupation, deplored what he saw. He wrote:

> Our nation, Joseon, became Buddha's Joseon when Bud-
> dhism was introduced to the nation, Confucius' Joseon
> when Confucianism was introduced, and Jesus' Joseon
> when Christianity was introduced. Why was it not Joseon's
> Buddha, Joseon's Confucius, and Joseon's Jesus?

No one will dispute his view. Neither the ancient Silla Dynasty's
one thousand years of Buddhism nor the Joseon Dynasty's 500 years
of Confucianism could arouse the Korean people to raise themselves to
play center stage to the world. We Christians should not repeat the past.
Koreans should be reborn as Christians, enlightened, and unified.
Christianity should lead us to make Korea a great nation.

To achieve this mission, the Korean church should commit itself to
the reunification on a foundation based on the truths of the Bible. It
should throw itself behind a mission to develop the nation to assume a
leading role in the history of the world.

WHAT IS A MISSIONARY KOREA? One theologian has said, "As fire needs
oxygen, the church needs a mission." A church is no longer a church
when it ceases to pursue missionary activities. What will be the next
step, once our people achieve reunification and bring about a Biblical
Korea? Should we cease our forward march, contenting ourselves with
our prosperity? Clearly, we should not. Our nation's founder, Dan-gun,
declared an ideal embracing the whole world when he built a holy city
and established a nation, saying, "Spread benefit for mankind, and in so
doing, transform the world."

This statement embodies a noble humanitarianism. The Bible is
regarded as great because every page of its sixty-six books reminds us of
God's will to bless and benefit mankind.

A Korean intellectual, the poet Kim Ji-ha, has said that Dan-gun's
ideology will lead the world in the 21st century. I do not agree. There is
no dispute about the greatness of the humanitarian ideal of spreading
good for mankind, but his notion of making the humanitarian ideal a
guiding doctrine is taking its meaning too far.

The world should be led for the next one thousand years by the
truths that are found in the Bible. I say this confidently. In the age of a
Reunified Korea and a Biblical Korea, people and church should work

to ensure that Jesus' principles govern the world. Through the DCM, we have campaigned to achieve this vision and have developed *Mokmin* theology to support it.

Mokmin theology is based upon our experience over the past 30 years. It is not a theology born in a library. Rather, it is a theology that has its foundation in people at the grassroots level. It is not a theology that has gone from someone's head straight to the written page. It was arrived at through experience. The foundation for *Mokmin* theology is the philosophy of Jeong Yak-yong, a visionary who lived a painfully hard existence 200 years ago. He was a man of great ability, but he had no opportunity to apply his principles. He developed *Mokmin* philosophy during an eighteen-year exile. The core of Jeong's philosophy is that to govern does not mean to rule, but to serve. His thought is laid out in his book entitled *Mok-Min-Sim-So (Book of Principles of Serving the People)*.

Doorae people are developing *Mokmin* theology, having *Mokmin* philosophy as a platform and the truth of the Bible as content. *Mokmin* missionary activity refers to educating people about *Mokmin* theology, a theology of service. All Doorae's campaigns and projects so far have embodied *Mokmin* missionary activity and have been aimed at implementing *Mokmin* theology in the evolution of history.

Doorae's *Mokmin* missionary activity focuses on four major areas —education, spreading the Gospel, healing, and helping people—and works to carry them out on the Korean Peninsula. These four missions have their roots in Jesus' life:

> Jesus went through all the towns and villages, teaching in their synagogues, preaching the good news of the kingdom and healing every disease and sickness. When he saw the crowds, he had compassion on them, because they were harassed and helpless, like sheep without a shepherd. (Matthew 9:35-36)

Jesus embraced people out of compassion when He saw them without leaders, like sheep with no shepherd. He embraced all people, but we pastors are concerned only with those in our congregations. We should extend our missionary activity to all the world, both inside and outside the church. Doorae people, who are committed to achieving the objectives of the Doorae Community Movement, see the future in a passage from Isaiah:

> Your people will rebuild the ancient ruins and will raise up the age-old foundations; you will be called Repairer of Broken Walls, Restorer of Streets with Dwellings. (Isaiah 58:12)

Workers who have been trained at the Doorae Community and who cherish their desire to build churches and serve in the name of Jesus Christ will rebuild our long-suffering country. They will rebuild the shelter for humankind, broken down over generations.

With the passage of time, people will say this about Doorae. "*They reconstructed the foundation for the future of Korea and built a home in which people could live a good and a blessed life.*"

APPENDIX

YEARLY AVERAGE RATES OF EXCHANGE

YEAR	WON/US $	YEAR	WON/US $
1955–1964	130.00*	1982	746.90
1964	255.80	1983	793.50
1965	271.00	1984	825.30
1966	270.40	1985	887.90
1967	267.80	1986	857.50
1968	281.10	1987	788.70
1969	303.60	1988	681.30
1970	315.90	1989	676.90
1971	370.00	1990	713.60
1972	398.10	1991	757.80
1973	396.50	1992	785.30
1974	483.00	1993	804.90
1975	483.00	1994	785.50
1976	483.00	1995	771.70
1977	483.00	1996	840.90
1978	483.00	1997	1,344.50
1979	483.00	1998	1,189.70
1980	657.50	1999	1,123.40
1981	698.30	2000	1,247.40

SOURCE: OFFICE OF STATISTICS, MINISTRY OF FINANCE AND ECONOMY

* Until the end of May 1964, the exchange rate was pegged at 130 *won* per US dollar. Beginning June 1964, the *won* was allowed to fluctuate within a band, until it was finally floated in late 1997.